FIVE CRIES OF PARENTS

Five Cries of Parents

Merton P. Strommen
and A. Irene Strommen

1817

Harper & Row, Publishers, San Francisco
Cambridge, Hagerstown, New York, Philadelphia
London, Mexico City, São Paulo, Singapore, Sydney

To Kathleen and Gilbert Wrenn
who have been loving surrogate parents
to hundreds of graduate students and their spouses

Ellen Goodman's column "For Tsongas and His Family, a Discovery of the Preciousness of Time," in the *Boston Globe* is excerpted and reprinted by permission of The Washington Post Company; copyright © 1984 The Boston Globe Newspaper Company/Washington Post Writers Group. "It's Time for Black Adults to Make Teenage Virtue a Necessity," by William Raspberry in the *Washington Post*, is excerpted and reprinted by permission of The Washington Post Company; copyright © 1984 Washington Post Writers Group. *Troubled Families*, Mathew J. Fleischman, Arthur M. Horne, and Judy L. Arthur, Champaign: Research Press, 1983, is excerpted by permission.

FIRST EDITION

Library of Congress Cataloging in Publication Data

Strommen, Merton P.
  Five cries of parents.

  Bibliography: p.
  Includes index.
  1. Parenting.   2. Parent and child.   3. Family—Religious life.
4. Youth—Conduct of life.   5. Youth—Religious life.   I. Strommen, A. Irene.   II. Title.
HQ755.8.S77 1985   649'.1   84-48231
ISBN 0-06-067747-3

85 86 87 88 89 RRD 10 9 8 7 6 5 4 3 2 1

Contents

List of Figures and Tables

FIGURES

TABLES

Preface

We would like to tell you about ourselves and our family. It may help your understanding of *Five Cries of Parents*.

We are the parents of five sons—Peter, Timothy, James, John and David. Our two eldest sons were adolescents when the last two boys were born. Because of the family age span, we have had adolescents in our home for twenty-two consecutive years. And this means that for twenty-two years we continually had five different stages of development around us.

We know firsthand about the power of peer pressure; the embarrassment of being fifteen and not wanting to be seen in the local ice cream store with your little brother in tow; the feeling of alienation when you get teeth braces the same year you make your debut at the big junior high; the resentment against your parents when you're told you have to say home with the family on Christmas Day instead of spending it at your newest girl friend's house; the desperation you feel when you're thirteen and trying to find your lost dog late at night; the awesomeness of your first brush with death when Grandpa dies; the rage when your brother eavesdrops on the other phone when you're talking to a girl.

We know how parents struggle for the right words when a son bursts with frustration after spending most of the basketball game on the bench; or loses a coveted championship game by a field goal that went over the goal posts after the buzzer sounded; or tears a ligament in his knee and is "out" for the season.

We know the shared sense of joy when a son gets the highest rating in original oratory at the state contest; or gets a lead in the school musical; or is voted Most Valuable Player at the end-of-the-season banquet.

We also know the irritation when brothers quarrel, when the police stop your son for throwing tomatoes at passing cars (from the roof of the church library!); or when a son sits sullenly at family devotions, refusing to participate (the same son, we might add who said not long ago, "Thanks, Mom and Dad, for being so persistent in bringing us the faith"). We know the unease of those first nights that the newly licensed driver drives the family car and parents lie awake waiting for the sound of the garage door closing. We know the exuberation of cramming all seven of us into a station wagon with tent equipment and sleeping bags, bound for vacation in the mountains. We also know about the tired father who wonders how he can make it to the first night's stop without collapsing from fatigue.

And so it follows that the adolescent years in our home have been blessed with the patchwork quilt of much discussion, laughter, competition, celebration, reflection, tenderness. It is because of our "boys" that we dare to write this book. And we thank them publicly here for sharing positive and negative observations about our family life, even giving permission at times to be quoted. Peter, Jim, John, and Dave did a preliminary reading of the manuscript for us. We also thank our three daughters-in-law—Norma Jean, Dawn, and Judy—for their openness and willingness to contribute their insights.

For over twenty years Irene's work world was the high school classroom. During Merton's professional career, he has taught, counseled, and researched adolescents. Our work settings have varied from rural and small-town communities to the urban and suburban areas of our country.

Over a span of twenty-five years we have had the privilege of being leaders of small groups of adolescents. Many of these groups met once a week in the form of a Bible study-discussion in the informal setting of our family room.

The chapters of this book represent the keystones of our personal philosophy of parenting. The promises of God in both the Old and New Testaments, our faith in Christ, and the presence of God's Spirit are a heritage we ourselves have been given and have tried to pass on to our sons.

Though we have worked together on writing assignments for many years, we have never before been co-authors. Naturally, some questions arose: "Will our writing styles mesh?" "Can we write at home where the dining room table is the desk?" "Where can we keep the hundreds of references and thousands of questionnaires?" Although we rented a room in a nearby school for a short time, the bulk of the work has been done in our home. It has indeed been easy to misplace data. In fact, one important file folder of references was found in the garage, slated for the garbage can! There were seemingly endless revisions—to the point where we said to each other, "Will we ever finish?" But now we can truthfully say it has been a rich experience to crystallize into words the thoughts on parenting that have accumulated in our hearts and minds for thirty-seven years.

We thank our extended family, which has always been a positive support to us in our life as parents.

We thank the 8,156 young adolescents and the 10,467 parents who gave the unprecedented information being shared in this book. We thank the thousands who allowed us to interview them through handwritten response or verbal sharing.

We thank the talented and hardworking team at Search Institute that carried out the Adolescent-Parent study, which forms a basic reference throughout the book. The people responsible for this study are: Peter L. Benson, Arthur L. Johnson, Phillip K. Wood, Dorothy L. Williams, and Janice E. Mills.

We thank Lutheran Brotherhood for the use of their computers in carrying out the complex analyses of data supplied by the young adolescents and their parents. We have been the recipient of this generous service over a period of 26 years.

We thank Elizabeth Kurak and Jean Wachs for their typing skills on the word processor.

We thank Andy Horne, and Shelby and Jim Andress for

reviewing preliminary copy and helping us set directions for our revisions.

It is with a special sense of gratitude that we acknowledge the hours spent by C. Gilbert Wrenn in perusing the manuscript carefully several times. His work as consulting editor for this book represents only one of many ways in which he has expressed genuine interest and affection for his former advisee, Merton, and the research he has carried out. Gilbert Wrenn has been a friend, mentor, and father.

A special thanks to Lilly Endowment, Inc. for their generous grant and the thirteen youth-serving national organizations for dedicated involvement in the Adolescent-Parent Survey. Their participation made possible the rich treasury of data that form the foundation of this book.

1. A Time of Danger and Opportunity

We have been parents for almost four decades now. Throughout those years we have uttered each of the five cries discussed in this book.

Because Merton is a research psychologist at Search Institute[1] in Minneapolis, Minnesota, we have had privileged access to a large amount of unique research data, accumulated over twenty-five years. Of special import are the findings of the massive study of Young Adolescents and their Parents, also called the Adolescent-Parent study, which was carried out by Peter L. Benson and the research team of Search Institute in 1983. Supplementing this research are data from a host of other studies, and insights garnered from scores of books and articles on parenting.

This introductory chapter deals with the following topics:

- The five cries
- Danger and opportunity
- Purpose of this book
- Our data base
- Our interpretive stance

The Five Cries of Parents

Parents of adolescent children often have searching and sometimes urgent questions. They want answers that will provide them with insight, guidance, and support. We call these searching questions "cries" because they represent the strong desire of parents for:

- Understanding
- Close family
- Moral behavior
- Shared faith
- Outside help

We also use the concept of cries to underscore just how stressful parenting adolescent children can be. A parent's need for answers during this period is perhaps more urgent than at any other stage in the family life cycle.

In 1983 a comprehensive sociological study of more than one thousand families[2] confirmed something that had been observed in other, smaller, studies: instead of improving over the years as parents gain in experience, there is actually a steady decline in most measures of family achievement from the childless stage to the adolescent-raising stage of the family life cycle. During these years, closeness and adaptability reach a low point, and communication between parents and adolescents is poorest. Where that occurs, one can expect to find a highly stressed family.

In 1984 a smaller study of 208 families[3] came up with similar findings. Virtually all parents view the adolescent stage in family life as the most difficult. Why? One reason is parental annoyance over issues of independence and control. A second reason is parental fears over the potentially undesirable consequences of their child's new-found independence. These fears may relate to drugs, reckless driving, or delinquent behavior. Though parents know they are supposed to encourage and facilitate independence, they find this responsibility difficult to carry out.

Added to the difficulty of managing teenage children is the difficulty of financial support. Today's parents are under increased strain to provide money needed to support and educate their growing children, whose needs grow right along with them. Thus financial and business strains are especially intense during this stage of family life.

Both parent and adolescent are simultaneously in unique cycles of growth and change—children in adolescence, and the parents in what some psychologists call "middlescence," the years between thirty-five and fifty. Gail Sheehy writes that wives past the age of thirty-five often experience a movement toward more independence.[4] During these same years, according to Eda LeShan,[5] the husband may become more aware of unfulfilled aspirations, mistaken decisions and choices, things left undone. He may realize that there will be no "big time" in his career. Hence this period of married life is ripe for anxiety, impatience, and misunderstanding.

Danger and Opportunity

Initially, we considered making "fear" one of the five cries of parents. On closer examination, however, we came to see that fear is not a separate cry, but rather a quality that gives urgency to the others. Parents have many fears because they know how susceptible children and young adolescents are to the social infections of our culture. This fear has been intensified by the many tragic accounts reported daily in the news media.

Another fear is generated by the word "epidemic," a term used increasingly in scholarly journals and popular press. The term refers not to diseases such as smallpox, cholera, yellow fever, or malaria, but to behaviors that are equally devastating to the lives of youth and adults. Almost half of all patients hospitalized today are there not because of a disease, but because of practices that are symptoms of an illness such as drug use, alcoholism, or child abuse. These social ills, all of which have appeared on the horizon as aggravated social problems, are like contagious diseases. They are passed on through peer pressure and through the mass media.

But a time of crisis, with its obvious dangers, can also be a time of opportunity. This awareness is incorporated into the two-part Chinese character for the word "crisis": one part means danger, and the other opportunity.

The response to an epidemic situation can involve three different actions: trying to eliminate the infectious disease, cutting off the ways by which the disease is communicated, and increasing the immunity or health of people through vaccines or improved nutrition. This book stresses the third strategy. There is much that parents can do to counter social infection by increasing the inner strength and immunity of their children.

Our studies have shown that adolescents are vastly helped if they can draw on five great sources of strength:

- Understanding, affirming parents
- Close, caring families
- Moral, service-oriented beliefs
- A personal, liberating faith
- An accepting attitude towards receiving help

Used correctly, they can at least partially deter negative behaviors and encourage a life of service and responsible action. These five sources of strength will be described in later chapters.

This hopeful stance is in tune with the feelings of parents in the Adolescent-Parent study. Though four out of ten parents admit they worry "very much" about their child's future, and an additional three in ten worry "quite a bit," they are still hopeful. When asked to describe their own child, they tended to reflect a positive attitude by a use of words such as "caring," "feeling for others," "happy," "respectful for authority," and "trouble-free." Though some parents described their child as hard to live with or rebellious, such parents are in the

minority. Most of the parents in the Adolescent-Parent study
enjoy their children and find considerable satisfaction in parenting.[6] This is seen in the responses fathers and mothers gave
to the statement "I get a lot of satisfaction out of being a
parent."

	Mother	Father
Almost always true	60%	53%
Often true	28%	33%
Combined answers	88%	86%

This finding of parental satisfaction is supported by other
studies. Catherine Chilman's 1980 study of 454 families found
the majority of parents (60 percent of the mothers and 68
percent of the fathers) "mostly happy" as parents.[7] In addition, the majority of mothers consider parenting more satisfying than outside employment.

In spite of the fear of the future that seems to dominate the
media, fewer than one in five parents in the Adolescent-Parent
study agrees with the statement "I sometimes wish I did not
have children." Though aware of the dangers facing adolescents, parents in the study seem strongly attuned to the opportunities and possibilities of parenting. Whether you think
them misguided or not, the fact remains that 85 percent of
these parents agree with the statement "I think I'm doing a
pretty good job as a parent." This positive attitude can only
help them be good parents, able to turn potentially dangerous
situations into opportunities for significant growth.

Purpose of This Book

This book is addressed to parents and other adults who are
in a parenting role with children and adolescents. Its purpose
is to provide a rationale for parenting, to encourage reflection,
and to supply clear directions regarding the help parents may
need.

We have tried to organize commonly held ideas about parenting into an easily remembered conceptual framework, supplied by the five cries and the essentials of parenting to which they point: understanding, close family, moral purpose, shared faith, and outside help.

We encourage you to reflect on parenting. Poor parenting can result from a parent's unresolved personal problems. There are brilliant psychiatrists and psychologists who know a great deal about the human personality, but are inept as parents. Their insecurities and needs, obvious to others but not to themselves, profoundly influence their actions. Though insightful and effective when helping others, they lose their effectiveness when dealing with issues that touch their own lives. Unresolved dynamics can cause them—as well as anyone—to act contrary to their better knowledge. Having observed this phenomenon again and again, we find it crucial to encourage all parents to reflect on themselves as people and mates, as well as parents. We believe every parent needs to work at examining and understanding his or her hidden feelings. For parents of adolescent children, in a time of stress and change, this is doubly important.

Although this is not a "how-to" book, we hope it will help parents change. Thus each chapter includes practical suggestions culled from interviews, scores of excellent books on parenting, and our own experiences as parents. Use these suggestions as presented, or allow them to help your imagination envision new ways to solve problems.

Our Database

To address the five cries and provide answers not previously available, we have used factual data from a number of studies involving parents. A principal source of information is the aforementioned Adolescent-Parent study, which involved 8,165 young adolescents and their 10,467 parents. This study, funded by Lilly Endowment, was based on thirteen national samples of young adolescents (grades 5 through 9), randomly selected from the membership rosters of thirteen national youth-service organizations (see Table 1 for more information on the sample). All groups used the same questionnaire of 319 items and the same procedures in collecting data. A separate but parallel questionnaire of 328 items was used to query the parents of these adolescents.

Table 1. Sample Sizes and Origins*

Grade in school	Young Adolescents			Parents		
	Boys	Girls	Total	Mothers	Fathers	Total
5	660	720	1,380			
6	807	852	1,659			
7	866	978	1,844			
8	888	1,010	1,898			
9	586	677	1,263			
Total	3,807	4,237	8,165**	6,076	4,391	10,467

Sample Origins

Sponsoring Agency	Percent of Young Adolescent Sample	Percent of Mother Sample	Percent of Father Sample
African Methodist Episcopal Church	3%	1%	2%
American Lutheran Church	10	14	13
Baptist General Conference	7	10	8
Churches of God, General Conference	4	5	5
Evangelical Covenant Church	6	8	7
4-H Extension	14	12	14
Lutheran Church—Missouri Synod	7	9	8
National Association of Homes for Children	7	0	0
National Catholic Educational Association	14	8	10
Presbyterian Church/U.S.	5	7	6
Southern Baptist Convention	8	8	9
United Church of Christ	8	9	9
United Methodist Church	8	10	9

*This table identifies sample sizes and their origins as well as the percentage each contributes to the composite sample. No reference is made in this book to information from any of the individual samples, only the total samples of 8,165 adolescents and 10,467 parents.
**Includes 121 young adolescents, grade or sex unknown.

The study is unprecedented in size of sample, scope of questioning, and specificity of information. Though the results of the composite sample based on these national groups can be applied only to the populations they represent (about 60 percent of the national population), the conclusions shared here have wide application. Care has been taken to find corroborative data (based on samples of the general public) to justify the making of generalizations that will apply to parents generally.

As a preliminary to the Adolescent-Parent study, we asked approximately two thousand parents to respond to a questionnaire consisting of thirty item stems, such as the following:

The worst thing about my family is _____ .
When my child does something wrong, I _____ .
I would be a better parent if _____ .
The best thing about our family is _____ .

Many parents wrote freely, describing their hopes, dreams, and difficulties. From these brief essays we extracted quotes to illustrate the thoughts and feelings that underlie the statistics used in this book.

In addition to reading the questionnaire results, we interviewed approximately two hundred young and older adults, as well as some high school youth. We asked them such questions as:

Describe the most important qualities in the parent you yourself want to be.

Describe your most positive experience as an adolescent in your home.

If you could change one quality of your home life as an adolescent, what would it be?

We were impressed by the comments of the people we interviewed, for they included many insights similar to those found in books written for parents. While they often acknowledged mistakes and failures, the interviewees seemed to know what constitutes good parenting.

Though this book is truly data based, it is not a research report. Rather, it represents our interpretation of the meaning inherent in a mosaic of research findings. We have used the data to broaden our understanding and increase our ability to see with clarity the significance of what parents and adolescents report about their families.

Our Interpretative Stance

Admittedly, our interpretations are biased by our values, beliefs, and personal experiences. As Christians, we reflect a distinct value orientation and world view. But the research findings on which our conclusions are based provide a measure of objectivity. They help to establish our basic points as something more than personal opinion.

As authors, we believe that each source of strength within the family contributes to the growth and development of an adolescent. We also believe that a liberating religious faith enhances each characteristic. We use the word "liberating" faith because our studies evidence two types: a forgiveness-oriented faith and a guilt-oriented faith. One is freeing and the other enslaving.

A liberating Christian faith fosters love and trust within a family; it encourages an open, understanding, affirming stance toward oneself and others. This openness makes it easier to accept help, acknowledging that supportive people, trained counselors, and studies on "parenting the adolescent" are all gifts of God.

In conclusion, we feel it is essential to emphasize that parenting is an ongoing process that begins at a child's birth. Each source of strength mentioned here, developed more fully throughout the book, has its roots in the early stages of family life. This means that preparation for the adolescent years begins in childhood. And parenting never ends. Though the role we play will change, as parents we are always parents. The umbilical cord is truly cut only when death separates us from our children.

In Letty Cottin Pogrebin's words, "If the family were a sport, it would be baseball: a long, slow nonviolent game that is never over until the last out."[8]

2. Cry for Understanding Yourself As a Parent

If you cry out for insight and raise your voice for understanding, *if you seek it like silver and search for it as for hidden treasure . . . wisdom will come into your heart and* understanding *will guard you.*

—PROVERBS 2:3, 10

Parents of two thoughtful children decided to invite a child from another culture and contrasting style of life into the warmth of their family. The eight-year-old Asian girl they adopted had been a procurer for her mother, whose livelihood came from serving as a prostitute for U.S. servicemen.

To understand their adopted daughter better, the parents met with others who had adopted Asian children. They read books and consulted with friends. Soon they observed that two personalities were embattled within the girl—one that responded to the love and caring of her new home and congregation, and one that wanted her former style of life. The latter attraction drew her toward people who were glad to exploit her. By the time she was in junior high, she was using drugs and sexually active.

"How can we help her to break with friends and practices that are destroying her future?" cried this girl's new parents. They visited school counselors and pastoral counselors, they read books—all in their search for insight and understanding. Over time, their persistent cry became, "How can we best parent a daughter whose childhood experiences are the determining force in her life?"

In their search for wisdom these parents discovered not only need for a better understanding of their child, but also of themselves as people and of each other as mates. As a result they joined Al-Anon and became a part of a parents' group with its weekly discussions.

This chapter takes a look at the forces and dynamics that influence our perception and response as parents within a family situation. They are the key to understanding adolescent behavior, which is the focus of the next chapter.

This chapter is divided into two sections.

- The emotional forces that move out of our past and into the present: forces from our family of origin; wounded memories; unmet personal needs; feelings of failure; and reactions of anger.
- The emotional forces that are intensified by stressful circumstances in a marriage situation: external trauma, such as death in the family; divorce and separation; single parenting; and establishing a step-family.

The Need for Understanding Hidden Emotional Dynamics

When the 10,467 parents in the Adolescent-Parent study were asked to rank the importance of sixteen values, two that received top billing were "to be a good parent" and "to have wisdom (mature understanding, insight)." The high ranking of wisdom and understanding does not seem to be an idle desire, but one that is matched by an awareness of its challenge. Four out of five parents agreed that "to be a good parent is one of the hardest things in life I do."

In other words, parents in the study do want to receive insight into the character and subtleties of their adolescent sons and daughters. They do want to grasp the meaning of their children's often cutting remarks and puzzling reactions. They do want to know when discipline is too severe or too lenient. They do want to be able to communicate better with their adolescent children.

Interestingly, however, the parents in the Adolescent-Parent study tend to minimize their own personal difficulties. True, some do admit they have problems in relating to others. Some do characterize themselves as very emotional, not able to devote themselves completely to others, very competitive, not at all kind, insensitive to the feelings of others, troubled with feelings of inferiority, or likely to go to pieces under pressure. But the number who thus describe themselves is few indeed.

The majority of parents characterize themselves as active, gentle, kind, confident, and warm in their relations with others. Fathers especially tend to see themselves as independent, able decision makers who stand up well under pressure. While they feel that they are less able than mothers to devote themselves completely to other people, they still see themselves as strongly helpful and "somewhat" aware of the feelings of others.

Mothers characterize themselves as quite emotional and at times prone to go to pieces under pressure. But they also stress that they are able to devote themselves "completely" to others, are highly aware of people's feelings, and are very warm in their interpersonal relationships.

One might conclude that the chief need for parents is to gain a better understanding of their children. This is important, but as parents we also need to get in better touch with our own feelings and those of our mate. There is an interrelationship between such disturbing questions as, "Why the antagonism between my son and me?" and the question, "Why does my mate overreact during a family crisis?"

Though parents may sense it, they seldom verbalize the truth that hidden dynamics do affect their behavior. One reason is that we can never be fully in touch with our feelings, drives, or motivations. Even parents trained in the area of human relations are not always aware of the emotional forces that cause them to treat their children insensitively. An emotional dynamic can subtly cloud the understanding of the most loving and insightful parent. The result is an inability to see that certain actions are inappropriate and even at times hurtful.

Family of Origin

Our family of origin determines much of what we do as parents. Recall, for instance, times when you have stopped in your tracks and realized you were reacting just as your own mother or father used to do when you were a child.

A friend says, "Whenever I get hurt and angry and I sense myself withdrawing in silence to lick my wounds, I say to myself, 'Don't do it. Remember how you hated when Mother did that.' " Another says thoughtfully, "What can I do about this habit of yelling at my kids? I don't really believe that's the way to handle a situation, but it was the way Mom did it at home. It frightens me a little when I think my children will do the same unless I change."

A 1983 *Time* magazine article on violence in the home spoke of the powerful dynamics that are established by abusive parents.[1] "Like a poisonous plant sending out spores," family violence tends to reproduce itself. Battered children grow up disposed to batter their own offspring. (See Chapter 7 for a fuller discussion on this subject.) As parents, we need to recognize the power of our family of origin—to be aware of its negative and positive patterns of behavior and their potential for continuing to shape our behavior. We may need consciously to break certain negative patterns and discipline ourselves to act otherwise. Of course, we may also try consciously to emulate some of the positive behaviors and attitudes our parents modeled so beautifully.

Wounded Memories

These memories are the hurtful remembrances of our past that still influence us today. Sigmund Freud dramatized the enduring power of early experience by showing how the effect of traumatic childhood experiences lingers on into adulthood. Our past experiences and decisions profoundly affect our present perceptions as parents and mates. For this reason, in a marriage relationship, mothers and fathers need to take time to recall and share experiences of their own youth with each other. Sometimes the memory of an experience helps us understand more clearly our present concerns, as was the case of the counselor in the following illustration.

Tom, a middle-aged man active in the ministry of counseling delinquent boys in a large private school, was in one of our study groups in which members were asked to reminisce about life in their parental home. "Think back on what life was like at dinner time when you were fifteen," they were asked. Tom was initially skeptical of the exercise; but as others contributed to the discussion, he became increasingly pensive. When his turn came to share, he spoke with a touch of sadness. "I had forgotten how much trouble I caused my parents when I was fifteen. It was a bad year."

Sometimes a painful memory of the past helps us respond sensibly in the present.

A soft-spoken elderly woman in our study group cringed when she remembered herself as a girl of fourteen, shouting angrily at her parents, "I'd like to kill you!" But because she remembered, she could understand when similar words came from her grandchild.

However, emotional reactions from the past are not always positive. Sometimes these wounded memories remain within us as negative forces, to cloud our perceptions. Knowing this, a parent who has unhappy memories would do well to discuss them with a professional counselor. Such a step becomes especially important if the experiences have included sexual abuse, or ill treatment by an alcoholic parent. The tragedy of these experiences is their tendency to be lived out again in the life of the child-turned-parent.

Unmet Personal Needs

Related to the dynamic of wounded memories is the emotional force generated by certain unmet personal needs or unfulfilled ambitions. In more than a biological way, children are extensions of their parents. When we as parents begin to live out our ambitions or unfulfilled dreams through them, we can become prey to emotional upheaval for each mistake or inadequacy of our child. Unless the dynamic of our own unmet need is understood, the force brought into play can cause a cleavage between us and our adolescent. Let's look at some illustrations.

Most of us are familiar with the "Babe Ruth" father, who continually shouts his instructions and reprimands to a son at second base. Those sitting beside the father on the bleachers cringe for the boy, to say nothing of his embarrassed mother. This father feels that *he* is out on the field making the mistakes that caused *him* to be cut from the team when *he* was a ninth grader.

Then there is the mother who wanted to excel scholastically in her adolescent years, and often felt inferior because she did not do as well as a brother and sister. Now she pushes her teenage daughter to get As in school. Reprimanded for not having As on her report card, the girl—who actually is an earnest student, though not able to come up to the parents' standards—says, with considerable insight, "I can't understand why you expect *me* to get such good grades. *You* didn't."

What about the father who rebelled against his parents in his youth? As an adult, he regrets this and realizes how much his attitude during his teen years is now tied to many unfulfilled dreams and aspirations. Now he desperately tries to keep his son from taking the same path. But the tactics he uses are heavy-handed, and, as a result, the element of trust is rapidly eroding between father and son.

Feelings of Failure

Though the feeling of having failed as a parent is at some time present within every father and mother, for many parents it is a persistent thought. For about half of the 10,467 parents in the Adolescent-Parent study, "I am not as good a parent as I should be" is a nagging thought. The greatest concern of most parents is that they will fail as parents. Of the fourteen worries listed in the survey, none draws as high a rating as the worry over "the job I am doing in raising this child."

Much of our self-esteem as parents is linked to the behavior of our children. We tend to interpret their failures as our failures. This dynamic, with its accompanying sense of guilt and self-blame, surfaced as a prominent element in the cluster of family concerns among American Lutheran Church women in a 1981 study.[2] It is sufficiently strong and widely enough felt to have caused the following items to cluster together:

1. I am sometimes too harsh in the discipline of my children.
2. I feel unable to cope with my children.
3. My children are not turning out as well as I had hoped they would.
4. My children aren't learning much in school.
5. My husband is sometimes harsh in his discipline of our children.

The power of this dynamic is shown also in its lingering effects on women years after the children have left home. Women over sixty-five are most plagued with these nagging regrets particularly if they are also widows.

Parents who have always been self-critical and troubled with feelings of low self-esteem are especially susceptible to this dynamic. They continue to be sensitive about their modest achievements and their self-perceived limited importance in the scheme of things. Such parents often will react strongly when their children fail to obey or show them proper respect, because they interpret this as another sign of failure. Such parents then tend to become more controlling and rule-oriented. When they have a flare-up with their adolescent child, these parents do not see that their reaction of wanting to punish might be a way of making up for their own feelings of inferiority. Over-strictness and overprotection are control reactions of parents fearful of failure. For how many parents is this especially real? Among the parents of adolescents in the Adolescent-Parent study, it is real for one in four.

Reactions of Anger

Involved in a parent's sense of guilt and failure is regret over having gotten angry. Half of the parents in the Adolescent-Parent study acknowledge that "once in a while" they punish their child more than he or she deserves. One in three admit to times when "I get so angry I might hurt my child." It should be noted that the parents who admit to these outbursts of anger are primarily church-related, conscientious people who very much want to be good parents. David Mace has some insightful statements that apply to both parents and adolescents in family relationships:

The failure to achieve love and intimacy is almost always due to the inability of the persons to deal creatively with anger. Marriage and family living generates in normal people more anger than they experience in any other social situation in which they habitually find themselves. The overwhelming majority of family members know of only two ways of dealing with anger—to vent it or to suppress it. Both of these methods are destructive.[3]

The first way Mace indicates of handling anger—to vent it—is the experience of the father who writes about an incident concerning his eighth-grade daughter:

The children were arguing back and forth. I said to stop but she wouldn't. I got upset and hit her on the side of her head. I wish I had not done it.

This kind of reaction only produces guilt.

A second way of handling anger is to suppress it. Psychologist Haim Ginott in *Between Parent & Teenager* makes an apt observation on this method.[4] He stresses that parents should not convey hypocrisy by being outwardly "nice" while feeling angry inside. Children are very sensitive to parents' reactions and may often sense anger, even when the parents themselves are not fully aware of it.

Ginott contends that anger "should bring some relief to the parent, some insight to the teenager, and no harmful after-effects to either of them."[5] There might be a harmful after-effect if, for example, children are disciplined in front of their friends. The father of an eighth-grade boy writes of this experience: "When my child does something wrong, I get angry and often embarrass him in front of his friends." Such actions only make the child act up more.

Ginott says that parents may effectively express their feelings of anger to an adolescent if they are able to acknowledge the following truths:[6]

1. We accept the fact that in the natural course of events teenagers will make us uncomfortable, annoyed, irritated, angry, and furious.
2. We are entitled to these feelings without guilt or shame or regret.
3. We are entitled to express these feelings with one limitation: No matter how angry we are, we do not insult teenagers' personality or character.

In a situation that creates anger, the parents should first explain to the adolescent what he or she has done wrong and how it makes the parent feel. The parent then needs to tell the teenager what has to be done to correct the situation.

If these steps are followed, the storm clouds evaporate much more easily. A parent does not want to perpetuate waves of anger, defiance, retaliation, and revenge. These can lead to some of the most serious problems in parent-adolescent relationships.

We have seen some of the hidden dynamics that can cause a parent to overreact in a way that surprises both the parent and child. The reaction may be out of proportion to the significance of the incident. A parent may get very angry, or very depressed—withdrawing into a lonely and self-condemning silence that the family senses, but does not understand.

Because these dynamics are usually hidden and not available for personal reflection, a parent needs help to bring these feelings to the surface. There is no substitute for times of conversation and reflection in which husband and wife, parent and pastor, or parent and counselor sit and talk. The amazing phenomenon of unthreatened and reflective conversation is that it provides the setting within which memories of the past can float to the top. These, when explored, may provide insight and release.

Understanding Your Marriage Situation

The dynamics that stem from one's family of origin, from wounded memories, unmet personal needs, feelings of failure, and reactions of anger may be intensified by a stressful marriage situation. Our disappointing personal reactions cannot be fully understood without taking this into consideration.

Stress has the power to worsen relationships between husband and wife or between parent and child. Because certain marriage situations create added stress, consideration will be given here to their possible effects.

Stress-Creating Circumstances

Parents in the Adolescent-Parent study were asked to name the stress-producing situations that have occurred in their family within the life-span of their adolescent son or daughter. They experienced the following stressful situations:

21%	Losing a job
18%	A parent having a serious accident or illness
16%	Severe financial hardship in the family
12%	Parents divorcing
11%	Parents separating
7%	A natural disaster that damaged or destroyed the home, farm, or crops
6%	A parent or child developing a disability or handicap
6%	A family member being arrested
3%	Death of a child

Although only a small percentage (3 percent) of the parents

reported the stress of having lost a son or daughter, we are using the example of a death in the family to show how external pressure may intensify the home situation. The same dynamics are often present in other stressful situations, particularly those in which a child "fails" a parent, as in the case of parents with children who are drug addicts.

Trauma of Death in the Family

In 1976 David M. Kaplan and a research team conducted a study of the impact on 40 families of losing a child to leukemia.[7] They found that within a year after the death, 70 percent of the parents showed evidence of serious marital problems. Forty percent of the families had a parent with a serious drinking problem, and 43 percent of the mothers showed significant difficulty in performing homemaking duties. Obviously, the trauma of the situation had negatively affected the parents. In almost all cases, the study reports that negative effects could have been lessened by better communication between husband and wife, situations where each was allowed into the other's thought life, feelings, and judgments. In this way an environment of safety would have been created, and no one would need to bury an experience for fear it would not be accepted.

Three common factors may hinder communication in this type of situation:

1. The *sense of guilt* parents feel as they endlessly think, "If only I had done this . . . " or "if only I hadn't done that . . . "
2. The *escape into a fantasy world*, imagining that everything is as it used to be.
3. The *use of drugs or alcohol* or both to blank out pain.[8]

The great need is for husband and wife to talk about what has happened and to share each other's pain. It is important that they do this immediately and as an ongoing practice. By talking about loss, the father and mother gain a healthy understanding of how each is bearing the grief. If they do not, two people who have lived together for many years may misunderstand each other's reactions and grow apart.

Because many men in our culture think they are not expected to show emotion (except perhaps anger), it is common for a man in grief to bury it by becoming preoccupied with his work. The wife may think he is uncaring, because he seldom speaks about the child who has died or "failed." On the other hand, the husband may become upset with his wife's reaction of depression, or her constant talking about what has happened.

A helpful structure for promoting communication between spouses after a stressful situation, such as the death of a child, is to set up the following type of family meeting:[9]

1. Let discussion be open-ended, allowing time for "all there is to say."
2. State the intention and willingness to hear the other express feelings.
3. Let one person talk until he or she has said all he or she wants, with no rebuttal.
4. Invite each person to tell what kind of support he or she wants from the other.
5. Make sure there are no interruptions, such as phone or doorbell.

After this period of communication, and a time for husband and wife to spend some time alone together, parents need to give each other space to process and integrate what has happened in their own individual lives during this stress period.

Divorce and Separation

Grief and shock, fear of the future, resentment, self-pity, frustration, and even rage are some of the emotions that cloud the perceptions of divorcing or divorced parents. These emotions place a separated parent under unusual pressures. In a pending marital breakup, parents often fear talking about the situation, so they avoid explaining to their children what is happening. This silence in turn creates fear and guilt feelings in the adolescent. Some parents subject their children to frightening confrontations and displays of verbal abuse, using their children as confidants, spies, and emotional pawns.

Parents can change this situation if they realize that their lack of cooperation is depriving their child of a vital relationship. If they care about the child, separating parents will seek a new framework for dealing with each other as people and a new framework for raising their children. A key element in this working relationship is forgiveness of the former spouse for past unhappiness. With that as the basis, the chances for success are multiplied. Once the trauma of an unhappy marriage is over, divorcing parents may be more free to become good parents. A friend, in reflecting on her divorce, had this to say: "I consider it of prime importance that I do not hate my former husband. If I should hate him, I know my daughters would develop feelings against men and it might affect their future marriages and homes."

As a beginning step, divorcing parents should sit down with their children and explain what is happening and how it will affect each of them. A strong affirmation of parental love is necessary at this time. Parents should not blame each other; and they should stress that the children are not to blame for the divorce, that they are free to love both parents, and that they will not be asked to take sides against either parent. Preteens—nine- to 12-year-olds—are especially vulnerable to being used as an ally by one parent against the other, and may become extremely angry at the parent they feel is to blame. Some children may react physically to this kind of stress, developing stomach aches, headaches, or asthma attacks. Other children may begin to steal or lie. Teenagers often act out anger at their parents by spending more time way from home; some become involved in sexual activity.

Children do not believe in no-fault divorce. They blame one or both parents, or they blame themselves. The need for understanding is great. But with the search for understanding comes the wisdom and insight that has enabled many divorced parents to establish close relationships with their children and enjoy a happy family life.

Single Parents

Because little is known about characteristics that tend to typify single parents, we made a special analysis comparing the responses of 482 single parents to those of parents of intact families (where there has not been separation, divorce, or death).[10] This information may help single parents realize how many of their parenting problems are intensified by their marital situation and not necessarily by poor parenting. It may also help family, friends, and support groups understand what the single parent is having to cope with. Such understanding can lead to supportive action.

Without question, the cry for understanding is strongest from those who valiantly try to be both father and mother. Single parents especially want to know how to communicate better with children, how to instill healthy concepts of what is right and wrong, and how to deal with the practice of drug use. Because their need is so strong, they are more likely than parents of intact families to seek out a specialist for help.

From the standpoint of numbers alone, single parents are a significant group. Approximately half (48 percent) of public school children in the Minneapolis, Minnesota, school system in 1983–84 came from homes with a single parent. A medium-sized city in California reported 63 percent of single-parent homes within the school system. With the divorce rate approaching 50 percent for those now marrying, there should be no decline in the percentage of children who will live, for a time at least, in a single-parent home.

Though every situation is different, certain characteristics do typify single parents. In 90 percent of divorces, children are assigned to the mother's care. For this reason, our findings deal with the mother's situation as single parent. Only one-third of these mothers receive any financial support from the absent mate. As a result, they become involved in downward economic mobility. Some move to more modest housing, often to another community; if they had not done so before, they must now take on full-time jobs. Thus their children suffer multiple losses—loss of father; loss of mother to a heavy work schedule; and often loss of the home, community, and former school friends. Needless to say, the burden such a mother assumes is enormous, not least because of the effect it has on the children.

One single-parent mother, speaking about her eighth-grade daughter's reactions to the divorce, says, "When we moved and changed schools, she went to pieces. All she did was cry and get sick—she missed eighteen days of school in three months. Before, she had perfect attendance. Her inability to adjust upset me. I sought professional counseling. We moved back to our old school district." It is in stressful situations such as these that the cry for understanding becomes a cry of desperation.

When single parents are asked, "How are things going for you and your family these days?" fewer than those of two-parent families in the Adolescent-Parent study are able to answer, "Fairly well" or "Very well." More of them feel their family life is having negative effects on their child, that "members of my family do not get along well with each other." Many more are worried about the job they are doing in raising their child. More single parents rate their child in the direction of being disobedient, rebellious, likely to get into trouble, disrespectful of authority, and not a good student. When trying to imagine what their child worries about, they are more likely (than married mothers) to assume their child has thoughts of suicide and worries about getting beaten up at school or losing a parent through death. Even worse, more think their child is worried about losing parental love, losing the parent to alcoholism, or being physically hurt by the parent.

Some single parents are very conscious of their inability to discipline their children. More often than married mothers, single parents in the Adolescent-Parent study will use extreme measures—either being too lenient when discipline is needed, or reacting in anger by yelling or hitting the child.

Mother-Son Conflict. Understanding and special consideration are needed where there is conflict between mother and son in a single-parent household. A number of studies have found that boys fare worse than girls in a single-parent home, and the negative effects seem to increase with age. This observation was confirmed through a large and comprehensive national study conducted by Guidibaldi in 1983 that compared the children of divorced parents with those in intact families.[11] It documents, for instance, that fifth-grade boys contrast strikingly with fifth-grade girls on a variety of measures. The boys show less peer popularity; greater pessimism; lower scores in reading, math, and classroom conduct; and greater likelihood to repeat a school grade. The contrasts are even more dramatic when boys of divorced parents are compared with girls of divorced parents and with boys of intact families. The consistent finding is that a boy in a single-mother family is more likely to be involved in aggressive acts toward his mother. The findings show that boys typically react with aggression to the stress of divorce, while girls tend to react by being more helpful than before. A single mother, writing about her fifth-grade son, says,

I was divorced when my son was five years old. When he has a problem, he seems to clam up and won't talk. He doesn't listen, and I have to tell him over and over to do something. I wish I knew why he defies me. He has been having a lot of difficulty with schoolwork and getting along with others. He seems to do things deliberately to get punished.

A surrogate father may provide the stabilizing ingredient needed by a fatherless boy. It is impressive to see how the attention and regular contact of a grandfather, uncle, or divorced father can bring about positive changes in an adolescent boy.[12]

Father-Daughter Reaction. It is generally observed that girls do not show the marked negative effects of single parenting found in boys. Nevertheless, the sense of loss is also powerful for girls.

One negative behavior found more often for high school girls living with a single-parent mother is a higher than normal desire for male affection. Such girls are especially vulnerable to the sexual advances of males. With mother gone all day to work, the empty house can become an attractive place for after-school lovemaking. The support of family, friends, congregation, or youth group may form a substitute family that supplies the missing elements of human love and care that adolescents need so desperately when only one parent is in the home.

Loss of Support Systems. A big void in single parenthood is the loss of social support systems. Following divorce, the single mother often significantly decreases her contacts and those of her children with the former husband's relatives. This means breaking relationships with grandparents, aunts, and uncles, who may still care a great deal about the children and mother. There may also be a sharp dropoff in the mother's former friendships, and hence a limited social life.

The 482 single parents who participated in the Adolescent-Parent study showed themselves to be less active in church and less involved in community organizations than intact families. This lack of involvement also holds true for their children. One divorced mother says,

Our family had always been active in church. My husband and I had even been youth leaders for a while. After our divorce, the children (all adolescents) didn't want to participate in church activities anymore. They felt strange and different, as though people no longer liked them and they didn't belong.

The tendency for single parents to withdraw from community institutions is seen in the fact that no more than one out of ten in the Adolescent-Parent study was a single parent (in a day when almost half of public school children are from single-parent homes). This disengagement from congregations, which are potentially important support systems, has been documented elsewhere. Most single parents do not identify with a religious institution.

The lack of adequate support systems places an added burden on the single parent. Perhaps this explains why single mothers are more often drawn to the emotional extremes of slapping, spanking, or yelling at their children. It also may explain why children of single parents find it harder to get along with each other and the parent with whom they live.

From his study, Guidibaldi provides some fascinating data on the importance of support systems.[13] He finds that children of divorced parents fare best in smaller schools—either private or parochial—and ones that use a traditional rather than open classroom structure. Children in these schools demonstrate better classroom adjustment and performance in school environments characterized as "safe, orderly, and predictable." Apparently, such classrooms operate as support systems.

Furthermore, he found that academic performance is significantly higher for children whose grandparents live nearby and are often around to assist with household tasks. The same is true for the children who are in continued contact with the relatives of their custodial parent. Where there is continued contact with relatives and friends among children of divorced parents, one is likely to find more independent learning, less irrelevant talk in the classroom, less withdrawn behavior, less blaming, and less inattention.

It is hard to overstate the benefit to single parents of being surrounded by a group of loving and concerned friends and relatives.

Stepparenting

Far less is known about the pressures common to step-families than to single parents and divorcing parents. However, due to the great increase in divorce and remarriage, step-families represent a growing phenomenon in our country. When single parents marry, each with children from a previous marriage, a new family unit emerges. Puzzling dynamics often operate in the new family situation, ones that make the parents cry out for understanding. As a result, there has been a burgeoning of support and study groups on this area of family life.

What does a father do, for instance, when his stepson views him as an intruder and the person responsible for his parents' break-up? The stepson may be intent on gaining revenge for the hurt he has suffered; he may refuse to go anywhere with his stepfather, or even to carry on a conversation with him. He may react negatively to whatever his stepfather does.

Likewise, it is not rare for a stepparent to have mixed, if not hostile, feelings toward a stepchild, especially if the child exhibits negative characteristics of the divorced mate. A woman referring to her eighth-grade stepdaughter says, "I don't like her. She has the same characteristics of her mother, the ones that caused the divorce in the first place." In the next breath, the same woman speaks of how guilty this attitude makes her feel.

Sometimes a child feels it would be disloyal to like the stepparent. One woman expresses this when she writes of her fifth-grade stepdaughter, "She is torn between me and her real mother."

Equally painful for the stepparent is the situation in which the adolescent feels rejected by the absent parent. "I need help," says one woman, "with a stepson who has been rejected by his father."

A review of current studies led Jolliff to conclude that "though the bonds between stepchildren and stepparents are seldom as strong as those between members of primary families, they can be quite positive and meaningful."[14] He reports that the effect of remarriage is least significant (negatively) for children under the age of eight, somewhat more significant for children between eight and twelve, and the most significant for adolescents.

If the stepparent has a child of his or her own, guilt feelings may arise over loving this child more than the stepchild. It is easy to feel, especially if one has gone through a painful divorce situation, "My poor child has gone through so much trauma. I must do everything I can to make up for it." It is not difficult to see where siding with one's own child in a conflict situation may cause problems with one's mate. This is why the husband-wife relationship is to be treated as primary.

Maturity and leadership are two qualities stepparents need in the "new" family. In trying to understand the stepchild, the new parent needs to recognize that the child probably has feelings of anger toward both stepparent and birth parent, and feelings of guilt over having caused or having failed to stop the divorce. The absent parent tends to be idealized and bad things forgotten. For the child, it is a struggle even to know what name to call the stepparent. But no matter how complex the dynamics, the child still longs to be accepted and to have a happy home, and the stepparent must never forget this.

When children of two families live in the same home, periodically or permanently, it is essential for parents to spend time together—alone. Difficult as this may be with the multiple duties of stepparents, it is of paramount importance. There are unusual stresses on the relationship of husband and wife in remarriage where there is a merging of two families. Therefore, times of sharing problems, learning to know and understand each other, placing priority on the relationship, may mean the difference between a marriage that works out or one that eventually dissolves. (Jolliff stresses, however, that issues of negative behavior are often part of a short-term adjustment, and overconcern can sometimes turn the situation into a long-term adjustment.)

C. Gilbert Wrenn, in *The World of the Contemporary Counselor*, has advice applicable to stepparents. The adolescent, he reminds us, is not a different person because he or she is in a new circumstance. Therefore, he or she should be treated normally, always with a positive emphasis on the future, not on the should-have-beens.[15]

This chapter has addressed the kinds of pressures that affect our ability to be the parent we want to be. In writing this book we have been impressed by how easily most parents can describe the characteristics of good parenting. Yet, the same parents exhibit attitudes and actions that contradict their ideals.

As indicated in the beginning of this chapter, the tendency of parents is not to acknowledge family or personal weaknesses or difficulties. This may be due to an attempt to be a tower of strength for the children, or a hidden desire to appear successful in child rearing. Whatever the reason, parents need to acknowledge that they fight the same battle as their children. They grapple with many of the same issues and want significance and recognition, just as their children do. In coming to understand themselves, they are better able to understand their adolescents. The developmental tasks identified for adolescents in Chapter 3 may be applied equally to parents.

3. Cry for Understanding Your Adolescent

It's hard to rebel when I know you're trying to understand me.
—TEENAGER TO PARENT

A MOTHER'S DIARY

I'm puzzled tonight—and a little bit scared. Up to now—Karen's just going into seventh grade—she's been a delightful girl to have around. She's a fun person and I've always thought she enjoyed being with her Dad and me.

I've tried to tell myself I'm getting too sensitive, but she really hurt me yesterday when she didn't want to go with us to see Grandma. For years we've done this on Sunday afternoons and Karen has loved it. She is her Grandma's pet.

But I distinctly heard her saying to her best friend, Cathy, "You know my mom—she wants me to go along *everywhere* she and Dad go. It's so boring. Sometimes I can hardly *stand* it." (We *don't* go everywhere together—it's only on Sunday afternoons!)

Then she's started wearing her hair like Cathy—long and untidy, and she has such pretty hair when it's neat and combed. But when I said something about it to her the other day, she flared right up at me.

She *knows* how I feel about that loud, awful music she plays when she comes home from school—just when I'm back from work and tired. Sometimes I ask her to *please* turn it down. The last time I did that she snapped back at me in a scornful tone of voice that made me want to cry,

"You're so old-fashioned I can't believe it!"

As parents, we need two pieces of equipment to help us know and understand our adolescents: one, a simple conceptual framework to help us understand the changes typical of this stage of growth; and two, listening skills to help us tune in and discover who our adolescent is and where he or she is in the maturing process.

Framework for Understanding Early Adolescence

A method of organizing our observations will provide a basis for evaluating the significance of what we see and hear as we live with our adolescent children. We need a framework for answering such questions as, "Is this behavior typical of a young adolescent or not?" "What constitutes 'normal, healthy growth'?"

We also need a framework for helping our adolescent answer such questions as, "Who am I?" "How should I understand the puzzling feelings I have?"

These questions relate to the developmental process experienced by every adolescent. Should a young person not progress through the stages of the maturing process, he or she might physically become an adult, but remain a teenager emotionally.

Following are the seven goals an adolescent intuitively seeks to achieve during the teen years.[1]

1. *Achievement.* The satisfaction of arriving at excellence in some area of endeavor.
2. *Friends.* The broadening of one's social base by having learned to make friends and maintain them.
3. *Feelings.* The self-understanding gained through having learned to share one's feelings with another person.
4. *Identity.* The sense of knowing "who I am," of being recognized as a significant person.
5. *Responsibility.* The confidence of knowing "I can stand alone and make responsible decisions."
6. *Maturity.* Transformation from a child into an adult.
7. *Sexuality.* Acceptance of responsibility for one's new role as a sexual being.

The initial letters of each catchword in this list form the acronym "AFFIRMS." Because a conceptual framework may be easily forgotten, using the word "Affirms" as a memory jog can help recall the *seven goals of adolescence,* as follows:

Adolescent Goals

A	Achievement realized
F	Friends gained
F	Feelings understood
I	Identity established
R	Responsibility accepted
M	Maturity gained
S	Sexuality understood

One of these goals is the overall goal of which the other six are parts. The goal of maturity encompasses all the others. We include it as a reminder that our ultimate goal is to see our child become a responsible, caring adult.

We have chosen "Affirms" as a key word because our studies of the helping professions show the concept to be of high importance in working with people. Search Institute carried out a large study for the Association of Theological Schools that involved over 4,000 clergy and lay members randomly selected from 47 denominations. One purpose of the study was to determine the criteria people use when evaluating the effectiveness of pastor, priest, or rabbi.

An open and affirming approach to people ranked highest in importance, irrespective of denomination. This style of relating to people, a pastor's most important quality in ministry, includes the following elements:

1. Remains positive and affirming to people even when handling stressful situations
2. Is willing to acknowledge own limitations and personal mistakes
3. Shows a flexibility of spirit in being willing to hear differing views and welcome new possibilities
4. Honors commitments and carries out personal promises

Thus an affirming approach—which applies equally to the parent-child relationship—reflects an attitude that is nondefensive (willing to admit mistakes), flexible (willing to hear differing views), and dependable (carries out promises).

Affirmation is a hopeful stance. As a mind-set, it conveys the conviction that every person is significant and has unique possibilities. A 1974 study found that what separates outstanding youth workers from the mediocre is not skill but an attitude of faith in their ability to change others.[2]

How can we affirm our adolescent child? A closer look at the seven goals for adolescents will show how parents may affirm their child in meaningful ways.

Goal 1—Achievement

Adolescents have a need to achieve, to excel in a tangible way (for example, in skills such as computer programming, playing football, sewing, painting, being a good mechanic). To know one does well in an activity vastly enhances one's sense of self-esteem.

The parent's task is to help the adolescent discover his or her "special gift" and then affirm each hesitant effort to develop this ability. The most devastating action of a parent is to fault, criticize, or demean the fumbling efforts of a child. In 1918 Charles Cooley said, "Pygmalion is alive and well in work with young people. Adults who convey a sense of futility to youth always seem to find their prophecy fulfilled, whereas those with great expectations likewise discover great potential in youth."[3] This is as true today as it was half a century ago.

Why should the parent not criticize the efforts of a child? Because the child's desperate short-term need is to gain a sense of achievement, to be seen as praiseworthy *now*. An adolescent needs affirmation and encouragement, not well-meaning criticism. An accurate critique can follow later.

An adolescent's need for parental praise and support can never be overestimated. Telling a child specific ways in which he or she has done well shows the adolescent that a parent has taken time to observe what he or she has done. Withholding affirmation or encouragement is often interpreted by children as an indication of parental lack of interest or even rejection. A friend recalls, "I can't remember ever getting a compliment as a teenager. I think my parents were afraid it would make me proud. But never knowing I did anything well made me feel like a nobody."

The opposite of this position, of course, is routine praise. "Don't praise every little thing," says a mother. "Kids can sort out what is phony or not. They also know what they can do well." If an adolescent has not done a task he or she was asked to do, or has performed poorly, we show we care by finding out why things did not work out. In the process, we may discover that the reason lies in a sense of inadequacy.

There may be situations, however, in which too much praise is hurtful. One young adult says, "I feel that I was praised more than necessary for my ability in athletics as a young adolescent. I think I developed the belief that I was more gifted than I really was. It caused some false hopes and expectations, which meant a long struggle with a sense of failure later on."

The adolescent's long-range need for achievement is centered in doing something significant in life, in finding a satisfying occupation or vocation. The 8,165 young adolescents in the Adolescent-Parent study were given a list of twenty-four values and asked to rank them in importance for their lives. Four top values (after a "happy family life") emerged:

1. To get a good job when I am older.
2. To do something important with my life.
3. To do well in school.
4. To make my parents proud of me.

The first two values (getting a good job and doing something important) are seen as being more important by ninth-graders than fifth-graders, whereas the next two (doing well in school and making parents proud) are regarded more highly by fifth-graders than by ninth-graders. Nevertheless, among the twenty-four values that adolescents of this age consider important, the average rank for these four values is from number two to number five. Clearly, the desire to achieve is a strong motivation for young adolescents. This means they will appreciate whatever their parents do to affirm and guide their exploratory thinking about a vocation or personal future.

Vocational choice becomes an increasingly important discussion topic as an adolescent matures. Figure 1 indicates the high ranking that adolescents grades five through nine give to the value of "doing something important with my life."

Studies show that the parent can be a child's best resource in evaluating career decisions. A helpful guide for parents interested in discussing their possibilities is found in a book by Luther B. Otto entitled *How to Help Your Child Choose a Career*.[4]

Talking about the child's future career may be a way by which parents can counter the marked decline of ninth-grade boys' desire to achieve at school. Though the interest of girls in doing well at school remains high from grades five through nine, it steadily declines for boys. It may be that some boys shift their interest to other types of achievement. In response to the item, "At school I try as hard as I can to do my best work," 39 percent of the ninth-grade boys answer "very often," as compared with 49 percent of ninth-grade girls.

Granting this difference in academic motivation, it is well to recognize that 69 percent of the boys and 81 percent of the girls in the Adolescent-Parent study still aspire to go on to college. Of these, 26 percent of the boys and 31 percent of the girls entertain ideas of training for a profession. This suggests that thoughts about advanced education are already well entrenched in the minds of middle-school adolescents.

We can help our adolescents find a sense of significance, but not by controlling them. Our data show that parental overcontrol, no matter how well-intentioned, has a dulling effect on the educational aspirations of adolescents. Even worse than this type of guidance is overcontrol motivated by the personal ambitions of the parent (this emotional dynamic was discussed in Chapter 2 under "Unmet Needs").

A father may wish very much that his son play football, but the son might rather play chess. Chess, not football, is what

Figure 1. Achievement: Value placed on "doing something important with my life."*

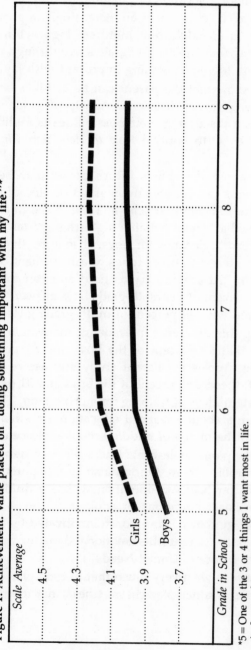

*5 = One of the 3 or 4 things I want most in life.
4 = I want this very much.
3 = I want this quite a bit.
2 = I want this somewhat.
1 = I don't want this much at all.

this boy needs to build confidence. A high school teacher expresses the problem:

I've been a high school drama and English teacher for five years now. My students have won top state awards in drama for the past three years. But my father feels I'm a failure because I'm not doing my medical residency at the Mayo Clinic.

The developmental goal of achievement is especially important for physically disabled adolescents. Though handicapped by cerebral palsy, Tom Janvier, while training for the Olympics, was asked, "What made the difference in your life?" Upon reflection, he decided that the more appropriate question would be, "*Who* made the difference?" Then he spoke of his parents as compassionate people who did not cease in their devotion to help him gain control over his uncontrollable muscles. In a speech entitled "I Don't Believe in Handicaps," he referred to his sisters, who loved him for himself; and to his speech teacher, who helped him share his feelings. These people helped him decide to be a winner when the odds against him were monumental.[5]

Goal 2—Friends

A second important goal for an emerging adolescent is gaining "friends I can count on." When asked about their interest in "learning how to make friends and be a friend," 52 percent of the boys and 69 percent of the girls in the Adolescent-Parent study say they "very much" wanted help in doing this. Why do they have this strong interest? Gaining friends is the adolescent's unconscious way of broadening his or her social base. In this way they can become integrated into a larger group without breaking from their parents.

Our task as parents is to affirm the adolescent's desire for friends and to open our home to these friends, thereby encouraging a broadening of the adolescent's social network. Peer friendships are extremely important. They help adolescents gain the skills needed for establishing lifelong friendships.

With increased skill in interpersonal relationships comes the ability to meet strangers, to feel comfortable in a group, and to be personally affirming of others. Unfortunately, in the 1970 Search Institute study of high school youth, we found that controlling parents show little interest in their child's friends, or, worse, are likely to disapprove of them. They actually discourage the widening of their child's friendship circle.

Boy-Girl Differences. As shown in Figure 2, marked differences do appear between the sexes on the goal of having friends. Girls are more concerned than boys about establishing friendships, a concern that for them does not change significantly by grade. Boys, who are less concerned about friends, also show less skill in interpersonal relationships.

Though parents notice the increase in their daughters' ability to relate well to people and to make friends, parents of boys do not see this improvement. As a result of having fewer social skills, boys do not cope as well in combating feelings of loneliness, being misunderstood, or being ridiculed. Clearly, social competence—the ability to make friends—is an important goal that tends to be underdeveloped among young adolescent boys. Skill in interpersonal relationships is at its highest for an adolescent boy when he is in seventh grade.

In contrast, ninth-grade girls are at their highest point in interpersonal relationships and lowest in their feelings of social alienation. It would appear that parents might enjoy a more comfortable relationship with their ninth-grade daughter than they may have had in her earlier stages of adolescence.

Parental Support. The adolescent's goal of gaining friends may be a turbulent road, as many parents know. A long-time teacher notes how prominently cliques figure in the lives of her fifth-graders. "The cliques sometimes change within a few weeks," she said. "And one thing I've noticed is the cruelty of some girls within a clique toward another. But the picked-on girl will stay because she wants to be a part of the friendship circle."

Parents may help make these friendship circles positive ex-

Figure 2. Friends: Value placed on friendship*

Percent "very much" or "at the top of my list"

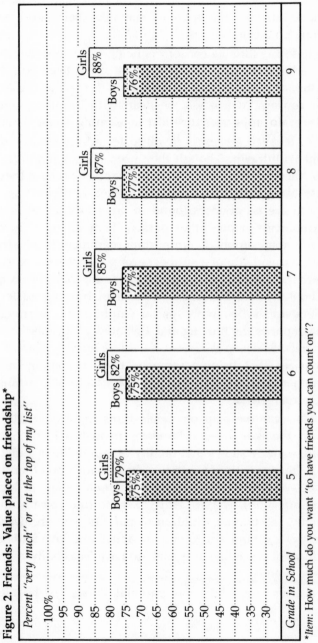

Grade in School

*Item: How much do you want "to have friends you can count on"?

periences by providing fun occasions for friends to be together. For instance, a parent who has a boat may invite his son's friend out for a ride; parents may take their daughter's friend along on a camping trip.

Today, justifiable concern is being expressed over the hours an adolescent may spend in front of the television, the computer, or playing video games. Though there are other reasons for concern, which will be dealt with in later chapters, our concern here is over time lost in learning social skills.

A deeper problem is involved for adolescents who are shy and withdrawn. Though they need friends more than others do, they make it hard for this to happen because they tend to stay away from social situations. Least threatening for such youth are experiences found in large groups, or in the companionship of one other person. Sometimes a church youth leader may supply this important ingredient and be the bridge to the friendship of a support group. A program originated by Barbara Varenhorst, a psychologist in the Palo Alto, California, school system, has been effective in training adolescents in friendship skills, with special emphasis on learning how to reach out to the hurting and alienated youth in school. In *Real Friends: Becoming the Friend You'd Like to Have*,[6] Varenhorst emphasizes that helping someone else—becoming involved in another person's life—is a necessary factor in learning how to be a real friend.

How can we help our adolescents mature socially and acquire the skills needed for close friendships? The Adolescent-Parent study shows that quality of family life is a distinguishing characteristic of youth who have many good friends. Wherever you find family closeness (parental show of love, trust, and affection), you are more likely to find socially competent youth. In contrast, children of parents who are overly strict, controlling, and apt to employ abuse and love withdrawal as a form of discipline, are likely to have less ability to make and keep friends.

Adolescents who know parental abuse, feel hostile toward

their parents, and are involved in antisocial behavior tend to have few, if any, friends. Such characteristics are also associated with drug use and suicidal tendencies, even for adolescents as young as ten years old.

The Adolescent-Parent study strongly indicates that the adolescents who are apt to make friends easily are those most certain of a personal religious faith. They are also likely to see religion as liberating, rather than as a restrictive force that hems a person in with "do's" and "don't's." Clearly, participation in the life of a religious institution helps adolescents achieve this second developmental goal of making and keeping friends. They learn to become part of a larger family in which friendships are established on the basis of a common faith and shared values.

Goal 3—Feelings Understood

Learning how to share personal feelings with a trusted friend means learning to describe one's emotions in words. Doing so makes it possible for an adolescent to deal rationally with puzzling emotions.

The importance of this third goal became apparent to the research staff at Search Institute during a youth survey in 1959. Using a questionnaire that presented the range of youth concerns, respondents read each description and then indicated how much each item bothered them. After finishing the survey, young people often stayed around to talk. One remarked, "I enjoyed taking the survey because the items describe how I really feel. Not until I saw the words did I know what some of my feelings were."

We have discovered that the inability to describe feelings is a child's major block to communication with parents. Though they might want to discuss problems with a parent, some adolescents simply cannot. They feel inadequate to find words that express how they feel. All they can do is make a few unsuccessful attempts and then walk away, saying, "You just don't understand."

Here is where an adolescent's peer group plays an important role. In the nonthreatening setting of their own age group, adolescents explore their feelings. They fumble for words that describe their anxiety-producing experiences, and hear others do the same. This sharing of secrets and emotion-laden experiences helps adolescents develop the ability to share themselves. In this process the seemingly interminable phone conversations between teenagers, which are such an irritant to parents, are ways in which adolescents learn to verbalize feelings and share them with peers; entrusting themselves to another in this way, they gain the capacity to express affection and love. This can also be a positive outcome of friendships between boys and girls at this stage of development.

The value of friends in achieving the goal of sharing feelings is apparent. Increasingly, as adolescents grow older, they also desire help from their peers in coping with concerns. The number of youth who want such help increases steadily by grade in school.

As parents, our task in all this is to affirm and encourage our adolescent's stumbling efforts at describing inner thoughts and feelings. It is important to take time to listen carefully. A good "listening posture" on the part of the parent, described later in this chapter, is vital in helping children learn to share their feelings with others.

Adolescents who have not developed this ability say, "I can't talk about personal things with my friends," "It is hard for me to understand what other people are feeling," "It is hard for me to share my feelings with other people." In contrast, adolescents who have learned to share themselves will often say, "I know what my best friend is feeling before he or she even tells me."

Growth in coming close to another person includes growth in "feeling with" and understanding. It brings a sensitivity that is vital if one is to become a caring person. By the ninth grade, as indicated in Figure 3, girls are well ahead of boys in this ability. As though to compensate, boys seem to prefer

Figure 3. Feelings: Ability to establish intimacy*

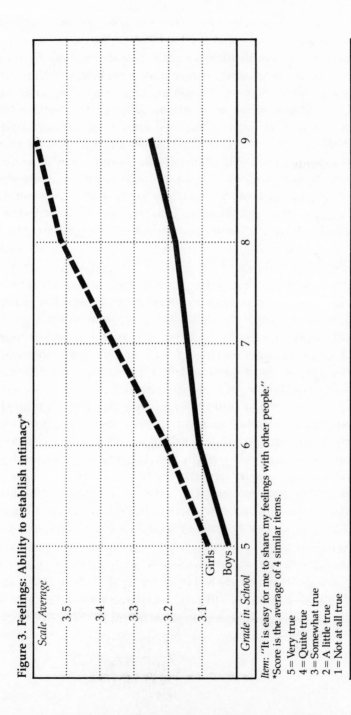

Item: "It is easy for me to share my feelings with other people."
*Score is the average of 4 similar items.

5 = Very true
4 = Quite true
3 = Somewhat true
2 = A little true
1 = Not at all true

moving in cliques or gangs that serve to increase their sense of independence.

An obvious difficulty for boys in learning how to express emotion is the "macho" image that says "boys don't cry." This public image encourages them to bury their feelings and tough it out. That is why conversations to help boys verbalize their feelings should begin when they are young children. By fifth grade, or even before, children show an eagerness to discuss adolescent issues with their parents. Parents would do well to enter this open door. It is also at age eleven and twelve that adolescent children show strong interest in a personal God and concern for world need. Helping one's child verbalize his or her feelings on these subjects is a worthy goal for parents.

Goal 4—Identity Achieved

A big question for young people entering puberty is, "Who am I?" Dramatic portrayal of this search for identity is shown in Figure 4, which illustrates the sharp upturn between sixth and seventh grades in the number of adolescents who "spend a lot of time thinking about who I am." If this preoccupation with self is surprising, consider the changes that force an adolescent to look for a new self-concept.

First, enormous bodily changes are giving the child the physical characteristics of an adult. Facial features and body shape are beginning to change markedly, while the voice deepens, especially in boys. Strength and stamina increase, and with this comes a greater capacity for work and play. In boys, the growth of the testes and scrotum is accelerated, and they experience their first ejaculation. In girls, the breasts begin to develop, and they experience their first menstrual period.

These physical changes, especially unsettling for girls, cause a sharp increase in the number of adolescents who say "no" to the item "I feel good about my body." A negative trend among girls from the fifth to the eighth grades indicates how difficult it is for girls to feel good about the changes they are experiencing.

Figure 4. Identity: Concern about one's identity*

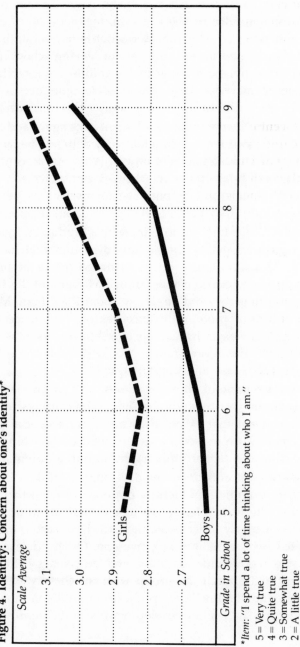

Scale Average

3.1

3.0

2.9 — Girls

2.8

2.7 — Boys

Grade in School   5   6   7   8   9

*Item: "I spend a lot of time thinking about who I am."

5 = Very true
4 = Quite true
3 = Somewhat true
2 = A little true
1 = Not at all true

A second major change that occurs relates to the role of the adolescent in society. An adolescent now is aware of leaving the child stage; he or she is aware, for instance, of drives for sexual expression. But the adolescent is not yet an adult. Society has defined minimum ages for leaving school, for being hired for a job, for serving in the military, for driving a car, for getting married. Thus young adolescents are in a transitional period in which they are neither children nor adults.

"Who am I?" the young adolescent asks again and again. In this search for identity, an adolescent depends heavily on the reactions and perceptions of others. Why? Adolescents tend to see themselves as others see them. When affirmed as significant individuals, adolescents see themselves as people who are respected; they begin to feel good about themselves.

Irene's family decided to express to a brother on his birthday some positive quality they admired in him that had been a source of inspiration to them. It turned out to be one of the most intimate occasions that family has ever had. Each of them learned things they did not know about the others. More than that, it was a profoundly encouraging experience for their brother. He was affirmed; he saw himself as others in the family saw him. Every family would do well to do this in a setting that is free and uninterrupted.

Most pervasive of all to an adolescent's future development and sense of worth is whether he or she can be strengthened in the concept that "God loves me. I am a special person. I have great worth in God's eyes." A good relationship is needed if the child is to absorb this truth through a parent.

Some adolescents delay the development of their own sense of self by adopting an identity opposed to what their parents stand for (for example, becoming a sexual adventurer in reaction to an overly strict home life). In these cases, the identity adopted is essentially a negative one. Other adolescents may slip into ready-made identities and proclaim by dress, mannerism, and speech the group with which they identify (the "jocks," the "brains," the "potheads"). In doing this, they are postponing the task of developing their own identity.

Adolescents who willingly identify with their families achieve positive self-identity more easily. The child who can find satisfaction and pride in knowing he or she is the son or daughter of the O'Briens, or the Johnsons, or the Taylors, can more quickly come to an awareness of who he or she is. But for children who have had several fathers or mothers in the course of growing up, identifying with a family name is less possible. For some adolescents, the resultant feelings of separateness and aloneness makes the goal of self-identity more difficult to achieve.

Slow developers (usually boys), for whom puberty is delayed until as late as the ninth grade, also have their problems. Small and undeveloped physically, they are easily shunted aside. Granted the status of neither children nor adults, they also are not viewed as adolescents. Those who mature late feel the impact of this nonidentity socially and personality-wise; they especially need the emotional support of parents and friends. Parents must help them understand that the "internal clock" may vary considerably from person to person.

Goal 5—Responsibility Accepted

One day, while we were seated in a restaurant in western Colorado, someone drew our attention to a nest of blue swallows outside the window. The fledgling birds were peering over the edge of the nest to the cement walk eight feet below. The mother bird, having decided it was time for her four offspring to try their wings, was nudging them ever closer to the edge of the nest. It was fascinating to witness the reluctance of these fledglings to leave their nest, and the insistence of the mother that they start flying.

The analogy of a bird nudging her offspring out of the nest is apt. While we tend to think that youth's drive for independence is rooted in rebelliousness, the drive originates just as much with parents. We found this to be true in our study: Most parents want their children to begin accepting adult responsibilities and making decisions on their own. Most parents want their children to leave home as self-reliant, responsible adults. Carrying out this conviction, however, is not easy. Many parents are afraid of how their adolescent will abuse this freedom. As a result, parents tend to shelter their growing adolescents and act in ways that make them unable to take independent actions.

The Adolescent-Parent study shows that youth-parent conflict is not a major issue during the junior high school years. Nor does conflict occur more for boys than for girls, nor does youth-parent conflict increase significantly from grades five through nine. What does change over the years, however, is the number of adolescents who want to "make my own decisions." Without question, there is a growing desire for independence during this stage in life. Figure 5 shows the rise in need for autonomy between the fifth and ninth grades, a change from 43 percent in fifth grade to 63 percent in ninth grade.

Clearly, the fifth goal for a maturing adolescent is to become behaviorally independent. Who achieves this goal best? Interestingly, it is those adolescents who view their parents with respect and affection. Although parents will note a greater resistance to authority as their adolescent moves toward ninth grade and, hence, occasions when sparks will fly, the increase in hostility is minimal. The change is primarily in an adolescent's reaction to parental roles.

The parent's task in helping an adolescent to accept responsibility is to avoid a smothering, rule-oriented, overcontrolling approach that keeps a child dependent on the parent or forces a rebellious response that results in rash and hurtful decisions.

The parent's task is to involve the adolescent in the basics of decision making, which should ideally begin in early childhood. Two young adults, when asked what ingredients they would consider essential in the homes they hope to establish, give some helpful insights into this process. One says,

I would teach responsibility, not by leading my child by the hand and telling him/her what should be done, but by teaching my child to think and make independent decisions. I would help him/her practice by creating a thinking situation, and then taking time to explain what

Figure 5. Responsibility: Desire to make own decisions*

Percent "very much" or "at the top of my list"

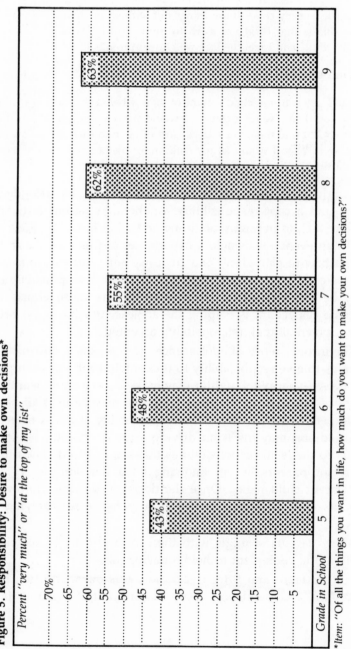

Item: "Of all the things you want in life, how much do you want to make your own decisions?"

I, as a parent on the basis of my experience, think are important things to consider and what are not, in making the decision. I would then ask that my child figure things out without my help. The reason I say this is that I did not learn to think in this way until I was a young adult, and I feel the lack was hurtful to me.

The other adds,

I would listen to my child's point of view when a decision has to be made and then give my position. I would say how important it is that we each listen to the other's ideas, sort of get into each other's shoes, as it were. Then I would let my child make his/her decisions without my butting in.

Taught in this way, the maturing child learns to make decisions and accept responsibility for them. A parent also can involve a child in family planning and what has to be done to make an event a satisfactory experience. In this way, the child learns how to plan ahead and creatively anticipate future tasks. As the child grows older, more and more adult responsibilities may be assumed. The parent who affirms these efforts to become self-reliant is helping the adolescent achieve the fifth developmental goal: responsibility accepted.

The inconsistency of adolescence often makes it difficult for parents to give responsibility to their adolescent. For example, a fourteen-year-old daughter may make a scene about wanting more responsibility; two days later, she may hand it all back or forget she had accepted the responsibility at all. A fifteen-year-old son may insist on driving a car or motorcycle, oblivious to the legal responsibilities that are involved. The difficulty for parents lies in knowing what decisions to let an adolescent child make. Once the decision is made, however, parents must hold the adolescent responsible for carrying it out.

Many parents struggle with the pros and cons of allowing their young adolescent to hold a paying job.

For fourteen- and fifteen-year-olds, this question often becomes an "independence" issue. According to Simmons Market Research Bureau,[7] three in five teenagers between fifteen and seventeen years of age and one in two twelve- to fourteen-year-olds are employed.

One positive aspect of teenage employment is that they learn to assume responsibility and help the family financially. One might also expect that the adolescent would learn the value of a dollar. This is not necessarily so, however; the University of Michigan's Institute for Social Research found that most of the high school seniors it surveyed used most or all of their earnings for immediate pleasure.[8]

Fifteen-year-olds who work more than fifteen hours a week on the average do less well in school and are less involved in school activities than those who do not work. Teens who have jobs, according to a study done at the University of California at Irvine, "tend to use cigarettes, alcohol, marijuana, and other drugs more often than unemployed adolescents, partly because they have more available cash and partly because they are subjected to more stress."[9]

A parent who gives an adolescent permission to get a job needs to help the child make the work experience a positive step in reaching maturity. This means considering such possibilities as taking a job that offers opportunities for learning; limiting the number of work hours so there is time for school and church activities on weekday evenings and Sundays; and encouraging long-term goals, such as saving for a college education. It could be a worthwhile experience for parent and adolescent to work out guidelines together, and have checkpoint times to see how the goals are being met. The end result could be progress toward the goal of achieving a sense of responsibility.

When parents talk of adolescents' accepting responsibility, they are often thinking of doing dishes, mowing the lawn, shoveling snow, cleaning the room, not as work for which they receive pay, but which is done as a member of the family. Other aspects of responsibility are overlooked. A young person grows in maturity by accepting responsibility for making an ill or unhappy family member feel better; or by accepting responsibility for reconciling family differences. This does not mean assuming the role of "the responsible one," but giving opportunities for each person in the family to struggle to a point of maturity. Of course, parents need to be aware of each adolescent's different abilities and not expect the impossible. Part of wisdom is expecting decision making only in areas where the adolescent is equipped to do it. Affirming a child's acceptance of responsibility is important.

Goal 6—Maturity

The end goal of all the developmental tasks, of course, is maturity—the state of having been transformed from a child to an adult. Though the onset of adolescence begins with a sharp break from childhood, the end of adolescence is not as clearly defined. Some adults never do complete their developmental tasks. They live as immature people whose behaviors are often quite adolescent.

Sexual maturity is another dimension of growing up. We asked the 10,467 parents of young adolescents to describe their child in relation to puberty. One question was, "To what extent has your child gone through puberty—that is, the period of time when the body takes on adult characteristics (for example, body hair grows, girls' breasts develop, boys' voices deepen). Which of the following is truest for your child?"

1. My child has not yet begun to go through puberty.
2. My child is in the beginning of puberty.
3. My child is in the middle of puberty.
4. My child is almost through puberty.
5. My child has completely gone through puberty.

Table 2. Parents' Estimates of Child's Reaction to Puberty

Grade in school	Boys					Girls				
	5	6	7	8	9	5	6	7	8	9
A. % Not yet begun puberty	86%	65%	38%	15%	5%	33%	14%	5%	1%	1%
B. % Beginning puberty	14	31	48	44	18	58	56	42	18	6
C. % In middle of puberty	0	3	11	26	41	7	22	31	31	21
D. % Almost through puberty	0	1	3	13	29	2	5	13	29	35
E. % Completed puberty	0	0	0	3	7	1	3	9	20	37

Note the growth trend in pubertal development indicated in Table 2. Two-thirds of the parents of girls believe their fifth-grader has entered puberty, and only fifteen percent of the parents of boys. Notice that the onset of puberty has not begun for some boys in eighth or ninth grade. There is a variability among young adolescents of at least five years. Interestingly, a few parents of girls think their child has completed puberty by the fifth or sixth grade (ages eleven and twelve), whereas over a third feel it did not happen until ninth grade (age fifteen). It is possible that parents themselves are not sure what constitutes entering or completing puberty.

Probably the most important fact to note is that girls mature sexually about two years earlier than boys. The average age at onset of menstruation is thirteen years; the average age at first ejaculation of semen is fifteen. See Figure 6.

Goal 7—Sexuality Understood

As already noted, a major component in the onset of adolescence is growth toward sexual maturity. This goal for an adolescent is acceptance of the new role of being a potential mother or father and acceptance of the responsibility sexual maturity implies. The task for the parent is to affirm the adolescent in this development and help him or her understand what is taking place.

The increased sex drive that accompanies onset of puberty is shown in the rising percentage of young adolescents who are interested in the opposite sex, as shown in Figure 7. The percentage who think "often" or "very often" about sex increases each year, from 24 percent for fifth-grade boys to 50

Figure 6. Maturity: Pubertal development by grade*

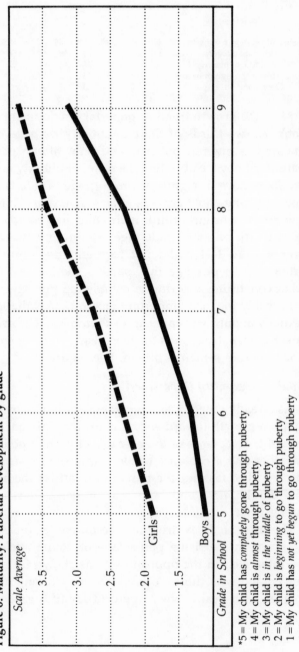

Scale Average

3.5

3.0

2.5

2.0 Girls

1.5 Boys

Grade in School 5   6   7   8   9

*5 = My child has *completely* gone through puberty
4 = My child is *almost* through puberty
3 = My child is *in the middle* of puberty
2 = My child is *beginning* to go through puberty
1 = My child has *not yet begun* to go through puberty

percent for ninth-grade boys. Though two years behind girls in their physical development, boys do not lag in the number who think often about sex. They respond more readily to sexual stimuli when alone, in contrast to girls, who respond more readily to affectional stimuli.

With thoughts of sex come an increased percentage who frequently talk about it. The number who talk "often" or "very much" with their friends about sex steadily increases from 26 percent (fifth grade) to 48 percent (ninth grade). It is a topic that new drives and emotions make exciting and daring. For many, talk about sex becomes a way of coming to understand and accept this new phenomenon in their lives.

A parent should know that the likelihood of an adolescent adopting a responsible attitude to sexuality is influenced by a variety of forces. The Adolescent-Parent data show that adolescents raised in families characterized by nurturance, warmth, and cohesiveness are significantly less likely to become attracted to sexually arousing stimuli or to become involved in sexual activity. The same is true for adolescents who view religion as important in their lives or who are raised by devout parents.

The adolescents who find it most difficult to accept a responsible approach to sexuality are those who as children have suffered sexual abuse. The tragic impact is the tendency of an abused child to repeat the cycle when he or she is older. For some reason not readily apparent to us, girls in the fifth grade are more likely (compared to girls in grades six through nine) to be afraid of sexual coercion.

Significantly, sexuality is a dimension of life adolescents wish they could discuss with their parents. When asked to indicate the one "to whom they most likely would turn for help or advice when having questions about sex," their overwhelming preference was parents. Though the percentage that prefer parents drops sharply following the seventh grade, there are still more ninth-graders who prefer their parents to personal friends or other adults for help or advice.

Figure 7. Sexuality: Frequency of Thinking About Sex*

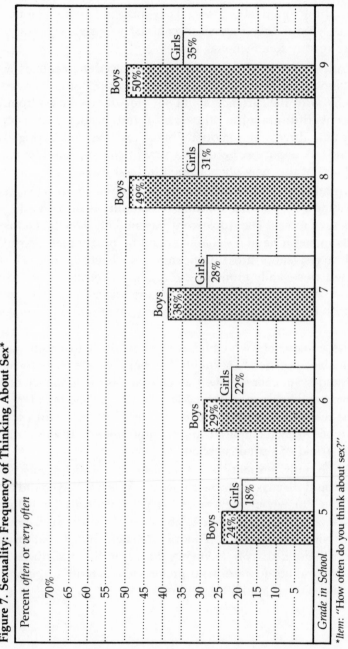

Percent *often or very often*

Grade in School

Item: "How often do you think about sex?"

Clearly, the time of opportunity for helping adolescents understand and responsibly accept their potential for creating life is in these early adolescent years. Unfortunately, most parents fail to take advantage of this opportunity. Only one-third of the adolescents in the Adolescent-Parent study say that they "have had good talks with my parents about sex." Yet, for half the young adolescents in grades six through nine, it is an especially pertinent topic of conversation. Fifty percent say they are "in love with someone of the opposite sex." The task of a parent is to affirm the significance of boy-girl attraction, a God-created phenomenon, and help the adolescent understand its meaning and beauty. Parents are most helpful to their adolescent sons and daughters when they can discuss not only the facts of sex, but the emotions and responsibilities involved. Parents need to evaluate their own feelings on sex issues in order to be the help they want to be to their adolescent.

A girl speaking about her mother's relationship to her in the matter of sex conversation says,

I'd like to talk to my mom more openly about my boyfriend, especially how to handle sexual desires so I can stay in keeping with God's Word. She doesn't have time for me. Or, when she does, I feel like she's not really understanding. I'm embarrassed to talk openly to her because I feel like she won't approve or accept my feelings. So, I feel like I always have to be my best. It doesn't give me any room to deal with my humanness and faults and to know that I'm loved.[10]

The conceptual framework for understanding early adolescence presented earlier can be helpful to us as parents if we use it to organize what we hear and observe in our children. It is important to allow conversation to go below the surface of routine exchange. To have such conversations we must sit down and listen with an attitude of truly wanting to understand our child. The following section discusses how this stance of understanding can be established.

Listening for Understanding

"Of course I know more than a child. . . ."

Adults typically think they know more than children. From such a vantage point, we relate to our children much as doctors relate to their patients. We ask questions (often probing ones) to locate trouble spots. Having heard the answers and made a judgment, we give a prescription as to what should be done. From our position of authority, we expect our prescription to be followed.

From this stance also, we may relate to our child as a teacher does to a student. We feel free to correct a mistake, or to give information. This may be a helpful way to operate with small children, but we need additional skills with adolescents. Because they are entering into adulthood, they will respond better to being approached as peers. Essentially, the path to such understanding is a *listening stance.*

Three Types of Listening Mistakes

The concept of a listening stance is well known. In fact, most of the parents in our study say they often listen to their adolescent. Unfortunately, however, listening is not easily practiced. Roland and Doris Larson, in *I Need to Have You Know Me*, describe common "listening mistakes" of well-meaning people.[11] These mistakes illustrate that the kind of listening most busy people do does not represent the "listening from the heart" that adolescents need.

Listening with Half an Ear. This is a common form of listening within a family setting. Let us imagine a scene wherein thirteen-year-old Barb storms into the house in angry tears. It seems that her best friend, Cindy, has broken a trust. Barb told her a personal secret and made Cindy promise she would tell no one. But Cindy did tell someone, and Barb is furious. "I hate her!" she cries. "I never want to see her again!"

Barb's mother is busy. It's only a few minutes before supper and she is making a tossed salad and keeping an eye on the roast in the oven. She is sympathetic, though, and asks a few questions. But then she says briskly, "Just a minute, Barb. I have to check on the meat." She turns away and opens the oven door. "Oh, dear, it's getting overdone! Keep talking, Barb; I can hear you." Barb does try to continue, but somehow it's not as easy to talk when someone isn't looking at you and is preoccupied with something else.

The mother faces Barb again. "Now, as you were saying about Cindy. . . ." Barb's face brightens and conversation picks up. Then suddenly the mother interrupts again. "Oh, oh, I forgot to put the broccoli on and your father will be home any minute. I'll be right back." She runs downstairs to the freezer. What has happened when she returns? Barb has gone up to her room. The mother has missed a chance to enter into a painful experience with her daughter. Moreover, this is the age when a friend's betrayal is crushing. Talking about it could have brought insight into the situation; it could have brought healing.

What can a parent do in a situation such as this? After all, the mother was legitimately busy. But if one is going to listen, one has to stop what one is doing and tune in to the other person's feelings. If possible, even at a busy time such as before supper, the mother needs to listen intently for a few minutes and then explain that this is a difficult time to talk. She and her daughter should then agree to have further conversation as soon as possible. The most important element is that the adolescent knows she is being heard. Her problem is important enough to warrant her mother's time later, if not right now. Self-worth is preserved.

"Yes, But" Listening. Let us imagine the same scene between Barb and her mother. This time the mother is attentive. She hears the story, asks a few questions, then quickly launches into her "advice" treatment.

"But Barb, don't you remember I told you that if you ever want anything broadcast all over town, tell Cindy? Her mother is just like her? There are some things you're going to have to learn in life, Barb. You're too trusting—just like your father. I don't mean you should be suspicious of everyone, but you have to be smart about things like that. . . ."

Barb has already left the room. Anger at Cindy is now mingled with anger at her mother. Reinforced inside her is the conviction, all too common for adolescents, that you can't tell grown-ups anything. They just scold you and tell you what you *should* have done.

There is a strong possibility that Barb's mother gave sound advice. After all, she has lived longer than Barb, knows her community and, no doubt, more about human nature. But she didn't give the gift of herself in listening; she merely gave advice. And she missed the opportunity to help Barb discover her own way of dealing positively with this painful experience.

"I Can Top That" Listening. In this instance, Barb's mother hears part of the story. Then she says, "That's tough, Barb, but you'll get over it. If you think this is bad, let me tell you what happened when I was your age—well, maybe a year older—I can't remember exactly what year it was. But I remember I lived at the house on 32nd Street. Anyway . . . " the mother is now very animated, thinking of the incident in her past " . . . I had a friend named Joyce. We were really close. I told her that I had a crush on a boy in our class and I swore her to secrecy and she promised. The next day when I came to biology class it was plastered all over the blackboard, 'Annie loves Jack'—Jack was the boy's name . . . "

The mother looks at Barb, whose face bears little expression. In fact, she is putting on her coat, ready to leave.

What has happened? The mother has taken all the limelight, shifted the attention to herself. She never entered into her daughter's problem.

A young man remembers:

My warmest feeling about home was coming back from school and talking to Mom, answering questions like, "What did you do today?" and "How did you feel about school today?" As I think about the family I might have in the future, I find myself wanting to give quality time listening to my children in a noncondemning way. I want to listen to *who they are* and how they feel.

As a mother, I remembered with fondness and gratitude the many long talks our sons and I had together in their growing-up years. One instance in particular comes to my mind now. When one of our sons was in seventh grade, he often would ask me to come into his bedroom after he had gone to bed just so we could talk. In that quiet, dark place, frustrations and dreams were listened to and shared, even though sometimes I was very tired and would rather have gone to bed myself. In eighth grade, he went through a turbulent, rebellious time. Not once during that time did he ask me to come in and talk at night. I never said anything about it, either. You can imagine what it meant to me when, at the beginning of ninth grade, he said one night, "Mom, can you come in and talk?"

How to Listen

Listening with the heart is a basic requirement for understanding our adolescent sons and daughters. It is the only way by which we as parents can come to understand the thoughts and concerns and feelings unique to adolescents. It is also the only way by which we as parents can come to understand that *person* who is our child, regardless of his or her age. Listening is a vital aspect of parenting. A careful empirical study, *Families of the Slums* by S. Minuchin and others, has documented that multiproblem families are groups of people who do not listen to one another. In those families there is no experience of making contact with each other, of counting as persons.[12]

In learning how to listen with the heart, consider the following insight from Barbara Varenhorst's book *Real Friends*:

Heart listening can be learned, but it cannot be practiced or done mechanically. You can listen mechanically with your ears, but not with your heart. Why? Because the essence of listening with your heart is to put your whole self into trying to hear what the other is saying, because you care that much. Unless you care, you won't stop talking, resisting, or ignoring long enough to hear what is being said. You won't sacrifice your time or convenience to hear the other's feelings behind the words or the twisted behaviors. If you care enough, you will learn the necessary skills, and then you will practice repeatedly, putting out the effort needed to learn to listen with your heart.[13]

Given below are three important guidelines for listening. These are not techniques you can pick up and use immediately as an instant solution. Rather, they represent an approach that must be learned and perfected over time. They shift the parent's approach away from being an authority figure to being that child's peer. The net effect is that the adolescent feels that he or she is being treated more like an adult. We have used these techniques ourselves, and have found them to be highly effective in our own family life.

Guide 1. Listen in Ways That Encourage Expression of Feelings.

Adolescence is a time of bewildering emotions and intense new feelings. This includes sexual desires, fantasies, grandiose ambitions, dreams, anger at being treated like a child, and strange feelings about bodily changes. Not until an adolescent *identifies these feelings with words* will he or she begin to handle them in a rational, mature way.

Years ago, in conducting five-day youth counseling seminars for pastors, we brought in young people to assist us in the training. For two separate evenings, the pastors sat and actively listened to these youth share their concerns (and later their evaluations of how well the pastors listened). We were impressed by the fact that many friendships were formed between the pastors and youth, friendships that often continued through the year via letters. When several youths were queried about these friendships, one said, "You don't understand. Never before in my life have I had an adult listen to me for forty-five minutes. It's a good experience." We came to realize there are few times an adolescent is able to speak freely to an adult without being stopped short by a reprimand or correction.

The first essential in listening is to convey an attitude of warm interest, free from a spirit of judgment or criticism. This cannot be faked. If a parent is unable honestly to adopt such a stance, it will be sensed. An adolescent is quick to judge a parent's attitude from the tone of voice, set of the lips, or facial expressions. A parent will be able to convey a nonjudgmental affirming attitude only if that is the attitude the parent has. Much of what is needed in a listening posture flows out of this attitude of warmth and unconditional regard.

A second essential in listening is to use two kinds of verbal responses, each of which tends to encourage conversation.

Affirming Responses. Adolescents, self-conscious because of their lack of skill in expressing themselves, appreciate comments that are accepting, approving, affirming. It is reassuring to the adolescent to hear a parent say, "I can understand what you're saying," or "I can appreciate your willingness to tell me that," or "Good! You're saying it well."

This type of affirming response can dispel fears adolescents have when talking about themselves with an authority figure: "Are my comments worth hearing? Do I make sense? Do I sound like a nut?" Once adolescents feel they are being heard and appreciated, their reaction is to talk more freely.

General Leads Instead of Specific Questions. Authority figures tend to use highly specific questions. These have the effect of placing an adolescent on the defensive or in a dependency role. Its observable effect is to reduce conversation to responses that become shorter and shorter.

Far better are "general leads" that give the adolescent freedom to share what he or she chooses. Some "general leads" might be: "Mind telling me about your game today?" or "Would you care to explain that more fully?" or "Could you give me a 'for instance'?"

These convey an open-endedness that allows an adolescent to share what he or she wishes. The net effect of this type of verbal response is to increase comments from the adolescent.

Guideline 2. Listen to Discern the Adolescent's Perspective.

This means listening to discern "where your adolescent is coming from." It means trying to understand how your child views life. It means trying to view a situation through the eyes of your adolescent.

It doesn't mean that at this point we stop being parents. But it does mean that we make a deliberate effort to know the inner life and feelings of our child. Such knowledge is a parent's best guide for determining how best to respond.

Listening to discern an adolescent's perspective is an active process that is helped by the use of two additional kinds of verbal responses. They are worth practicing because they are effective in helping one listen more sensitively and in establishing a close relationship.

Feedback Responses. It is helpful when a parent responds to an adolescent's comments by saying, "Let me tell you what I am hearing, to see if I am on target," or, "In other words, you. . . . Does that sound right?"

These responses convey the idea that you as an adult are trying to understand what is being said. All you are doing is using your own words to restate or summarize what the other person has just said. If you have heard correctly and stated it well, the adolescent's reaction will be to say, "That's right," and then continue telling his or her story. If you are not accurate in your feedback, you might hear, "No, that's not what I meant." Your response has given the child a chance to clarify what has been said.

Clarification Responses. Clarification means going further than just restating or summarizing what you have heard. It means trying to interpret what you hear. It involves listening for the feelings being expressed through words. It is listening with a third ear. You might indicate your interpretation of what you hear by comments such as these: "You resent Dad's absence from your games. Is that correct?" or, "You feel we're picking on you. Is that it?"

It does not matter that the clarifying response may be off-target. If you are not grasping what your child is saying, you have encouraged him or her to go into greater detail in explaining the situation. Adolescents feel complimented if a parent takes the time to hear them out while intently trying to understand.

The net effect of this kind of "listening from the heart" is a closer relationship between parent and adolescent.

Guideline 3. Approach Each Conversation with a Sense of Hope.

The adolescent may be fearful and deeply troubled. Trapped by peer pressure, he or she may have become involved in problems created by drug or alcohol abuse, sexual activity, vandalism. It is important that we as parents are able to reflect the conviction that there is hope, regardless of the situation.

This hope can be based on our faith in the child and the possibilities we see that can be unlocked. Adolescents sensing this confidence in them will receive it as "good news" of the highest order.

For some parents, this hope finds its ultimate source in the belief that God can change things and is seeking to do so for their child. This confidence in God gives a sense of hope to the conversations they have with their child.

4. Cry for a Close Family

> If the family were a container, it would be a nest, an enduring nest, loosely woven, expansive, and open.
> If the family were a fruit, it would be an orange, a circle of sections, held together but separable—each segment distinct.
>
> —LETTY COTTIN POGREBIN

When they were children, there had been much togetherness in their family—long trips and weeks of camping. But as the years wore on, the closeness eroded. Father was frustrated because his children were not developing in the directions he would have chosen, and his reaction was interpreted by his adolescents as failure on their part. Because he didn't take time to develop a listening stance, Father missed chances to "read" his children. The "Yes, but . . . " response (see Chapter 3) often came too quickly in his conversations with his adolescent children.

Mother saw the gap widening, but her warnings went unheard. The family became fractured, and there was a distance of spirit between sons, daughters, and father. But Father was a caring man. Sensing things had gone awry, he began to create opportunities for the children to be with him individually and with the family as a group. Gradually, the old sense of camaraderie began to reappear; the grown children began to look forward to being together. Most of all, the children began to understand their father. . . .

This father's cry for the closeness that he and his family once knew exemplifies the theme of this chapter: the deep desire of parents and children alike to experience the happiness of a close family life. In the Adolescent-Parent study, both groups gave "a happy family" the highest rank of importance.

But the ideal of a "happy family life" is neither easy to

achieve nor to maintain. In evaluating *how well* members of their family "get along with each other," and *how true* it is that "there is a lot of love in our family," adolescents' and parents' combined ratings decline as the children grow older (see Figure 8).

Does this mean that ninth-graders are more disruptive and harder to handle than fifth-graders? No. Repeated measures show the opposite to be true: Parents report less difficulty in handling ninth-graders than fifth-graders. Why, then, the decline in family closeness? Because there is also a decline during these years in:

- Parental harmony
- Parent-youth communication
- Parental discipline or control
- Parental nurturing

These are four essential elements for a close family life. When present they serve as a source of strength for adolescents.

Parental Harmony

The relationship between husband and wife changes noticeably as their children grow older. Adolescents entering the ninth grade notice less exchange of affection (for example, hugging and kissing) between their parents, and they are aware that their parents argue more and get "mad at each other." When evaluating how well their parents "get along with each other," adolescents' rating decreases significantly from fifth-grade to ninth-grade.

Do the 10,467 parents in the study agree with their children's evaluation? Yes. When the parents rated the happiness of their marital relationship, the number who agreed that their relationship was "very" or "extremely" happy dropped from 67 percent for parents of fifth-grade youth to 61 percent among parents of ninth-graders. That difference, though a significant

Figure 8. Change in Family Closeness*

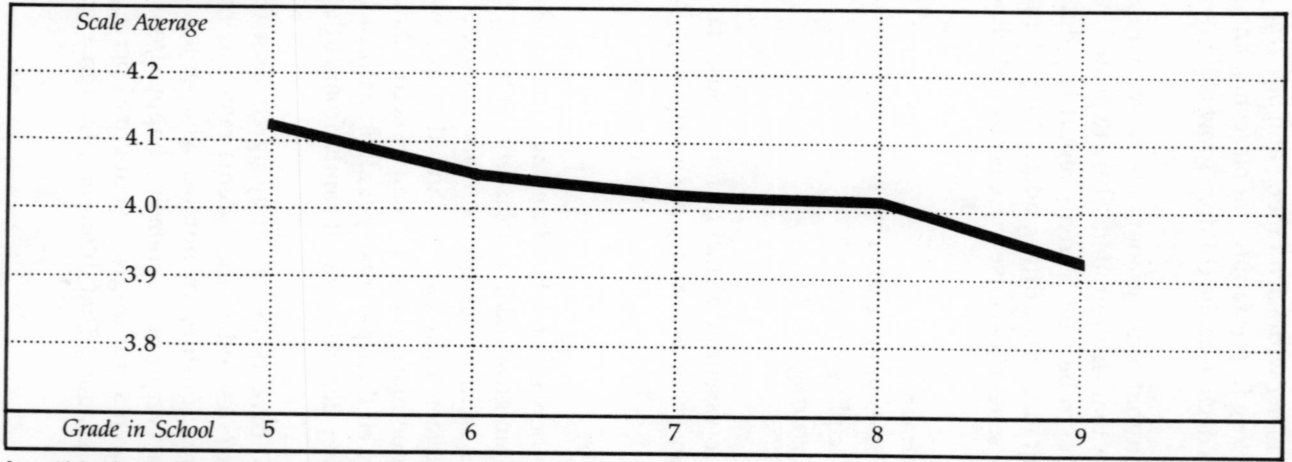

Item: "Members of my family get along well with each other."
*Based on the average of 4 items

5 = Almost always true
4 = Often true
3 = Sometimes true
2 = True once in a while
1 = Never true

drop, is not a great one. Probably more important is the fact that one in five of the 10,467 parents admitted that their marital relationship is not happy. One in two report times of arguing or "getting mad at" each other. Of these, one in eight says it happens "often" or "very often."

We also asked several specific questions in the survey about how adult partners handle their disagreements or arguments. Two out of three mothers acknowledge times when they were given the "silent treatment." One out of four mothers said that there were at least six times during the year when a partner "raised his voice, insulted me, or swore at me."

One in five remember times in the past year when a husband threw, smashed, kicked, or hit something in the home. One in ten mothers admit to having been pushed, shoved, or grabbed; and a few report having been hit (7 percent) or beaten up (2 percent).

These occasions illustrate what sociologists David Olson and Hamilton McCubbin call the "storm and stress" stage in the family life cycle.[2] Pressures on parents are such that during the children's adolescent years, parental harmony drops to its lowest point.

In Chapter 2 we discussed parental stresses under the topic "Understanding Yourself as a Parent." There we identified emotional forces and types of stressful circumstances that can cause parental disharmony and encourage a strained, cold, or embattled relationship. When parents don't get along, it causes real distress for adolescents. In *Five Cries of Youth*, we reported that almost 60 percent of the youth who feel like psychological orphans in their home (due to parental disharmony) sometimes consider suicide.[3]

Even though parents may try to hide their conflict from the children, it is doubtful that they really succeed. In *The Family Crucible*[4] family therapist Augustus Napier says he frequently finds that the problems of a troublemaking child or adolescent can be traced to some strain in the husband-wife relationship that is upsetting the balance of family life. For instance, where there is parental conflict, a parent may begin to get needed affection from a child rather than the spouse. This shift may be a subtle one, but it shows that outside help may be necessary to gain the needed insights into what is happening within such a family structure.

In our 1971 survey of high school youth we pursued the issue of factors that predict family disunity. Through a complex analysis of the data, we found that one item outranks all other factors: "My father and mother do not get along with each other. This bothers me very much." *This simple statement is our most powerful indicator of family disharmony.* Where father and mother are at odds with each other, the whole family suffers. The children become psychological orphans.[5]

An added problem for children is the common but debilitating fear that they are to blame for their parents' fighting. For this reason, as well as for their own sakes, parents embroiled in conflict will do their children a favor by seeking outside counseling.

Family closeness actually fortifies children with an inner resistance to the toxins of life. The Adolescent-Parent study shows that adolescents in a close family unit are the ones most likely to say "no" to drug use, pre-marital sexual activity, and other antisocial and alienating behaviors. They are also the ones most likely to adopt high moral standards, develop the ability to make and keep friends, embrace a religious faith, and involve themselves in helping activities. All of these characteristics pertaining to adolescents from close families are significant—which means that the evidence cannot be attributed to mere chance.

Parent-Youth Communication

The importance of good parent-youth communication has been evident to us from the very beginning of the Adolescent-Parent study. When 2,000 youth filled in answers to item stems beginning "I wish . . . ", they often responded, "I wish

I could talk to my folks about some of my problems." The frequent response of 2,000 parents to the same item stem was, "I wish I could talk with my teenager about the things troubling him."

The responses point up the impasse in communication that both parents and adolescents wish could be broken. Some parents indicated specific areas in which they had poor communication with their children:

The hardest thing to talk to my child about is racial relationships and social standings.

The hardest thing to talk to my child about is what he should expect to encounter in the areas of drugs, sex, alcohol, and relationships with other people as he approaches adulthood.

The hardest thing to talk to my children about is their father's drinking behavior and the time he and I spent at a treatment center. They don't want to talk about it.

The young adults we interviewed talked freely about communication problems they faced as teenagers:

I would have liked to have been able to talk easier with my dad—in a more chummy way, not just 'this should be done' or 'that should be done.' "

The hardest thing to talk to parents about was relationships with boys, questions about sex. Talks on these subjects were not deep enough. I wish I could have discussed this more with my parents."

Fortunately, some families have succeeded in establishing meaningful communication, and thus common understandings, on difficult subjects. For example, about one-third of the adolescents in our study say they "have had good talks with their parents about sex." But this figure is well below the number of youth who wish they could discuss this and other troubling issues with their parents (for example, "deciding what to do with my life," "wondering how to handle my feelings"). Boys want these conversations as much as girls do. And even more than youth do, parents wish they could have such talks. In fact, 60 percent say they "definitely would like to talk more" with their children about worries and concerns, hopes and dreams. An additional 37 percent said they "probably" would welcome such opportunities.

Decline in Interest

Since it is evident that family closeness requires communication between members, it is important to note that youth's interest in discussing adolescent issues with their parents steadily declines between fifth grade (58 percent) and ninth grade (37 percent). The number who want more communication with their parents on five youth topics shows a marked decline (see Figure 9).

This decline may simply be a function of the growing up process: a teenager needs to mature, to become more independent, to develop a broader social network of confidants. But this process does not require breaking off communication with his or her parents. Figure 9 shows an increase in the percentage of youth who would prefer turning to both friends and parents for advice on "very important decisions" as they grow older.

Young adolescents in the Adolescent-Parent study are more parent-oriented than peer-oriented. They prefer being able to talk with their parents about issues that bother them. Grade five is a time of special opportunity for parents to help the young adolescent initiate conversations and learn how to communicate on a feeling level (see Figure 10).

As parents, we have learned that entering into meaningful conversations with adolescent children adds a new dimension to family life. At Search Institute we had a striking illustration of the excitement parents feel once conversations do begin in the home. We had just launched a project involving over 400 young people in Minneapolis and St. Paul. Its purpose was to train them in the friendship skills needed for reaching out to lonely and alienated peers. Also involved in the training were exercises in which the youth practiced starting conversations

Figure 9. Change in Youth's Desire for Communication with Parents*

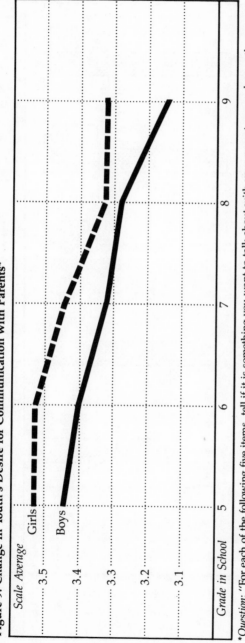

Question: "For each of the following five items, tell if it is something you want to talk about with your parents more, less or the same as you do now." (Participants in the survey were then to answer this question for issues relating to drugs, friends, school, ideas of right and wrong, and sex.)

5 = much more
4 = a little more
3 = about the same
2 = a little less
1 = much less

Figure 10. Sources of Advice: Peers vs. parents*

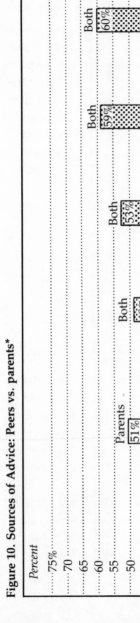

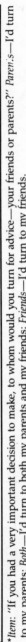

**Item:* "If you had a very important decision to make, to whom would you turn for advice—your friends or parents?" *Parents*—I'd turn to my parents; *Both*—I'd turn to both my parents and my friends; *Friends*—I'd turn to my friends.

with strangers and "authority figures" (parents and teachers). We wanted parents to feel comfortable with what was being done and therefore invited them to an open house. They could meet the training faculty and raise whatever questions they might have about the project.

We didn't know how many parents would come to our sessions, offered on two consecutive evenings, and planned to serve coffee and cookies for fifty people. To our surprise, 200 showed up, eager to learn about the project. Why? One after another said, "Whatever are you doing in this project? My child has actually initiated conversations in our home! We've had some long talks as a result. We love it! Keep it up!"

This incident convinced us that aided by some training, conversations can take place in the home with initiative being taken either by parent or adolescent.

Four Aids to Parent-Youth Communication

Four aids to parent-youth communication deserve mention here:

- Recognize the natural blocks to communication
- Take time to establish relationships
- Share thoughts and feelings
- Focus on the adolescent's concerns and interests

Recognize the Natural Communication Blocks. It is difficult to initiate communication with an adolescent because of certain traits that characterize adolescence itself.

1. *Growing self-consciousness.* As noted in the previous chapter, adolescents are preoccupied with themselves, and for good reason. They are trying to understand the enormous physical changes occurring within them—changes that often make them feel self-conscious. Anything that could be interpreted as a criticism or correction makes them feel as though they have been slapped on a sunburned back. This touchiness is too easily interpreted by a parent as a signal to "leave me alone."

In reality, the adolescent's hypersensitivity only underscores the need for the listening stance described in Chapter 3.

2. *Limited verbal skills.* A second roadblock to parent-youth communication is the difficulty adolescents, particularly boys, experience in describing feelings and emotions.

As parents we can help our adolescents develop this ability. Simply asking a "feeling" question, such as, "How do you feel about . . . ?" may open new dimensions in conversation. One father tried this technique one day when his ninth-grade son came home from school. The father asked him about his *feelings* concerning a disturbing situation that had come up in class. To his amazement, his son answered him on that level—about his feelings. "We talked for two hours!" said the father. "This has never happened before." Engaging one's adolescent in conversation requires patience, time, and the choice of a nonthreatening situation for conversation. These facts all help establish more comfortable communication and a closer parent-child relationship.

3. *Growing resistance to authority.* Parents also need to realize that an adolescent's desire to make personal decisions increases with age. Though the Adolescent-Parent study indicated only small increases in the percentage who disagree with parental rules, there is an increase from fifth to ninth grade in the percentage who reject authority. Thus it would seem that when an adolescent exhibits growing resistance to authority within the family structure, parents should make sure they talk with the child on a peer level. This kind of relationship reduces the social distance—and the defenses—between parent and adolescent. Children whose parents relate to them as peers, regardless of age, often refer to their mother or father as "a friend" or "my best friend." The beauty of this relationship is that it can begin early and endure for life. Very young children blossom when they are spoken to without condescension, as people whose opinions and ideas are respected and listened to.

Take Time to Establish Relationships. Over half (53 percent) of the adolescents in the Adolescent-Parent study spend less than 30 minutes a day with their fathers; and 44 percent spend less than 30 minutes with their mothers. That's the same amount of time parents take for watching the news on TV. Even more alarming, one-fourth of the ninth-graders in this study spend less than five minutes (on an average day) alone with father to talk, play, or just be together. No doubt this neglect is one reason why 46 percent of the fathers in the study admit they worry ("quite a bit" or "very much") about how their child feels about them.

The following story of Paul Tsongas, as told by Ellen Goodman in the *Boston Globe*, is a poignant and heartwarming illustration of how a man regards time with his family as a top priority.

I met Paul Tsongas once on a late-afternoon flight from Washington to Boston. The senator from Massachusetts was traveling light that day. No bags, no briefcase, no aides. All he had with him was a daughter.

It was rare enough to see a man alone on a plane with a preschool child. But Tsongas's reason was even more unusual. He was going to Boston for a meeting and he wanted to spend some time with his middle daughter. So he was taking her along for the ride. Together they would get the late plane back.

I've thought about that scene a dozen times, with mixed feelings of admiration and poignancy. Here was a father struggling with the demands of work and family. Here was a father who had to capture minutes with his child, on the fly, at 35,000 feet.

This scene, repeated over and again in Tsongas's life, seems somehow symbolic of a whole generation of men and women: parents with schedule books. It is barely even a parody of the way many of us cram work and children into calendars that won't expand to fill the needs, into lives that cry out for more hours. Tsongas was one of us, trying to make it all fit together.

But last October, the senator and father of three young girls discovered something that wasn't on his agenda. He had a tumor that was "not benign." . . . The statistical average life expectancy for those with this disease (mild lymphoma), as he related it, is eight years, and he is planning for more. . . . But Tsongas decided not to run again. He is coming home to Lowell, Mass., and home to his family in a way that politics doesn't allow.

. . . Tsongas never forgot the older colleague who stopped by his table when he was a freshman congressman and said, "Let me tell you one thing. I was in your shoes. I was here and I really devoted myself to my job and I ignored my kids and they grew up and I never knew them. It makes me very sad. Whatever you do, don't do that."

[Tsongas] had to hear the words "not benign" to finally focus on priorities, on mortality, on time itself. . . . There are times when we all end up completing a day or a week or a month, as if it were a task to be crossed off the list with a sign. In the effort to make it all work, it can become all work. We become one-minute managers, mothers, husbands. We end up spending our time on the fly.[6]

As Paul Tsongas did that day on the plane, a number of parents arrange for special time when *one* child is "alone" with *one* parent. This time alone together is important for building self-confidence in the adolescent. It is, however, of the essence in this kind of setup that the parent shows no partiality, and attempts to make each child's time equal in amount or quality.

In Charlie Shedd's book *Promises to Peter*, he relates that during his children's growing-up years he took each child out for dinner—alone—monthly. The kids chose the restaurant. After they'd had a good talk, they went to the dime store and picked out something they wanted. Shedd says that even when his children reached adolescence, when they didn't talk much to the family, they still enjoyed these monthly talks with their father.[7]

Some parents arrange for regular times when the family discusses any issues they wish. In this way, parents come to understand what their children are thinking on personal matters, the church, the community, and the world.

In thinking about taking time to be with our children, it is well to remind ourselves also that *listening*, of which we spoke at some length in Chapter 3, is a vital form of communication, even though it is basically silent.

Share Thoughts and Feelings. Some parents find it hard to admit to their adolescent that they have personal struggles and failures, too. The young woman in the following illustration wishes her father could have shared some of his inner struggles with her and her sister during their teen years. Because he did not, the father and the younger sister went through some rough years of alienation. Said the young woman,

When I was an adolescent, my father seemed to us to be strong, domineering, opinionated, sarcastic, ambitious, and successful. Since I have become an adult, my father has shared some of his fears and problems with us. I wish he could have been like that when my sister and I were teenagers at home.

The very nature of the early relationship between parent and child dictates that the parent controls most situations and decisions. Thus the parent may feel that he or she cannot reveal weaknesses or talk about personal problems; this, the parent reasons, might weaken the traditional position of authority, confuse the child, or make the child think the parent is inadequate. But it seems important that this stance change so that both parent and the child are free to reveal their humanness, their capacity for failure and struggle. That is a vital part of parent-youth communication, one that creates an attitude of mutual understanding and trust.

Some parents find it difficult to verbalize their love for their children. Strangely, the existence of love cannot be assumed. If it is unspoken, it may be doubted. Parents need to tell their children they love them. A counselor speaks of being in his office one day with a small family group troubled with parent-child conflicts. Suddenly the father turned angrily to his teenage son and said, "But you *know* I love you." To which the young man replied with equal emotion, "No, I don't. You've given me just about everything I've ever wanted, but I don't remember you *ever* telling me that you loved me!"

Some parents find it difficult to receive correction or insight from their teenager. Actually, teenagers may be very helpful to a parent in giving both negative and positive insights.

I well remember the time when one of our teenage sons said to me, "Mom, there's something I want to tell you. I hardly ever hear you saying bad things about people, but your tone of voice changes when you talk about certain kinds of people. I can tell that you think of them in a belittling way and it bothers me."

This was a jolting critique. In this situation, it would have been easy for me to have become defensive and counter with, "You're a fine one to talk. You've got some shaping up to do yourself." Instead, I asked him to clarify and give an example of what he meant. He did. It was a humbling and helpful insight.

Focus on Their Concerns and Interests. Adolescents want to talk about the very issues parents wish could be discussed, namely, their worries (See Table 3). For parents, these concerns can provide openings to discuss numerous topics. One thoughtful young man whose father was a reserved, busy

Table 3. The Worries of Young Adolescents

Percent responding *very much* or *quite a bit*

Item	All Youth	Grade 5	Grade 6	Grade 7	Grade 8	Grade 9
School performance	57%	54%	54%	57%	59%	60%
About my looks	53	42	48	56	60	57
How well other kids like me	48	43	46	51	50	48
Parent might die	47	50	48	49	47	41
How my friends treat me	45	42	43	46	47	45
Hunger and poverty in U.S.	38	52	41	39	32	31
Violence in U.S.	36	43	37	38	33	30
Might lose best friend	36	40	35	39	34	29
Drugs and drinking	35	40	38	35	33	32
Might not get good job	30	31	28	31	28	30
Physical development	26	31	28	27	24	17
Nuclear destruction of U.S.	25	29	28	27	22	21
Parents might divorce	22	30	26	22	17	13
That I may die soon	21	26	24	24	17	13
Sexual abuse	19	24	21	19	17	15
Friends will get me in trouble	18	25	21	18	13	13
Drinking by a parent	15	21	18	14	11	11
Get beat up at school	12	18	16	12	9	9
Physical abuse by parent	12	17	13	12	9	9
That I might kill myself	12	16	12	11	9	9

school administrator, regretted that during his adolescent years he saw his father as aloof, not really interested in him. He knows now that this observation was wrong. But consequently, this young man has a strong feeling that a parent must be aware that a young person often has neither the courage nor the know-how to *initiate* conversation about his or her worries. To adolescents, personal problems are mountainous obstacles; they are afraid parents will consider these same problems as insignificant, and so the parents are never made aware of the worries and given a chance to help.

One woman remembers as a teenager trying to get up enough courage to approach her mother on a question about sex. "If only there had been a word, a 'lead' on my mother's part," she said, "the floodgates of sharing a painful problem would have been released." A general question or comment on any one of the following topics may become the occasion for a good conversation.

1. *School performance.* Fifth-graders especially want to talk about the top worry of young adolescents: "How I'm doing in school." It is important for them to make their parents proud by doing well both at school and in extracurricular activities. They even want to talk with their parents about trouble at school. If parents do not make use of this chance for open, two-way conversations, it will be more difficult in the years ahead—especially with boys, whose desire to do well in school declines as they near the ninth grade.

2. *My looks.* Worry about one's physical appearance, the second greatest worry of young adolescents, reaches its highest point among eighth-grade girls. Among fifth-graders, "looks" rates seventh as a worry. Because teenagers are preoccupied with how they look to their peers, fads in clothes and styles need not be a subject of parental censure. Rather, the parent might make efforts to affirm those styles that compliment the adolescent. The question parents might ask themselves here is, "So what if I don't like that outfit? Is it worth breaking a relationship to get my way?" Chances are good that the fad

will assume its proper perspective for the adolescent if the parent doesn't nag about it.

Since looks are a concern, parents might do well to open doors for positive interchange if an adolescent in the family is, for instance, overweight. No amount of nagging or ridicule will help. But talking frankly about the struggles of dieting, affirming positive features—these are the gifts of communication a parent can bring to these situations.

3. *That a parent might die.* This fear, high among fifth- and sixth-graders and ninth-grade girls, touches a tender part of the spirit. Adolescents are often afraid to tell their parents about this fear. Such was the case with one of our sons, who remembers as a fifth-grader "standing by the window for what seemed like hours waiting for you to get home. If it got late, I was sure you had been killed in a car accident." Verbal expression of fears such as this present an opening for caring communication between parent and child.

4. *How friends treat me.* This fifth-ranked worry mounts each year to its highest peak among 45 percent of eighth-graders. Parents might use this concern as the basis for discussing with the adolescent what it means to be a friend to someone else, shifting the emphasis away from "what my friend can give to me" to "what I can give my friend."

The problem of being "picked on" and getting into a fight is a great worry to fifth- and sixth-graders. Instead of getting angry at the child or at the others who involved the adolescent in a fight, a parent may find in this situation an opportunity to learn how the fight started and what are the child's feelings about the incident.

6. *Hunger and poverty.* Interestingly, this is the number-one worry of fifth-graders in the Adolescent-Parent study, suggesting how conscious they are of the suffering of others. Significantly, the worry declines with age, and becomes sixth-ranked for those in grades seven to nine. This subject, which parallels a comparable decline in concern for people, will be considered again in Chapter 6.

7. *Violence in our country.* Again, fifth graders—the "worry-warts" among adolescents—are most conscious of this problem. In ways parents might not expect, adolescents of this age are very aware of their community and nation. Current events could well be topics at the dinner table. Fears about incidents of violence might be brought into the open. If local incidents of violence have occurred, parents might discuss safety measures in the home and rules for self-protection.

8. *Lose best friend.* This eighth-ranked worry peaks for seventh-graders and declines to its lowest point among ninth-graders. The concern is closely related to "how other kids like me" and "how my friends treat me." It is a reflection of the adolescent's longing to be seen as a "fun" person, a significant person. A teacher says, "One of the most painful things I see in a classroom is the cruel ways teenagers treat each other, and especially the one who is on the fringe of things." Parents do well not to ignore a child's "loss of a best friend." By conveying the impression that "This is kid stuff," a parent shuts the door to good conversations on subjects of self-image and sharing feelings with others.

9. *Drinking by friends.* This is a genuine worry for 35 percent of the youth in our study, one which adolescents would prefer to discuss with their parents. Surprisingly, those most worried about the subject are sixth-graders. Most parents do not see their sixth-graders as being old enough to talk about the use of alcohol; but the results of the Adolescent-Parent study, as well as many others, indicate that this age is crucial for discussion on this topic. The adolescent's concern here may be a mingling of worry about peer relationships, peer pressures, and the tremendous battle of ambivalence: "My parents don't like this," or "What if the kids get me to do it?" or "Does it mean I can't go out with my friends to parties?" or "Should I try it?" Girls especially want parental communication on this subject.

10. *Locating a job.* Even among early adolescents, vocational goals are important, and with this concern comes worry about

not being able to "get a good job when I am older." This tenth-ranked worry is highest for ninth-graders. It is wise for a parent to find out how much importance the adolescent attaches to advanced education and then, depending on the ability and interest of the young person, discuss the value of working for a junior college degree, a vocational technical degree, or a higher degree.

One young adult tells of his parents taking him as a teenager to the Mayo Clinic for a visit, because he had expressed a strong desire to study medicine. Some parents arrange to have their son or daughter meet a person who is in a vocation that interests the child. Parents and adolescents grow in understanding of each other as they explore the question, "How does one develop one's career potential?" Everyone knows that adolescents' ideas on vocation may, and most likely will, change many times before adulthood. This process, however, is an important beginning in learning to make decisions.

Parental Discipline or Control

A third major factor in close family life is parental discipline. How parents treat their children powerfully shapes not only the emotional climate of the home, but also the children's personality, character, and competence. In the Adolescent-Parent study a shift occurs in type of discipline as the adolescents grew older. Ninth-graders report more inflexible or autocratic treatment from their parents, another factor that contributes to a decline in family closeness. Parental control is an important factor in how parents and adolescents relate to each other.

Through careful studies, Diana Baumrind was able to identify three types of parental discipline and demonstrate how each disciplinary pattern shapes the child in a different way. Data from the study of 10,467 parents confirm that these three types of discipline are being used in families: autocratic, permissive, and democratic (authoritative); each is associated with contrasting kinds of behavior. The first two methods create distance between parents and adolescents, whereas the third—the democratic or authoritative—encourages family closeness. Parents who value a close family life might well evaluate the approach they now use. The way parents treat their children either inclines them toward a loving response or toward a rebellious rejection of behavior that the parents may idealize.

Autocratic-Type Discipline

Baumrind identifies the authoritarian (hereafter referred to as an autocratic) parent as one who values obedience as a virtue and favors punitive or forceful methods to curb the self-will of a child.[8] The parent does not encourage verbal give-and-take, believing rather that the child should always accept the parent's position as right. Autocratic parents may be either very protective or very neglectful.

Although many of the 10,467 parents in this study are inclined toward the autocratic stance, it is a matter of degree; some parents are more rigid, controlling, and demanding than others. When it comes to verbal give-and-take, one in ten say it "often" happens that "I will not allow my child to question the rules I make." Three in ten say it happens "sometimes."

Similarly, 14 percent of the mothers and 20 percent of the fathers say it happens "often" that "I do not let my child question my decisions." An additional three in ten say this happens "sometimes."

The clearest expression of an autocratic parent comes in the response given to the survey item, "I expect my child to believe I am always right."

One in five mothers (19 percent) and one in four fathers (25 percent) say they "often" take this position. If we include the "sometimes" response, we find half of the parents trying to give children the impression of being "always right." This need may stem from the idea that admission of error by parents weakens their authority.

Parents who "overcontrol" usually punish for wrong behavior. Here is how parents in the study thought they would react when presented with the following imaginary situation: If their adolescent (age ten to fourteen) came home at 10:30 P.M., though the curfew was clearly understood to be 9:00 P.M., 34 percent said they "probably" would yell at their child; 7 percent were "very sure" they would yell. Yelling suggests anger, and is a common response of autocratic parents. One third of the parents (33 percent) admit to times when they get so angry they are afraid they might hurt their child. This strong response reminds us of how much an autocratic approach is linked with personal feelings or reactions to stress. Findings in *Study of Generations* show that parents who are autocratic in treatment of their children tend also to be law-oriented in their understanding of religion.[9] This means they view Christianity as basically a set of rules and standards that must be obeyed. Such parents find it hard to forgive and hard to admit they are wrong. Their religion tends to be self-centered and self-serving.

The issue of the autocratic parent appeared prominently in our study of 7,050 high school youth (discussed in *Five Cries of Youth*). Two out of five young people (39 percent) were bothered either "very much" or "quite a bit" by the fact that "My parents are too strict." In that study we found that one result of extreme strictness was greater tension in the home. In comparisons between groups, we found greater family disunity and more distance between parents and youth in the families of overly strict parents than any other group. We found the effect of overcontrol on youth to be lower self-esteem and heightened feelings of self-condemnation. Another frequent outcome is parent-youth conflict, with life in the home becoming an ongoing power struggle.[10]

Similar effects are seen in our analyses of data from the Adolescent-Parent study. Adolescents raised under autocratic control are more likely to be characterized by the following behaviors: hostility to parents; age prejudice; antisocial activities (for example, stealing, lying, fighting, vandalism); feelings of social alienation; rejection of traditional moral standards;

and inability to relate well to people. An overly strict approach also encourages a more prejudicial and judgmental spirit in the adolescent.

These outcomes are similar to those reported in many other studies. Punitive approaches to discipline—including verbal and physical abuse, and unreasonable deprivations of privilege—have negative effects. More of the children in homes characterized by this approach react with attitudes of noncompliance and a compulsion to transgress.

Permissive-Type Discipline

It must not be inferred from the above comments that parents should operate without controls. Permissiveness in discipline can be as negative in its effect on children (and on close family life) as an autocratic approach.

Baumrind identified a permissive parent as one who sees him or herself as a resource to be used as the child wishes—not as one responsible for shaping the child's future behavior. The immediate aim of such a parent is to free the child from restraint and allow the child to develop as he or she chooses.[11] Whereas the autocratic parent expects a child to act as an adult, the permissive parent believes the child should have all the privileges of an adult.

A fair number of the 10,467 parents in the study lean toward permissive parenting. When asked, "How often is it true that you 'let your child do whatever he or she wants to do'?" a little over one-third (37 percent) said "often" or "very often." A total of 22 percent acknowledge being "too lenient"; and about that many (20 percent) admitted "I often let my child off easy."

This approach of under-control has its negative effects. Children who live in overly permissive homes have trouble believing their parents really care about them. Permissiveness is sometimes interpreted as a form of rejection. This may be one of the reasons that our measures show that a number of negative behavior patterns are associated with a permissive approach. Adolescents whose parents assume little responsibility for their behavior show more of the following characteristics: Fewer are likely to go out of their way to help people (helping a peer with homework, mowing lawns for those who cannot do it themselves, helping someone pick up dropped groceries); fewer are willing to live by the moral standards of their parents (with respect to stealing, lying, drinking); more are likely to become involved in hedonistic behavior (use and abuse of alcohol, sex, drugs); more will seek out movies that are sexually explicit and erotic. Permissiveness seems to encourage a hedonistic and antisocial behavior that brings its own tragedies. Clearly, a child needs firm limits.

More important than these negative behaviors is the loss of desired, positive behaviors. Adolescents of parents who use permissive-type discipline are not as likely to be concerned about people, to relate well to others, or to be religiously or ethically motivated.

Authoritative (Democratic) Discipline

The disciplinary approach that seems to work the best falls between autocratic and permissive. We use the terms "authoritative" and "democratic" to describe this third form of parenting. The firmness of an authoritative parent is combined with the freedom found in a democratic setting. The parent who uses the authoritative approach exerts firm control; at the same time, this parent does not hem the child in with restrictions; he or she values both independence in the child and disciplined conformity. The authoritative parent affirms a child's own qualities and style; at the same time, this parent sets standards for future conduct.

The comments of a young adult, reminiscing about his upbringing, reflect this balance: "In our family, there was a delicate balance between allowing the children to make mistakes and be their own person on the one hand, and setting helpful, protective boundaries and values for them on the other hand."

One indication of the number of parents in our study who

use this authoritative approach to parenting is found in their response to the item, "I give my child a chance to talk over rules he or she does not like or understand." Over half say they do this "often"; of these, 18 percent said they do this "very often."

Three out of four parents say it is "often true" that "When I tell my child I am going to punish him or her, I follow through and do it." Whether or not practice is equal to report we do not know. But clearly half or more identify themselves as having characteristics of an authoritative approach to discipline.

Baumrind concludes, on the basis of her research on pre-school children, that authoritative patterns of upbringing are more beneficial to children than autocratic and permissive patterns.[12] From our analyses of Adolescent-Parent data, we come to the same conclusion about young adolescents. The children of parents using the democratic or authoritative approach to discipline are more likely to be service-oriented, concerned about people, free from feelings of alienation, and committed to a religious faith. Where this approach to family discipline is used, one is more likely to find family closeness, parental affection, and parental reward-giving.

A striking illustration of the contrasting effects of the auto-cratic-permissive versus authoritative (democratic) approaches to parenting is seen in a study of college students. Its purpose was to see if there was any connection between parents' use of social control and their offspring's involvement with mari-juana. The findings showed high use of marijuana by students whose parents were perceived to have been permissive, and medium use among students who saw their parents as auto-cratic. The students for whom use of marijuana was low per-ceived their parental relationship as democratic. The researcher saw the parent-child interaction, parents' respect for the child's participation, and the mutual sharing and listening stance of the democratic parental relationship as fostering a personal commitment to the values of the parents.[13]

Guidelines for Practical Applications of Authoritative (Democratic)-Discipline

Based on this analysis of parental discipline styles, we think that the following guidelines show the kinds of parenting that make for a close family.

1. *An adolescent needs clear, firmly established rules.* This means a clear definition of acceptable and unacceptable conduct, as well as a clear statement of consequences if the rule is broken. Interestingly, young adolescents in the study do not rebel against parental rules. Acceptance of rules remains the same from the fifth to the ninth grades, even though there is an increase in resistance to authority over these years.

2. *A flexible stance, blended with good judgment, is important.* A young adult recalls an experience in his teen years:

My friend and I took our family boat without asking permission of our parents, and I was grounded for a month. I became rebellious because I felt it was too strong a punishment. My parents, when they saw my reaction, lowered the punishment. I think this was very important. Parents need to be flexible when the situation warrants it.

A mother says:

If you realize you have made a wrong decision about something involving your child, be willing to change that decision, if need be. What I do first, if the child thinks it is unfair, is tell him I will think about changing it. Then I come to him later and tell him I have done so.

3. *Consistency in defining and applying discipline is essential.* In a supermarket one day, we heard a classic illustration of inconsistency in discipline. The characters in this minidrama were a mother with two young children:

"Brian, if you don't behave, I'm going to put you and Susie out in the car."

Less than a minute later:

"If you don't do what I say, I'm never going to take you shopping again."

One aisle later:
"Brian, if you don't come right over here, I'm going to spank you."

A confused concept of what the parent wants and expects, and a confused concept of punishment is disturbing to a child. Preliminary findings from Francis J. Ianni's recent eight-year study on adolescents show that most teenagers studied were looking for consistent rules in families, schools and communities. "In fact," says Ianni, "they are often desperately seeking those rules."

His study attempted to determine what rules parents, school officials, and others in a community thought they were imposing on the adolescents. The initial studies were in a New York City neighborhood where residents were poor and mostly black, Hispanic, or Chinese. In urban settings the researchers found families, schools, social agencies, and criminal justice workers in conflict, often blaming each other for society's failures. As a result, these institutions set highly conflicting rules for teenagers, who responded to them with resistance and rejection. It is out of this conflict that street gangs emerge "almost destined," says Ianni, "to put these kids in future conflict with society." He adds, "But there is a consistent set of rules to follow."[14]

4. *Disciplining must be a private affair.* To be humiliated or embarrassed in front of friends or in a public place touches one of the most sensitive spots for an adolescent, namely, concern about the opinion of others, especially peers. The humiliation from such an experience can linger on into marriage situations and become one of the "wounded memories" referred to in Chapter 2. This is evident in a husband's words to his wife one evening after she had taken issue with him in front of a social group, "When you criticize me in front of others, it touches something very painful for me, since I was shamed frequently as a kid, and I feel like hiding."[15]

5. *The use of sarcasm or "rubbing it in" brings negative results.* One teenager said,

When I do admit I was wrong about something or say I'm sorry, my parents cut me down. They say, "Oh, she admitted she was wrong? Mark that on a calendar . . . " or something like that. And it makes me feel bad and makes me not want to talk to them.[16]

To "rub it in" and not allow the adolescent to forget that he or she transgressed drives children and parents apart. Sometimes these cutting words, often spoken in front of others, pretend to be in jest, but their meaning is clear. The adolescent has every right to ask that it be stopped.

6. *Conflict can be handled in a positive way.* It is easy for parents to withdraw or react angrily when a teenager espouses a value different from that of the parent. Even though hurt, afraid, angry, and disappointed, parents cannot afford to panic in such a situation and thus allow communication to break off. When adolescents know that their parents are trying to understand and appreciate their feelings, even if they don't sanction the behavior, a spirit of closeness develops between generations.

Even in "ordinary" arguments, in which a break between generations is not imminent, it is important to state clearly to each other what has been the cause of irritation, and to try to work for a solution. A young woman, looking back on her teen years, speaks rather wistfully:

When there was an argument at home (and there were many), nobody would speak to each other for about two days. It was awful. Then we'd get friendly again, but there was no settling of anything, no resolving of issues.

Parental Nurturance

Nurturance has been defined as caretaking—parental acts and attitudes of love that are directed at enhancing the well-being of the child. We found in the Adolescent-Parent study that nurturance is a powerful force for good. Adolescents in homes characterized by love and affectionate caring are better able to resist negative behaviors and more free to develop in positive ways. For instance, there is significantly less social alienation among adolescents whose parents emphasize nurturance, as well as less involvement in drug or alcohol use and sexual activity. In nurturing homes we find more adolescents who know how to make friends and maintain good relationships with them; more who are involved in helping-type behaviors and more who tend to view religion as a liberating and challenging force in their lives.

Although nurturance can be expressed in many ways, we have chosen to discuss it under the following headings:

- Showing affection
- Building trust
- Doing things together
- Developing support systems.

Showing Affection

The decline in family closeness discussed at the beginning of this chapter is paralleled by a decline in how often parents show affection to adolescents. When asked, "How often do you say things to your child like 'I love you' or 'I'm proud of you'?" parents' answers show a dramatic decline by year in school, as seen in Table 4.

As one would surmise, the percent who express this verbal affection only four times a month (or less) increases with each year in school.

Table 5 illustrates that decline also occurs with measures of touching, caressing, and embracing. For some reason, parents

Table 4. Parents Expressing Verbal Affection Every Day

Child's Grade in School	Mothers	Fathers
5	61%	40%
6	57	37
7	50	30
8	45	29
9	37	24

become less affectionate as their children enter the adolescent period.

Table 5. Parents Expressing Physical Affection Every Day

Child's Grade in School	Mothers	Fathers
5	83%	64%
6	75	59
7	67	47
8	60	43
9	49	33

Nonverbal communication is important in expressing closeness. Holding a child's hand, stroking hair or forehead, leaning over to put a hand on the shoulder are examples of gestures that create strong bonds and often speak louder than words. A touch can say "I care," "I love you," "I'm here." Every parent needs to find a way of showing affection that is natural and comfortable for both parent and child.

Demonstrating affection is not always easy for parents. Perhaps it was not done in their own parental homes. Yet many parents wish they could free themselves to express affection toward their adolescent. Said one father, "I would be a better parent if I could express myself more freely with hugs and kisses."

This parent is right. He would be filling a definite need in his adolescent's emotional development if he could show affection. Figure 11 shows evidence that fathers are less demonstrative in showing affection than are mothers. Expressions of love and caring are especially needed from both parents during the adolescent period. Struggling to know who they are and how they are regarded by others, adolescents need the affirmation found in both verbal and nonverbal physical signs that they are loved.

Building Trust

Respect for the privacy of adolescents, an important aspect of nurturance, indicates parents' belief in their children's right

Figure 11. Change in Demonstrative Affection by Parents*

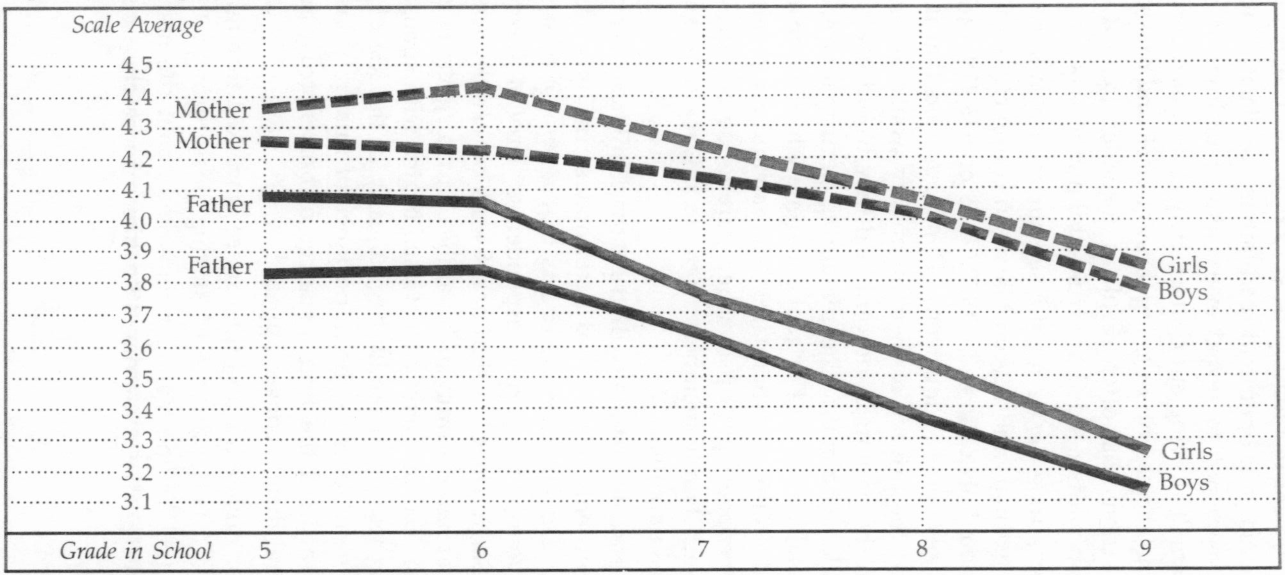

Item: "How often does your mother/father hug or kiss you?"

5 = Daily
4 = Couple of times a week
3 = One to four times a month
2 = Less than once a month
1 = Never

to have a life space of their own. More than that, it is an important ingredient in building trust. Parents who listen to phone conversations or open and read letters are violating the adolescent's desire not to reveal every aspect of himself or herself to others. Throwing out clothes, magazines, or records belonging to the adolescent, or going through desk and dresser drawers, are actions that often result in alienation instead of togetherness. What is needed are trust-building efforts.

Adolescents' strong desire for privacy surfaced in a survey done by Jane Norman and Myron Harris in conjunction with Xerox Education Publications in 1977. Out of 673,479 early adolescents (ages eight to fourteen), 41 percent said that if a parent violated the privacy of their room they would discuss the issue with the parent; 26 percent said they would use the "hide and lock technique." The remaining participants said they would retaliate in kind or make a scene when the invasions occurred. In this questionnaire, Norman and Harris also learned that teenagers get upset when parents do not affirm and enforce each family members' right to privacy from siblings as well as parents.[17]

"Snooping parents" basically distrust their children. When trust is not present, relationship deteriorates. In *Traits of a Healthy Family*, Dolores Curran reports that a *sense of trust* is rated number four by 551 survey respondents.[18] Jerry M. Lewis, author of *No Single Thread*, a significant work on healthy families, found that parents from such families have a strong need to *preserve trust*, and that family trust itself begins with spousal trust. Building trust in a family begins early in the life of a child. Yet for many parents the importance of this trait does not become real until the first instances of broken trust between them and their teenager appear.[19]

If respect for private life and time space is worked through, the family has a better chance of staying close through the adolescent years. As one teenager remarked about the home she would like to have some day, "I'd like it to be close *and* open."

Doing Things Together. Love and caring is shown by taking an interest in the activities of one's children and doing things together with them. Interestingly, there is no appreciable decline in the number of hours families spend each week in doing things together. Apparently, patterns established when the children are young are maintained as they enter the adolescent period. It is significant, however, that about one-third (36 percent) of the families in the Adolescent-Parent study spend less than five hours in an average week doing things together.

Perhaps in our culture, family time together is possible only if a conscious decision is made to find time. Just as a budget is planned, so time together needs to be planned. Hamilton McCubbin and David Olson,[20] in their study of families that cope well under stress, found that one characteristic of such families is "they set aside time to be together." A tremendous learning opportunity is created by the family which discusses and prioritizes its family time.

One of our sons recalls how this was done in our family:

We set aside a definite evening for planning, with all family members participating, giving their suggestions as to what they would like to do. Granted, some plans did not work out, but we had a fail-safe. Sunday noon dinners, which were our council time, were occasions for regrouping.

Even though mealtimes have traditionally been "together" times, there are evidences that American families are robbing themselves of this valuable time for talking and listening to each other. Fast-food dining is becoming an American way of life, a symbol of shortness and intensity in our social encounters. Work schedules and organized activities are culprits in limiting family mealtimes, and perhaps television viewing is equally guilty.

Author George Armelagos[21] reminisces about the significance of the dinner hour in the past. He regards it as having been one of the major times that the parents included children in family and societal affairs. Often dinner began with a prayer, which then put the food in a symbolic and ritualistic context. In the process of talking during the meal, social relationships, attitudes and beliefs were all enforced.

Armelagos expresses sadness over the death of the family table. Yet parents who care about the values of doing things together have it in their power to reverse this decline in their own home.

When interviewed, a number of young adults and adolescents alike speak of certain mealtimes during the week as being a highlight in family memories. This is especially interesting because therapists often ask a patient to think back to his or her memory of a family dinner during childhood. It is a way of finding out how much general communication and interaction there was in a patient's early life. Therapists maintain that there is a relationship between the love in a home and the richness of the family table experience. "It is to the table that love or discord eventually come."

As parents, our image of teenagers is frequently that they are champing the bit to throw off some of the traditions of home, those hundreds of little rituals of togetherness unique to each family. Sometimes when children leave home and establish their own families, they perpetuate traditions that did not seem to interest them when they were living at home. In our own family, with its Scandinavian roots, we have a tradition of serving lutefisk each Christmas Eve. To our knowledge, our second-oldest son never deigned to taste it. But a year after he was married, we had a long-distance call from South Dakota: "Say, how do you prepare lutefisk?"

Teens may go through a period of pulling away. They are, after all, in a separation process. But ultimately, when they form a new family, some old and some new traditions will be part of their lives. Every experience parents give their children becomes part of their future. It will be heartwarming for parents to note that, when interviewed, adolescents and young

70563

adults alike listed as most important, regardless of the activity, ingredients such as these: "we were all together," "Dad played with us," "we joked and laughed a lot," "we talked about funny things that happened in our family," "we all went and helped somebody," "our parents let us work with them on fixing things."

A recurring theme of these interviews was the memory of Christmas:

We lived on a farm, and I remember my sister and I going with my mother every Christmas Eve to a neighbor's home. They were very poor. Mother always made special food for that family. I try to do things like that myself every Christmas—and other times, too.

Vacations are special times too. One of our sons shared the following insight:

Family vacations have been very important in our family. When I think of how they have helped shape me, I would say that going to new exciting places (as we did) together with the family has given me a powerful sense of belonging. I was co-existing with my family while at the same time branching out into unfamiliar territory. Somehow it could be seen as risk-taking with security.

Developing Support Systems

A caring family unit forms its own support group. As one young adult says, "We pull for each other." Another adds, "We have a commitment to each other."

One of our sons relates the following incident:

I remember when I was a little boy and my brothers were teenagers. We were setting camp at Mt. Rainier and I was so enthralled by the surroundings that I set out to explore them. When I realized I had gone so far that the family was nowhere in sight, I became frightened and cried out. I can still remember vividly the family converging on me. Some came running up the path. My older brother took the shortest route and climbed the cliff. I can remember seeing his face appearing over the rock. It was a warm, wonderful memory of family support.

In fact, families that report having quality relationships with relatives and friends dealt best with the stresses of family life. David Olson,[22] professor of family science at the University of Minnesota, was surprised to find how much the nuclear family of parents and children in his study relied on relatives for emotional support. Our interviews with young adults and adolescents bore out this finding:

My warmest memories are of my extended family. I was my grandfather's special person.

I like my mother's family. Somehow they always notice me at family gatherings. They make me feel important.

Our many Sunday dinners at my uncle and aunt's house said to me, "You're important to us."

When we were in very bad financial straits as a family, there would always be a substantial check for Christmas from two of my uncles.

My aunt and uncle shaped my concept of caring. When my brother, who was a teenager, was dying, they spent hours and hours at his bedside and supported our family in every possible way.

Curran, in *Traits of a Health Family*, finds that in black families particularly "grandma" establishes a close, lifelong relationship with her grandchildren, a relationship missing in many white, middle-class families. Often grandma is the early caregiver to these children whose parents, out of necessity or desire, have to go to work. The grandchildren develop a basic trust in grandma in their infancy years. As they grow up and move away, they come back for support and affirmation both from their own parents and from grandma.[23]

Community and friends are also part of the extended support systems. A young man writes,

My high school basketball coach was extended family. He was my model. He was the first person I could discuss my faith with.

Our next-door neighbors were always there if I got in trouble and my parents weren't home is the comment of another young person.

Conclusion

Close family life is one of the major sources of strength for adolescents. Measures of nurturance, authoritative (democratic) control, good family communication, and parental harmony show that this resource of family closeness gives adolescents an inner strength for growth and development as well as for more responsible living. A close family characterized by parental affection, trust, doing things together, and strong support systems provides an inner resistance to the toxins of life. It provides an atmosphere within which an adolescent best matures toward the seven developmental goals described in Chapter 3.

This resource is eroded, however, by parental disharmony and by styles of discipline that are either autocratic or permissive. Their negative effect on a family unit are too important to ignore.

The issue in this chapter is one of building close relationships. Those who work with troubled youth report that "quality of human relationships is the most powerful determinant of successful programs in the education and treatment of troubled children.[24] The principle applies to all types of adolescents. Nothing is as powerful as the love of parents. And as indicated in this chapter, love is more than feeling. It is action, and a process of giving. It is caring, feeling responsible, showing respect, and learning to know the feelings of another. Love, acceptance and understanding are not the rewards of good behavior (to be used as social reinforcers) but as prerequisites to behavior.[25]

It is love and caring that establish the setting within which adolescents come to adopt the value orientation discussed in Chapter 5, and to know and understand the liberating faith discussed in Chapter 6.

5. Cry for Moral Behavior

The human mind has no more power of inventing a new value than of imagining a new primary colour, or indeed, of creating a new sun and new sky for it to move on.

—C. S. LEWIS

"What have we done differently in raising this child than his older brothers and sisters?" ask the parents of a teenage boy.

"Maybe we babied him," suggests the father.

"Maybe we left him alone too much," says the mother.

"He's caused a lot of trouble to us." The father's voice is heavy.

"He started using drugs around ninth grade—maybe before that, for all I know. It's both drugs and alcohol now."

"You've gotten help for him?" the friend asks.

"Oh, yes," replies the mother, "a whole year, every week. We were all involved."

"But something's wrong yet." The father's voice is somber. "It's like he has no respect for us, no understanding of our problems, no appreciation of what we've done for him. It's like we're just here to pay any price he wants us to pay for what *he* is doing."

"He's downright cruel," says the mother.

The experience of these parents culminates in an anguished cry: What did we do wrong? Is it too late to develop healthy concepts of right and wrong? If children have learned it "right" in childhood, does it become unlearned? If they have learned it "wrong" in childhood, can that be changed? These cries are borne out of sleepless nights, bitterness, and heartache.

Where and how do our children find the inner conviction and strength to live moral lives?

"It's the lying I can't stand," says another mother. "My daughter goes to school in the morning and skips out as soon as she can. But she tells *me* she's gone to school all day." The mother turns to her friend, searching her eyes for an answer. "Doesn't it make any difference that you teach your child not to lie when she is small? I can't understand what has happened."

The parents in these vignettes express the dilemma being faced by countless parents: How do we cope with a child whose way of living is the opposite of what we tried to teach?

This anguished cry is real, and it is a difficult one to deal with. In this chapter, we approach the subject of moral behavior by means of these topics:

- Deciding what is moral
- Becoming concerned about two critical issues in moral behavior
- Realizing how we communicate values and beliefs
- Working to internalize moral beliefs

Deciding What Is Moral

Everyone has a different idea about how people should live their lives. Some people follow traditional moral beliefs, and others follow a morality based on personal preferences or the norms of their peer group.

The conflict between these views is one that concerns many parents.

When C. S. Lewis, Oxford don and Cambridge professor, saw traditional values being debunked as "sentimental" in an English school textbook, he became very conscious of this conflict. In a book that has now become a classic, he insists that an ethic based on "I want" (a view he found espoused in the textbook) could result in nature's conquest of man. In letting instincts become one's guide, he says further, a person loses the basis for making judgments, because instincts sometimes lead one in contradictory directions. Lewis believed separation from traditional moral values introduces the demise of humankind. Hence the title of his book, *The Abolition of Man*.[1]

Lewis contends that there never has been more than one judgment of values embedded in the civilizations of this world. This judgment is found in the writings of all time—pagan and religious alike. Whether one reads the writings of ancient Babylon, Rome, China, India, or any other civilization, one finds a moral stance that includes judgments such as the following:

- The "law" of mercy
- The "law" of magnanimity
    Generosity in forgiving
    Willingness to die for another
- The "law" of doing good
- The "law" of caring for one's family
    Duties to parents and others
    Duties to children
- The "law" of justice
    Sexual justice
    Honesty
    Justice in court
- The "law" of good faith

Over the centuries, a general consensus has evolved as to what is "good." It is morality that is refined and enhanced in the writings of the Old and New Testaments. These value judgments define the moral structure or universe within which we live. It is the conviction of C. S. Lewis that the "human mind has no more power of inventing a new value than of imagining a new primary colour, or indeed, of creating a new sun and a new sky for it to move on."

C. S. Lewis's view of morality as being mercy, justice, magnanimity, caring for one's family, and the like, draws attention to the fact that there is a moral structure to our universe.

Certain generally accepted standards of goodness and rightness in conduct or character make for happy living.

As we write this chapter, for example, a number of adults are on trial for sexual abuse of children. These adults are accused of sexual acts. If convicted, they will serve prison sentences. Sanctions against child abuse, rape, indecent exposure, polygamy, and child neglect are present in civil laws because such conduct violates community values. These values are built into the fabric of life; they are necessary if a civilization is to survive. Some of these might be called intrinsic values:

- Respect for the personal dignity and freedom of individuals
- Respect for the basic human ties of family
- Respect for the physical and psychological health of people
- Respect for the rights of individuals

Parallel with these intrinsic values are moral values:

- Fidelity—keeping promises
- Honesty—being truthful
- Sexual restraint—control of sexual appetite
- Social justice—protecting the powerless

Moral values are not matters of personal preference. Rather, they are judgments about life that every civilization has found necessary for survival. E. Stanley Jones, renowned missionary and author, once said, "We don't break the Ten Commandments. If we ignore them, they break us." Schools teach moral values when they make it clear that cheating, stealing, vandalism, and fighting are not allowed. These are accepted norms, rules, or sanctions common to schools.

A parent may wonder, however, if moral behavior is not more than conformity to the generally accepted standards of right conduct or character. Granted, many parents would be enormously relieved if their son or daughter did accept and live by these standards. But one wonders if moral behavior might be more than conformity to accepted standards of goodness and rightness of conduct.

Lawrence Kohlberg, a moral theorist, thinks so. He views moral development as reflecting six distinct levels or stages in which the first stage is being good to avoid punishment. His sixth and highest stage identifies morality with the recognition of the rights of others. This recognition of people's rights centers in the principles of fairness, justice, and respect for people. Kohlberg illustrates this concept of morality with a young man's answer to the question, "What does the word 'morality' mean to you?"

I think [morality] is recognizing the rights of individuals, not interfering with those rights. Act as fairly as you would have them treat you. It means the human being's right to do as he pleases, without interfering with somebody else's rights.[2]

A crass example of this concept of morality can be heard in comments by advocates of adolescent rights. One popular psychologist, who counsels people by the radio, said this during a broadcast:

Do not meddle in the sex life of a teenager. That is their private domain. If they wish to be sexually active, that is their right and privilege.

Carol Gilligan, in her book *In A Different Voice*, presents a contrasting view by defining morality as a feeling of responsibility for the welfare of others. In her interviews with women she finds this concept of morality emerging in a striking way. An illustration of this concept surfaces in the following interview with a twenty-five-year-old law student. He was asked, "Is everybody's opinion, with respect to moral problems, equally correct?"

No . . . There are situations in which I think there are right and wrong answers that sort of inhere to the nature of existence. We need to depend on each other, to be enriched by cooperating with other people and striving to live in harmony with everybody else, to find fulfillment in ourselves. To that end, there are right and wrong things that promote different courses of action that obviously promote or harm that goal.[3]

Gilligan champions a morality that is primarily concerned about people, those suffering and in need; a morality of trying to live responsibly and contribute to the health and well-being of others. This concept of morality equates responsibility with caring.

Kohlberg, aware of this critique, refers to her morality of responsibility as an ethic of responsible, universal love (*agape*). It involves an interpenetration of religion and ethical action which he does not view as competitive with his principle of fairness. Each needs the other.

In his discussion of the highest stage of moral development, Kohlberg wonders if there might be a seventh stage—a morality motivated by religion. Religion, he sees, helps people to be moral even though acting morally may not give the person any tangible rewards or pleasure. To him, ultimate moral maturity requires a mature solution to the question of the meaning of life.[4]

Why be moral? That is a question adolescents often ask parents. Why should I try to act in ways above the behavior of my classmates? Why should I be concerned about what is fair, right, or an expression of love?

We recognize there may be several answers to this question. But one that emerges powerfully in the studies of Search Institute is the motivation of a personal faith. Though motivation for a morality of responsibility can be a humanistic love for people, our studies show it to be strongly associated with a consciousness of God's presence.

In a 1971 study of 7,050 high school youth,[5] we found that a sense of moral responsibility strongly correlates with both a consciousness of God's presence and participation in the life of a congregation. The high correlations ($r = 0.53$ and 0.55) make it clear that for youth identified with the church, morality can be more than conformity to other people's expectations. Morality can be a life of responsible caring for others that is motivated by a personal faith. Morality can be living a life of service that gives a sense of joy and meaning in life. The focus of this concept of morality is on life-enhancing activities instead of on the "don'ts" of wrong behavior.

Becoming Concerned About Two Critical Issues in Moral Behavior

We have identified two different levels or moral behavior: (1) seeking to live according to the traditional values of a moral universe; and (2) seeking to rise above laws and human expectations to a life of responsible living. Both are important and each poses a critical issue.

The Issue Involving Traditional Moral Beliefs

Parents and youth in the Adolescent-Parent study evidenced a high degree of acceptance of the traditional moral beliefs presented in the survey. They were asked to read descriptions in paragraph form of typical situations that involve issues of public morality (e.g., shoplifting, racial discrimination, premarital intercourse) and then rate them "right" or "wrong," Nine out of ten parents agreed on the wrongness of each behavior, with one exception. On the abortion issue, almost half the parents (45 percent) either expressed uncertainty or declared abortion justifiable.

The responses of the adolescents on issues of public morality were much the same. Agreement as to what is "wrong" behavior characterized over four out of five in the study. Only on the issue of abortion was there confusion. (An average of 39 percent were "not sure" whether an abortion was "right" or "wrong.") However, there was a change in perception from fifth to ninth grade—the percent "not sure" decreased from 48 percent to 34 percent. The shift was toward coming to view abortion as "wrong."

It is significant that we found widespread agreement on these aspects of public morality. And it is noteworthy that young adolescents seek to clarify their belief position on new issues.

Evidence of Erosion. The issue centers in the fact that the Adolescent-Parent data reflect a discernible shift in the adolescents' acceptance of some of the traditional moral beliefs. The three available to us from the survey relate to issues of national concern: drug use, sexual activity, and honesty. A decline occurs in the number of adolescents who regard the use of alcohol (Figure 12), premarital intercourse (Figure 13), and lying to parents (Figure 14) as wrong. Though their beliefs about the wrongness of shoplifting and racial discrimination remain continuously high, beliefs about the wrongness of activities that are of special concern to parents decline sharply from fifth to ninth grade. Take, for instance, the use of alcohol. The number of boys who view drinking beer as being wrong for them at their age drops from 76 percent for sixth-graders to 61 percent for ninth-graders; and the same relative decline in percentage occurs for the girls.

With respect to premarital relations, the number of boys who "don't think" they will have sexual intercourse before marriage drops from 50 percent for sixth-graders to 36 percent for ninth-graders. On this issue, the differences in response between boys and girls is one of the largest found in the study. The percent of girls who "don't think" they will have sexual intercourse before marriage remains high, with 61 percent of the ninth-graders maintaining this position.

With respect to lying, the great majority of early adolescents are agreed that lying to their parents is wrong. What is significant, however, is the erosion of this conviction (see Figure 14).

Though these changes in moral beliefs are obviously due to many factors, one can neither ignore the deliberate efforts of mass media to exploit the youth market nor the power of peer pressure to alter youth's moral convictions. David Rosenthal, writing in the *Rolling Stone Yearbook*,[6] sharply criticizes the "bad films aimed at 12-year-olds." His article takes the same position as that of Harry Haun in his article "Loss of Innocence

Figure 12. Belief About Drinking Alcohol*

Percent *wrong* or *very wrong*

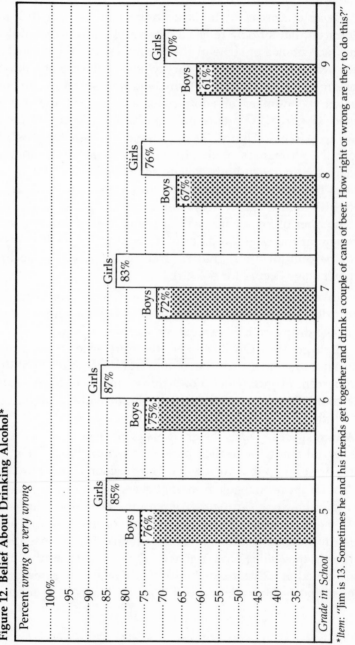

Grade in School

*Item: "Jim is 13. Sometimes he and his friends get together and drink a couple of cans of beer. How right or wrong are they to do this?"

Figure 13. Percentage Opposed to Premarital Intercourse*

Percent *strongly agree* or *agree*

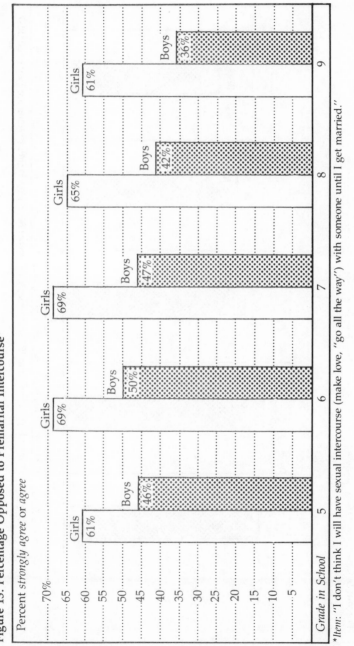

Grade in School

Item: "I don't think I will have sexual intercourse (make love, "go all the way") with someone until I get married."

Figure 14. Belief About Lying to Parents*

Percent believe wrong or very wrong

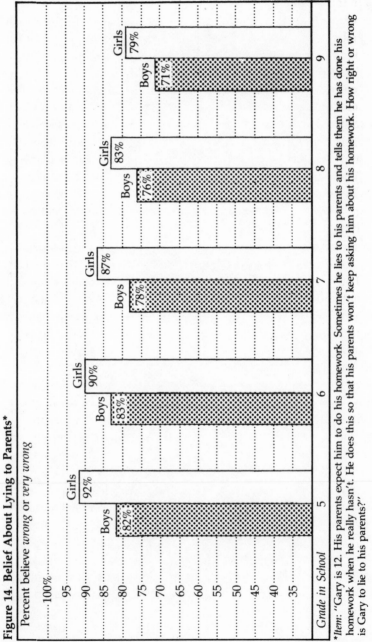

Grade in School

Item: "Gary is 12. His parents expect him to do his homework. Sometimes he lies to his parents and tells them he has done his homework when he really hasn't. He does this so that his parents won't keep asking him about his homework. How right or wrong is Gary to lie to his parents?"

Remains a Commercial Constant."[7] The concern of both writers is the sexploitation of the youth market.

Beer companies are using mass media to capture the youth alcohol market. Their unabashed effort to cultivate the youthful drinker has resulted in their being characterized by the Center for Science in the Public School as predators in "the business of creating drinkers." The use of sports heroes to promote the excitement and camaraderie of using alcoholic beverages can scarcely go unnoticed by highly vulnerable young adolescents.

Parents should be concerned over the values being presented through mass media. Our study of adolescents shows a strong relationship between exposure to mass media and the following: hedonism (seeing pleasure as the highest good); use of drugs and alcohol; sexually arousing activity; and rejection of traditional moral beliefs.

A factor related to erosion of moral beliefs is the power of a peer group on its members. In 1983 a Search Institute study of 10,505 randomly selected students in Minnesota high schools dramatized this power.[8] It found that the overwhelmingly favorite time for drinking is a weekend party of peers, a time when peer pressure is greatest. This factor has shown up also in studies regarding use of marijuana. These studies identify peer pressure as the number one predictor of marijuana use. Inasmuch as half of the adolescents in the Adolescent-Parent study worry much about being liked, and 60 percent worry about how their friends will treat them, it is not surprising that young adolescents will acquiesce to group pressure when there is drinking.

Do such factors as mass media impact and peer group pressure have an eroding effect? It is difficult to prove conclusively the determining factors; but the Adolescent-Parent study clearly shows that an erosion in certain moral beliefs is occurring.

Parental Concern. Voices are being raised today in protest of adults who don't expect young people to resist temptation.

William Raspberry, columnist for the *Washington Post*, wrote an article entitled, "It's Time for Black Adults to Make Teenage Virtue a Necessity."[9] In addressing the alarming rise in pregnancies and child-bearing among unmarried teenagers (55 percent of all black children born in 1982 were born to a single mother), he quoted from a study by Harriet McAdoo. Though 80 percent of the teenagers recognized that having a baby was terribly disruptive to their educational and economic prospects, and half saw it as "ruining" their lives, 20 percent of the girls still expected to get pregnant and 44 percent of the boys expected they would get a girl pregnant. The conference where this study was reported toyed with the idea of introducing counter-incentives to getting pregnant. One proposal was to pay girls $200 every birthday as long as they avoid pregnancy and $2000 on their eighteenth birthday if they haven't gotten pregnant by then. Raspberry wrote:

What fascinates and dismays me is how seldom the question of morality enters any of these discussions. That adolescents will be sexually active is taken as a given, and the only question seems to be how to avoid the natural consequences of that activity.

I have the feeling that unless we get back to the old-fogey notion that teen-age sex is wrong (in the religious context, a sin) that morality demands the postponement of sexual activity, that virtue and decency are real concerns, the pragmatic approach is doomed to fail.

The 10,467 parents in the Adolescent-Parent study give top priority to the task of instilling moral beliefs in their children. Two out of three are much concerned about this task and wonder how best to carry out their responsibilities. They sense the conflict of values between their home and church on one hand, and society on the other. For that reason, when asked what help they would prefer, their top choice is "To help my child develop healthy concepts of right and wrong." A total of 70 percent say they are "very" or "quite" interested in programs that would equip them to give this help. The concern of over two-thirds of these parents is to instill in their children *a sense of morality* regarding what is right and wrong.

The need for greater attention to the issues is also being seen by professionals in the field of family counseling. Dolores Curran, in *Traits of a Healthy Family*,[10] speaks of being pleasantly surprised to see how highly 551 professionals rated the traits "teaches a sense of right and wrong." These professionals, who touch families through their work in education, church, health, and family counseling or voluntary organizations, rank it number seven on a list of fifty-six possible characteristics of a healthy family. Strikingly, in a day when development of self takes precedence over the development of a moral life, these workers give priority to the teaching of morality.

Supportive Power of Moral Beliefs. Parents can find encouragement in the fact that there is the potential in moral beliefs to provide inner strength and support to adolescents. We find that as acceptance of traditional moral standards or beliefs goes up for young adolescents, antisocial behaviors, drug and alcohol use, norm violations, and promiscuity go down.

This link between moral beliefs and behavior has appeared in other Search Institute studies as well. In fact, it forms a major conclusion of *Study of Generations,* a 1972 national study of Lutherans between the ages of fifteen and sixty-five.[11] The study shows that the best indicator of what people will say or do is their values and beliefs system. Additional evidence of this power of values and beliefs to influence behavior is strikingly apparent in a 1982 study of the religious beliefs and values of the 96th Congress by Peter Benson and Dorothy Williams of Search Institute.[12] From interviews (averaging thirty-five minutes in length) that include 72 percent of those drawn in an exact random sample, we gain unique information. We find that the beliefs and values of people in Congress are as good an indicator of their voting behavior as their party affiliation. When party affiliation and type of religious beliefs and values are combined, one can quite accurately predict how people in Congress will vote on matters such as defense, civil rights, humanitarian efforts, and foreign aid.

For a parent, the implications of these findings are highly significant. It means that adolescents (as well as adults) who are helped to internalize moral beliefs and values, are likely to adopt behaviors compatible with these values.

A parent naturally wonders about the reliability of this kind of information. Therefore let us add that well over a hundred studies can be summoned to show a significant correlation between acceptance of traditional moral beliefs and moral restraint. Conversely, loss of traditional moral beliefs can be shown to be associated with a rise in immoral, illegal, and self-destructive behaviors.

In a separate study of data on youth ages fifteen to twenty-nine,[13] we analyzed what best predicts a young person's willingness to reject temptations such as alcohol abuse, swearing, premarital sexual intercourse, X-rated movies, and pornographic literature. We introduced thirty-nine different possibilities (variables) into the computer and let them compete with each other to see which variable best indicated a willingness to delay gratification. Interestingly, it was a moral belief that won out. Youth who believe that premarital sexual intercourse is "not permissible" are the ones most likely to show restraint in the many other behaviors related to moral behavior.

The Issue Involving a Sense of Moral Purpose

Our discussion now shifts to consideration of a higher expression of morality—feeling responsible for the needs of others. As was true for traditional moral beliefs, the majority of the young adolescents do accept a sense of responsibility for others. The Adolescent-Parent study gives clear evidences of a serving stance, particularly among the girls. Two out of three of the early adolescents speak of doing things for others. This is most encouraging.

Erosion of Moral Purpose. It is sobering to note that this sense of responsibility is not one that increases with age, but rather shows a decline from fifth to ninth grade. Take, for instance, the high concern fifth-graders show over hunger and poverty found in the United States. A total of 52 percent say they worry "very much" or "quite a bit" about this tragedy. It is something these fifth-graders are concerned about. But a steady decline appears in these percentages as the adolescents grow older. Only 31 percent of the ninth-graders identify this topic as a major concern. The same drop occurs in the value these young adolescents place on having a "world without war" (it ranks third in importance for fifth graders and eighth for ninth graders).

The critical issue is the apparent decline in a concern for people during these young adolescent years. A measure involving three items—adolescents' doing things that help people, wanting a world without war, and wanting a world without hunger or poverty—shows a discernible decline between the fifth and ninth grades (Figure 15). One might conclude from this and other changes that during early adolescence youth became increasingly self-oriented. The diminishing sense of moral purpose, however, centers primarily on boys, who appear to be less concerned with the needs of others.

Figure 16 suggests that girls differ from boys in their involvement in serving and helping activities. Not only are more of them involved in this way, but also there is a strong rise in the extent to which girls give aid to people in trouble, share money and food, give volunteer time to charities, and assist friends or neighbors. Girls are clearly more responsive to this aspect of a morality of responsibility than boys. The two issues we have identified emphasize the reason why parents in the Adolescent-Parent study need to give first priority to the teaching of healthy concepts of right and wrong. The challenge is to see that children become not only intelligent and healthy, but virtuous. As noted by Harvard psychiatrist Robert Coles,[14] parents need to inspire in their children a desire not only to get ahead and get along, but also to give to and help others. What children need as much as food, clothing, and a good education is moral purpose.

Adolescents need value judgments with which to critically evaluate the values and morality of the society in which they live. As parents we need to evaluate our own stand on controversial moral issues. By sharing them with our adolescents, we can help them learn to say "no" to unethical behaviors. Youth generally want this kind of direction-giving. Two young

Figure 15. Concern for People*

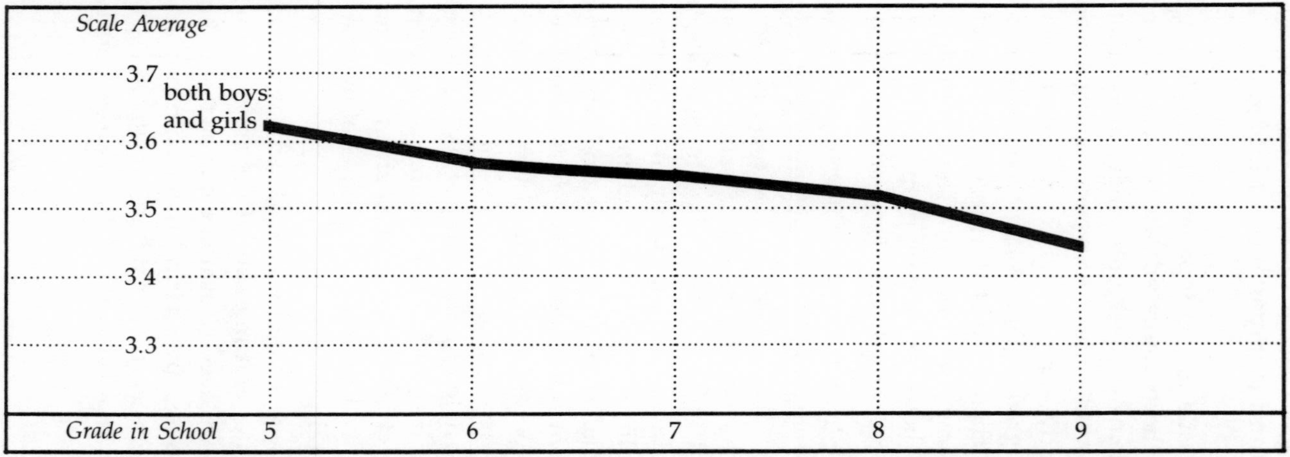

*Item: "I worry about all the people who are hungry and poor in our country." Based on the average of three similar items

4 = Very much
3 = Quite a bit
2 = Somewhat
1 = Not at all

Figure 16. Prosocial Behavior*

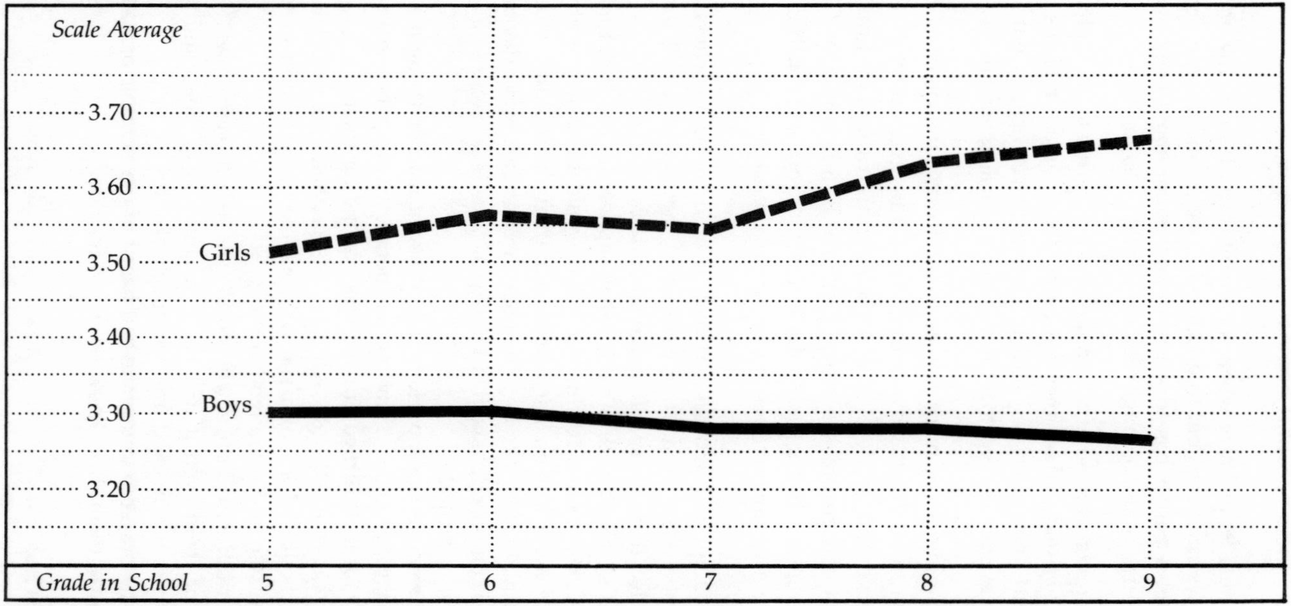

*The Prosocial Behavior scale is based on the average of six survey questions. The scale range is from 1 (low) to 5 (high).
Item: "How many hours did you give during the last month to help people outside the family (such as the poor, sick, aged, handicapped)?"

adults make their observations on this subject, based on experiences in their parental homes:

A parent should let us know when we are off track. It's true that most of the time we need freedom to decide what we should do in a given situation. But a parent has to warn an adolescent about some dangers. Otherwise he or she might realize it when it is too late.

I feel my parents were so afraid to step on our rights as individuals that they never told us how they felt about decisions or problems we had to face. I knew they had strong feelings or convictions but because they never expressed them it made me feel *alone* sometimes.

The following account of six-year-old Ruby, one of the first black children to be involved in school desegregation in the South during the sixties, is a striking illustration of how a young child can embrace a moral purpose in a heroic way. She did this because her parents took their stand on a difficult moral issue and encouraged Ruby to do the same.

Every day [Ruby] and another girl had to be escorted to school by federal marshals facing shouting mobs who threatened to kill them and who called them every vile name imaginable.

As a psychiatrist trained to study what happens to children under stress, Dr. Coles wanted to find out what would happen to Ruby's psychological development. The teacher admitted she couldn't understand how Ruby could take it. "She goes through hell every day and yet seems so composed," she told Dr. Coles. "She is so eager to learn and is such a nice child."

Dr. Coles said he was puzzled, too. When a teacher thought she observed Ruby talking to some of the people haranguing her, she asked her about it. It turned out she was praying for them.

When Dr. Coles asked Ruby why she was praying, she said it was "because I should." He found she was praying at the behest of her parents, minister, and grandmother.

"Do you think it will do much good?" she asked. Her reply: "We must pray for them even if it doesn't do any good." She admitted she prayed even when she didn't feel much like it.

She said she prayed because she had heard of the example of Jesus: "Father, forgive them, they know not what they do."

"That was her moral education," Dr. Coles said, noting that people come to develop some of the most admirable qualities in response to pain, suffering, and hardship.[15]

How Values and Beliefs Are Communicated

Moral actions develop from our moral beliefs. In other words, moral actions are the outcomes of the value orientation we hold. Our life priorities (values) and convictions (beliefs) are the soil out of which our actions emerge. Granted, there may be times when social pressures and stressful situations cause us to act out of emotion and without due restraint. But over time, our pattern of behavior is basically a reflection of our value orientation. This is true for us as parents and true also for our adolescent.

Sin as a Value Orientation

Where is the word "sin" in this picture? After all, sin figures prominently in both the Old and New Testaments. Does the concept of "sin" relate to the issue of one's value orientation? We believe that it does.

Sin can be defined as primarily a state of being, an orientation to life that centers on oneself, that places one's own interests in a position of top priority. That is why pride can be called the primary sin from which all others are derived. What we call unethical behavior or immoral acts are "sins" that result from the primary sin of self-interest or a self-centered value orientation. True, it is necessary for a parent to be concerned over behaviors or "sins" that are self-destructive (such as lying, stealing, drinking, vandalism, and fighting). They need to be restrained. But more important than these behaviors, and hence of greater potential concern to parents, is the value orientation out of which they arise.

It is not by chance that young adolescents involved in drug and alcohol use tend also to be involved in antisocial behaviors. These activities are highly intercorrelated.

The Adolescent-Parent study shows that associated with these activities are preferences for certain kinds of music, violence on television, and sexually arousing movies. The interlocking pattern of behaviors points to an underlying set of values that bring with it a tendency to reject the moral beliefs and standards that may be treasured by a parent. The Adolescent-Parent study shows a high correlation between youth whose pattern of behavior is as described above and those who reject traditional moral beliefs. The issue for us as parents is to help our children find the set of values that focuses on a moral purpose—a life contributing to the well-being of others, a life of significance.

If a child's orientation can be directed to a life of caring and concern for people—a life of moral purpose—the hoped-for positive behaviors will increasingly appear. On the other hand, the more a child's values center in self and personal gratification, the more he or she will show negative behaviors.

The Parents' Values

Values, a quality we can't see and certainly find difficult to define, are communicated most powerfully by parents. Though a child's friends may be influential, their power usually emerges as dominant only if the relationship of love and caring between parents is broken or vastly diminished. The prime communicator of values is still the parent.

When asked, "Whom do you enjoy more—your friends or your parents?" the answer is surprising. Sixty percent of the 8,165 adolescents say they enjoy both equally; 15 percent indicate a preference for their parents. The fact that no more than one in four prefer their friends suggests that for most adolescents a strong parent-child relationship exists along with their peer relationship.

The issue, then, is "What value orientation am I communicating to my child?" It is not enough to say that lying, cheating, and vandalism are wrong. These "sins" are simply expressions of a set of values that the child holds. The most important element of communication is the life direction a parent is giving the child through what he or she does and says.

One life direction or value orientation a parent can communicate is an approach of over-strictness that assumes that morality comes through controlling people by rules and regulations. It results in an authoritarian, restrictive approach to parenting and use of severe punishment. It tends to be unloving, unforgiving, and rigid. Though it may use the words of Scripture and orthodox Christianity, its spirit is poles apart from a Christianity of grace (unmerited love). Its focus is on external behaviors and the do's and don'ts of a personal morality.

Tragically, this well-intentioned and often earnest approach to parenting tends to drive children to do the very things that are forbidden. Our data consistently show that young people under such a regime seek out friends of contrasting standards and adopt behaviors that stand in defiance of their parents. Though they may not be able to put their feelings into words, they are repulsed by the relentless condemning spirit that lowers their self-esteem and causes them to battle with overwhelming feelings of guilt and no resolution of these emotions.

A contrasting value orientation is what Allen Keith-Lucas[16] calls a Christianity of Grace (meaning unmerited love). This stance focuses not on behaviors but on the underlying motivation of thankfulness for the love, the promise, and the presence of a living God. Parents with this value system know what it is to experience God's forgiveness and love themselves. In turn they can approach their children at a time of wrongdoing with an uncondemning spirit. If parents can give this value orientation to a child, they are giving a priceless gift. A sense of moral responsibility and concern for other people is a characteristic of this orientation.

An incident occurred in one of our studies that convinced us of how the values of respected adults are communicated to adolescents with whom they work. We were involved in a government-funded study that trained high school youth in friendship skills in order to reach out to lonely and alienated peers. The purpose of the study was to test the relative effectiveness of three different approaches to training these youth.

Because the project was government funded, care was used not to include any "God talk" or to sponsor any type of religious activity on its retreats. Likewise, when choosing the trainers of friendship skills, no thought was given to the value orientations of those selected—only to their skill and competence. By chance, one turned out to be an agnostic (a refugee from a moralistic background), the second a nominal member of a mainline denomination, and the third a psychotherapist who was also an ordained clergyman. Each person, highly skilled in human relations, developed a training program unique to his or her discipline. Each person, using the methodology unique to his or her specialization, taught friendship skills to a group of young adults, who in turn taught a group of high school students.

At three different times during the field experiment (beginning, middle, and end), a battery of forty-six scales or measures was given the high school youth. One of the questionnaires (an assessment of twenty-five scales) included measures of religious interest, participation, and belief. Though these three measures were not germane to the project, they were used because their items were intermingled with the others.

When comparing scores from the three training approaches, we were surprised to discover that changes had occurred in the religious interest and participation of the young people of two groups. There was a measurable drop in religious interest and involvement of youth being trained under the agnostic, and an increase for those trained under the ordained clergyman. Our best explanation for this unexpected change in scores on the religious measures was that these highly respected trainers had communicated a life direction and value orientation. Though they did not work directly with the high school youth, the power of their lives moved to them through the young adults. Their personalities were a contagion, particularly during retreats on weekends. This finding, confirmed by other studies, illustrates how values and beliefs are communicated when the authority figure is able to establish a congenial relationship. They are communicated by the modeling or lifestyle of a person as well as by verbal sharing. Values are primarily caught—not taught. They are unconsciously absorbed from those one loves and respects.

A strong incentive to moral living and a powerful inhibitor of living for the instant gratification of one's desires is found in the expectations of an adolescent's parents. Where love and respect is the common bond, the opinions and wishes of the parent carry considerable force. One young man, reminiscing on past behavior says, "What helped me decide against doing something I knew was wrong were the expectations of my folks. I respect and care for them and did not want to do something I knew would hurt them."

Working to Internalize Moral Beliefs

As parents we must know our position regarding what is right and wrong, and then be able to explain the reasonableness of this position. Such an approach to moral teaching is called induction. It relies on discussion and exploration, and in this process a child is helped to internalize a moral code. This method does not use compulsion or the common device of love withdrawal—"I won't like you if you do that." Rather, it attempts to explain why certain moral laws are important, that breaking them can violate some inner personal needs, and that breaking them can bring unhappiness to someone else as well. Induction appeals to a child's own internal resources for controlling and monitoring behavior. Over time, it creates internal standards an adolescent will use to control behavior.

The Adolescent-Parent study is conclusive regarding how a parent's behavior is tied with an adolescent's moral behavior.[17] Clearly, three parenting behaviors—demonstrative affection, authoritative (democratic) control, and inductive discussion—

are strongly tied with self-esteem, helping others, internalization of moral values, and a concern for people. Furthermore, when these parental approaches are used, one is less likely to find norm-breaking behavior, chemical use, and aggressive behaviors with one's adolescents. Granted, these parental behaviors do not assure moral behavior, because each adolescent makes his or her own decisions. But they do influence behavior.

Parents should also know that autocratic and permissive control, coercive discipline, and withdrawal of one's love consistently correlate with opposite behavior. Where parents use these approaches, one is more likely to find adolescents with low self-esteem, aggressive behaviors, chemical use, and a lack of interest in helping others.[8]

Parents who help their child to internalize moral beliefs that find their own focus on love of oneself, one's neighbor, and God gives the child an important source of strength. It equips the person to fight today's social epidemics. An adolescent can grow strong by resisting the pressures of an ethic of "I want" and adopting the ethic of what is helpful to both self and others.

6. Cry for a Shared Faith

Each morning I saw my father take his Bible and go into his study for private devotions. I felt that if it was important for him as a grown-up, it must be for me, too.

—COLLEGE STUDENT

"Do we have family devotions?" Janet repeated the question after her interviewer. Then she looked over at her husband Bob and they exchanged a helpless laugh.

"I haven't heard that word for a long time," said the husband. "We had it when I was a kid."

"Don't you remember, Bob," said his wife, "we started out having something like that when the children were small?"

"Yeah, we were idealists, then, I guess."

"There are problems, aren't there?" The interviewer was tentative, waiting for a response.

"You bet there are," said Bob. "The last years I've traveled a lot in my business—days at a time, so Janet is alone with the kids."

Jane chimed in quickly. "I work part-time now, and when I get home, I'm a chauffeur. First I bring Betty to her cheerleader's practice—it's every day after school, you know. John's in cub football now and then he'll start hockey. There's no time for *anything*, let alone something structured like family devotions. We scarcely eat together. I'm a short-order cook."

Bob was a bit meditative. "I can see where it would be a good thing. I hardly know what my kids are thinking anymore. But," and he gave that helpless little laugh again, "time is the problem. Time."

Some readers may find such expressions as "private devotions," and "family devotions" archaic. What meaning do they have for today's parent or today's adolescent? Aren't they merely throwbacks to an earlier age?

The desire for a shared faith is only a muted cry. Though religious faith ranks high in importance for parents in the Adolescent-Parent study, it is seldom a topic of discussion in the home. This chapter is called "The Cry of Shared Faith" because 68 percent of the parents do express interest—"very much" or "quite a bit"—in learning "how to help my child grow in religious faith." There is a longing expressed here. The cry is a real one.

The purpose of this chapter is to draw attention to the critical need for parental sharing of faith within the family. The chapter considers four topics:

- The issue of sharing faith
- What faith can mean to an adolescent
- Why sharing faith is needed in a family
- How faith is shared

The Issue of Sharing Faith

In the Judeo-Christian tradition, the command to teach one's children about God goes far back in the life of God's people. When Moses, the leader of the Israelites and giver of the Ten Commandments, spoke to his people about entering the Promised Land, he told them they were to keep alive the story of how God had led them out of slavery in Egypt. They were to tell of how God promised to bless his people. Moses' instructions were clear: They were to teach these commands and promises to their children *at home.* How were they to accomplish this? Through conversation, symbol, and ritual.

You shall therefore lay up these words of mine in your heart and in your soul, and you shall bind them as a sign upon your hand, and you shall teach them to your children, talking of them when you are sitting in your house, and when you are walking by the way, and when you lie down, and when you rise. And you shall write them upon the doorposts of your house and upon your gates, that your days and the days of your children may be multiplied in the land. . . . (Deuteronomy 11:18–21)

Faithfully, devout parents through the centuries have followed these very commands—using different methods, perhaps, but keeping the theme of what God has done for them and how he continues to show his power and love.

A teenager of today speaks of how this kind of teaching was used in her home:

We learned about God chiefly through Bible stories in our family devotions and at night before we went to bed. When I have a family of my own, I would want to do the same thing. I love Bible stories, and I can remember them well from when I was a little girl.

In 1982, 551 professional counselors and educators were given a list of fifty-six traits characterizing a healthy family. They were told to rate them in order of importance. In the resulting book, *Traits of a Healthy Family*, author Dolores Curran reports that the trait "a shared religious core" ranked number 10.[1] Similarly, when Hamilton McCubbin studied the effects of war on the families of men who were killed, missing, or prisoners in Vietnam, he found that families were more resilient if they had strong religious beliefs.[2]

One would expect parents in the Adolescent-Parent study to be discussing their faith at home. When ranking sixteen values, they give fourth place to "having God at the center of my life." This is outranked only by their desire to have a happy family life, to be a good parent, and to have wisdom. Six in ten of these parents attend church once a week or more, two in three pray most days or every day, and one in two report being active in their church (See Figure 17). Thus it's not surprising that such a high value is placed on God-centeredness. When these 10,467 parents were asked, "Over all, how important is religion in your life?" the overwhelming majority—80 percent of the mothers and 67 percent of the fathers—affirmed that "it is the most" or at least "one of the most important influences in my life."

Figure 17. Specific Religious Behaviors of Parents

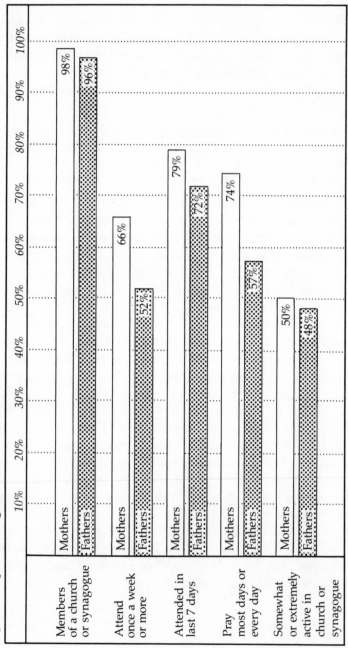

Table 6. Importance of Religion to Parents

Response	Percentage Mother	Percentage Father
It is the most important influence in my life	36%	26%
One of the most important	44	41
Somewhat important	18	26
One of the least important	2	6
The least important	0	2

Do their adolescent children rate the religious interest of their parents similarly? Interestingly, yes. When asked to rate "How important do you think religion is in your mother's/ father's life?" their ratings agree fairly well with their parents' rating. Ratings of mothers do not differ on the average more than 5 percent. Fathers were not as easy to judge; this shows up with an average discrepancy rating of 9 percent. One-fourth of the adolescents assumed that a religious faith was not important to their father.

Adolescents in the study share the personal conviction of their parents about the importance of religion.

A majority of the young adolescents say it is the most important or one of the most important influences in their lives (See Table 7).

Table 7. Importance of Religion to Youth

Response		Grade in School				
		5	6	7	8	9
The most important influence						
	Boys	29%	23%	17%	18%	17%
	Girls	27	25	20	17	20
One of the most important influences						
	Boys	31%	31%	32%	31%	29%
	Girls	33	32	35	38	35

The enigma, however, is this: though religion is identified as important by both parents and adolescents, it is almost a taboo subject in the home. When asked, "How often does your family sit down together and talk about God, the Bible

. . . or other religious things?'' 42 percent of the young adolescents say this never happens; 32 percent say this topic is discussed once or twice a month, 13 percent say it is discussed once a week. And this, it must be noted, is the finding from a survey of largely church-connected families, of whom 97 percent are members of a church.

Apparently, the Old Testament command to parents, "You shall teach these words of mine to your children, talking of them when sitting in your house, and when you are walking by the way, and when you lie down, and when you rise," is largely ignored. The concept of the father as priest in the home is a relic of the past in most homes—a discarded practice. No more than 13 percent of the adolescents are aware of such conversations. (This finding is supported by other studies. A 1980 study of Lutherans showed that only 8 percent of the families maintain the practice of sharing, discussing, or praying together as a family.)[3]

These low percentages of active sharing in the home are part of a larger national trend. Gallup's 1980 poll of Americans showed a decline in the proportion wanting their children to have religious training, a decline that has been in process since the mid-1960s.[4] Since the subject is of top importance to parents who participated in the Adolescent-Parent study, one wonders why there has been a decline in home conversations about matters of faith.

One answer might be that the fruits of declining instruction in faith in the mid-1960s are now appearing. Parents who have received scant biblical training and little opportunity to verbalize what they do believe, feel inadequate to teach at home. They reason that if their child should begin to question them and they do not know the answer, it would be humiliating and confusing.

As illustrated at the beginning of this chapter, there are homes today, in which there may be very good intentions of having a "Christian home," complete with talks about one's faith. Attempts may have been made when children were young, but as they near adolescence, the family begins to fragment: social life and work obligations become more complex; children begin participating in extracurricular activities and working at part-time jobs. A meal is scarcely ever eaten when everyone is together; if the family is together, someone is watching a TV program at the same time. "How can we even have time to talk about such things?" parents cry out. "We know we should, but it's impossible!"

Some parents regard church and confirmation instruction as the proper and only place for religious training. It is argued that pastors and their lay assistants are the only qualified teachers of religion.

Still another reason might be that there is no agreement between parents concerning matters of faith. One parent may be interested; the other may not, or may be of another faith. So, for the sake of harmony, this subject is omitted from discussion in the home. Some parents find it impossible to communicate their faith to their children, because it is not real for the parents themselves.

Parents' desire to learn. Though religious discussions are rare, most parents of the 10,467 wish it were different. When asked in the Adolescent-Parent study about training programs that a school, agency, or church might provide, strong interest is expressed in several possible subjects. The top two were the programs described in Table 8.

Furthermore, parents in the survey were asked if they wished they could talk more with their children about "God and other

Table 8. Preference of Training Programs for Children

Subject	Percent "Very" or "Quite" Interested
How to help a child develop healthy concepts of right and wrong	70%
How to help a child grow in religious faith	68%

religious topics." As shown in Table 9, 40 percent of the mothers and 28 percent of the fathers said "definitely."

Table 9. Desire to Talk More

Response	Percentage Mother	Percentage Father
Would like to talk more about God and other religious topics		
Definitely	40%	28%
Probably	47	47
Not sure	8	15
Probably not	5	1
Definitely not	1	1

The reluctant dragon in this area seems to be father. Nevertheless, a significant proportion of both parents "definitely" want more conversations about religious issues, and an additional 47 percent "probably" do. The cry for greater sharing is clear: almost four out of five are interested. It is highly significant that fewer than one-fifth of the parents resist this subject.

What most parents do not realize is that a mature religious faith has resident power to create what they want their children to be, namely, caring, other-centered people.

What Faith Can Mean to an Adolescent

Religion is largely ignored in most books on adolescent development. It is a dimension few research psychologists consider when trying to understand the adolescent. Hence little has been known about the importance of a religious faith in the life of an adolescent.

This study of 8,165 young adolescents does give information regarding their religious faith and provides evidence as to its possible impact in their lives. Four measures of religious perception were used for both adolescents and parents. These perceptions are described below.

Four Religious Perceptions

Variety appears in the religious perceptions of young adolescents and their parents. By reflecting on the following themes or emphases developed by Peter Benson of Search Institute,[5] parents may sense which theme best characterizes their adolescents.

1. *Liberating religion* is experienced as freeing and enabling. People for whom religion is liberating tend to place a good deal of emphasis on the fact that God accepts them just as they are and that salvation is a gift, not something earned. It is an orientation sometimes referred to as a "Gospel" orientation, as opposed to a "Law" orientation.

2. *Restricting religion* is experienced as stressing limits, controls, guidelines, and discipline. Whereas liberating religion stresses freedom, restricting religion emphasizes limits.

3. *Vertical orientation* has to do with how one interprets one's responsibility as a person of faith. Those with a vertical orientation (later referred to as Centrality of Religion) tend to see that the believer's priorities should be to establish and maintain a close relationship to God. The emphasis is on prayer, worship, and other activities that keep one's focus on God.

4. *Horizontal orientation* is typically an emphasis on themes of love and justice, and those with a horizontal orientation tend to reach out and care for others.

Our measures of each theme show that young adolescents in this study tend to experience religion more as liberating than restricting. In part, this means that young adolescents focus more on God's love than on God as judge or rule-giver. Most adolescents in this study affirm that religious responsibility includes a horizontal commitment—reaching out to help others. Finally, three of the scales discussed in this chapter—religious centrality, liberating religion, horizontal orientation—are tied to desirable values and good patterns of behavior.

Behaviors Associated With Each Perception

The Adolescent-Parent study gives clear indications that moral behaviors, service activities, and the avoidance of self-destructive practices tend to be found among religious adolescents. Specifically, where religious faith is central and important, one is more likely to find helping and serving adolescents. Such youth are more likely to have high self-esteem and a positive attitude toward church. They are also more likely to refrain from drug and alcohol use.

Adolescents characterized by a liberating faith will not only evidence the behavior indicated above, but also will be less racially prejudiced and less likely to be involved in antisocial activities such as fighting, vandalism, shoplifting, cheating at school, or lying to parents (see Table 10).

Where a horizontal religion's emphasis is strong, one is likely

**Table 10. How Religious Orientations Correlate
With Attitudes and Behaviors***

Youth's Values, Motivations, Identity	Liberating	Horizontal	Restricting
Self-esteem	+		−
Moral internalization	+	+	−
Acceptance of traditional standards	+	+	
Achievement motivation	+	+	−
Ageism		−	
Sexism			+
Racial prejudice	−		+
Positive attitude toward church	+	+	
Value world peace			
Youth's Behaviors			
Prosocial behavior	+	+	−
Drug and alcohol use	−		+
Antisocial behavior	−		+

* + means that the higher the religious orientation, the more likely that the other variable is high.

− means that the higher the religious orientation, the more likely that the other variable is low.

(Correlations range from .12 to .38 and are statistically significant.)

to find young adolescents who place a high value on world peace and show a value orientation that emphasizes concern for people.

By way of contrast, adolescents who view religion as restricting are linked to a number of undesirable characteristics. Those high on this measure tend to be high on antisocial behaviors and alcohol use. They are linked also to racial prejudice and sexism. Among these adolescents who feel tied down by religion one can also expect to find low self-esteem, failure to internalize moral standards, and a lower achievement drive.

This highly significant measure of religion shows that a misperceived religion—one focused on standards and prohibitions—can have a negative effect. Its impact is similar to that of an autocratic approach to parenting.

Why Sharing Faith Is Needed in a Family

Why should parents break the silence and initiate conversations about spiritual or religious issues? There are three compelling reasons: religious doubt, decline in religious interest, and the relationship between religious faith and style of parental discipline.

Religious Doubt

One reason for bringing discussion into the home relates to the emergence of religious doubt during adolescence. The percentages who attribute some truth to the statement "I'm not sure what I believe about God" are indicated in Table 11.

Table 11. Youth Who Attribute Some Truth to Statement of Doubt

Response		Grade in School				
		5	6	7	8	9
I'm not sure what I believe about God.						
	Boys	45%	46%	51%	55%	62%
	Girls	42	46	52	53	54

For boys as well as girls, the percentage who are unsure of what they believe about God increases with grade in school. This increase is accompanied by a sharp decline in the percentage who claim that religion is "the most important influence in my life." These measures indicate a possible erosion in the faith that many parents highly prize for their children.

For over twenty-five years we had groups of youth in our home to discuss issues in the light of Scripture. Many years after they had been members of a group, we invited them back to our home to tell us what they remembered and what they especially appreciated. We learned that what youth expressed at the time when they were teenagers held true in their memories years later. "I appreciated being able to speak openly of my doubts and differing ideas and not be immediately jumped on and told, 'You mustn't talk like that,' " said one young adult. Another said, "I was confused in my beliefs as a teenager and said some rather blasphemous things, but the group cared enough to hear me out, and because of their acceptance and understanding, I am a believer today in Christ and his Word."

The issue of doubt can actually become a plus in conversations about faith. Usually an adolescent's doubts are rooted in a need for answers. Opportunities to probe, make distinctions, examine, and scrutinize actually further a function of doubt encouraged in the New Testament. Doubt can be a state of openmindedness in which faith is asking the intellect for help.

Relation of Belief to Faith. Beliefs are not the same as faith. In her book *To Set One's Heart*,[6] Sara Little expresses this in an interesting way. She says that beliefs are components of faith. They might be described as "inferences about what is going on within a person" as it pertains to one's relationship to a personal, loving, redeeming God. The struggle, then, is to *understand* those inner realities and *verbalize* them. Beliefs take form when faith "asks the intellect for help" in explaining what one has experienced. In *saying* the words of faith we clarify our understanding of relationship to God. One reason it is hard to discuss faith issues at home is that neither parents nor children have struggled to verbalize the words of faith—in other words, their *beliefs*. We need informal and structured discussions about matters of faith in order to clarify this for ourselves and each other. As noted earlier, putting concepts into words is difficult for some boys, in particular.

Parents who have trouble verbalizing their faith would do well to seek help in this area themselves. The built-in sharing during adult Bible discussions, for instance, can make a great deal of difference. This was the case for David, who himself had grown up in a largely nonverbal family. His children remember him as "the silent one" during their adolescence. A small-group Bible study at church, however, has helped him verbalize his faith. Today communication between David and his grandchildren is a heartwarming thing to see.

Decline in Religious Interest

The Adolescent-Parent study shows a marked decline for religious interest during adolescence, which usually finds its lowest point with ninth-grade boys. A striking portrayal of this decline is seen in an eight-item measure of the centrality religion holds in the life of an adolescent. From seventh grade on, the average scores drop each year for boys, indicating a growing alienation from the faith of their childhood years (see Figure 18).

This decline is matched by a changing attitude toward the church. Here again, the interest of fifth-graders represents a high point that steadily erodes to ninth grade (see Table 12).

Table 12. Youth Attitudes Toward the Church

Response		Grade in School				
		5	6	7	8	9
How important is	Boys	54%	49%	45%	42%	40%
your church or	Girls	58	53	49	48	51
synagogue to you?*	Total	56	51	47	45	46

*Percent "very important" or "extremely important."

Figure 18. Centrality of Religion*

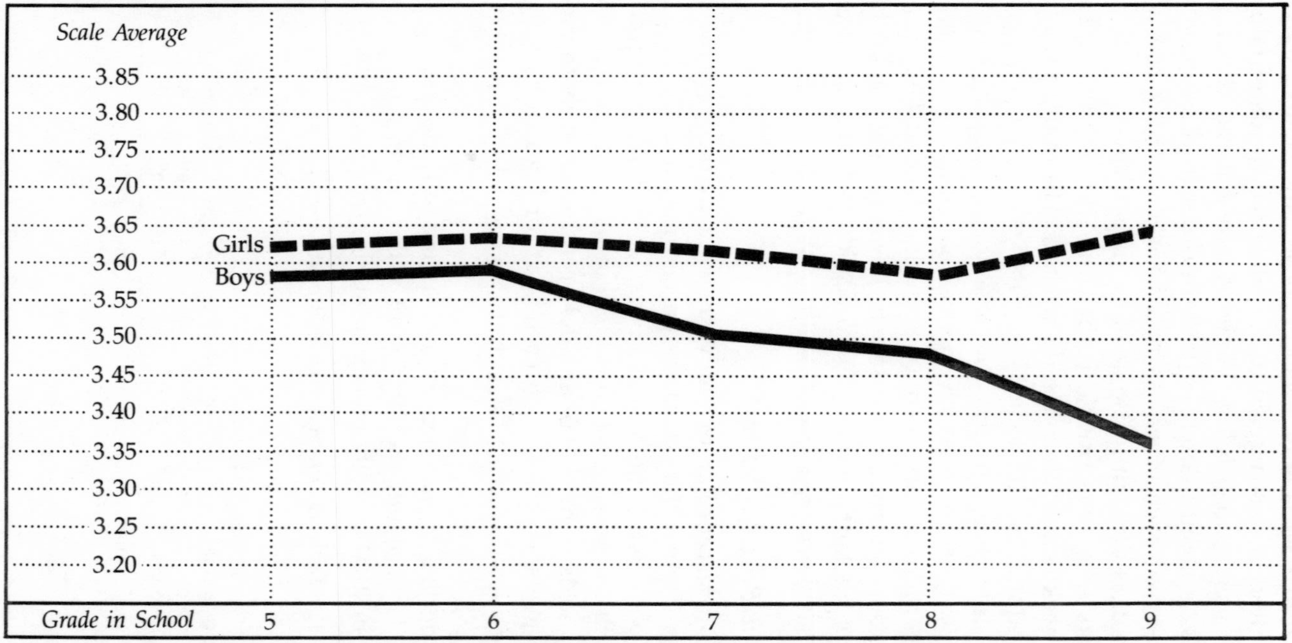

*Centrality of Religion scale is based on the average of eight items. The scale range is from 1 (low) to 5 (high).
Item: "Overall, how important is religion in your life?"

These indices of religious interest are paralleled by answers to two direct questions: "How much do you want God at the center of your life?" and, "How much do you want to be a part of a church?"

The answers are revealing. There is a steady decline until the eighth grade in adolescents' desire to have God as central in their lives or to be a part of a church or synagogue (see Figure 19).

What accounts for this erosion of interest? There is no reason to attribute the decline merely to characteristics of adolescence. On the contrary, there is reason to anticipate a rise instead of a fall. Why? Adolescence is a time of unfolding, which historically has been identified with religious conversion or commitment. The studies of Starbuck in 1899, replicated thirty years later by E. J. Clark, identify the ages of twelve and sixteen as times of religious awakening or conversion to the faith.[7]

This decline of interest may be due to neglect with respect to the historic functions of the father as religious leader in the home; or it may be because this age group is neglected in the life of the church. In most denominations, these youth are regarded as being too old for Sunday school and too young for the high school youth program.

Another possible explanation for decline of interest is youth's vulnerability, or susceptibility to temptation. During this age, which has been identified as one of greatest vulnerability, adolescents are being exposed to powerful media presentations that teach a contrasting value system. This exposure is significant. One-half (51 percent) of the adolescents in the Adolescent-Parent survey say that on an average school day they watch TV three hours or more.

The significance of an adolescent's exposure to mass media gains added strength when one sees the kind of movies many enjoy. One-third of the adolescents already have acquired a taste for "R" or "X" rated movies. One in three (32 percent) say they like "very much" or "quite a bit" to gain entry into

Figure 19. Value Placed on God and Church*

Percent very much or at the top of my list

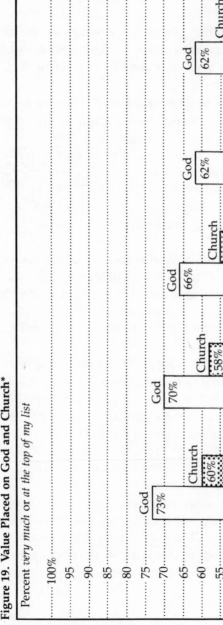

Item: "How much do you want 'to have God at the center of my life'?"
Item: "How much do you want 'to be part of a church or synagogue'?"

such movies. A third of the boys have a similar preference for media violence—that is, movies that show people getting hurt or killed.

Whatever the reason, we as parents need to initiate ways of reversing the downward trend if we do not wish to see our children dissociate themselves completely from the religious resource of the family.

Religious Faith and Style of Parental Discipline

A third compelling reason for becoming attentive to the business of sharing faith as a family is related to the issue of how parents discipline their children. As indicated in the previous chapter, almost half the parents in the Adolescent-Parent study take a moralistic stance toward Christianity. Their orientation is toward rules and regulations. The statement "I believe that God has a lot of rules about how people should live their lives" was agreed with by 52 percent; and 41 percent agreed "I believe God is very strict."

A consistent finding here and in other studies carried out by Search Institute is that adolescents raised under an autocratic style of control are less likely to experience religion as a liberating power. On the contrary, they are likely to see it as restricting. If adolescents see it in this way, their obvious reaction is to move away from religion. This is precisely what boys in the sample are doing. As was shown in Figure 18, religion and the church are becoming less and less prominent in their lives.

Parents should know that a caring stance of parental nurturance and democratic (authoritative) control both correlate with a liberating, challenging, and people-oriented (horizontal) faith. Ranking a close second in encouraging a living, action-oriented faith are the two other dimensions found in a democratic (authoritative) approach, namely, trust by parents and family closeness. In other words, if we as parents engender a caring, affectionate, trusting atmosphere in the home, our adolescents will not be trying to escape. Instead, they will be likely to accept our beliefs and values.

How Faith Is Shared

This chapter has led from the question of the what and the why of shared faith to the critical climax—how it is done. Faith is shared in family life in three ways: (1) during daily interaction, (2) during structured times of worship, and (3) by "doing the truth together."

Faith Is Shared in the Natural Flow of Home Life. In Deuteronomy 11:19, the writer says, "You shall talk about these things when you are sitting in your house and when you are walking by the way, and when you lie down and when you rise." Here our attention is drawn to the fact that the focus of Scripture is on daily life; the Word gives us divine insight, which reorganizes our whole perspective on life. This experience of sharing the faith as a natural flow of home life does typify some families.

Several young adults we interviewed speak of the atmosphere in their parental home as being open to talking about God in the ordinary routines of life. In fact, as one young man put it, "It happens all the time. There's no specific point when we say, 'Now, let's talk about God.' "

A teenager who was a dinner guest in such a home remarked afterwards, "They were talking about just ordinary things, and all of a sudden you realized they were involved in a theological discussion." When questioned further as to her interpretation of "theological," she described it as, "Oh, you know, how something related to a Christian view of things. It was interesting to see that everyone was talking, not just the parents."

These are the homes in which children "pick up" on religion as being important to their parents. They feel free to ask questions themselves and venture opinions. As one young woman from such a home expressed it, "For my mother, when

I was growing up, there were no unaskable questions about faith."

Fifty-one percent of all adolescents in the Adolescent-Parent study expressed much interest in receiving more help on what it means to be a Christian. Young people of this age, struggling for identity, warm to the freedom of expressing doubts and asking questions without feeling stupid, getting hurt, or being put down. They like the freedom to debate with people who have an opposite opinion. It is a way to arrive at a personal belief and know why.

When young people learn that parents are committed to open discussion carried on in a spirit of humility, they will grow in their ability to share personal experiences and ideas. It is in this kind of atmosphere also that the strength of a parent's faith comes through to a child, as, for instance, in a time of great stress.

A young woman remembers, "I was a teenager when my brother was killed in a plane crash. The witness of my parents' faith during that time was a pervasive one." Sharing beliefs may mean sharing together deep hurts and pain so that healing may come to the whole family. Parents need not fear showing hurts to their children.

Another young adult tells of the death of a teenage brother who was close to her in age. Her father, an ardent Christian, appeared through the whole experience always "radiant and strong," even though he deeply loved his son.

I used to wonder how he could be that way—kind of superhuman, while I was often bitter and resentful. Then one day, after my brother had been dead for some months, I happened to walk by the room where my dad was taking a shower. I realized he was sobbing loudly, and I heard him shouting out to God, "Why? Why? Why did you take him from me?"

Something happened inside of me that day. I felt so bad for my dad, but I felt warm and released, too. My dad couldn't understand "why?" either. He was human, too.

Unplanned conversations may become counseling times. Our

study shows that adolescents are often eager to discuss problems concerning their friends. But sometimes the problem comes closer to home—when the young person in the family is the one who needs help, and comes with a confession. At such times parents may struggle with a sense of disappointment or shock at what is confessed. Our emotions may make it hard to continue the conversation in the same open manner as before. But it is exactly at this point that our child needs us most.

Disappointment in another person, failure, anger, shame, illness—all are unplanned circumstances, but they demand that families talk about them. Vocational goals, losing a job, good grades and bad grades—these represent the endless flow that is woven into the warp and woof and faith of a family. If parents talk about them together with children, pray about them, and even cry about them if need be, family members are reaching out together for the hand of God.

A friend says, "We have shared bad financial reverses, my husband nearly died in a terrible accident, we have lived many years with a child who is ill with a fatal disease. But through it all my husband and I are thankful for the faith that has sustained all of us and brought us closer together."

This openness also makes it possible to laugh together. By laughing we do not mean getting sarcastic delight from another's discomfort, or giving flip answers to another's seriousness. Rather, we are referring to the ability to laugh at "the fool" in oneself. If members of a family are able to do this, they will be able to see humor in countless everyday situations and share them with each other.

There is a deeper sense in which use of humor is a freeing experience: when persons can see the comic side of a painful, frustrating, or hurtful situation. They see it because they can see "the fools" in themselves and others. When one can no longer laugh at the difficulties of life, one is cutting off a source of God-given freedom, one which parents can give as a heritage to their children. An old Jewish proverb expresses it thus:

There are three things which are real: God, human folly, and laughter. The first two are beyond our comprehension so we must do what we can with the third.

A sense of humor is a "saving grace," as one family member described it—a gift of God to be enjoyed in the context of our lives as God's children.[8]

The natural flow of life may be full of beautiful and laughing times. But there may be ugly times, too, when tempers flare and words are said that can never be recalled. The glory of shared faith lies in the stumbling words of forgiveness—sometimes hard to come by—between father and son, brother and sister, mother and daughter.

The open home, the place where friends and relatives can come and go, talk and eat together—that is part of the natural flow, too. Karen Mains, in *Open Heart, Open Home*, says of these times, in her own girlhood experience, "Food on family occasions . . . was sharing, a communal expression. There was not much emphasis on elegance or finery, but a high priority on how hot the verbal debates could wax, how riotous the laughter would rage, how deeply the discussions would range." During such times, she adds, "We shared life and being."[9] We noted as Bible discussion leaders for our youth group that when we had several potluck suppers in a row, sharing of self and faith became a much more natural process.

Faith Is Also Shared During Structured Times. Within the family, it means believing "This is an important part of our life together." From Old Testament times, devout Jews and Christians have continued some form of family "worship." People who have seen *Fiddler on the Roof* on film or on stage, for example, will have vivid memories of Sabbath worship in the home of Tevye and Golda. Recently, we participated in a Passover meal (family Seder) and were reminded again of the sense of celebration the family experiences in this ritual, and the repetitive beauty of saying together, "Blessed art thou, O Lord our God, King of the Universe, Who has kept us in life, Who has preserved us and has enabled us to reach this season."

Granted, in the pioneer days of our land, family devotions may not have had much beauty or drama about them; in fact, they may have been very prosaic. But if done in an atmosphere of love, they were still remembered fondly.

Such was the case with Uncle Clarence Strommen, now ninety years of age, who clearly remembers family devotions in the farm home when he was a teenager:

I remember my father and mother gathering us children for family devotions after chores and supper. Pa had been a heavy drinker who had sometimes treated us pretty bad when he was drunk. But after he became a Christian, when I was about twelve, he really changed. No, he never preached, he never said anything in church, but it was in our *home* we saw the change. It was like he had said to himself, "From now on, we will have devotions every day."

Even though he did not verbalize the thought, perhaps Uncle Clarence's Pa sensed that this might be his most lasting memorial and witness to his children.

I (Irene) remember my own family a generation later, in the 1930s. Saturday morning after breakfast was "special devotions time" for us. Each child in the family took turns reading the Bible story and was given the privilege of asking questions of everyone else. And while the emphasis of my parents was on free prayer, every once in a while my father would say, "Today you may read the prayer of the church." And so, ingrained in us also would be prayers for the government and for leaders of church and state, a wide scope that went way beyond our little world. We also had a favorite one-stanza hymn we often sang; then we prayed the benediction together. These are powerful memories even today. I remember that my younger sister was sometimes reluctant to come inside from play. Occasionally, my father would say, "Let her play." He remembered his own youth, when he felt the rules had been too strict, the devotions too long.

In our contemporary society, methods of presenting Scripture in family devotions may include using the family's creative gifts in acting, drawing, singing, and discussion. Whatever the format used, it seems right that the family's creative gifts be made an integral part of the experience.

Lawrence Richards, in *Religious Education*,[10] has some interesting observations on teaching the Word to children and youth that apply to any structured form of devotions in the home. He says he has come to understand when teaching children, he does not worry that he is giving them something that is beyond their ability to grasp. For even though they may not be able intellectually to understand forgiveness, he is helping them *experience* the reality of receiving forgiveness and extending it to others. In other words, regardless of age and stage of development, he is inviting the children to experience what scripture teaches. The challenge, Richards continues, is to link the Word with the *life* of the child so that he or she sees life from God's point of view. In this way, when temptation comes, anger surges, or alienation hurts, the experience triggers a biblical truth that will give the right perspective and help the child respond in a positive way.

Encouraging our children to use the privilege of free prayer is an important parental role. A friend says, "I remember my mother gathering us children around her so we could pray about problems that troubled her." Not only in confession of sin, not only in times of discouragement and fear, not only in intercession for others, Christian parents teach that prayer is "what you do." Parents teach that prayer also belongs to the exuberance of life, the "thanksgiving" days.

A life in which prayer is a big factor does not come easily. That is why we can help our children by encouraging the sharing of specific people and situations about which to pray. It is, for instance, indelibly imprinted on a child's memory if he or she hears a parent say his or her name in a prayer. And a parent gives a great gift to a child by encouraging what Frank Laubach[11] calls using "the chinks of time" for prayer—the in-between moments when one is walking down the corridor between classes at school, or waiting for a bus; in other words, in the normal flow of life as well as the structured times.

At a recent prayer breakfast for Search Institute, Barbara Varenhorst, author of *Real Friends* and *Peer Counselor Training*, shared the following story from memories of her own family life.

Each Saturday evening we had a family prayer service. Here is where I learned to pray for people who were in need, people who were in difficult situations. As a teenager I sometimes groaned when my mother prayed because her prayers were so long. My brother would try to get around this by saying quickly, "Barb, you pray tonight!" Nevertheless, my mother has been a model for me in her prayer life. She used prayer cards; she prepared prayer calendars for each day of the year, way up to the time of her death in her eighties. She did not just name the person or situation, she made one aware of the particular reason she brought their name before God.

Another specific way Mother's prayer life has been an example to me is that she encouraged my praying for a person who was making it difficult for me in some way. When I do that I have found that my attitude toward that person changes; I make constructive ways to settle our differences.

This is a heritage each parent can give his or her child.

Structured devotional times are planned by some families on celebration days. The Christmas festival, baptisms, birthdays, graduations, confirmations, anniversaries—all can attest to the fact that celebrations of life for the Christian family are inextricably linked with belief and faith.

In our family, we have a ritual each Christmas Eve. After reading of Scripture and singing—planned by different members of the family each year, and which all have a part in—the Christ Candle is lit. Then, one by one, beginning with the youngest, they go to the low table where the Christ Candle is surrounded by as many unlit candles as there are people present. Each in turn lights his or her candle from the Christ Candle and says, "I am lighting my candle because I want Jesus to light my way."

Structured devotional times during vacations capitalize on a period of the year when a family has time to be reflective. It is also a ritual in our family to set aside an hour at the end of a vacation to reflect on our experiences in relation to our faith. Equally meaningful statements come from the young child and the early adolescent as from the older teenager.

We have also observed the custom of having our own family service on Sunday mornings when on vacation. In this service, everyone has a chance to participate. The worship service has taken place in many settings. We've climbed on a Sunday morning to a point above a 12,000 foot pass, where we overlooked the formidable peaks of the Sawatch Range in the Colorado Rockies. As we sang the hymns, our voices were reminders of our smallness and God's greatness in this vast universe. We have sat on a rock in a cove of the Pacific Ocean beach as the tide came in. We have transformed an ordinary motel room into a place of worship. Each has served to provide a structured time of meaning and close fellowship.

Doing the Truth is Not an Adjunct to Shared Faith—It Is an Integral Part of It. Children in a family may learn their Bible stories very well, sing the songs of faith, feel a warmth in praying for each other, sense the kinship of believers in the family circle. But the totality of the shared faith experience is more than that. It is a combination of believing and doing. Sara Little, in *To Set One's Heart*, calls it "doing the truth."[12]

This third aspect of shared faith, namely, *doing the truth*, emerges in the study as a concept little thought about and seldom carried out. In spite of the fact that nearly 80 percent of the parents in the study indicate that religion is "the most important" or "one of the most important influences in my life," many do not see the connection between that and performing acts of love for others. Jesus' words, "I was hungry and you gave me food, . . . I was a stranger and you welcomed me, I was sick and you visited me," have seemingly not been attached in their minds to "religion."

We have given considerable emphasis throughout our book to the power of modeling. Yet, here we come to a situation in which the adolescents in the Adolescent-Parent study rank higher than the parents. Parents are considerably less likely than their children to believe that religious responsibility includes a horizontal dimension, that is, reaching out to help people in acts of love and mercy.

It is worthy of note that among adolescents in the Adolescent-Parent study who have a *concern for people*, one tends to find the following characteristics:

- Religious certainty
- The belief that religion is important
- Achievement motivation
- Positive self-image
- Concern about friendship
- Acceptance of traditional moral values.

Among fifth-graders and sixth-graders, there is a high correlation between a concern for people and a desire to work against poverty and for peace. As the march continues toward the ninth grade, however, this type of interest lessens. One possible reason for this is that parents tend to underestimate the interest and maturity of a child of eleven or twelve, and consequently do not give them opportunities to be part of a helping ministry. Wayne Rice, in *Junior High Ministry*, speaks of this age group as idealists even in the midst of their struggles, failures, and doubts.

For this reason it is important they be given many opportunities to serve and use the gifts God has given them. Their idealism, while it may be strong during the early adolescent years, will diminish over the years if not given expression, or it may be diverted into undesirable and destructive living. [Parents] should find as many ways as possible to channel the energies and enthusiasm of junior highers into service projects and other activities that allow them to give of themselves and to see the results of their efforts. They need to feel the significance and affirmation that such activities can give them. Junior highers desperately need to know that they are important and that God can use them right now.[13]

We remember a chance meeting with friends at an elegant restaurant some years ago. Their eighth-grade daughter had given them a bad time about their going out to eat that evening. She had learned at school about all the hunger in the world, and thought the money her parents were using to eat out should rather have been given to help someone in need. The mother especially was troubled and felt guilty. As we reflect on the incident now, we realize the greatest help we could have been to our friends and to ourselves would have been to discuss how we could involve our families in helping the hungry.

Such was the case with the father in the following true story,[14] told in the March 9, 1984 edition of the *Minneapolis Star and Tribune*. Frank Ferrell lived in a "well-off" suburb of Philadelphia. After seeing a TV presentation shortly after Christmas, he decided to take his eleven-year-old son, Trevor, into the downtown section so he could see firsthand how the street people live. They brought only a blanket and pillow to give to a needy person. The son was so profoundly moved and interested that he wanted his father to take him into town many nights a week with coats, jackets, soup, coffee, perhaps a bag of sandwiches. The boy "connects" his faith with these acts—he talks of being a minister when he grows up, and of establishing a permanent home for street people. But equally moving as the eleven-year-old's interest is the father's sensitivity in providing the opportunity for the boy to evidence his concern in concrete ways. By allowing children to give, we help them achieve a sense of worth.

To see one's acts of service as acts of faith are extremely helpful to an adolescent. Even in early childhood, families can have structured times of sharing faith which include Bible stories that tell of Jesus' caring for others. The next step is to relate the concept of caring to family life *in concrete ways*.

Edith Schaeffer, in an article entitled "What is a Family?" has this to say:

Human relationships on all levels are derived from essential child-hood experiences. How to treat people is not a subject to be lectured about; it should be taught in real-life situations within a family.[15]

If parents were to take this statement seriously, they would be directly involved with their children in performing acts of service to others. One father and mother of young children tell of bringing the whole family along whenever they go to visit an elderly person who is homebound; the father, when he goes to remove snow from a neighbor's driveway, takes his five-year-old boy with him.

Bruce, a public school superintendent of a large suburban school district, now father of several adolescents himself, re-calls a powerful modeling experience from his own youth.

July 17, 1961 was a hot humid Central Illinois day. My father, a farmer, was up at dawn to work in the fields. I was in graduate school and studied in the morning and helped him in the afternoon. About 5:30 P.M. Dad took me out to a neighbor's farm to get his truck. As I followed him back home, I saw him stop his truck on the edge of town where Harry Smith lived. Harry was considered a "bum," at least a person with no money, no friends, and no one who cared. As I drove by, Dad was walking around Harry's rundown house to see if he needed any food, transportation, or had needs of any kind. I remembered thinking as clearly as if it were yesterday, "who besides Dad, tired as I know he is, would care so about another person's needs, especially when humanly speaking there is *nothing* in the world Harry could do in return.

Bruce goes on to say that his father had learned a lesson that the son is still learning—how to focus on another's needs, not his own. This example has caused the son to ask many times, "How can I show a person who is hurting that I care?" not "What's in it for me?" or "How will this affect me?"

Performing acts of love, if one sees the reason for doing so, can become a way of life. Alec Allen and Martin Mitchell, administrators of the Starr Commonwealth Schools in Albion, Michigan, had this demonstrated for them when they worked with troubled students who reside in family-style units. These students are part of an atmosphere designed to emphasize the positive values of caring, helping, trusting, and being responsible. These students learn that even if they are frightened in carrying out a project of helping someone else (e.g., a physically handicapped person), the thought that they can make that person's life better and safer by their act helps them overcome fear. Very positive things happen to these troubled students as a result of their service-learning. It would not be difficult to imagine some of the same benefits within a family unit under similar circumstances:

- They developed a bond of togetherness.
- They developed sensitivity to the needs and struggles of the mentally and physically handicapped, to the elderly, and to those facing death and disaster.
- They experienced the joy of helping.[16]

One young man said to a staff member, "Thank you for giving us the chance to know what it is like to help someone else." The staff noted that learning to help had long-lasting effects. A student named Eric left Starr to return to his home in Detroit, Michigan. Not long after, he went on his own to a section of Detroit where there were many nursing homes. He visited several of them to find out whether there were any residents who had no relatives or friends to visit them. Then he openly volunteered to visit those who needed a friend.

It is easy for a parent to fall into the trap of "arranging" for an act of kindness to be done by the adolescent for someone else. One mother, for instance, would offer her teenage daughter for babysitting, with no pay. Another mother and father invited a homeless family to stay with them for a period of time. As a result, night after night a resentful teenage daughter stood long hours in the kitchen washing dishes for the expanded family unit. In neither case was the adolescent girl part of the planning. Consequently, the acts of service were only negative experiences for her.

A positive experience occurred for Carolyn and Carl when, with the consent of their own two children, they welcomed four young brothers from Vietnam into their home. These four

boys, all of whom were adolescents, had spent seventeen un-
believable days and nights on a boat, and two years in a camp
in the Philippines. Now, a congregation witnesses the miracle
of togetherness and love that has come as a result of the gift
Carolyn and Carl gave of an open heart and open home.

To summarize, this chapter has drawn attention to a much
neglected and overlooked source of strength—a shared faith.
Though idealized as an important dimension of family life, the
practice of sharing a religious faith in one's home is practiced
by only a minority of church members.

The Adolescent-Parent study shows why this ancient tradition from Old Testament times ought to be revived. It can
counteract a trend characteristic of early adolescents, namely,
their growing disinterest in a religious faith. It provides also
an opportunity for adolescents to deal with their growing issues of doubt and religious uncertainty. More importantly, a
family-shared faith becomes a source of strength for young
adolescents. It encourages them to avoid life-threatening behaviors and embrace those which are life-offering.

This chapter has drawn attention to the fact that sharing
one's faith as a family can be done in a number of ways. It
can be integrated into the everyday conversation of the family
and made a part of the natural flow of the day. Or, matters of
faith can be highlighted through structured times such as
family devotions or festival times. Not least are the times when
parents teach their children how to "do the truth" by participating with them in acts of service or kindness.

The data make it convincingly clear that families that take
seriously the issue of sharing a religious faith give their children a remarkable legacy of strength.

7. Cry for Outside Help

I can remember nights when we didn't sleep at all. I remember nights when I cried myself to sleep.

—A DISTRAUGHT FATHER

Where does a parent turn for help?

That was the question asked by a perplexed father and mother who had "given up" on their seventh-grade boy. Even the public school would no longer keep him.

He had been changing in ways they thought were only the marks of adolescence. But now he was becoming unmanageable: at times withdrawn, unwilling to study or go to school; at times belligerent, hostile to authority, "spaced out," irresponsible.

Both mother and father—devout, caring and loving people—spoke of sleepless nights filled with tears of despair, frustration, and guilt.

"Where have we failed?" they cried.

In desperation they consulted psychiatrists; this in turn led to psychiatric clinics, a detoxification center, an adolescent treatment center, a drug treatment center. There were parent therapy sessions, too, and support group sessions. There was Al-Anon. Things had gone out of control for mother and father by this time. The distance between two people who cared deeply for each other had been widening. Father blamed mother; mother blamed father; and an older son and daughter blamed them both.

Outside help? They grasped at it as they would a lifeline.

This chapter explores four important topics:

- Parents can't "go it alone"
- Four ingredients needed in outside help

- Six critical situations demanding outside help
- Clergy—a trusted resource

Parents Can't "Go It Alone"

If we stop to reflect, we will realize that as parents we have been the recipients of outside help all through our parenting lives. The nurse-friend who stayed with us around the clock during the birth of our first son . . . the neighbor who took a son to the hospital at midnight for emergency surgery when his father was out of town . . . the community uncles who coached the ball teams.

These are examples of the taken-for-granted forms of help we all accept, to one degree or the other, in the normal ebb and flow of family life.

Another stage of outside help is more consciously and deliberately accepted and used by parents. It is the information we gain about ways of parenting: the knowledge we seek in order to strengthen our children mentally, physically, and spiritually. Such meaningful help comes from books, workshops, seminars, and videotapes, which give both information and a conceptual framework for interpreting what we read and hear and see. This book itself is an example of outside help. Thirty-seven percent of mothers and 27 percent of fathers in the Adolescent-Parent study rate this kind of help highly.

In a recent session in which information on parenting was given, a couple who had celebrated their fiftieth wedding anniversary the year before were in attendance. Their reaction was very clear: "I wish we had had this kind of help fifty years ago, before we began raising our kids."

Today there is an added sense of urgency to know more about preventive measures in parenting. Our society has undergone a radical shift in values since 1965. This shift has been a movement to greater individualism, personal freedom, and tolerance for diversity, particularly personal indulgence. Some old moral absolutes have become quite relative. Many adolescents feel that "What I'd like to do is okay for me to do."

These changes have brought about serious problems for both youth and parents especially in six main areas: (1) drug use, (2) alcohol use, (3) sexual activity, (4) suicidal tendencies, (5) child abuse, and (6) other out-of-control behaviors.

We know that some of the desperate cries, such as we hear described in the illustration that begins this chapter, echo many times throughout the world of parenting. In this chapter, therefore, we are giving some pertinent information on each of these areas, some suggestions for home treatment that professionals who work in these fields have found helpful, and some guidelines for knowing when and where to go for professional help.

Especially in situations where it may mean loss of face, it is hard for a parent to ask for help outside the family. This is particularly true for parents whose own families never discussed family ills with "outsiders." Old timers know the hands-off expression, "Never soil your nest," meaning "Never say anything bad about your family." Asking for help is viewed by some parents as a sign of failure; this leaves them wide open to the assumption that every parent should be an expert in parenting.

Fortunately, parents today are coming to realize that it makes sense to draw on the skilled resources of an outsider when something needs to be fixed. If it's an income tax report, consult an accountant. If it's a car that gives trouble, see a mechanic. It's a sign of hope that of the 10,467 parents in the study, when asked whom they would turn to if facing a serious problem in their family, only 20 percent answered "nobody." The remainder said they would go to a relative, friend or neighbor, clergyman, medical doctor, school official, or community agency, depending on the problem involved. Figure 20 clearly identifies the clergy as a trusted source for parents. The relative few who would single out a school official (13 percent), medical doctor (17 percent), and community agencies (12 per-

Figure 20. Parents' Choices of Preferred Help on Problems*

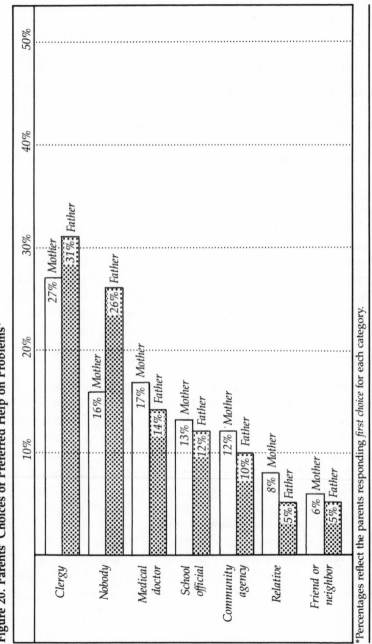

*Percentages reflect the parents responding *first choice* for each category.

cent) for preferred help may only indicate a general lack of awareness of the rich assortment of services available in a community. The pastor is often the facilitator for providing information on sources of help available; he or she can help parents gain access to remedial or educational programs.

The mother and father at the beginning of this chapter eventually availed themselves of many sources. For most communities, the principal ones are the pastor or a member of a church staff; a school counselor; a doctor or worker in the community health center; a family service agency (state or private); and youth-serving organizations such as the Y, Boy Scouts, Girl Scouts, Campfire, 4-H, Alcoholics Anonymous, Al-Anon, or Al-Ateen. Each one of these organizations has a surprising number of programs and services available to the family.

As parents our task is to discover the service that meets our special needs. It's like looking for a good restaurant. You don't give up on going to restaurants simply because one place served a bad meal. Likewise, parents should not let a poor experience with one person or program deter them from trying another source of help.

Four Ingredients Needed in Outside Help

No matter what problem parents are having with their adolescent, four elements are needed in the help they seek:

- Helpful support groups
- Esteem-building activities
- Positive belief system
- Own insight into self

These four comprise a model developed by Dr. Philip Shapiro.[1] Each ingredient supplies an important element in the healing process. We might mention, too, that in every instance of a parent-adolescent problem *both* parent and adolescent benefit from help.

Helpful Support Groups

Of importance to a person who needs help is to feel respected and esteemed, cared for and loved by a network of people. A social support group serves as a buffer during times of stress brought on by problems within the family; at the same time it provides healing and strength. This was the experience of the couple in the beginning illustration. The most powerful positive outcome for them came through a parent support group.

The universal experience is that just being in a support group has a calming effect. The invisible hand of human kinship is a therapeutic agent. A young woman who had been struggling with a number of decisions regarding personal morality remarked after a group meeting in which none of her own problems had been discussed, "I *needed* to come tonight. This was a great strength for me." In our nation today, there are over 40,000 national organizations of self-help groups. Their popularity proves that people who care about each other can be of mutual help without drawing on the expertise of professionals. The central ingredient of adult love and caring must figure prominently in any help a parent gives and receives.

Esteem-Building Activities

A second basic element is a set of activities that builds self-esteem. These may be work projects, recreational activities, training programs, or service projects. The essential element is that they breed a feeling of satisfaction and well being. They should give the troubled adolescent a feeling of accomplishment and significance.

A striking example of such activity is found in a service-learning program developed at the Starr Commonwealth Schools for troubled adolescents.[2] These youth are referred to the Starr presidential program because of police records, problems in family life, or poor school adjustment. At the same time as they are receiving treatment, they carry out more than one hundred community service projects during the year. They may serve as teacher aides, or work with retarded children, or chop firewood for the disabled, or visit shut-in senior citizens. The youth are shown how valuable their services are to the people involved; and intermingled with service they learn of constructive skills. The teachers of Starr Commonwealth report that these service-learning activities have helped their troubled adolescents develop increased responsibility and self-esteem. In fact, careful measures have shown striking gains in self-esteem over a three-year period. Parents themselves may find that becoming involved in a volunteer helping project at a time of family trouble is useful in giving them a sense of worth.

Positive Belief System

A third essential element in Shapiro's model is a positive belief system. It is a system of thought that one can use to gain a stable view of the world. It can also be used to determine one's identity, interpret life, maintain a sense of direction, and in general gain a sense of control and continuity in life.

There are two kinds of belief systems—one is pathological and the other healing. The pathological belief system consists of negative ideas, delusions, and incorrect conclusions held in a rigid and unyielding way. These can be held about oneself, one's family, one's world or one's God. We described in Chapter 6 how this is expressed theologically as a moralistic, guilt-producing concept of religion. The task for the help-giver is to correct the wrong ideas, change the person's beliefs about self, and help the person to accept the possibilities of desired changes.

One illustration of a pathological belief system is commonly seen in adolescents who are caught in a drug habit, alcoholism, sexual activity, or suicidal depression. They tend to believe they are no good, that they are not loved, and that the future holds no possibilities for them. They doggedly hold to the idea they are in control when using drugs, that peer acceptance will not allow the word "no," and that personal gratification ought not be delayed.

What is needed for these adolescents is the kind of help that brings another belief system into their consciousness—one that uses logic, includes adult love, and stresses a moral position. Often it is not the *words* of this new belief system, but *loving concern* that leads an adolescent to believe he or she is important, is loved, and has a future. Adolescents who are helped to internalize a moral code and identify with a personal God show the greatest likelihood of living responsibly and with the fewest hang-ups.

Ruth speaks of her experience with depression as a young woman: For me, as a Christian, the belief that I had infinite worth in the sight of God, that Christ had removed the element of judgment from me because of his redeeming love was life-giving for me. Scripture verses saying that nothing could separate me from the love of God, that the love of God had been poured into me, were powerful positive beliefs.

Own Insight into Self

A fourth component in the healing process of the troubled adolescent is self-knowledge or insight. For instance, if an adolescent is troubled with anxiety and depression after the death of a parent, he or she may be helped to see that these feelings are a natural aftermath of such a wrenching experience. The insight gained through such counseling can calm the fears the person may have had that he or she was "going mad." Even more, the adolescent may be helped to cope with depression by an awareness of the constant loving presence of God.

Perhaps the greatest, and the most necessary, help a professional counselor can give is in the area of a deeper level of insight, where the adolescent comes in touch with buried feelings long forgotten. This kind of insight can resolve, for instance, the strange dilemma of holding the belief "I love my mother," while at the same time battling strange feelings of rage and hatred for her.

This last component of the healing process, namely insight into oneself, may not come without pain. It is at this point that the supportive group, the esteem-building activities, the strength found in positive beliefs about oneself and one's God, are the bulwarks that bring the adolescent—and perhaps the parent, too—into a state of mental and spiritual health.

As parents look at these four basic ingredients needed in an outside help program, they might ask themselves the following questions about a program they are considering or are already participating in: Are supportive groups developed or used? Does the program make use of activities to develop a sense of self-worth? Are positive beliefs about oneself and God being established? Does the program encourage and lead one into greater self-knowledge and insight?

Notice that these four ingredients, placed in a certain order, spell the word HOPE.

Helpful Support Groups
Own Insight into Self
Positive Beliefs
Esteem-Building Activities

Six Critical Situations That Demand Outside Help

Drug Use

During the 1960s and 1970s, use of all illicit drugs increased twenty-fold, and the use of marijuana increased thirty-fold. What began with university students in the early 1960s spread downward in age through high school to junior high school. When Dr. Armand Nicholi finished his scholarly review of the research on drug abuse, he chose as subtitle for his article the words "A Modern Epidemic": "Use of psychoactive drugs has spread with explosive force into an epidemic of extraordinary scope, involving all regions of the country, all socio-economic classes and all age groups."[3]

Marijuana, the most used drug (next to alcohol) and the most defended in the past, has effects that justify serious national concern. It affects intellectual functioning, memory, sensory and perceptual functions, and reaction time—a fact that contributes to the high incidence of automobile accidents among young people. Its use can precipitate psychotic reactions, impair lung function, and affect the immune and reproductive systems. Those using the drug regularly have less motivation, perform more poorly in school, have fewer religious convictions, and are more involved in antisocial and delinquent behaviors such as stealing, vandalism, and truancy. Though use of marijuana was declining in the early 1980s, 66 percent of the 1981 class of high school seniors reported some use of this illicit drug.[4] Two out of three parents in the Adolescent-Parent study (64 percent of fathers and 68 percent of mothers) say they are much interested ("very" or "quite" interested) in learning more about drugs and how to cope with adolescents who are using them.

Behavioral scientists have consistently found that student drug use is largely a social activity. But Richard and Shirley Jessor at the University of Colorado have found that while experimentation with drugs is related mainly to environmental opportunities, deep involvement correlates best with low self-esteem.[5] Young people with poor self-images are drawn to drug use whenever it occurs, finding in it a common bond with other troubled youngsters, which may lead them into increasing isolation from non-drug-involved peers and activities. These processes generally start between the sixth and twelfth grades. It is usually most helpful to give students who have a firm sense of self-respect accurate information about the physical and psychological risks of drug use.

What Parents Can Do. The biggest hurdle for parents is to accept the fact that the child they love and care for has become involved in the use of drugs. Denial is an almost universal defense mechanism. It is a common experience to hear a mother say of her teenager, "I can't understand it; Judy used to get such good grades in school. This year she just doesn't seem to care." Or, "I don't like the friends Judy is running around with. They're all different from the ones she had last year." Yet this mother is quick to add, "But I know she isn't using drugs. She'd never do that," even though the evidence clearly points in that direction.

Parents are advised to bring their teen to a drug counselor if they suspect a problem. It is much better to be told by a counselor that you don't need professional help than to let a problem become more severe, and consequently more difficult to deal with. There should be no hesitation about seeking a therapist immediately if your teenager is using amphetamines, barbiturates, Angel Dust, cocaine, acid or heroin. Use of marijuana shows up in behavior such as lack of responsibility, grades dropping off in school, or a change in circle of friends.

Because the family is involved, drug education must begin with parents. In the booklet *Never Too Early, Never Too Late*, members of a Chemical Awareness Committee in a Minnesota school district have given a number of guidelines for parents who suspect more than incidental use of drugs by their teenager. This set of guidelines is furnished by Hazelden, a drug treatment center.

- *Confront the issue.* Be open and honest about your feelings.
- *Don't minimize and deny.* Parents want to believe otherwise.
- *Set standards.* Parents need to say "no" clearly and firmly.
- *Don't ask why.* Work with what's happened rather than trying to determine why it happened.
- *Ask for help.* There are many confidential sources available to parents. Call your school, police, or community agency for information on sources of help.[6]

Although only one person in the family may be singled out as an abuser, the whole family needs to be involved in treatment. A family is an interactive system in which all members affect and are affected by each other. A strong tendency found in addictive families is a dependent need for each other. As a result, addicts tend to continue living with their families of origin well into their late twenties. They use drugs to escape their family without actually leaving them.

Because families are such an interactive system, the treatment of choice for drug addiction is family therapy. It provides a way by which parents can be helped to relinquish control and the addicted member helped to establish a sense of autonomy. The goal of family therapy is to enlist the family as an ally in the treatment process. Through participation, the family learns how to survive without needing a chemically abusive member.[7]

Alcohol Abuse

Because of groups like Mothers Against Drunk Driving (MADD) and Students Against Drunk Driving (SADD), the public is now aware of the immense social and personal costs of alcohol abuse. As many as 15 million Americans have severe drinking problems. Three million are under 18 years of age. For motorists sixteen to twenty-four years old, alcohol-related car crashes are the leading cause of death. In a given two-week period, almost half the high school seniors of our country have been drunk. Search Institute confirms this finding in a 1983 study[8] of 11,000 high school students in Minnesota (through a random sample of public and private schools.) It finds that 46 percent of the twelfth-grade students reported having had five drinks or more in a row some time during the previous two weeks. Significantly, 51 percent expect to be drinking as much or more a year later. The implications of widespread teenage drinking are disturbing and the stories being told are tragic.

In the spring of 1983 one of the authors met with the Division Director of Mental Health and Developmental Disabilities in the state of Alaska, Dr. Philip Shapiro. Though experienced in the ghettos of Harlem, he was profoundly shaken by a three-day visit to an Alaskan village. There he found three hundred natives in despair over the fact that in a period of six months, thirteen young people had died of suicides or alcohol-related deaths.

Though alcohol-related problems have always been with us, at no time in our history has the issue been one of such magnitude and pervasiveness. What has been suspected for centuries is now a known fact. Fetal alcohol syndrome, a severe and irreversible syndrome of birth defects, is one of the three most common causes of mental retardation.[9] A fair approximation of the situation in 1983 is that alcohol abuse is linked to half of all automobile accidents, half of all homicides, 25 percent of all suicides, and about 40 percent of all problems brought to family court. It is estimated that the cost of alcholism to society is about $10,000 per problem drinker.[10] Yet in today's society, athletic heroes do TV commercials telling youth its OK to drink; their peers are insisting that a weekend party is dull without plenty of beer or hard liquor.

Virginia Edwards writes:

Ours is a drinking society. All the great rites of human passage are celebrated with booze. Births and christenings, birthdays, graduations, weddings, promotions, divorces, deaths and funerals all include drinking of alcohol. Holidays and festivals revolve around the fellowship of the glass. We even have parties where alcohol is the guest of honor—the cocktail party, the beer bash, and the wine-tasting party make no secret of that. We drink to promote a deal and to close one, when the team wins and when it loses, when we're relaxed with friends and tense with strangers. It's when kids get the impression that we *need* to do this that they're off to a bad start.[11]

That message is being heard. In 1983, 84 percent of Minnesota's eighth-graders had already tried drinking, and 24 percent had done so 20 times or more.[12]

The cry for outside help arises out of real, not imagined concerns. It relates to a threat that is being intensified by profiteering adults anxious to sell their products. The tragedies connected with their use is sufficient to justify an all-out war. That is how parents, banding together under the title MADD, view their activity. Incensed over deaths of their children caused by drunk drivers, they are working for more stringent legislation to restrict drivers that drink.

"No alcohol for kids under drinking age except in the case of religious or ceremonial use," decrees Dr. Neil Hartman of Cornell University Medical College, New York City. A specialist in substance abuse, he sees so many adolescents in deep difficulty with drugs that he has no patience with parents who play alcoholic games with their children. "Offering kids drinks or sips of drinks shows psychopathology in the parent that is akin to child abuse," he says firmly. "Total abstinence for those under 18 is a good goal. These are the years when personality is forming, and alcohol interferes with sound social and sexual development."[13]

Parents need to realize that teenage drinking often is a reflection of adult drinking habits. Families that have a tradition of heavy drinking can expect the same from their adolescents. Teen drinkers follow a well-developed set of folk rules in their drinking that corresponds to the unspoken social rules followed by adults.[14]

What Parents Can Do. The best way to help adolescents avoid alcohol abuse is to provide them with accurate, undistorted information about alcohol, a good example, and firm moral guidelines.

Parents ask, "How can I tell if my child is drinking?" Experts and cynical young drinkers have a counter-question. "How can you *not* know?" Parents' resolute blindness to their youngsters' drinking is one of the most familiar aspects of the alcohol problem.

A wild tirade, specialists warn us, isn't the answer. Postpone the talk until the youngster is sober and you are calm and in control. Encourage the youngster to analyze the reasons for his or her loss of control.

If the incident is repeated, it's time to show a different kind of concern. Drunkenness is not natural or understandable; it is a state of illness. In the opinion of Ellen Morehouse, a third incident should bring punishment, swift and immediate (denial of going to an event the youth may have looked forward to). More than three incidents calls for strong intervention, she feels. "Point out that 'we're a family with a problem. You are drinking, and I am not getting through to you.' Don't wait until the situation is out of control and the kid's marks are dropping, he's cutting classes, getting into fights, seeing a whole new world of friends." Typically, parents do wait until the problem is entrenched.[15]

As parents, it is vital that we allow youngsters to suffer the consequences of their irresponsible drinking. Experts agree on this. Don't try to "squash" traffic tickets, or hush up incidents involving the police "for the family's sake." For the kid's sake, let him or her deal with the results of his or her own actions.

Adolescents, not the parents, should make amends for property damage, either by making repairs or earning the money to pay for them. They should deal directly with the people they have injured when out of control. *"Don't do anything to make it easier for the kid to drink,"* urges Betty Karnay, specialist in adolescent treatment at Princeton House, Princeton, NJ.

When reasoning, firmness, and strong limits—and even a couple of bad experiences—haven't stopped out-of-bounds drinking, parents must seek outside help.[16]

Where to Get Help. Following is a list of people to contact. Assume that a person and a program can be found that fits your situation.

School. Contact the chemical health coordinator or community educations director of your local school district. If these do not exist in your school system, consult the school counselor or principal.

Work. Contact your employer as to whether or not your place of work has an employee assistance program.

County. Contact your county social service and health service agencies. They can refer you to public and private treatment centers, counseling and mental health clinics, detoxification centers, half-way houses, and services for assisting in chemical dependency.

Community Groups. Check into groups such as Alcoholics Anonymous, Al-Anon, and other support programs. Your local service organizations such as Jaycees, Kiwanis,

Knights of Columbus, and local youth serving organizations such as 4-H, Campfire, or Boy Scouts may have
programs.

Church Pastor. Remember, this person can be of great assistance in helping you find the right help for a specific adolescent or family situation.

Sexual Activity

A third critical issue is the growing incidence of premarital
sexual activity among adolescents. Some profound changes in
our society have occurred with respect to sexual freedom.
Between the years 1967 and 1974 nonmarital intercourse rates
increased about 300 percent for white females and 50 percent
for white males.[17] Since then there has been a continuing rise
in nonmarital intercourse, with adolescents becoming involved
at younger and younger ages. Illegitimate births are seen as
undermining black families. The percentage of fatherless black
families tripled between the 1960s and the early 1980s.[18]

The Adolescent-Parent study found that one in five ninth-
graders have had sexual intercourse at least once. This was
true for 28 percent of the boys. These statistics and trends
alert us to the fact that a sexual revolution did indeed occur in
the late 1960s and early 1970s.

There are factors in the life of an adolescent that break down
good resolves, making sexual activity not only desired, but
inevitable. Chilman, in her comprehensive review of studies
on adolescent sexual activity, singles out the following major
factors associated with nonmarital intercourse: "low level of
religiousness, permissive societal norms, racism and poverty,
peer-group pressure, friends who are sexually active, low educational goals and poor education achievement, deviant attitudes, strained parent-child relationships and minimal parent-
child communication, age (older than sixteen) and early
puberty.[19]

Most parents are not willing to acquiesce to the idea that no
matter what we say, "teenagers are going to be sexually ac-

tive." This assumption, they maintain, sells young people short; for it is telling them in effect that they're incapable of self-discipline and they're not intelligent enough to make choices for purposes greater than self-gratification. A society that settles for teenage sexual activity also fools adolescents into thinking they're mature enough at age thirteen and fifteen and seventeen to handle all the emotional, psychological, social, and moral consequences of premature sex.

What Parents Can Do. Teenagers want to hear a clear statement, with reasons, as to why they should resist teenage pressures to become involved in sexual intimacies. Parents should realize that the most important sex organ is still the one found between an adolescent's ears: the brain. Because feelings begin in the brain, young people can back away from being overwhelmed by pressures and peer society norms.

Most parents want help in learning how to talk with their adolescent about sex. Some are uncomfortable when talking about the facts and feelings of sexuality, especially when it involves their children. Others, though willing to be their children's teachers, have questions concerning *when* children should be taught about sexuality, *what* details should be conveyed, and *how* the information should be presented. Few parents want to admit their ignorance about human sexuality, or to sound ignorant on the subject before their children. As a result many parents feel the need for support and training in communicating a stance on sexuality that commends both responsibility and restraint.

Where to Get Help. An aid to parents is available in video-assisted programs of instruction in sexuality, for use in schools and churches. Each course, introduced first to parents, is a values-based program designed to develop a sense of reverence for this aspect of God's creation and to promote responsible restraint. The tapes are used to introduce difficult-to-discuss topics, thus making it easier for parents to talk about matters of sexuality with their adolescents. Dr. John Forliti, has developed the training program for use in public schools and Roman Catholic congregations and schools. Dorothy Williams has developed a similar program entitled "There Is a Season" for use in Protestant churches.[20] For some parents, certain sexual issues may be more difficult. Emotionally charged sexual issues such as homosexuality, incest, or rape require professional helpers.

Parents should take advantage of resources such as these:

Denominational Social Services. Major denominations have excellent staff and programs in major cities and towns to serve parents and teenage parents. Your pastor can help you locate the appropriate one.

Family Services. A network of 250 Family Service agencies provides confidential services at fees based on ability to pay. Information about them may be obtained by contacting United Way in your community. Crisis intervention services for families and individuals are available immediately for those whose situation is seen as critical.

Adolescent Suicide

Throughout history, suicide has been considered a mysterious act and, in most societies, a taboo subject. But the sharp rise in adolescent suicides since the 1960s has made it a subject of great concern. The dramatic rise in adolescent suicides from 4 per 100,000 in 1957 to 12.2 in 1975 represents a 300 percent increase in a period of eighteen years.

In an article in *Lutheran Standard*, Steve Swanson cites illustrations from both a wealthy suburb and a rural area.

Psychiatrists in Chicago speak of the suburban North Shore—one of the richest areas on the country—as the Suicide Belt. With median family incomes exceeding $60,000, teenagers there grow up in beautiful neighborhoods, go to the best schools, and materially at least, have much of what they want. Porsches and Jaguars pepper the high school parking lots. Yet 28 North Shore teenagers in a 17-month period killed themselves—18 by gunshot, eight by hanging, and two by lying down in front of trains.

This isn't only a problem that threatens suburban youth. A small town in North Dakota has been touched by this tragedy, too. In a seven-month period, three young people killed themselves. A fourth youth, age 16, died of a handgun wound that authorities believe was self-inflicted. As that rural community struggled with the issue of suicide and its prevention, a hospital chaplain cautioned the people against 'denial of reality' and a feeling of not wanting to talk about this concern for fear of disrupting the community.[21]

Causes. The causes of suicide are complex and numerous. Each case involves a different combination of reasons, but they are mainly cradled in the difficulties of adolescent years. Here, in order of importance, are the major causes that current research has isolated.[22]

Depression. This is the most common emotion felt by a suicidal person, but it is not always easy to detect.

Loss of parent. Loss by death, divorce, separation, or extended absence can have a devastating impact on an adolescent. While loss of parent usually does not precipitate a suicide, it can influence adolescents in that direction.

Alienation from family. When family ties are close, suicide rates are low; and where the ties are not close, the rates are high. Alienation comes when communication breaks down because of family conflict or stress on high achievement in school, sports, or social relationships.

Other contributing causes. For some adolescents, death holds a mystical or magical attraction. For others, strong sex drives create inordinate feelings of guilt. Still others are frightened by world events and have lost all hope of a significant future. Some have an overwhelming need for perfection. Change of address, breakup with a girlfriend or boyfriend, and inability to cope with a situation are all additional factors.

Warning Signs. Given these major causes, what does a parent watch for as warning signs?

Verbal signs include frequent comments similar to these: Di-

rect comments like "I wish I were dead"; or indirect statements such as "No one around here needs me" or "Why
is there so much unhappiness in life?"

Behavioral signs include extreme mood shifts, sudden changes
in behavior, an unsuccessful suicide attempt.

Depression is the most prevalent indicator of suicide. Symptoms of depression are varied: fatigue; loss of appetite and
energy; marked drop in quality of schoolwork and grades;
withdrawal from friends; spending much time alone; difficulty in sleeping or, in some cases, excessive sleeping;
preoccupation with talk about suicide; giving away prized
possessions; feelings of guilt; helplessness or anxiety;
expressions of hopelessness; despair; low self-esteem; delinquent behavior; sexual promiscuity; drug and alcohol
abuse.

What Parents Can Do. When parents become aware of warning signals, the best preventive measure is to listen. Give the
adolescent a chance to talk freely. (See Chapter Three on Listening for Understanding.) For a suicidal person, friendship
from a peer can avert disaster. It may be difficult for a peer to
give this friendship to a person at school who may be labeled
"weird" or "unfriendly" because he or she feels alienated; but
we as parents need to encourage this kind of friendship on
the part of our adolescents. *At the same time*, parents should
contact a person skilled in suicide prevention and bring the
adolescent into a counseling relationship.

Where to Get Help. Over two hundred suicide prevention
centers across the country are staffed around the clock, seven
days a week. These centers operate an immediate crisis service
by telephone. The purpose of this service is to provide emotional support to the caller and direct the person to sources of
help. A list of suicide prevention centers may be obtained by
writing to the American Association of Suicidology, 2459 South
Ash, Denver, Colorado 80222.[23] In addition, help is available
at community health centers located throughout every state,

at county health services, and denominational social service agencies.

A remarkable story of hope was found in a *New York Times* article about William Fox, an officer in the New York police department.[24] He was successful in persuading Michael Buchanan, a young teenager, not to jump from a Bowery flophouse roof, while people in the street below shouted, "Jump, jump!" The appeal that got through to the boy, whose mother died when he was two and whose father was an abusive alcoholic, was this: the bachelor police officer promised to take him to his home, where he could have a room and could go to school. When he was finally rescued, the boy, with tears in his eyes, asked William Fox, "Did you really mean what you said?"

William Fox did. Michael became his foster son and was soon attending school and drawing respectable grades. Finding an adult who would love and care for him changed his life dramatically. A book written about the two, entitled *To Make a Difference*, became a two-hour CBS television movie.

Child Abuse

The September 1983 issue of *Time* magazine[25] focused on the serious national problem of interrelated private acts of violence known as child abuse, wife-beating, and rape. Of these, child abuse was singled out as being the "ultimate betrayal."

Murray Straus, in a research study of 1,146 families,[26] found that approximately fourteen of every one hundred children between the ages of three and seventeen experience an average of 10.5 episodes of violence per year. These alarming data are supported by statements of many reporting agencies that the instances of child abuse and neglect are not less than the above, but more. The growing awareness of the magnitude of child abuse has led to it also being labelled a "disease epidemic."

The Search Institute study showed that one in five of the 8,165 young adolescents worry that "someone might force me to do sexual things I don't want to do." One in four worry ("somewhat," "quite a bit," or "very much") that "one of my parents will hit me so hard that I will be badly hurt." A physical abuse index in this study showed that parents who are abusive also tend to be coercive, nagging, drinkers who use autocratic methods of control and excessive punishment. Their children tend to rebel against their authority, acquiesce to peer pressure, and be fearful of sexual aggression. Each of the characteristics identified above with parents and youth correlates well with the index of physical abuse.

Mary Otto, in her review of the research on child abuse notes that abusive parents are not necessarily poor or uneducated, though poverty and lack of knowledge do cause additional stress in families, and therefore account for a somewhat higher rate of abuse in poor families.[27] Child abuse exists at all social levels.

Typically, abusive parents are lonely, isolated, insecure individuals who have very little psychological or social support from their families. They lack meaningful communication with their partners, parents, or siblings. They usually have few friends or valued social outlets. They have an overwhelming sense of isolation. Though they may wish to stop their abusive behavior, they lack the skill and support to make and maintain constructive changes.

Physical abuse carries the most visible scars and draws the most outraged reactions. But it is second to emotional and sexual abuse in its devastating effects on a child.

Linda Halliday, in her autobiographical account entitled *Silent Scream*,[28] tells of her emotional reactions to sexual intercourse with her father from the ages seven to sixteen. The experience drove her to attempt suicide several times; she turned to alcohol and prostitution, and then to date only men who were physically and sexually abusive to her.

Like a poisonous plant sending out its spores, family violence reproduces itself. Most rapists were preyed upon sexually as children; most violent criminals were raised in violent homes. Battered children grow up disposed to batter their own offspring.

What Parents Can Do. These frightening, ugly details are difficult for parents to read or agree to. To have sexual abuse come from a stranger is easier to accept and warn against than when it occurs within one's own walls or within one's larger family or neighborhood unit.

Those who work in the area of child abuse suggest that parents begin to use preventive measures when a child is very young. For example, a parent could teach a child at an early age how to distinguish between a "good touch" and a "bad touch," between feeling "safe" in the company of an adult or feeling "threatened." A number of good books and teaching aids available through libraries and child protection agencies give helpful suggestions in carrying out preventive measures. It is important that children are taught to *tell someone* if they feel confused or bad about something someone has done to them. A parent might explain that sometimes people we love have problems and don't act appropriately. When we feel confused or unhappy about what someone says or does to us, we should talk about it.

Children find it extremely difficult to "tell" if the offender is a parent, because often the only form of security, livelihood, and love they know is tied up in their home. In some cases, an offending parent has put an unbelievably heavy burden on a child by saying, "If you tell, I will be put in jail, and it will be your fault." For that reason alone, it is rare for a child to lie about sexual abuse.

A parent should believe the child, even if it hurts. A child may throw out hints, hoping the parent will guess; perhaps an ambiguous statement elaborated on from time to time. This is called testing the parent to see if the subject could be open for discussion. At this point *reflective listening,* as discussed in Chapter 3 could be put to good use.

A child protection assessment worker in Dakota County, Minnesota, gave this advice at a workshop:

If you as a neighbor, friend or relative, hear a child, however obliquely, refer to his or her parent as abusive, listen carefully to what is being said and attempt to ask sensitive questions that will not frighten the child. It's important not to promise the child that action will be taken to stop the abuse. Broken promises are something that the child may be all too accustomed to. Rather, you might reassure the child that you care, that you will continue to listen and would like to ask the help of someone accustomed to handling such problems. While only certain professional people are mandated to report suspected child abuse and neglect to the authorities, any person may do so.[29]

Symptoms of sexual abuse are also indicators of other problems. It is the combination of these symptoms that may lead to an unfolding of the problem and subsequent help. Symptoms that have sexual overtones are the ones most likely to mean the presence of sexual rather than physical abuse.

Possible Symptoms of Child Abuse. The following are symptoms you should watch for in your child.

1. Dramatic changes in school behavior; withdrawal, depression, acting-out
2. Moderate to severe depression or anxiety
3. Fear of going home
4. Fear of being touched
5. Excessive fear of adults (male or female)
6. Running away from home, especially when it is habitual
7. Chemical/alcohol abuse or dependency
8. General self-destructive tendencies: includes chemical addiction, involvement in delinquency, suicide attempts or ideation, involvement in destructive relationships, adolescent prostitution
9. Poor peer relationships
10. Extremely low self-esteem
11. Inability to trust others, fear of the outside world
12. Poor personal-care skills
13. Regressive behavior such as bedwetting, thumb-sucking
14. Frequent nightmares
15. Unusual disgust for sexual matters
16. Sexual acting out, lack of appropriate boundaries
17. Unexpected sexual utterances (sounds or words, phrases) especially from small children

18. A facade of maturity; especially in teenage girls who are given adult roles to fill in the family
19. Excessive masturbation in children
20. Regression in developmental milestones
21. Clinging behavior
22. Open sexual behavior after age five to seven
23. Physical symptoms:

   - burns, cuts, bruises appearing regularly or on unlikely parts of the body
   - fractures that don't fit the description of the incident
   - unexplained abdominal pain
   - body mutilation (self-inflicted tatoos, cigarette burns, cuts)
   - venereal disease—oral, genital, anal
   - adolescent pregnancy
   - pain on defecation
   - vaginal discharge in girls, urethral discharge in boys
   - oral fissures or other unexplained lesions, gagging response or chronic sore throat
   - sudden weight gain or loss—especially in teenage girls

Where to Get Help. Most communities have child protection agencies, community mental health centers, or police departments who can give needed help. If the abuse is occurring within your own immediate or extended family, you should confront the offender as well as seek outside help. Breaking the secrecy that surrounds the abuse is therapeutic. However, it is also important to recognize that the root causes underlying abusive behavior and its scarring effects usually need professional intervention in order to break the cycle of abuse.

Because abusive parents are consistently described as being isolated, lonely, and lacking in support, the help given them must be a response to these conditions. Although individual counseling offers help in some areas of the parents' life, it does not provide the ongoing support system that alleviates the isolation and loneliness.

A more helpful approach is *group counseling*. Membership in such a group provides parents with an immediate support system and a chance to reduce their overwhelming sense of isolation. In such support groups, parents are encouraged to contact each other between meetings and they are required to call a specified person when they are about to abuse a child. This making of a definite break between feeling and behavior reduces impulsiveness. The result is a sharp reduction in physical and verbal abuse, even after only two sessions of the group.

Group counseling provides a mechanism by which abusive parents can be distracted from themselves and their problems, learn to share with others like themselves, and come to understand how best to handle their anger. A peer group is effective because it not only supports parents but also demands the reduction of violent behavior.[30] A national association of support groups called Parents Anonymous (patterned after Alcoholics Anonymous) is an available help.

Parents should know that if sexual abuse has been a factor in the home, in most cases it indicates the lack of a loving, supportive discipline system. The children have heard many angry and abusive words; physical violence has often been used to control them. Parents in such homes may be suffering from depression, anxiety, and problems of controlling their anger. They need outside help in learning how to redirect anger and aggression into appropriate behaviors. They need help in learning to show love to their children. There may be marital conflicts in such a home, alcohol abuse, difficulties in relationships with friends and relatives. Sometimes there is the stress of poverty, poor housing, employment problems, and single parenthood. These factors are often a part of the vicious cycle of perpetuating family violence.

Other Out-of-Control Behaviors

More than half the cries for help that reach child-guidance clinics are for problems such as defiance, fighting, lack of cooperation, and lying. Characteristic signs of such out-of-control children include:

- Physical: hitting, vandalizing, stealing
- Verbal: sarcasm, yelling, defiance
- Attitudinal: negative, defeatist
- Emotion: lack of affection, manipulative use of affection

Children who *frequently* display these behaviors are often called "incorrigible," or "social deviants," or "problem children."

Every parent has seen these behaviors in a child. What distinguishes out-of-control adolescents is the frequency with which these behaviors occur. In the study of 8,165 adolescents, 5 percent admitted to having damaged property or stolen from a store six times or more during the year. Twice that many (11 percent) acknowledged having hit or beaten another six times or more. One out of four (23 percent) admitted to having lied to one of their parents six times or more during the last twelve months. These are the kind of adolescents who are candidates for the label "out-of-control" youth. Accompanying their norm-breaking or aggressive tendencies are often the following characteristics:

- They associate with peers who are prone to the same kind of deviance
- They are frequently in conflict with their parents
- They are uninterested in school
- They are conscious of their peers violating school regulations
- They report high exposure to movies and TV

Significantly, a 1982 report by the National Institute of Mental Health, which reviewed a decade of studies on the effects of television on children especially scored television violence. It found almost all studies that were reviewed support the conclusion that watching violence on television leads to aggressive behavior by children.[31] Television viewing has the effect of heightening a state of general arousal—it can produce an emotional respone.

Need for Discipline. Studies have found that out-of-control children *do* respond to discipline that is consistent, nonabusive, and rationale-giving. The solution seems to lie in helping parents to become more effective disciplinarians.

For discipline to be effective, it should be used consistently and then, after the punishment is over, the parents should emphasize the child's positive responses.

What Parents Can Do. An excellent program for parents with out-of-control difficult children has been developed by Fleischman, Horne and Arthur, the authors of *Troubled Families*.[32] With minimal additional training, professionals with a B.A. or M.A. degree can make this training available in a religious institution, community mental health center, child guidance clinic, protective service agency, juvenile department, or school. The program, aimed to assist parents with behavior problems, emphasizes home-based rather than institutional treatment. It can be conducted in groups and used in a variety of social service, congregational or psychological settings. It uses a step-by-step sequence for building skills and transferring responsibility for change from teacher to parent. When tested over a two-decade period, it has proved highly effective in altering the behavior of out-of-control children. In bringing children to accept adult authority and control, it accomplishes what they want of their parents—clearly identified limits. (Described below are six disciplinary procedures recommended to parents in the program, with special emphasis on handling difficult children. Though uniquely effective with out-of-control children, parents should note that these procedures can be preventive medicine, applying equally well to children not out-of-control.)

Time-Out is a type of punishment often used when a child hasn't done what he or she has been told to do and has a defiant attitude. It also is an effective discipline when there is fighting going on between siblings. In time out, a parent isolates the child for a few minutes after each instance of misbehavior. Children who are six years or older who refuse to go to time-out should be warned once. If they still refuse to go, then a privilege is taken away.

Grandma's Law is a good procedure for enforcing various rules, routines and responsibilities set up in a household. It is essentially non-confrontative, deriving its name from the legendary grandmother who told her grandchild, "First you eat your vegetables, then you can have some pie." What the rule really means is that parents insist children do whatever has been asked of them or expected of them. Then and only then can the children do what they want. If a child ignores the parent and follows his or her own wishes, a time-out results. Sometimes the alternative is to lose a privilege or be assigned extra work.

Natural and Logical Consequences. "Natural consequences" could be defined as what would normally happen with no adult intervention, and "logical consequences" as letting the punishment fit the crime. These are ways to deal with children who act irresponsibly or like to let the parent do the work for them. Using such consequences means that the parents will no longer cover for the children or protect them from the negative consequences of their behavior. For example, a parent refuses to join in a frantic hunt for schoolbooks that have been misplaced by a child, or a mother won't rewarm a meal for a child who comes home late, or a parent requiring a child who damages something to pay for its repair. Following natural and logical consequences works best when these irresponsible actions have become patterns of behavior, and thus the parents have opportunity to decide well beforehand how they will carry out the intended consequences.

Some parents, especially those who tend to be overly protective, may find it hard to let their children suffer the consequences of their actions. The parents feel guilty about not coming to help their child. For this reason, parents who seriously consider using natural or logical consequences as a form

188 / FIVE CRIES OF PARENTS

of discipline should discuss between themselves the pros and cons of this technique; they may develop a list of positive self-statements to assist them in following through without feelings of guilt.

Withholding Attention as a procedure works best with small children who pester their parents for attention, sometimes by whining, pouting, or pretending to cry. If parents consistently ignore these behaviors, they usually will see a dramatic decrease in their occurrence. The child will increasingly use attention-getters when the parents first withhold attention, thinking it will eventually "work." Parents need to withstand this initial *increase* in annoying behavior by recognizing that their child is testing this new discipline. Should the child's testing get too severe, the parent should be prepared to use time-out as a punishment.

Taking Away Privileges. When a child tests the parents' use of time-out, Grandma's Law, or withholding attention, then parents can remove privileges. Loss of privilege is also a good consequence when a family member fails to attempt or complete part of an agreement. Used this way, it's the most appropriate consequence for older children ("If you're home late, you can't watch TV after dinner.") Allowing no desserts or snacks, denying use of the telephone, not letting the child ride his or her bike, not letting an adolescent play the stereo are all common procedures of removing privileges. A discipline especially difficult for a gregarious teenager is to take away the privilege of having friends over. When using this method, most parents make the mistake of taking away too many privileges and for too long a period of time (grounding a child for a week). It's generally more effective to withdraw fewer privileges for a shorter time—for example, losing an hour of TV time or having to go to bed 30 minutes early. Except in special circumstances the privilege should be lost for no longer than twenty-four hours after the misbehavior has occurred. This is important for parents to remember.

Assigning Extra Work. With more serious offenses, including lying, stealing, damaging property, and causing problems at school, this procedure is effective. The amount of extra work should be based on the seriousness of the behavior. For example, white lies might earn fifteen minutes of work; stealing one to two hours. To discourage the child from simply dawdling over the assigned chore, the parents should identify the amount of work they expect to be done (for example, if one is asked to clean the bathroom, it means scouring the sink, tub, and toilet, and mopping the floor). Observing this simple procedure can save angry words between adolescent and parent. Parents should also expect the work to be done well and, until the job is finished to the parents' satisfaction, they should deny the child access to any privileges.[33]

These methods, developed over time and proven to be effective, illustrate parenting that is firm, rational, and caring. They establish the parent as being the person in charge.

This matter of learning to accept the authority of one's parents is a basic ingredient in the life of an adolescent. When it is missing, one tends to find adolescents who rebel against any requirement that crosses their wishes. As a result of such rebellion the adolescent often becomes involved in at least one of the six critical behaviors described here. Living without clear limits and a firm authority figure is similar to living under an extremely permissive type of parental control. The effect is to encourage a self-centered and self-indulgent child. By way of contrast, a discipline that teaches young people to accept and respect authority prepares them for the realities of life, the authority of the workplace, of marriage, of living under governments, of a moral universe.

Clergy—A Trusted Resource

Over the years, people have sought out clergy as their first choice when turning to someone for help during a personal crisis. Clergy are a trusted resource. When faced with seven problem situations involving their adolescent, and asked who would be their first choice for help or advice, parents in the

Adolescent-Parent study gave clergy the highest average response. Of course, the answers vary according to the problem. For instance, if the problem is depression, a medical doctor is the first choice. The same is true when one's child is asking difficult-to-answer questions about sex (though other professions may be more knowledgeable regarding the emotional, moral, or spiritual aspects of sex). The one problem most parents assume they can best handle alone is the problem of their child hanging around with kids the parents don't like. Here they are inclined to ask nobody. Aside from these exceptions, the pastor is clearly seen as a preferred source of help.

When these parents rated the help given by their clergyperson, nearly half used the rating of "very" or "quite" helpful. Clearly, a significant proportion of today's population is pleased with the help made available to them through their pastor. One can conclude that many members of the clergy, through their programs of clinical pastoral education, have become skilled in providing support and making referrals to agencies that specialize in certain services.

As one distraught woman explained, "I was so depressed over the problem with my fourteen-year-old son that I couldn't think of a single place to go for help—except to my pastor. I called him and found the help I needed. He was great!"

It is an expectation of church members that they can look to clergy and the community of faith for help in times of stress. In fact, it is associated with their concept of effective ministry. Documentation for this comes from the Readiness for Ministry study conducted by Search Institute and referred to in Chapter 3. When laity and clergy who were randomly selected from forty-seven denominations indicated which characteristics they regarded as most important in a clergyperson, their second-from-the-top choice was "ministry to people in times of stress." People in congregations want their pastor to be especially sensitive to people who are going through times of physical, emotional, or spiritual stress. They also want members of the congregation to be equipped to serve as a caring community and as a friendship/support network. Though this form of ministry in most congregations is an emerging service, whatever exists is appreciated. The evaluations given by parents in the Adolescent-Parent study show that programs, books, and printed materials made available by congregations have been helpful.

Help is wanted as much by parents of girls as of boys. Though fathers lag behind mothers in saying they are much interested in the kinds of help identified in the survey, more that half say they are "very" or "quite" interested in key services related to the five cries of parents. A responsibility of parents is to make this desire known to the clergy and local church councils. Here are the average percentages of 10,457 parents declaring much interest in:

70%   How to help a child develop healthy concepts of right and wrong (Moral Purpose)

68%   How to help a child grow in religious faith (Shared Faith)

66%   More about drugs (Outside Help)

62%   How to communicate better with one's children (Close Family)

47%   Effective discipline (Close Family)

44%   More about sex education (Understanding One's Adolescent)

42%   How to participate in a parent support group (Understanding Oneself)

It is interesting to note that the percentages of parents wanting this help show little variation from fifth to ninth grades. The kinds of help parents want do not vary by the age of their child. More importantly, they relate directly to the issues discussed in this book.

As parents we should note that adolescents are also open to help from their congregation—help related to the very areas of special concern to parents. Half of the adolescents declare much interest in programs that coincide with their parents' top interests, namely, help related to

- figuring out what it means to be a Christian
- learning about what is right and wong

Two out of five adolescents want to "learn how to talk better with adults."

Of special note is the adolescent's interest in topics related to their own greatest concerns:

- learning how to make friends and be a friend (61 percent)
- finding out what is special about me (51 percent)

Without question, clergy and their congregations form a unique and trusted resource for the parent.

A Final Word

This book has identified five desires or cries of parents. Each cry represents a parent reaching out in order to become a better parent. Each cry focuses on a basic issue in the home. And each cry points to a highly significant and available source of strength.

This book addresses parents in a day of epidemics—a time when social diseases are laying claim to an increasing number of adolescents. Rather than try protecting our child from the toxins of life, we should concentrate on strengthening the inner life of the child.

In summary, these sources of strength include the following:

A close but open family life

This is possible when parents

- demonstrate love and affection in their relationships with each other
- communicate well with their adolescent and each other

- teach responsible living through consistent authoritative-type discipline
- show affection, respect, and trust to their child

Moral beliefs and purpose

Encouraged by parents who

- seek to live within the universe of traditional moral beliefs
- have a life orientation that is not moralistic or self-centered
- model a life that carries a sense of responsibility for others' needs
- help adolescents internalize moral beliefs by using rational explanations of what is right or wrong

A personal, liberating faith

Encouraged by parents who themselves

- have a faith that is liberating rather than moralistic and restrictive
- share their experiences of faith with members of the family
- discuss the Scriptures and pray together with their adolescent
- model "doing the truth" by helping where there is need

The support of caring people

Made possible by a parent's willingness to

- accept the help of others
- become part of a support network of caring adults
- seek help when one's adolescent is involved in:
  — drug abuse
  — alcohol abuse
  — sexual activity
  — suicidal tendencies
  — child abuse
  — other out-of-control behaviors

- learn methods of discipline that are consistent, firm, and fair.

These are the sources of strength adolescents need.

These are the elements of parenting which we as authors have experienced as sources of strength. We share them not only because they have enriched and enlivened our family but also because research based on thousands of families identifies them as sources of strength. Parents who feel beleaguered while battling against seemingly impossible odds, should take heart. The sources of strength presented here are live options for every parent. They can be answers to the cries which occasioned the writing of this book. Undergirding these answers is the caring God who revealed himself in Jesus Christ. We have found that "He is faithful who promised." He does intervene in the life of a family, to reshape values, attitudes, and relationships, and to unite members in a bond of love.

Notes

Chapter 1. A Time of Danger and Opportunity

1. Search Institute is a nonprofit organization, founded in 1958. Its mission is scientific, pioneering research on issues faced by service and religious organizations and action based on the research to effect desired changes. During its 25-year history, SI has been located in Minneapolis, Minnesota. Its mission is carried out through three separate activities: searching for answers to questions involving human need by means of research; sharing this information with those who need it; and consulting with organizations to help them act on the information they receive.

   Though Search Institute has specialized in the study of young people, it also conducts major studies of institutions and people who serve youth. Hence, the institution has conducted such studies as a Readiness for Ministry project involving the seminaries and congregations of 47 denominations, a study of Catholic high schools in the '80s, and a study of the religious beliefs and values of the 96th Congress.

2. David Olson and Hamilton McCubbin, *Families: What Makes Them Work* (Beverly Hills: Sage Publications, 1983), 219, 221.

3. Kay Pasley and Viktor Gecas, "Stresses and Satisfactions of the Parental Role," *Personnel and Guidance Journal* 62 (1984): 400–404.

4. Gail Sheehy, "The Crisis Couples Face at 40," *McCalls* 103, (May 1976): 107.

5. Eda LeShan, *The Wonderful Crisis of Middle Age* (New York: McKay Publishing Company, 1973).

6. Documentations for all references to the Adolescent-Parent study can be found in the following publication, available through Search Institute: Peter L. Benson, et al., *Young Adolescents and Their Parents* (Minneapolis: Search Institute, 1984).

7. Catherine Chilman, "Parent Satisfactions, Concerns, and Goals for Their Children," *Family Relations* 29 (1980): 339–345.

8. Letty Cottin Pogrebin, *Family Politics* (New York: McGraw Hill, 1983), 25–26.

Chapter 2. The Cry for Understanding Yourself as a Parent

1. Kurt Andersen, "Private Violence," *Time* 122 (September 5, 1983): 19.

2. Robert Reineke, *Report to the National Board of American Lutheran Church Women on a Study of Attitudes of Women* (Minneapolis: Search Institute, 1981).

3. David Mace, "Love, Anger and Intimacy," *Light* (April-May 1980): 2.

4. Haim G. Ginott, *Between Parent & Teenager* (New York: Avon Books, 1969), 96.

5. *Ibid.*, 97.

6. *Ibid.*, 100.

7. Joan Bordow, *The Ultimate Loss* (New York: Beaufort Books, 1982), 52.
8. *Ibid.*, 81.
9. *Ibid.*, 89.
10. This analysis is based on data from the Adolescent-Parent sample. The 482 single parents who participated in the study were compared to the entire population of mothers from intact families.
11. John Guidibaldi, "The Impact of Parental Divorce on Children: Report of the National NASP Study," 1983.
12. *Ibid.*
13. *Ibid.*
14. David Jolliff, "The Effects of Parental Remarriage on the Development of the Young Child," *Early Child Development and Care*, 13, (1984): 321–334.
15. C. Gilbert Wrenn, *The World of the Contemporary Counselor* (Boston: Houghton-Mifflin, 1973).

Chapter 3. Cry for Understanding Your Adolescent

1. We have adopted these goals from a conceptual scheme developed by John Hill in *Understanding Early Adolescence: A Framework* (Carrboro: Center for Early Adolescence, University of North Carolina, 1980).
2. Larry K. Brendtro and Arlin E. Ness, *Re-educating Troubled Youth* (New York: Aldine Publishing Company, 1983), 15.
3. *Ibid.*
4. Luther B. Otto, *How to Help Your Child Choose a Career* (New York: M. Evans and Company, 1984).
5. Amy Harris, "He Doesn't Believe in Handicaps," *Faith at Work* 91 (October 1978): 51.
6. Barbara Varenhorst, *Real Friends: Becoming the Friend You'd Like to Have* (San Francisco: Harper & Row, 1984).
7. Grace W. Weinstein, "Should Teenagers Work?" *McCalls* (June 1983): 54.
8. *Ibid.*
9. *Ibid.*
10. Fritz Ridenour, *What Teenagers Wish Their Parents Knew About Kids* (Waco: Word Books, 1982), 40.
11. Roland Larson and Doris Larson, *I Need to Have You Know Me* (Minneapolis: Winston Press, 1979), 35–36.
12. Francis Iaani, *Eight-Year Study of Teenagers* (New York: National Institute of Education, 1984).
13. Varenhorst, *Real Friends*, 58.

Chapter 4. Cry for a Close Family

1. Letty Cottin Pogrebin, *Family Politics* (New York: McGraw Hill, 1983), 25.
2. David H. Olson and Hamilton McCubbin, *Families: What Makes Them Work* (Beverly Hills: Sage Publications, 1983), 231.
3. Merton P. Strommen, *Five Cries of Youth* (San Francisco: Harper & Row, 1974), 47.
4. Augustus Y. Napier and Carl A. Whitaker, *The Family Crucible* (New York: Bantam Books, 1978).

5. Strommen, *Five Cries of Youth*, 42.
6. Ellen Goodman, "For Tsongas and His Family, a Discovery of the Preciousness of Time" *The Boston Globe*, (17 January 1984).
7. Charlie Shedd, *Promises to Peter* (Waco: Word Books, 1970), 116.
8. Diana Baumrind, "Authoritarian vs. Authoritative Parental Control," *Adolescence* 3, no. 11 (Fall 1968): 261.
9. Merton P. Strommen, Milo L. Brekke et. al. *A Study of Generations* (Minneapolis: Augsburg Publishing, 1972), 390.
10. Strommen, *Five Cries of Youth*.
11. Baumrind, "Authoritarian vs. Authoritative Parental Control," 256.
12. *Ibid.*, 269.
13. Dave Capuzzi and Lindy Low Le Coq, "Social and Personal Determinants of Adolescent Use and Abuse of Alcohol and Marijuana," *Personnel and Guidance Journal 62*, no. 4 (December 1983): 200.
14. Francis J. Ianni, "Community, Adults Mold Teens, Study Says," *Minneapolis Tribune*, 25 March, 1984.
15. David Augsberger, *When Caring Is Not Enough* (Scottdale: Herald Press, 1983), 270.
16. Fritz Ridenour, *What Teenagers Wish Their Parents Knew About Kids* (Waco: Word Books, 1982), 83.
17. Jane Norman and Myron Harris, *The Private Life of the American Teenager* (New York: Rawson, Wade Publishers, 1981), 37.
18. Dolores Curran, *Traits of a Healthy Family* (Minneapolis: Winston Press, 1983), 99.
19. *Ibid.*, 103.
20. Lee J. Stromberg, "Meet Hamilton McCubbin: He's Testing Family Tension," *Correspondent* (Winter 1983): 9.
21. George Armelagos, "Culturally Speaking: A Tasty Tale," *Weight Watchers Magazine 14* (February 1981): 9.
22. Olson and McCubbin, *Families*, 150.
23. Dolores Curran, *Traits*, 102.
24. Larry Brendto and Arlin Ness, *Re-Educating Troubled Youth* (New York: Aldine Publishing, 1983), 63.
25. *Ibid.*, 63.

Chapter 5. Cry for Moral Behavior

1. C. S. Lewis, *Abolition of Man* (New York: Macmillan Press, 1946), 95–121.
2. Lawrence Kohlberg, "Continuities and Discontinuities in Childhood and Adult Moral Development Revisited," in *Collected Papers on Moral Development and Moral Education*. Harvard University, 1973.
3. Carol Gilligan, *In A Different Voice* (Cambridge: Harvard University Press, 1982), 19–20.
4. Lawrence Kohlberg, *The Philosophy of Moral Development*, Vol. 1 (San Francisco: Harper & Row, 1981), 345.
5. Merton P. Strommen, *Five Cries of Youth* (San Francisco: Harper & Row, 1974), 106.
6. David Rosenthal, "The Year in the Movies," in *Rolling Stone Yearbook 25* (1983), 25–26.

7. Harry Haun, "Loss of Innocence Remains a Commercial Constant," *Denver Post*, 12 August 1983.
8. Peter L. Benson, *Report on Drug Use and Drug-Related Attitudes, State of Minnesota* (Minneapolis: Search Institute, October 25, 1983).
9. William Raspberry, "It's Time for Black Adults to Make Teenage Virtue a Necessity," *Washington Post*, 7 August 1984.
10. Dolores Curran, *Traits of A Healthy Family* (Minneapolis: Winston Press, 1983), 185.
11. Merton P. Strommen, *A Study of Generations* (Minneapolis: Augsburg Publishing, 1972), 287.
12. Peter L. Benson, Dorothy L. Williams, *Religion on Capitol Hill: Myths and Realities* (New York: Harper & Row, 1983), 154–163.
13. Strommen, *A Study of Generations*, 243.
14. Robert Coles, Lecture at Westminster Presbyterian Church, Minneapolis, Minnesota, February 1984.
15. *Ibid.*
16. Alan Keith-Lucas, *The Client's Religion and Your Own Beliefs in the Helping Process.* Group Child Care Consultant Services, Aug. 1983, 12–15.
17. Peter L. Benson, *et al. Young Adolescents and Their Parents* (Minneapolis: Search Institute, 1984), 288.
18. *Ibid.*

Chapter 6. Cry for a Shared Faith

1. Dolores Curran, *Traits of a Healthy Family* (Minneapolis: Winston Press, 1983), 216.
2. Lee J. Stromberg, "Meet Hamilton McCubbin," *Correspondent* 81, no. 520 (Winter 1983).
3. Carl Reuss, *Profiles of Lutherans* (Minneapolis: Augsburg Publishing House, 1983).
4. Princeton Religious Research Center. *Religion in America*, 1981.
5. Peter Benson, *et al., Young Adolescents and Their Parents* (Minneapolis: Search Institute, 1984).
6. Sara Little, *To Set One's Heart* (Atlanta: John Knox Press, 1983), 13, 15, 17.
7. Paul Johnson, *Psychology of Religion* (Nashville: Abingdon Press, 1959).
8. David Augsburger, *When Caring Is Not Enough* (Scottdale: Herald Press, 1983), 110–111.
9. Karen Mains, *Open Heart, Open Home* (Elgin: David C. Cook, 1975), 16.
10. Lawrence Richards, "The Teacher as Interpreter of the Bible," *Religious Education* 77, no. 5 (Sept.-Oct. 1982): 515, 516.
11. Frank Laubach, *Prayer* (New Jersey: Fleming H. Revell, 1946), 56.
12. Little, *To Set One's Heart*, 76.
13. Wayne Rice, *Junior High Ministry* (Grand Rapids: Zondervan, 1978), 112–113.
14. Associated Press, "Boy, 11, Who Aids Street People is Honored by Philadelphia Council," Minneapolis *Star and Tribune*, 9 March 1984.
15. Edith Schaeffer, "What is a Family?" *Living and Growing Together* (Waco: Word Books, 1976), 22.
16. Alec J. Allen and Martin L. Mitchell, "Helping the Community: An Untapped Resource for Troubled Children," *The Pointer* (Fall 1982): 1-4.

Chapter 7. Cry for Outside Help

1. Philip Shapiro, "A Treatment and Management Model," *Coping Magazine* (April 1983): 11–20, 27–30.
2. Larry K. Brendtro and Abraham W. Nicolaou. "Hooked on Helping," *Synergist* 10 (Winter 1982): 38–41.
3. Armand Nicholi, "The Nontherapeutic Use of Psychotic Drugs," *New England Journal* 308: 925–933.
4. Peter Benson. *Report on 1983 Minnesota Survey on Drug Use and Drug-Related Attitudes* (Minneapolis: Search Institute, October 25, 1983).
5. Jeffrey Mervis, "Adolescent Behavior: What We Think We Know," *Monitor* (April 1984): 24, 25.
6. Hazelden Foundation, *Never Too Early, Never Too Late* (Hazelden Foundation, 1983), 14–15.
7. Russell A. Haber, "The Family Dance Around Drug Abuse," *Personnel and Guidance Journal* (March 1983): 428–430.
8. Search, *1983 Minnesota Survey on Drug Use.*
9. Sheila Blume, "Prevention of the Fetal Alcohol Syndrome," Paper prepared for National Council on Alcoholism (June 1983).
10. *New York Times*. "High Cost of Alcoholism Staggers Economy," November 1983.
11. Virginia Edwards, "Teenage Drinking," *Scouting* (October 1982): 76.
12. Search, *1983 Minnesota Survey on Drug Use.*
13. Edwards, "Teenage Drinking," 78.
14. Dave Capuzzi and Lindy Low Le Coq, "Social and Personal Determinants of Adolescent Use and Abuse of Alcoholism and Marijuana," *Personnel and Guidance Journal* (December 1983): 199–205.
15. Edwards, "Teenage Drinking," 80.
16. *Ibid.*
17. Catherine S. Chilman, "Coital Behaviors of Adolescents in the United States: A Summary of Research and Implications for Further Studies." Prepared for meetings of APA, 1983. Unpublished paper.
18. Ray Marshall, "Youth Employment/Unemployment/Underemployment: A Continuing Dilemma," (St. Paul: Center for Youth Development and Research, 1983).
19. Chilman, "Coital Behaviors."
20. John Forliti and Dorothy Williams. These courses are designed to facilitate several of the elements we consider helpful to family relationships. They help both young people and parents verbalize questions and answers about social relationships and sexuality. They provide a kind of support group for parents of teenagers, as well as try to raise the young person's self-esteem. And they help parents and teens talk to each other about their feelings and their identity as sexual beings. "There Is a Season" is particularly helpful in opening lines of communication between young persons and their parents, with specific weekly assignments for parent-child conversation on various topics of personal concern to them both. More information about these video-assisted training programs is available by writing to Search Institute, 122 West Franklin Avenue, Suite 525, Minneapolis, Minnesota 55404.

21. Steve Swanson, "Teen Suicide," *Lutheran Standard* 24, no. 3 (February 3, 1984): 11.
22. Lynda Y. Ray and Norbert Johnson, "Adolescent Suicide," *Personnel and Guidance Journal* (November 1983): 132–133.
23. F. Wenz, "Self-injury behavior, economic status and the family anomie syndrome among adolescents," *Adolescence* 14, 387–397.
24. Judy Klemesrud, "Officer Saved A Life and Gained A Son," *New York Times* Appeared in *Minneapolis Tribune* 4 April, 1982.
25. Ed Magnuson, "Child Abuse: The Ultimate Betrayal," *Time* (September 5, 1983): 20–22.
26. Murray Straus, Family Patterns and Child Abuse in Nationally Representative American Sample, *Child Abuse and Neglect* U.S. Government Publication Report printed in 3, 1979.
27. Mary Otto "Child Abuse: Group Treatment for Parents," *Personnel and Guidance Journal* (February 1984): 336.
28. As quoted in Magnuson, "Child Abuse," 21.
29. Judy Strommen, Child Protection, Dakota County, Minnesota. Talk given to Parish Education Directors, Minneapolis, Minnesota, November, 1982.
30. Otto, "Child Abuse," 338.
31. Eli Rubenstein, "Television and Behavior," *American Psychologist*, July 1983, 820–821.
32. Matthew J. Fleischman, Arthur M. Horne, and Judy L. Arthur, *Troubled Families* (Champaign: Research Press, 1983).
33. Quoted from disciplinary procedures presented in *Troubled Families* by Fleischman, Horne and Arthur, 1983.

Bibliography

Allen, Alec J. and Martin L. Mitchell. "Helping the Community: an Untapped Resource for Troubled Children." *The Pointer* (Fall 1982): 1–4.

Andersen, Kurt. "Private Violence," *Time* 122 (September 5, 1983): 18–19.

Armelagos, George. "Culturally Speaking: A Tasty Tale." *Weight Watchers Magazine* 14 (February 1981): 9.

Associated Press. "Boys, 11, Who Aids Street People is Honored by Philadelphia Council" *Minneapolis Star and Tribune*, March 9, 1983.

Augsburger, David. *When Caring is Not Enough*. Scottdale: Herald Press, 1983.

Ausubel, David P., Raymond Montemayor, and Pergrouhi Svajian. *Theory and Problems of Adolescent Development*. 2d ed. New York: Grune and Stratton, 1977.

Baruch, Dorothy W. *How to Live With Your Teenager*. New York: McGraw Hill, 1953.

Baumrind, Diana, "Authoritarian vs. Authoritative Parental Control." *Adolescence* 3 (Fall 1968): 255–270.

Benson, Peter L. Highlights from 1983 Colorado Survey on Drug Use and Drug-Related Attitudes, a project conducted by Search Institute, Minneapolis, in cooperation with KRHA-TV, Colorado Department of Education. Research Report.

Benson, Peter L. Report on Drug Use and Drug-Related Attitudes. State of Minnesota. Minneapolis: Search Institute, October 25, 1983.

Benson, Peter L. and Dorothy L. Williams. *Religion on Capitol Hill: Myths and Realities*. New York: Harper & Row, 1982.

Benson, Peter L. et al. Young Adolescents and their Parents. Minneapolis: Search Institute, 1984.

Better Homes and Gardens, eds. *What's Happening to American Families?* Los Angeles: Meredith Corp., 1983.

Blume, Sheila. "Prevention of Fetal Alcohol Syndrome." Paper prepared for National Council on Alcoholism, Washington, D.C., June 1983.

Bordow, Joan. *The Ultimate Loss*. New York: Beaufort Books, 1982.

Brekke, Milo L., Merton P. Strommen, and Dorothy L. Williams. *Ten Faces of Ministry*. Minneapolis: Augsburg Publishing, 1979.

Brendtro, Larry K. and Arlin Ness. *Re-Educating Troubled Youth*. New York: Aldine Publishing, 1983.

Brendtro, Larry K., and Abraham W. Nicolaou. "Hooked on Helping." *Synergist* 10 (Winter 1982): 38–41.

Briggs, Dorothy Corkille. *Your Child's Self-Esteem*. New York: Doubleday, 1975.

Buntman, Peter H. and Eleanor M. Saris. *How to Live With Your Teenager*. Pasadena, California: Birch Tree Press, 1977.

Bustonoby, Andre. *The Readymade Family*. Grand Rapids: Zondervan Publishing, 1982.

Capuzzi, Dave and Lindy Low LeCog. "Social and Personal Determinants of Adolescent Use and Abuse of Alcohol and Marijuana." *Personnel and Guidance Journal* 62 (December 1983): 199–205.

Chilman, Catherine. "Coital Behaviors of Adolescents in the U.S." Paper prepared for meeting of The American Psychological Association, 1983.

Chilman, Catherine. "Parent Satisfactions, Concerns, and Goals for Their Children." *Family Relations* 29 (1980): 339–345.

Collins, Gary. *How to Be a People Helper*. Ventura: Vision House, 1976.

Collins, Gary, ed. *Living and Growing Together*. Waco: Word Books, 1976.

Cunningham, Susan. "Abused Children are More Likely to Become Teenaged Criminals." *APA Monitor* (December 1983): 26, 27.

Curran, Dolores. *Traits of a Healthy Family*. Minneapolis: Winston Press, 1983. Discussing in particular fifteen traits commonly found in healthy families by those who work with them, this book is easy to read and full of practical insights and personal illustrations on what constitutes a strong, vibrant family.

Dickson, Charles. "Parents Can Help Their Children Learn to Live." *Lutheran Standard* 22 (February 1983): 10.

Dobson, James C. *Hide or Seek*. Old Tappan, New Jersey: Fleming H. Revel Company, 1974.

Dobson, James C. *Straight Talk to Men and Their Wives*. Waco: Word Books, 1980.

Donnelly, Katharine Fair. *Recovering from the Loss of a Child*. New York: Macmillan, 1982.

Duvall, Evelyn Millis. *Faith in Families*. New York: Rand McNally, 1970.

Edwards, Virginia. "Teenage Drinking." *Scouting* (October 1982), 76–80.

Elliott, David J. and Norbert Johnson. "Fetal Alcohol Syndrome: Implications and Counseling Considerations." *Personnel and Guidance Journal* 62 (October 1983): 67–69.

Fleischman, Matthew J., Arthur M. Horne, and Judy L. Arthur, *Troubled Families*. Champaign: Research Press, 1983.

Gallup, George, and David Poling. *The Search for America's Faith*. Nashville: Abingdon Press, 1980.

Gelles, Richard J. *Family Violence*. Vol. 4, Sage Library of Social Research. Beverly Hills: Sage Publications, 1979.

Gilligan, Carol. *In a Different Voice*. Cambridge: Harvard University Press, 1982.

Ginott, Haim G. *Between Parent & Child*. New York: Avon Books, 1969.

Ginott, Haim G. *Between Parent & Teenager*. New York: Avon Books, 1969.

Gordon, Sol and Judith Gordon. *Raising a Child Conservatively in a Sexually Permissive World*. New York: Simon and Schuster, 1983.

Greenfield, Guy. *The Wounded Parent*. Grand Rapids: Baker House, 1982. Written by parents whose children (teenagers and young adults) have rejected the spiritual values of their parents, this book attempts to provide both immediate and long-range help. It suggests ways in which parents might rebuild the channels of communication with their children and construct new relationships with them after the "break" has occurred.

Guidibaldi, John. "The Impact of Parental Divorce on Children." Report of the National Association of School Psychologists (NASP) Study. 1983.

Haber, Russell H. "The Family Dance Around Drug Abuse." *Personnel and Guidance Journal* (March 1983): 428–430.

Harris, Amy. "He Doesn't Believe in Handicaps." *Faith at Work* 91 (October 1978): 20-21, 51, 63.

Hazelden Foundation. *Never Too Early, Never Too Late*. Center City, MN: Hazelden Educational Materials, 1983.

Hill, John P. *Understanding Early Adolescence: A Framework*. Carrboro: Center for Early Adolescence, University of North Carolina, 1980.

Johnson, Paul. *Psychology of Religion*. Nashville: Abingdon Press, 1959.

Jolliff, David. "The Effects of Parental Remarriage on the Development of the Young Child." *Early Child Development and Care*, 13 (1984): 321–334.

Kamerman, Sheila B., and Cheryl D. Hayes, eds. *Families that Work: Children in a Changing World*. Washington, D.C.: National Academy Press, 1982.

Keith-Lucas, Alan. *The Client's Religion and Your Own Beliefs in the Helping Process: A Guide for Believers and Non-Believers*. Group

` Child Care Consultant Services, Chapel Hill, NC, 1983.

Kohlberg, Lawrence. "Continuities and Discontinuities in Childhood and Adult Moral Development Revisited." *Collected Papers on MoralDevelopment and Moral Education.* Cambridge, Harvard University Press, 1973.

Kohlberg, Lawrence. *The Philosophy of Moral Development. Vol. 1 of Essays on Moral Development.* San Francisco: Harper & Row, 1981.

Lagaard, Nora G. and Robert P. Goelz. "The Best-Kept Secret: Sexual Abuse." *Campfire Leadership Magazine* (October–December 1983): 5–7.

Landorf, Joyce. *Change Points.* Old Tappan, New Jersey: Fleming H. Revell Company, 1981.

Larson, Roland and Doris Larson. *I Need to Have You Know Me.* Minneapolis: Winston Press, 1979. This workbook, containing fifty exercises for couples to complete together and alone, is an excellent book for couples who want to take a look at their relationship. Participants evaluate their communication skills, measure their relational progress, and discover ways to enrich their marriage relationship.

Laubach, Frank C. *Prayer.* New York: Fleming H. Revell Company, 1946.

Lerman, Saf. *Parent Awareness.* Minneapolis: Winston Press, 1980.

LeShan, Eda. *The Wonderful Crisis of Middle Age.* New York: McKay Publishing Company, 1973.

Lewis, C. S. *The Abolition of Man.* New York: Macmillan, 1947.

Lewis, Margie M. *The Hurting Parent.* Grand Rapids: Zondervan Publishing House, 1980.

Lipuma, Ann. "The Forgotten Child." *McCall's* 110 (September 1983): 32.

Little, Sara. *To Set One's Heart.* Atlanta: John Knox Press, 1983.

Mace, David. "Love, Anger and Intimacy." *Light* (April-May 1980): 2.

McGinnis, Alan Loy. *Friendship Factor.* Minneapolis: Augsburg Publishing, 1970.

Magnuson, Ed. "Child Abuse: The Ultimate Betrayal." *Time,* 122 (September 5, 1983): 20–22.

Mains, Karen Burton. *Open Heart, Open Home.* Waco: Word Books, 1971.

Markun, Patricia Maloney. *Parenting.* Washington, D.C.: Association for Childhood Education, 1973.

Marshall, Ray. "Youth Employment/Unemployment/Underemployment: A Continuing Dilemma." St. Paul: Center for Youth Development and Research, 1983.

Mervis, Jeffrey. "Adolescent Behavior: What We Think We Know." *APA Monitor* (April 1984): 24, 25.

Naisbitt, John. *Megatrends: Ten New Directions Transforming Our Lives.* New York: Warner Books, 1982.

Napier, Augustus Y., and Carl A. Whitaker. *The Family Crucible.* New York: Bantam Books, 1978. In a fictional account of a family in therapy, Napier shows how each member of the family is involved when even one member is troubled, and how the trouble often stems from the relationship between father and mother.

Narramore, Bruce. *Why Children Misbehave.* Grand Rapids: Zondervan, 1980.

Nicholi, Armand M. "The Nontherapeutic Use of Psychoactive Drugs: A Modern Epidemic." *New England Journal of Medicine* 308 (April 1973): 925–933.

Norman, Jane and Myron Harris. *The Private Life of the American Teenager.* New York: Rawson, Wade Publishers, 1981.

Oates, Wayne E. *Pastoral Counseling in Grief and Separation.* Philadelphia: Fortress Press, 1976.

Offer, Daniel, Eric Ostrov, and I. Kenneth Howard. *The Adolescent: A Psychological Self-Portrait.* New York: Basic Books, 1981.

Olson, David H., and Hamilton I. McCubbin. *Families: What Makes Them Work.* Beverly Hills: Sage Publications, 1983.

Otto, Luther B. *How to Help Your Child Choose A Career.* New York: M. Evans and Company, 1984.

Otto, Mary L. "Child Abuse: Group Treatment for Parents." *Personnel and Guidance Journal* 62 (February 1984): 336–338.

Pasley, Kay, and Viktor Gecas. "Stresses and Satisfactions of the Parental Role." *Personnel and Guidance Journal* 62 (March 1984): 400–404.

Pogrebin, Letty Cottin. *Family Politics.* New York: McGraw-Hill, 1983.

Ray, Lynda Y. and Norbert Johnson. "Adolescent Suicide." *Personnel and Guidance Journal* 62 (November 1983): 132–133.

Reineke, Robert. Report to the National Board of American Luthern Church Women on a Study of Attitudes of Women. Minneapolis: Search Institute, 1981.

Religion in America. Princeton: Princeton Religion Research Center, and Gallup Organization, 1981.

Religious Community and Chemical Health. Minneapolis: Minnesota Prevention Resource Center, 1983 Report.

Report on 1983 Minnesota Survey on Drug Use and Drug-Related Attitudes. Minneapolis: Search Institute, 1983.

Reuss, Carl F. *Profiles of Lutherans: An Interpretive Summary of an Inter-Lutheran Research Project.* Minneapolis: Augsburg Publishing, 1983.

Rice, Wayne. *Junior High Ministry.* Grand Rapids, MI: Zondervan, 1978. An honest and compassionate presentation of the difficulties of working with youth between the ages of twelve and fifteen, this book is as valuable for the parent as for the church youth worker.

Richards, Lawrence. "The Teacher as Interpreter of the Bible." *Religious Education* (September 1982): 515–516.

Ridenour, Fritz. *What Teenagers Wish Their Parents Knew About Kids.* Waco: Word Books, 1982. Informally, humorously written, this book helps parents to bridge the gap between their own thinking and that of their teenager. This author has used illustrations freely from his own family, not hesitating to show both the ups and downs of family life. Discussion questions follow each chapter.

Rosenthal, David. "The Year in the Movies." *Rolling Stone Yearbook* 25 (1983).

Rubenstein, Eli. "Television and Behavior: Research Conclusions of the 1982 NIMH Report and Their Policy Implications." *American Psychologist* (July 1983): 820–825.

Search Institute. *Young Adolescents and Their Parents Project Report.* Minneapolis: Search Institute, 1984.

Schuller, David S., Merton P. Strommen, et al. *Ministry in America.* San Francisco: Harper & Row, 1980.

Schuller, Robert H. *Self-Esteem: The New Reformation.* Waco: Word Books, 1982.

Shapiro, Philip. "A Treatment and Management Model." *Coping Magazine* (July 1983): 27–30.

Shedd, Charlie. *Promises to Peter.* Waco: Word Books, 1970.

Sheehy, Gail. "The Crisis Couples Face at 40." McCalls 103 (May 1976): 107.

Smith, Barbara. "Adolescent and Parent: Interaction Between Developmental Stages." *Quarterly Focus*, Center for Youth Development and Research (1976).

Straus, Murray. Family Patterns and Child Abuse in Nationally Representative American Sample. U.S. Government Publication Report reprinted in *Child Abuse and Neglect* 3, 1979.

Stromberg, Lee J. "Meet Hamilton McCubbin." *Correspondent* no. 520 (Winter 1983): 8, 9.

Strommen, Merton P. *A Call to Ministry.* Summary of 1981 Study Involving American Lutheran Church Women. Minneapolis: American Lutheran Church Women 1981. This book makes use of research into high school age adolescents, revealing the cries of self-hatred, being a psychological orphan, social protests, prejudice, and joyous faith. The book, useful for personal reading or group discussion, has been effective in training youth leaders.

Strommen, Merton P. *Five Cries of Youth.* New York: Harper & Row, 1974.

Strommen, Merton P., Milo L. Brekke, et al. *A Study of Generations.*

Minneapolis: Augsburg Publishing, 1972.

Study of Work-Family Family Issues in Minnesota: An Educational Resource for the Business Community. Minnesota Department of Education, 1983.

Swanson, Steve. "Teen suicide." *Lutheran Standard* 24 (February 3, 1984): 10–12.

Teenage Birth Rate Fact Sheet. Facts on Women Workers. U.S. Department of Labor, Office of the Secretary, Women's Bureau, 1982.

Tournier, Paul. *To Understand Each Other.* Richmond, Virginia: John Knox Press, 1962.

Varenhorst, Barbara B. *Real Friends: Becoming the Friend You'd Like to Have.* San Francisco: Harper & Row, 1983. Written by a nationally recognized authority on peer counseling, this heartwarming book shows how to become a friend. Parents will learn much about understanding and developing relationships with their own children through reading it, as well as learn a great deal about themselves. Adolescents will welcome it, since "how to make and keep friends" is a major concern of adolescence. It is written for young people in language they understand, and makes effective use of illustrations.

Walters, Richard P. *How to Be a Friend.* Ventura: Regal Books, 1981.

Watts, Judy Humphrey and Susan Lapinsky. "When Divorce Divides a Family." *Redbook* (April 1983): 67–69.

Weinstein, Grace W. "Should Teenagers Work?" *McCall's* (June 1983): 54–55.

Welter, Paul. *How to Help a Friend.* Wheaton, Illinois: Tyndale Press House Press, 1978.

Wenz, F. "Self-injury, Behavior, Economic Status and the Family Anomie Syndrome Among Adolescents." *Adolescence* 14, 387–397.

Wetzel, Laura and Mary Anne Ross. "Psychological and Social Ramifications of Battery: Observations Leading to a Counseling Methodology for Victims of Domestic Abuse." *Personnel and Guidance Journal* (March 1983), pp. 423–427.

Wilt, Joy. *Raising Your Children Toward Emotional and Spiritual Maturity.* Waco: Word Books, 1977.

Wrenn, C. Gilbert. *The World of the Contemporary Counselor.* Boston: Houghton-Mifflin Company, 1973.

Wynne, Edward A. "Long-Term Trends Among Young Americans in Self- and Other Destructive Conduct." Paper presented at 1983 annual meeting of American Education Association, College of Education, Chicago.

"Youth and the Family." Center for Youth Development and Research, University of Minnesota Seminar Series #7 (September 1976).

Index

A TALE of TWO
CASTLES

GAIL CARSON LEVINE

A TALE of TWO

CASTLES

HARPER

An Imprint of HarperCollins*Publishers*

Thanks to all the creative writers who posted title
possibilities to my blog. Special thanks to
April Jo Ann Mack for the actual, final, *ta da!* title.
Thanks to Renée Cafiero for the many fixes to many books.
Such security you give me!
And thanks to David Macauley
for his crystal clear book *Castles*

A Tale of Two Castles
Copyright © 2011 by Gail Carson Levine
All rights reserved. Printed in the United States of America.
No part of this book may be used or reproduced in any manner whatsoever
without written permission except in the case of brief quotations embodied in
critical articles and reviews. For information address HarperCollins Children's
Books, a division of HarperCollins Publishers, 10 East 53rd Street, New York,
NY 10022.
www.harpercollinschildrens.com

Library of Congress Cataloging-in-Publication Data
Levine, Gail Carson.
  A tale of Two Castles / Gail Carson Levine. — 1st ed.
    p. cm.
  Summary: Twelve-year-old Elodie journeys to Two Castles in hopes of
studying acting but instead becomes apprentice to a dragon, who teaches her
to be observant and use reasoning, thus helping her to uncover who is
plotting against the ogre Count Jonty Um.
  ISBN 978-0-06-122965-7 (trade bdg.)
  ISBN 978-0-06-122966-4 (lib. bdg.)
  [1. Apprentices—Fiction. 2. Dragons—Fiction. 3. Reasoning—Fiction.
4. Kings, queens, rulers, etc.—Fiction. 5. Mystery and detective stories.
6. Fantasy.] I. Title.
PZ7.L578345Tal 2011
[Fic]—dc22   2010027756
                                                                    CIP
                                                                    AC

Typography by Andrea Vandergrift
11 12 13 14 15   LP/RRDB   10 9 8 7 6 5 4 3 2 1
❖
First Edition

To David, to whom I cannot dedicate too many books

mansions

Jonty Um's castle

Owe Street

town wall

menagerie

ogre's farm fields

Owe Street

south gate

N

king's castle

KINGDOM OF LEPAI

lair

...reet

...ue

CHAPTER ONE

other wiped her eyes on her sleeve and held me tight. I wept onto her shoulder. She released me while I went on weeping. A tear slipped into the strait through a crack in the wooden dock. Salt water to salt water, a drop of me in the brine that would separate me from home.

Father's eyes were red. He pulled me into a hug, too. Albin stood to the side a few feet and blew his nose with a *honk*. He could blow his nose a dozen ways. A honk was the saddest.

The master of the cog called from the gangplank, "The tide won't wait."

I shouldered my satchel.

Mother began, "Lodie—"

"*Elodie*," I said, brushing away tears. "My whole name."

"Elodie," she said, "don't correct your elders. Keep your thoughts private. You are mistaken as often—"

"—as anyone," I said.

"Elodie . . . ," Father said, sounding nasal, "stay clear of the crafty dragons and the shape-shifting ogres." He took an uneven breath. "Don't befriend them! They won't bother you if you—"

"—don't bother them," I said, glancing at Albin, who shrugged. He was the only one of us who'd ever been in the company of an ogre or a dragon. Soon I would be near both. At least one of each lived in the town of Two Castles. The castle that wasn't the king's belonged to an ogre.

"Don't finish your elders' sentences, Lodie," Mother said.

"*Elodie*." I wondered if Father's adage was true. Maybe ogres and dragons bothered you *especially* if you didn't bother them. I would be glad to meet either one—if I had a quick means of escape.

Albin said, "Remember, Elodie: If you have to speak to a dragon, call it *IT*, never *him* or *her* or *he* or *she*."

I nodded. Only a dragon knows ITs gender.

Mother bent so her face was level with mine. "Worse than ogres or dragons . . . beware the whited sepulcher."

The whited sepulcher was Mother's great worry. I wanted to soothe her, but her instruction seemed impossible to

follow. A sepulcher is a tomb. A whited sepulcher is someone who seems good but is, in truth, evil. How would I
know?

"The geese"—Mother straightened, and her voice
caught— "will look for you tomorrow."

The geese! My tears flowed again. I hated the geese, but
I would miss them.

Mother flicked a gull's feather off my shoulder. "You're
but a baby!"

I went to Albin and hugged him, too. He whispered
into my hair, "Be what you must be."

The master of the cog roared, "We're off!"

I ran, leaped over a coil of rope, caught my foot, and went
sprawling. Lambs and calves! Behind me, Mother cried out.
I scrambled up, dusty but unharmed. I laughed through my
tears and raced up the plank. A seaman drew it in.

The sail, decorated with the faded image of a winged
fish, bellied in the breeze. We skimmed away from the
dock. If fate was kind, in ten years I would see my parents
and Albin again. If fate was cruel, never.

As they shrank, Mother losing her tallness, Father his
girth, Albin his long beard, I waved. They waved back and
didn't stop. The last I could make out of them, they were
still waving.

The island of Lahnt diminished, too. For the first time it
seemed precious, with its wooded slopes and snowy peaks,

the highest wreathed in clouds. I wished I could pick out Dair Mountain, where our Potluck Farm perched.

Farewell to my homeland. Farewell to my childhood.

Mother and Father's instructions were to apprentice myself to a weaver, but I would not. *Mansioner*. I mouthed the word into the wind, the word that held my future. *Mansioner*. Actor. Mansioner of myth and fable. Mother and Father would understand once I found a master or mistress to serve and could join the guild someday.

Leaning into the ship's bulwarks, I felt the purse, hidden under my apron, which held my little knife, a lock of hair from one of Albin's mansioning wigs, a pretty pink stone, a perfect shell from the beach this morning, and a single copper, which Father judged enough to feed me until I became apprenticed. Unless the winds blew against us, we would reach Two Castles, capital of the kingdom of Lepai, in two or three days, in time for Guild Week, when masters took on new apprentices. I might see the king or the ogre, if one of them came through town, but I was unlikely to enter either castle.

I had no desire to see King Grenville III, who liked war and taxes so much that his subjects called him Greedy Grenny. Lepai was a small kingdom, but bigger by half than when he'd mounted the throne—and so were our taxes bigger by half, or so Mother said. The king was believed to have his combative eye on Tair, Lahnt's

4

neighbor across the wide side of the strait.

Queen Sofie had died a decade ago, but I did hope to see the king's daughter, Princess Renn, who was rumored to be somehow peculiar. A mansioner is interested in peculiarity.

And a mansioner observes. I turned away from home. To my left, three rowers toiled on a single oar. The one in the center called, "Pu-u-u-ll," with each stroke. I heard his mate across the deck call the same. Father had told me the oars were for steering and the sail for speed. The deck between me and the far bulwark teemed with seamen, passengers, a donkey, and two cows.

A seaman climbed the mast. The cog master pushed his way between an elderly goodman and his goodwife and elbowed the cows until they let him pass. He disappeared down the stairs to the hold, where the cargo was stored. I would remember his swagger, the way he rolled his shoulders, and how widely he stepped.

The deck tilted into a swell. I felt a chill, although the air was warm for mid-October.

"Go, honey, move. Listen to Dess. Listen, honey, honey." A small man, thin but for fleshy cheeks and a double chin, the owner of the donkey and the cows, coaxed his animals into a space between the bulwark and the stairs to the rear upper deck. He carried a covered basket in his right hand, heavy, because his shoulder sagged. "Come, honey."

His speech reminded me of Father with our animals

at home. *Good, Vashie,* he'd tell our cow, *Good girl, what a good girl.* Perhaps if I'd repeated myself with the geese, they'd have liked me better.

The elderly goodwife opened her sack and removed a cloak, which she spread on the deck. Holding her husband's hand, she lowered herself and sat. He sat at her side on the cloak. The other passengers also began to mark out their plots of deck, their tiny homesteads.

I wasn't sure yet where I wanted my place to be. Near the elderly couple, who might have tales to tell?

Not far from them, a family established their claim. To my surprise, the daughter wore a cap. In Lahnt women wore caps, but not girls, except for warmth in winter. Her kirtle and her mother's weren't as full as mine, but their sleeves hung down as far as their knuckles, and their skirt hems half covered their shoes, which had pointed toes, unlike my rounded ones.

The cog dropped into a slough in the sea, and my stomach dropped with it. We rose again, but my belly liked that no better. I leaned against the bulwark for better balance.

My mouth filled with saliva. I swallowed again and again. Nothing in the world was still, not the racing clouds nor the rippling sail nor the pitching ship.

The son in the family pointed at me and cried, "Her face is green wax!"

My stomach surged into my throat. I turned and heaved

my breakfast over the side. Even after the food was gone, my stomach continued to rise and sink.

Next to me, a fellow passenger whimpered and groaned.

I stared down at the foamy water churning by, sicker than I had ever been. Still, the mansioner in me was in glory. Lambs and calves! I would remember how it was to feel so foul. I wondered if I could transform my face to green wax without paint, just by memory.

The cog rose higher than it had so far and fell farther. I vomited bile and then gasped for breath. The bulwark railing pressed into my sorry stomach.

The person at my side panted out, "Raise your head. Look at the horizon."

My head seemed in the only reasonable position, but I lifted it. The island of Lahnt had vanished. The horizon was splendidly flat and still. My insides continued bobbing, but less.

"Here." A hand touched mine on the railing. "Peppermint. Suck on it."

The leaf was fresh, not dried, and the clean taste helped. "Thank you, mistress." My eyes feared to let go of the horizon, so I couldn't see my benefactress. Her voice was musical, although not young. She might be the old goodwife.

"I've crossed many times and always begun by being sick." Her voice lilted in amusement. She seemed to have found respite enough from her suffering to speak more than a few words. "I've exhausted my goodman's sympathy." She sighed. "I still hope to become a good sailor someday. You are young to travel alone."

Mother and Father didn't have passage money for more than me. "Not so young, mistress." Here I was, contradicting my elders again. "I am fourteen." Contradicting and lying.

"Ah."

I was tall enough for fourteen, although perhaps not curvy enough. I risked a sideways peek to see if she believed me, but she still faced the horizon and didn't meet my eyes. I took in her profile: long forehead, knob of a nose, weathered skin, deep lines around her mouth, gray wisps escaping her hood, a few hairs sprouting from her chin—a likeable, honest face.

"Conversation keeps the mind off the belly," she said, and I saw a gap in her upper teeth.

The ship dropped. I felt myself go greener. My eyes snapped back to the horizon.

"We will be visiting our children and their children in Two Castles. Why do you cross?"

She was as nosy as I was! "I seek an apprenticeship as"—I put force into my hoarse, seasick voice—"a mansioner."

"Ah," she said again. "Your parents sent you off to be a mansioner."

I knew she didn't believe me now. "To be a weaver," I

admitted. "Lambs and calves!" Oh, I didn't mean to use the farm expression. "To stay indoors, to repeat a task endlessly, to squint in lamplight . . . ," I burst out. "It is against my nature!"

"To have your hands seize up before you're old," the goodwife said with feeling, "your shoulders blaze with pain, your feet spread. Be not a weaver nor a spinner!"

Contrarily, I found myself defending Father's wishes for me. "Weaving is honest, steady work, mistress." I laughed at myself. "But I won't be a weaver."

The boat dipped sideways. My stomach emptied itself of nothing.

She gave me another mint leaf. "Why a mansioner?"

"I love spectacles and stories." Mansioning had been my ambition since I was seven and a caravan of mansions came to our country market.

Then, when I was nine, Albin left his mansioning troupe and came to live with us and help Father farm. He passed his spare time telling me mansioners' tales and showing me how to act them out. He said I had promise.

"I love theater, too," the goodwife said, "but I never dreamed of being a mansioner."

"I like to be other people, mistress." Lowering my pitch and adding a quiver, I said, "I can mimic a little." I went back to my true voice. "That's not right." I hadn't caught her tone.

9

She chuckled. "If you were trying to be me, you were on the right path. How long an apprenticeship will you serve?"

Masters were paid five silver coins to teach an apprentice for five years, three silvers for seven years. The apprentice labored for no pay during that term and learned a trade.

"Ten years, mistress." Ten-year apprenticeships cost nothing. Our family was too poor to buy me a place.

The cog dipped lower than ever. I sucked hard on the mint.

"My dear." She touched my arm. "I'm sorry."

"No need for sorrow. I'll know my craft well by the time I'm twenty-two . . . I mean, twenty-four."

"Not that. In June the guilds abolished ten-year apprenticeships. Now everyone must pay to learn a trade."

I turned to her. Her face was serious. It was true.

The boat pitched, but my stomach steadied while a rock formed there.

CHAPTER TWO

"hat will you do?" the goodwife asked.

"I will think of something." I sounded dignified. Dignity had always eluded me before. I excused myself from the goodwife's company and found a spot on the deck closer to the cows than to the human passengers. My curiosity about them had faded. I removed my cloak from my satchel, spread it out, and sat.

If our farm weren't so out of the way, we'd have learned the apprenticeship rules had changed and I would still be home. I'd probably have stayed on Lahnt forever.

Word might reach Mother and Father in a few months or a few years. When they found out, they would be wild with worry.

I hadn't enough money for passage back, nor did I want

to return. I would send word as soon as I was settled. No matter what, I would still be a mansioner.

Perhaps a mansioner master or mistress would take me as a fifteen-year apprentice. No one but me would give free labor for fifteen years. Who could say no?

My mood improved. Curiosity returned, and I watched the people on deck. The rowers rested their oars when the cog master's attention was elsewhere. The oddly clothed mother and daughter were squabbling. The goodwife had recovered from her nausea and joined her husband. I liked best to watch the two of them. Sometimes she leaned into his shoulder, and he encircled her with his arm. Her expression showed peace, eagerness, and patience combined. If I were ever to play a wife, I would remember this goodwife's face.

Night came. I curled up, hugged my satchel close, and wished desperately for home. But why wish? I mansioned myself there, under my woolen blanket in my pallet bed on a floor that didn't roll, with Albin only a few feet away and Mother and Father in their sleeping loft over my head. Yes, that was their bed groaning, not the mast.

Soon I was asleep. In the morning I felt myself a seasoned mariner.

At intervals the animal owner walked his beasts around the deck. "Come with Dess," he'd say in his sweet voice. "In Two Castles Dess will buy you fine hay, feed you fine grass. How happy you will be."

I decided that he and the goodwife were the most worthy passengers on the cog.

Master Dess's heavy basket turned out to contain kittens. He'd reach in for one at a time, stroke it from head to tail, and speak softly to it. Early in the afternoon of the second day, when even the gentle breeze died away, the cog master let Master Dess release them all.

The seven kittens, each striped black and white, burst out to chase one another between legs, around the mast, up and down the deck. A kitten played with the end of a coil of rope, batting it to and fro. The tiniest one climbed the rigging to the top of the mast and perched there for half an hour, lord of the sea. My heart rose into my throat to see it, so tiny and so high.

On its way down, it lost its balance and hung upside down. Frantically I looked around for something to help it with—a pole, anything. No one else was watching, except Master Dess and the goodwife, whose hands were pressed to her chest.

An oar might reach the kitten. I rushed toward the rowers just as the kitten scrambled upright and minced down the mast with a satisfied air. I returned to my cloak. Soon after, Master Dess collected that kitten and its mates.

When they were all in their basket, the goodwife came to me, bearing a small package wrapped in rough hemp. I jumped up.

"May I sit with you?"

I made room for her and she sat, tucking her legs under her. She placed the package in her lap.

What a pleasure to have her company!

"May I know your name, dear?"

I could think of no harm in telling her. "Lodie. I mean, Elodie."

"And I am Goodwife Celeste. My goodman is Twah."

"Pleased to meet you." I rummaged in my satchel. One must show hospitality to a visitor, even a visitor to a cloak on the deck of a cog.

She was saying, "You and I both feared for that brave kitten." She paused, then added, "Have you heard of the cats of Two Castles?"

I shook my head, while drawing bread and cheese and a pear out of my satchel. With the little knife from my purse, I cut her chunks of the bread and cheese and half the pear.

"Thank you." She tasted. "Excellent goat cheese." She unwrapped her own package.

"Cats in Two Castles?" I said to remind her.

"The townspeople believe cats protect them from the ogre. There are many."

"Many cats or ogres?" How could a cat save anyone from an ogre?

She laughed. "Cats." Her package held bread and cheese, too, and a handful of radishes.

14

We traded slices and chunks, observing custom, according to the saying, *Share well, fare well. Share ill, fare ill.*

Goodwife Celeste's cheese wasn't as tasty as mine, but the bread was softer, baker's bread. I wondered where my future meals would come from, once my food and my single copper ran out.

Goodwife Celeste returned to telling me about cats. "You know that ogres shift shape sometimes?"

"Yes."

"Cats know they do, too. The cats sense that an ogre can become a fox or a wolf, but they're not afraid."

Our cat at home, Belliss, who weighed less than a pail of milk, feared nothing.

"They're aware that an ogre can also turn into a mouse." She finished eating. "More?" She held out her food.

"No, thank you." I offered her more of mine, too, and she said no.

As I wrapped my food and she wrapped hers, her sleeve slid back. A bracelet of twine circled her left wrist. Were twine bracelets the fashion in Two Castles? She probably wouldn't have minded if I'd asked, but I didn't want to reveal my ignorance.

"Can an ogre shift into any kind of animal?" I said. "A spider or an elephant?"

"I believe so."

"Can an ogre shift into a human?"

15

Her eyebrows went up. "I doubt it." She returned to the subject of cats. "A cat will stare at an ogre and wish him—*will* him—to become a mouse. They say one cat isn't enough, but several yearning at him, and the ogre can't resist."

I pitied the ogre. "Is that true?"

"Many believe it. What's more, people train their cats. They don't train them to try to make an ogre become a mouse. It is in the cats' nature to do that, and the ogre must cooperate by giving in. But folks train cats to perform tricks and to stalk anything, including an ogre. Some make a living at cat teaching. With the flick of a wrist . . ."

She showed me, and I imitated her—nothing to it.

"With this gesture, anyone can set a cat to stalking."

"If there were no cats, what would the ogre do?"

"Nothing, perhaps. Or dine on townsfolk."

My stomach fluttered. "Does he live alone, or are there more ogres in his castle?"

"Alone with his servants. Count Jonty Um is the only ogre in Lepai. Likely there are others in other lands."

"He's a count?" You couldn't be a count unless a king made you one or made one of your ancestors one.

"A count."

"What happened to the rest of the ogres in Lepai?"

She turned her hand palm up. "I don't know. They may have become mice and been eaten. And ogres sicken and die, just as people do."

16

How lonely I would be if I were the only human. "Mistress? What about dragons? Are there many? Are any of them noble?"

"Just one in Two Castles, and IT is a commoner. Dragons don't generally dwell near one another." She straightened her left leg. "My old bones don't like anything hard."

I wished I had a cushion for her. She was so nice. I thought of Mother's warning, but Goodwife Celeste couldn't be a whited sepulcher. We had been together all this while, and she had done nothing to raise my suspicions.

"Beyond Two Castles," she continued, "Lepai has a few dozen dragons, here and there."

"Do people protect themselves from the dragon, too? Not with cats, with something else?"

"No. Everyone is used to IT. IT's lived in the town since IT was hatched a hundred years ago."

"So old?"

"IT is in ITs prime."

We fell silent. I leaned back on my arms and looked up at the blue sky. Summer weather in October. No clouds, only a breath of a breeze. How safe I felt, like a twig floating in a quiet pond.

Goodwife Celeste picked shreds of cheese and bread crumbs off her lap in a housewifely way. She walked to the bulwark, tossed them over, and returned to me. Back at my cloak, she knelt. "Crossing is a holiday. For a few days we're as safe as the kittens in their basket." She gestured at the cog around us.

I had been thinking exactly the same thought!

"I'm sorry I won't be able to help you in Two Castles."

That startled me. I hadn't thought of asking for aid.

Was she telling me in a roundabout fashion of her own troubles? Were she and her goodman too poor to feed themselves, or were they in some other sort of difficulty?

She put a gentle hand under my chin. "You have a determined face. Nothing will easily best you." She stood. "My goodman may well be wondering what we had to gossip about for so long." She left me.

That night, when I curled up on the deck, worries came and refused to be pretended away. The mansioners would not take me. I would starve. In the winter I would freeze, fall ill, die. Mother and Father would never know what had become of me.

CHAPTER THREE

he weather remained uncommonly warm. The cog master complained about the still air and our slow progress. I feared we would arrive after Guild Week, and then what would I do?

We'd set out on a Sunday, the only day the cog left Lahnt. Masters in Two Castles began seeing boys and girls on Monday, and by Friday all the places would be taken.

At noon on Tuesday I lunched on the last pear, the end of my provisions. By nightfall the wind freshened, although the air remained warm. When I awoke the next day, I sensed a change in the motion of the cog. The troughs weren't as deep, the crests not so high. I rushed to the foredeck.

An uneven triangle broke the horizon. Our cog now

sailed amid fishing boats, a whale among minnows.

I folded my cloak and pushed it into my satchel with my spare hose, chemise, and kirtle—my entire wardrobe, except for the clothes I wore and the shoes on my feet. My hand encountered the only other item, a list in Mother's small, neat writing on a sheet of parchment. I took it out.

HALF DOZEN RULES FOR LODIE

1. *Be truthful.*
2. *Act with forethought, not impetuously. Your mother and father depend on your safety.*
3. *Neither stare nor eavesdrop.*
4. *Do not interrupt or contradict your elders or finish their sentences or think you know more than they do.*
5. *Do not befriend anyone until you are certain he or she is worthy of your trust. Beware the whited sepulcher.*
6. *Know always that you have our love.*
7. *Be generous (an extra, generous rule).*

I patted the page seven times before returning it to my satchel.

Half the morning passed as we drew closer to land. From behind, the other passengers pressed against me, as impatient as I. I touched my apron and felt the familiar bulge of my purse. The stink of fish assailed my nose.

I took in the tiers of houses ahead, a few built of stone,

most of wattle and daub—clay and wood. Above town, on the right, a cluster of towers poked the sky. To the left, barely cresting the hilltop, were the tips of more towers, the other castle. Which was king's and which ogre's, I had no idea.

What I sought most I didn't see—the mansioners' wagons or at least the three pennants: the pennant that showed a laughing face; the one with a weeping face; and the one with a hushing face, a finger over the lips. No mansions, but the entire town could not be on view from here.

The cog master shouted instructions to his seamen. Passengers called to people waving from the dock. Someone touched my elbow. I turned.

The goodwife held a bundle of black-and-white fur. "Here. I bought you a kitten. It's good luck to bring a cat to Two Castles."

"Thank you, but—"

"You can leave it on the wharf. No cat starves here."

The kitten was asleep and didn't waken when Goodwife Celeste handed it over. It filled my two hands but weighed almost nothing, its ears huge, its pink nose tiny. I knew from the white left ear that this was the kitten who had climbed the rigging.

"Thank you, mistress."

"You're welcome. I hope to see you in the mansions someday soon."

"Do you know where they are?"

She pointed upward. "Beyond the town. See, there is King Grenville's castle." Her finger moved rightward to the jutting towers. "The mansioners are east of his castle and"—her finger shifted to the left—"east of his menagerie." Left again. "They are northeast of Count Jonty Um's castle, which is farther south but less than a mile from town."

"I see. Thank you."

She smiled and threaded her way back to rejoin her husband.

Farewell, my only friend, my kind friend who cannot help me any longer.

My stomach growled despite the fish stench. The cog bumped against the pier, causing the kitten to waken and squirm in my hands.

"Be still," I whispered. "I'll set you free soon enough."

As if it understood, it quieted and peered out at the world of solid land.

A seaman lowered the gangplank. I hung back and let the other passengers descend first. The girl in the odd apparel and her family were embraced by another family. Travelers were passed from hug to hug. Seamen rushed by me, joking to one another.

If anyone awaited me, this would be less an adventure. I remembered Albin's wisdom: A mansioner is always alone. If a hundred people had come to meet me, I would still be separate.

The goodwife and her goodman set off together into an alley. I wondered why no one had been here to greet them.

The kitten sniffed my wrists. I followed the last passenger and stepped onto the pier. How unaccustomed my legs were to a floor that didn't move. I wondered if seamen ever fell land-sick after weeks at sea.

I set the kitten down between an empty bucket and a mound of fishnet. "Be well. Live a happy cat life." I touched its nose. "Bring me luck."

It mewed briefly, then fell silent. I walked the length of the pier to the wharf. Where the two met, I stopped.

To my left a woman hawked muffins out of a handcart. My mouth watered, but I didn't go to her. I was sure to find better if I waited.

In a doorway a man and a woman sat on stools mending nets. Nearby a fishing boat lay upended, its owner busy applying oakum and pitch.

Stalls lined the wharf and people ambled along, stopping to examine the wares or to buy.

The women were clad as the mother and daughter in the cog had been, in narrow kirtles with long sleeves and long hems and with colored aprons tied round their waists. As at home, the tunics of the men ended just below their knees, revealing a few inches of their breeches. Everyone—men, women, and children—wore hoods or caps that tied under their chins.

I tugged on my sleeves to make them seem longer. I am a mansioner in costume, I told myself, not outlandish, not a bumpkin.

Two dogs chased each other to the edge of the water and back again. On the pier, a plump black cat with a white tail ambled to my kitten and began to lick it all over. Other black-and-white cats sunned themselves here and there on the wharf. If this had been a town for yellow cats, my kitten might have been snubbed.

I heard applause.

Mansioners? Here?

Three young women and four in middle age stood in a loose row on the wharf, backs to me, blocking the reason for their clapping. When I reached them, I saw two black-and-white cats at the feet of a young man perhaps seven or eight years older than I.

Yellow hair flowed from his cap down his sturdy neck. His skin seemed to glow. Large gray eyes, fringed by thick lashes, and curving lips might have made his face feminine but for the strength of his jawline and chin. Powerful arms pulled tight the sleeves of his frayed tunic. His hands and bare feet were long and graceful. The bare feet, the hollows in his cheeks, and his worn tunic bespoke desperate poverty.

Twisted around the fourth finger of his right hand was a ring of twine, knotted in front where the jewel of a silver ring would be. Goodwife Celeste wore a twine

24

bracelet. Was this fashion, or did twine-jewelry wearers belong to some confederacy?

The young man's hands described a circle in the air, and the two cats rolled over. The women clapped as enthusiastically as if he'd stopped the sun. I clapped softly.

"Ooh, Master Thiel. Again, if you please."

His name was Thiel, pronounced *Tee-el.*

He bowed, rewarded each cat with a tidbit, then obliged. The cats obliged, too. We clapped again. I touched the purse at my waist—still in place.

Here was a cat teacher, as Goodwife Celeste had said there would be, although he seemed not to be earning much at it. A wooden bowl on the ground held but four tins.

"Mistresses, here is the cats' newest trick." He raised his hands high above his head. The right-hand cat leaped straight up, like a puppet on a string. The left-hand cat licked its paw.

"Tut, tut." Master Thiel crouched. He rewarded the cat who'd leaped and snapped a finger against the other cat's scalp, chiding it in cat parlance, I supposed. The cat shook its head and became attentive again. This time when the young man raised his hands, both cats jumped.

More tricks followed. The cats waved, shook his hands, and even leaped over sticks held a few inches above the ground.

My stomach rumbled. I wrenched my eyes away. Across

from where I stood, a broad way marched straight uphill. Chiseled into the stone of the corner house was the street name, Daycart Way. This seemed the likeliest route to food and mansioners.

I set out, my satchel slung across my chest. People strolled on my right and left. A boy herded three piglets. Children and cats and dogs chased one another. The dogs came in every size and color, but the cats were always black and white. I watched my feet to avoid the leavings of the animal traffic—not merely dogs, cats, and piglets, but also donkeys and the occasional horse, bearing a burgher or a person of noble rank.

At the first corner, I came upon two more cat teachers, these hardly older than I. They practiced just the rolling-over trick. I wondered if Two Castles boasted a guild of cat teachers. These two might be apprentices and the young man on the wharf a journeyman.

I angled close to the merchants' stalls at the edge of the avenue. If I had been rich, my fortune would soon have been spent. The first table I passed was spread with belt buckles, most iron, but a few brass and one silver, the silver one hammered in the shape of a rose. How Father would cherish such a buckle.

In the next stall a knife-and-scissors sharpener sat at his wheel, waiting for custom. "Sharp scissors and knives!" he cried.

Beyond him a shoemaker shaped leather on a last. Shoes stood in double file up and down the table at his elbow. Mother might express wonder that the natives of Two Castles had such pointy feet.

How I wished they could be here, saying whatever they really would say, wanting whatever they really would want.

In the shoemaker's shop, which opened behind the shoemaker's chair, his goodwife sat on a bench while a boy and a girl near my age stood and addressed her. From the attitudes of the two—leaning forward from their waists—they were vying for an apprenticeship. I supposed both had the necessary silvers.

I heard a voice I knew coming from behind. "Step lively, my honeys, my cows, my donkey. Come with Dess."

Next I passed a table heaped with leather purses and touched the lump in my apron where my linen purse hung. A leather purse never needed darning or leaked its contents. I had double backstitched mine before leaving home.

My feet refused to pass by the next stall, a clothes mender's. On her table were neatly sorted piles of chemises, kirtles, aprons, tunics, breeches, hose, garters, capes, hoods, and caps, all in linen or wool. Of course everything had belonged to someone else, and likely death or poverty had brought the goods here to be repaired and made ready to wear again.

Rich folks' new garments were soft. Poor folks' garments became soft after long use. At the beginning they were stiff enough to stand unaided. My grandmother first wore my chemise, which now slid against my skin as gently as rose petals.

From behind the table, the mending mistress disputed with a goodwife over the price of a cloak. The mending mistress's right shoulder sloped upward. The goodwife had a hairy mole above her upper lip. A cat prowled in and out and around the legs of the table.

An orange kirtle caught my eye, pretty, adorned by three wooden buttons at the neck. I held it up. Narrow with long sleeves. Fashionable. I folded it again. My copper wouldn't be nearly enough.

Closest to me on the table were the caps. I moved two aside to reach a madder-red one, faded to the same color as my kirtle. A copper might buy a cap. If they were here, Mother and Father and even Albin would tell me to keep my coin, which would doubtless buy me food for several days. But I wanted a cap. Wearing a cap, my head at least would belong in Two Castles.

A cap might help persuade a mansioner master to take me, while a bareheaded girl would be turned away.

The mending mistress and the goodwife agreed on a price. When the goodwife paid, her sleeves slid back and I saw no twine jewelry.

The mending mistress scratched her chin as the cat brushed against my leg, back and forth.

"I have a copper." I held up the cap.

Her hand dropped from her chin, and her lips turned from down to up. "Ah. Are you an apprenticeship girl?" She emphasized her consonants and drawled her vowels long enough for me to think the next letter impatient. Two Castles talk, I supposed, and wondered if I could imitate it.

I nodded.

"Have you settled your place yet?"

I shook my head.

"Which one are you trying for?"

"I'm going to be a mansioner." I spoke my consonants decisively and stretched my vowels.

She looked puzzled.

I must not have done it right. I repeated myself more slowly, even harder on the consonants, even longer on the vowels.

"No matter," she said. "A cap will keep you cool in summer, warm in winter. Not that one." She took the madder cap from my hands. "It won't show off your pretty face."

I wished I could subtract her lie from the price of the cap. I wasn't pretty. My eyes were too big, my eyebrows too thick, my mouth too wide, my jaw too pronounced. *But* if you were in an audience, even standing behind the benches, far from the mansion stage, you would still be able to make out my features. At that distance, the distance that mattered, I was pretty.

I tried the accent again. "Mother tells me my eyes are the color of moss."

Perhaps that was better—or not. She said nothing, but picked through the caps, discarding half a dozen until she found the one she wanted, a woad-blue cap, hardly faded, the color of a bright blue sky, with cunning scallops along the edge. "Here. Let me tie it on you." She did so. "Hmm." She pulled two forehead curls from under the cap. "Ah. You are fetching."

No, I wasn't. The cat mewed, probably agreeing with me.

I abandoned the accent. "Will there be enough left over to buy my luncheon?"

"I will give you back five tins, young mistress."

In Lahnt five tins would buy two meals at least.

The second rule on Mother's list warned me not to be impetuous.

Mother, I'm not. I need a cap! "My coin is hidden." I half turned from the mending mistress and hunched over, so she wouldn't see, as if my purse held jewels.

When I straightened, I held out the copper. The cat leaped up. Its paw batted the coin from my hand.

CHAPTER FOUR

dived after the coin, but the cat took it in its teeth and scampered into the crowd. I shoved people aside and gave chase. A streaking cat with a coin in its mouth should be easy to spot.

But there was no streaking cat.

I stood still in the middle of the street and looked about. A cat sunned itself on a windowsill, its mouth empty. A cat crossed an awning pole, its mouth empty. A cat washed itself in a doorway. I wished I'd noted the robber cat's markings when I'd had the chance.

I returned to the mending mistress.

"Did you get it?"

"No, mistress." I took a deep breath for courage. I had never spoken to an adult as I was about to. "Your cat owes me a copper." Another breath. "Or you do."

"The cat wasn't mine." She entered the shop behind her. Parley ended?

But she returned with a fat cat in her arms, all black except for a white patch on its back. "I'm sorry, young mistress."

She could have ten cats. But I could prove nothing against her. Still, I wanted someone to blame. "What kind of cats live in Two Castles?"

"Here we have thieves of every sort. You should have been more careful."

More careful? My ears grew hot. It was my fault? More careful than bent over, hiding my purse? No one had warned me of animal robbers.

"I can't give you a cap."

My ears were going to catch fire. I untied the cap, dropped it back on the table, and walked to the next stall, a tallow candlemaker's. Now I had no money for food.

"Honey! Girl! Wait for Dess."

I turned.

Master Dess and his beasts had progressed as far as the shoemaker's stall. He waved to me. "Too bad. I saw the cat. Terrible bad." He toiled upward, his cows at his side, his donkey lagging. "Come, honey."

"You saw?" I said as he reached me. We hadn't exchanged a word on the cog, but in this town of strangers he felt like family.

"What a shame." Letting go of his animals, who didn't budge, and putting down his kitten basket, he opened his cloth purse. "The goodwife gave me three tins for your kitten. Here they are, maybe not the same three tins." He took my hand and put the coins in it. "I have your kitten again. It's an even exchange."

"Thank you!" The exchange wasn't even. I hadn't returned the kitten or paid the tins. "You're very kind."

He hefted his basket and opened it. Only three kittens remained, one with a white ear. It extended a paw at me. "She knows you."

I touched the pink nose.

"You should have her. Everyone has a cat. I'll give her to you."

"I have no way to feed her."

"Too bad! Cats must eat." He closed the basket and resumed his upward trek.

People must eat, too. If I were one of Master Dess's animals, I would have no worries.

I started back downhill, hoping to question the cat teachers. But when I reached the corner, the two of them were gone. I wondered if they might have sent a cat to rob me and left when they had my coin. On the wharf, the young man had also departed.

Had they all been in league? Perhaps they'd noticed my capless self and singled me out as easy prey.

But my thieving cat had been under the table when I arrived.

I looked out at the strait, where cloud reflections moved across the water. White fishing boat sails bit into the bottom of the sky.

No more dallying. First food, whatever three tins would buy, then the mansioners. I headed uphill again. A grand lady outstripped me on a palfrey. I saw her and her mount only from behind: the lady's straight back, her bright green kirtle, the dark hair spilling from her cap down her shoulders, the horse's dappled rump, and its tail braided with scarlet ribbons.

How lovely it would be to ride, especially to ride to a castle or a burgher's house, where a big meal was laid out for me.

I wished this were a food vendors' street. Nothing sold along Daycart Way was edible.

Behind me, coming from farther down the hill, a bass drum of a voice boomed, "Make way! Make way!"

The crowd fell silent. Was King Grenville passing by?

The throng closed around me and pushed me until my back pressed against a vendor's table. A woman and I were separated by her five young children, who leaned into her skirt and mine. Because the children were shorter than I, my view wasn't completely blocked by the adults surrounding them.

"Make way."

My neighbor, the mother, whispered, "Turn into a mouse."

The ogre! My breath stuck in my throat. If he plucked me for his cauldron, what could I do?

"Very thin here," I squeaked. "Not worth the trouble."

The voice roared, "I want no broken bones or flattened heads."

Flattened heads! Had that happened?

"Ogre coming. Dog coming."

I heard the full, echoing bark of a big dog.

Count Jonty Um's voice gentled to a rumble. "Hush, Nesspa."

He smelled like a clean ogre, perfumed with cinnamon and cloves, pounds of them. As he climbed farther up the hill, I began to see him. First came a thatch of black hair, cut so haphazardly that his barber was blind or couldn't keep his hands from shaking. Like me, the ogre wore no cap. Next came an ear as big as a slice of bread. He turned his head my way.

He was a young man ogre! Shrunk down, he could have been anyone. But as himself, he was eleven feet tall or more, puffed up as a pudding. His face might have been pleasant if it hadn't been so red with anger or blushing. He had round cheeks, level eyebrows, a square chin, brown eyes, and freckles across the bridge of his nose.

"Freckles," I murmured. I wanted to yell to Mother and Father across the strait. Freckles on an ogre!

Sweat lines streaked his forehead and cheeks. "Make way!"

An angry voice rang out. "We're crushed, Count Jonty Um." The voice paused. "Begging your pardon."

The crowd squeezed closer. Behind us, the table fell over. The ogre drew almost even with me so I could see down to his chest. Of course his dog remained out of sight.

His tunic, dyed a wealthy deep scarlet, was silk. A silver pendant on a gold chain hung around his neck. The pendant and chain together probably weighed ten pounds and would be worth a hundred apprenticeships.

He passed on. People spaced themselves apart again. Someone complained that Count Jonty Um strolled only at the busiest time of day.

Behind me a familiar voice spit out, "Monster!"

The mending mistress's table lay on its side. Piles of clothing had slid to the ground. I righted the table and began to pick up garments.

She took a tunic and attempted to brush it clean while making a sound of disgust in her throat.

I tried the accent again. "What a pity!" I folded hose for her.

"Don't think you can pretend to help and make off with a cap."

I raised my empty hands. My voice rose, and my attempt at an accent vanished. "As if I would! Lambs and calves! The ogre has more manners than you!" I moved away.

Her indignant voice followed me. "You compare me to an ogre? How is that for manners?"

I felt my face turn as red as Count Jonty Um's had been. People gave me a wide berth.

One could speak however one liked to an unknown young person with no coppers in her purse. In a mansioner's play, the impoverished unknown woman was often a goddess in disguise. If this were a play, the goddess (me) would transform the mending mistress into stone or into a deer. I grew more cheerful.

The ogre could actually shape-shift into a deer. How curious that he went about the town in his own form. If he turned himself into a cat, everyone would love him.

Might he have done so earlier? Could he have been the one to take my coin? Might his wealth be cat plunder?

Noon bells rang from the direction of the king's castle, joined in a moment by more distant ringing. Then other bells tolled closer by, sounding from somewhere in town, likely the Justice Hall. Last came the harbor bells, chiming out across the strait.

I stopped my climb to listen—bass bells, tenor bells, bright soprano bells, all in harmony—pealing and pealing, calling to anyone with ears, but saying to only me, *Two Castles, king's town, big town, thief town, stay, Lahnt girl, stay.*

Or maybe they said, *Starve, Lahnt girl, starve.*

The bells faded. I continued on my way.

CHAPTER FIVE

market square opened before me, more crammed with stalls and people than the street had been. The odors of sweat and spoiled eggs hung over all, but they were redeemed by the aroma of baking bread, roast meat, and the faint but heady fragrance of marchpane—sugared almond candy.

What would three tins buy?

Nothing, it seemed. A muffin cost four tins, and I couldn't wheedle down the price. My nose drew me to a man frying meat patties over a brazier. Though he had no customers, he still wouldn't sell me a quarter patty.

The marchpane perfume grew stronger. An old woman walked by, carrying a tray of the candies.

I hurried after her and tried again to speak with the

heavy consonants and dragged vowels of a Two Castler. "May I see, Grandmother?"

"What's that?"

I repeated myself without the accent.

"Looking's free." She held the tray out.

Each candy was cunningly fashioned as a fruit or a flower, the tulip looking just like a fresh bloom, the pear green but for a hint of pink. The tiniest candy, a strawberry one, would probably cost more than a copper.

I had tasted marchpane once. I'd found a marchpane peach on the ground at the Lahnt market. It was grimy and partially flattened where a shoe had trod. Father saw me pick it up. He took it, brushed off the dirt, kept the flattened part for himself, and gave the rest to me.

"Don't tell your mother," he'd said, and I wasn't sure if he thought she'd disapprove or if he didn't want to share three ways.

The marchpane mistress moved away. I followed as if on a string. Perhaps I would have died of starvation in the marchpane mistress's shadow if I hadn't tripped over a cat, who *mrrow*ed in protest. Jolted out of my reverie, I looked about and saw, just a few yards away, an enormous reptile's huge belly and front leg.

A dragon!

I skittered backward. People filled in between IT and me. Conversations continued. The smell of rotten eggs all but overpowered me.

If others weren't afraid, neither was I, despite the tingle at the nape of my neck and my breath huffing in and out. I sidled closer.

A little clearing surrounded the dragon. I hovered on the border, as close as I dared, midway between head and tail. ITs long, flat head faced forward, so I felt free to inspect. IT stood on stumpy legs. The tip of ITs tail, which was as long as the rest of it, curled under a dye maker's table.

Poor creature, to be so hard to gaze upon. Imagine being covered in brown-and-orange scales except for a wrinkled brown belly that hung almost to the ground. ITs spine crested at half the height of a cottage, and ITs claws ended in long, gray talons. The wing facing me was folded, but judging from the rest, that was probably hideous, too.

ITs head thrust aggressively forward, hardly higher than my own. The head thrust seemed masculine. Was IT a *he*?

Wisps of white smoke rose from ITs half-closed mouth and ITs nostril holes. A pointed yellow tooth hung over ITs orange lip. ITs long head rounded at the snout. The skin about ITs eyes puffed out.

The cat between me and IT licked a paw.

At my elbow a goodwife said, "My achy knee augurs rain."

Her goodman laughed. "Your achy knee sees clouds."

IT turned ITs head and stared at me. ITs eye, flat as a coin, glowed emerald green. I felt IT take stock of me, from my overwide, too-short kirtle and round-toed shoes to my bare head and my smile, which I maintained with *good dragon, nice dragon* thoughts. IT faced away again. I resumed breathing.

A line of men and women stretched away from IT, waiting their turn for something. Two baskets rested by ITs right front leg, one basket half full of coins, the other holding wooden skewers threaded with chunks of bread and cheese.

Third in the line was Master Thiel, the handsome cat teacher from the wharf. Draped around his neck, a cat lolled, as relaxed as a rag. Might this cat have robbed me, taught by his cat teacher?

The cat had a black spot above his left eye. Three big spots dotted his back. His legs were black to the knees, as if he wore boots. The rest of him was snowy white. Copper-colored eyes, the hue of my stolen coin, examined me examining him.

Barely opening ITs mouth, the dragon spoke in a nasal and hoarse voice. "Step up, Corm."

A stoop-shouldered man at the head of the line dropped coins into the coin basket and took a skewer, which he held out boldly. "I've waited long enough, Meenore."

IT had a name, Meenore, a nasal name. Sir Meenore? Lady? Sirlady? Master? Mistress? Masteress?

"Everyone savors my skewers." IT opened ITs mouth into a singer's round O and blew a band of flame, which engulfed the food.

The man danced backward. "Toasted, not cindered, if you please."

Enh enh enh.

Dragon laughter! The corner of ITs mouth curled up in a grin that reminded me of our dog Hoont at home, when I pulled her lips back toward her ears.

The flame shortened and lightened from red to orange. The fat in the cheese spit and crackled. How rich it smelled!

After a minute Meenore swallowed ITs flame, revealing the bread and cheese, toasted golden brown, beautiful.

Master Corm blew to cool his meal. I licked my lips. He put the skewer to his mouth and pulled off the first morsel with his teeth. Oh! Even untasted it tasted good.

Next, a boy tugged his mother toward the basket. The mother took two skewers.

"Can I, Mother?"

She gave him the coins, and he dropped them one by one into the coin basket. Ten *clinks*. Five tins for a skewer. Too bad for me.

Although he begged, the mother wouldn't let her son

toast his own skewer. When the food was cooked, the two moved off.

A fine drizzle began to fall. The cat teacher stepped up.

I wanted to ask him if cats were ever taught to steal, but my tongue turned to wood, a doubly timid tongue: afraid to draw ITs attention again and bashful about addressing this perfect young man.

Clink clink clink clink. Only four tins! Maybe I could get by with three.

Meenore swallowed ITs flame. "The price is *five* tins, Thiel. Pay up or leave the coins as tribute." *Enh enh enh.*

The cat purred.

Master Thiel bowed with a dancer's grace. "Apologies. My fingers miscounted." His voice was as gentle as a gemshorn, the shepherd's horn that calms stampeding sheep.

Four coins, five, an easy mistake. His purse jingled as he pulled out another tin. Lambs and calves! Bare feet, hollow cheeks or no, he was far richer than I.

"Make way!" Count Jonty Um emerged from a side street into the square.

Silence fell. The crowd parted. I backed away. The waiting line spread out. Only Meenore remained motionless. The cat on Master Thiel's shoulders stood up, back arched.

The count's dog, a Lepai long-haired mountain hound, pranced along, taking no notice of the cat but frequently looking up at his master. Though big as a wolf, his head came only to Count Jonty Um's knees. He was a beauty, with a coat of golden silk and a regally large head matched by a big black nose.

The count approached IT. "Three skewers, if you please."

What about everyone on line? That was no true *If you please*. Clearly an ogre did what he liked, no matter the inconvenience to small folk.

"It isn't fair!" burst out of me.

The silence seemed to crystallize.

Enh enh enh, IT laughed, possibly in anticipation of seeing me squeezed to death in one enormous hand.

Count Jonty Um turned and lowered his gaze until he found me. "I am unfair?"

I attempted a Two Castles accent again. Perhaps he wouldn't hurt me if he thought I had parents here. "*It* isn't fair." Not you.

"Meenore unfair?" he roared.

I was still alive. "Not IT." I gestured at Meenore. The accent came and went. "It."

Enh enh enh.

The ogre looked puzzled.

"Er . . . ," I said. "Others were ahead of you."

"Oh. I apologize. Thank you for telling me." How stiff he was. There was no feeling of gratitude in his voice, but he stepped back, three giant steps. "Proceed."

In continued silence, the people in line eased back into

their places, the man who had been at the end treading on the heels of the fellow in front of him to avoid closeness to the ogre. I realized that everyone would have preferred Count Jonty Um to go first and leave.

People resumed their strolling and buying, while giving the ogre a wide berth. At the head of the line, Master Thiel took his skewer from the basket.

Meenore said, "Young Master Thiel, I commiserate with you on the death of the miller."

Count Jonty Um boomed in, "I am sorry for your loss."

A polite ogre.

"Thank you." Master Thiel nodded at the dragon but not at the ogre. "My father will be missed. He had many . . ."

His father, dead? How he must be grieving. I thought of Father, and my eyes smarted.

"Missed by you most of all." *Enh enh enh.*

How could IT laugh? What a churlish dragon!

Master Thiel answered with dignity. "Masteress, my good father had confidence in my abilities."

Ah. A masteress.

Master Thiel continued. "My father believed—"

His cat jumped from his shoulder and strolled off. "Pardine!"

The cat didn't return. I knew I should leave, too. The sooner I found the mansioners, the sooner I might eat. But so much drama was passing here and the food smelled so tasty that I remained rooted in place.

Master Thiel held his skewer out. In a moment it was done. He stepped aside to eat. Masteress Meenore swallowed ITs fire and turned my way, which brought that smoking snout uncomfortably close.

I stood my ground.

"I commiserate with your loss, too, girl from the island of Lahnt."

CHAPTER SIX

y loss?" Had Mother and Father died, and IT could divine their deaths?

"You are a thief's victim."

I felt weak with relief. But how could IT tell I'd been robbed? "How can—"

"Simple." IT raised ITs voice. "Gather and hear. Masteress Meenore, finder of lost objects and people, unraveler of mysteries, will now exhibit, gratis, ITs skill at deduction, induction, and common sense, which in other circumstances would cost ITs customary fee."

Luckily no one stopped to listen. The ones on line had to hear, which was bad enough.

Count Jonty Um blared, "A demonstration. I will enjoy this."

"Your Lordship," IT said, "my demonstrations are always enjoyable if one is not their object."

The object today would be me!

IT continued. "You may ask the guests at your coming feast to recount my many other displays of intellect, which will entertain everyone." IT swiveled ITs head toward me. "What is your name, girl of Lahnt?"

I didn't have to tell! I hugged my satchel as if it could protect me. "Unravel the mystery of my name, if you can, Masteress Meenore." My legs tensed to run from ITs flame.

Enh enh enh. "The girl from Lahnt is clever, hasty, brave, and lacking in respect for her elders."

IT described me exactly as Mother would! Might IT be a mother, a *she*?

"Great faults and perhaps greater virtues," IT said.

Mother would not have agreed about *greater virtues.*

"Your name is of no consequence. You started your journey with something in your purse that you considered valuable. Whatever it was, was taken. In your distress you forgot to tuck your purse away afterward, evidence of the theft."

I pushed the purse under my apron.

Master Thiel, who'd finished eating, spoke. "Perhaps no one steals on Lahnt, so she didn't anticipate her danger." He smiled at me, showing pearly white teeth.

"Few do steal at home, Master Thiel." I smiled back,

a fourteen-year-old's smile, I hoped, perhaps even a fifteen-year-old's.

"If no one steals *there*," IT said, "more reason for caution *here*. Despite the theft, her purse still contains coins, four or fewer tins."

Could IT see through cloth? I asked, "How do you conclude that, Masteress?"

"Next in line," IT said.

How rude, to ignore me! How interesting!

Leaning heavily on a cane, a tall man hobbled forward. His payment tinkled into the basket. "I like my cheese well done, Meenore."

Instead of flaming, IT said, "By hiding your purse now, girl, you revealed that you still have something in it, which I had already surmised."

"I am waiting," the lame man said.

"You are safe in your guess, Masteress Meenore," Master Thiel said, laughing charmingly. "She will hardly show us what her purse holds."

Indeed, I wouldn't. I was glad to have Master Thiel on my side.

The lame man held out his skewer.

"My customer waits. I will explain my conclusions in a moment." Masteress Meenore toasted the food, to my eyes less thoroughly than IT had the other skewers. IT was eager to prove ITs brilliance. "She needn't open her purse for me to know the contents. If she—"

"More flame, Meenore."

IT toasted the skewer again and then continued. "If she never had more coins, the few she has now would be precious to her, and the purse would have been hidden from the start."

The lame man spoke while chewing. "How do you know she has fewer than five coins?"

"Surely Master Thiel must have come to the same conclusion as I," Masteress Meenore said.

Master Thiel shook his head, smiling.

But I knew, and I wished I'd departed the moment I saw IT. Rather than be shamed, I would shame myself. "Masteress Meenore observed me counting the tins as they dropped into ITs basket. If I had five coins or more, I would have joined the line. If I had no coins, I would not have bothered to count."

"Ah," IT said. "The girl without a name has inductive and deductive talents herself. She is poor and starving, from the way her eyes have dwelled on my excellent skewers. I have now explained in full."

I hurried away before I could see Master Thiel's pity. As I went, I made myself chuckle instead of weep. Good luck to bring a kitten to Two Castles? What would ill luck have been?

The drizzle increased to a light rain. Above the market, the stalls and the crowd thinned. A lark sang from its perch on an iron torch holder. I couldn't help wishing the bird roasted and set before me.

The upper half of a tower showed beyond the end of the way. I had almost reached the top of town, and soon I would see the castle whole.

Here the homes belonged to wealthy burghers. The houses were taller, as befitted their owners' elevated rank, with an extra story for servants.

The midafternoon bells chimed, muted by the rain. At the next corner I found a well. The water smelled sulfurous, but I drank anyway. The Two Castlers seemed healthy enough, and the water made my belly feel less empty. I rinsed my hands and face and neck, braided my damp hair, and tucked the braid into a knot at the back of my neck.

Then I looked down at myself. The hem of my kirtle was gray from the cog's bilgewater, and gray stains splashed up my apron. My apparel was unfashionable and, of course, I lacked a cap. What would the mansioner master make of me?

I heard a strange call that rose and fell, high-pitched, low-pitched, and bubbling. The sound troubled me until I remembered the king's menagerie.

The rain became heavier, and the air began to chill. I hurried, pressing my satchel against my chest. I could have put on my cloak, but then it would be wet, too.

If I was near the menagerie, I was on my way to the mansioners. Soon I reached the final row of houses, then behind them, kitchen gardens bordered by the town wall, much too high for me to climb. But here, at the top of Daycart Way, was the south gate, open and unguarded in peacetime.

I stepped through. Daycart Way became an oxcart road that soon forked. The right branch led to King Grenville's castle, which was so close that I could see the shape of a head in the outer gatehouse window.

According to Goodwife Celeste's description, the left-hand road would take me to the mansioners. I started up it. On either side of me, a meadow of late-blooming golden patty flowers glistened up at the wet sky.

Perhaps the mansioners were enjoying a snack and I might be invited to join in—join the troupe and partake of the meal.

The road was turning to mud. I avoided the wheel ruts and stepped from one higher, dryer patch to another. A wooden enclosure, taller than I was, lay ahead on my right, likely the menagerie, because I heard the eerie call again.

I reached the enclosure, which abutted the road. The gate stood open. I would have liked to glimpse a few of the creatures, but the view within was blocked by evergreen shrubbery trimmed in the rough shape of a bull.

After the menagerie, the road forked again. To my right it wound upward, likely leading to the ogre's castle. Straight ahead, perhaps a quarter mile off, five theatrical mansions stood in a row, appearing from here as boxes painted in rain-dulled hues: at the head of the line, purple for ceremonial scenes, then green for romance, black for tragedy, yellow for comedy, red for battles. From the side of the purple mansion, the mansioners' pennants hung limp in the rain. When the troupe traveled, the mansions would be hooked together and pulled by oxen, a stirring sight with the pennants in the lead.

Rain had probably ended rehearsals, but someone must be there, I thought, to keep watch. Better to arrive when the place was quiet, and the master or mistress would have time for me.

What would I do if I were turned away? I was already half starved. How would I keep from starving completely?

I wouldn't be turned away. I would say how hard I'd labor, how far I'd traveled, how much I loved the mansioners' tales, how I'd practiced them at home.

Might I start with a meal? Porridge would do.

Thunder growled in the distance. I felt something pass overhead and smelled rotten eggs.

Masteress Meenore landed between me and the mansions. Steam rose from ITs nostrils. *Enh enh enh.* "Here is the clever girl who will not reveal her name."

My heart skipped beats. It was one thing to be near a dragon in the midst of a throng, another to be alone with IT. I ran around IT, hoping to see someone, hoping IT wouldn't pursue.

CHAPTER SEVEN

o you wish to be a mansioner." I heard the rustling of ITs wings as IT caught up with me. "Perhaps no one has informed you that the free apprenticeship has been abolished."

"I know."

Was IT going to the mansions, too? Might IT put in a good word for me? Or reveal me as the bumpkin victim of a thief?

IT spread a wing to shelter me from the rain, an unexpected kindness. I looked up and stopped hurrying to stare. IT halted, too.

The wing was a mosaic of flat triangles, each tinted a different hue, no color exactly the same. Lines of sinew held the triangles together, as lead holds the glass in a stained-glass window. The tinted skin, in every shade of pink, blue, yellow, and violet, was gossamer thin. I saw raindrops bead on the other side.

"My wings are my best feature." ITs voice took on a sweeter, lighter tone than I'd heard before.

A lady dragon?

"You cannot see until I fly, but the wings are not identical. The pattern and arrangement of colors differ."

"It's beautiful, but . . ."

"But what?" ITs smoke tinged purple.

"Can't a branch poke through? Wouldn't an insect bite tear your skin?"

The smoke bleached to white. "The skin is as thin as a butterfly's wing yet strong enough to turn aside the sharpest sword."

The pride in ITs voice made me smile. Then I wondered if IT was ashamed of the rest of ITself, and that made me want to pet IT.

I set off again, staying within the shelter of ITs beautiful wing. As we walked, the rain waxed into a downpour. I wondered what time it was. Near dusk, I guessed.

IT craned ITs head toward me. "You will offer yourself for a longer free apprenticeship." IT must have seen my surprise, because IT added, "First I used inductive reasoning, in that you are headed for the mansions and you have no silvers and you attempt an accent not native to you. The rest is deductive. What can you offer but lengthy labor and talent, if you really are talented? The mansioner master is called Sulow."

"Do you know him well?"

"Without exception, I know people better than they think. Most I know better than they know themselves."

"Is he a kind master?"

Enh enh enh. "Try your Two Castles accent on him."

I couldn't tell if this was good advice or the opposite.

"Your robber was a cat, was it not?"

"Yes."

"You wonder how I know."

I was sure IT would tell me.

"You are a sensible girl, aside from desiring to be a mansioner. You would not have let a human thief near you."

"Thank you." I wished Mother could hear someone call me *sensible*—without knowing the someone was a dragon.

The road ended in mud and patches of grass. We approached the mansions from the rear. Each one was a huge rectangular box on wheels, though the wheels had been stopped with chunks of wood. During performances and rehearsals, the front long side of the mansion would be taken away, revealing the mansioners and the scenery. I heard no voices and guessed that the boxes had been shut against the weather.

Cats huddled under every mansion, waiting for fairer

weather or for a hapless field mouse.

"If he is here, Sulow will be in the yellow mansion."

Yellow for comedy. I wondered what that might signify.

We circled the mansion. A procession of jesters had been painted on the outside: juggling, beating drums, playing flutes, turning somersaults. Rounding the corner to the front, we found the door open just a crack.

Masteress Meenore folded ITs wing. I was soaked instantly.

The drenching gave me inspiration. Every year I had seen the mansioners of Lahnt perform *The Princess and the Pea*. I had tried the princess role at home, and Albin said it was my best. Now here I was, sufficiently bedraggled for a dozen true princesses.

I spoke the princess's first line soundlessly because my voice had fled. My knock on the door was a whisper tap.

But after a moment the door creaked, and I heard, "Meenore?" in the round, sonorous tones of a mansioner.

I didn't trust IT enough to attempt an accent. "Throw wide the castle doors"—by lucky accident, I sneezed three times as the door finished opening—"to admit a young princess of exalted lineage."

A man of middling height stood in the doorway. He was thin, but with a moon face, flat nose, tight mouth, and shrewd, heavily lidded eyes that slid past me. "Go away, Meenore. I haven't reconsidered."

"Wait!" I cried.

"Sulow," IT said, catching the door with a claw, "have I asked you to reconsider?" Raindrops sparkled in the red glow of ITs nostrils. "Here is an aspiring mansioner."

Master Sulow's eyes took me in at last. Puzzlement or annoyance creased his brow. "Yes?"

I spoke in a rush. "I seek an apprenticeship, a fifteen-year, *free* apprenticeship. I will labor harder and longer than—"

"There are no free apprenticeships. How old are you?"

Be truthful, Mother said. "Fourteen."

Enh enh enh.

How I hated IT!

"Your name?"

"Lodie. I mean, *E*lodie, Master Sulow."

"Can you wield a paintbrush?"

Be truthful. "Certainly."

"A needle?"

That I could. "Yes."

"You would toil without a tin for fifteen years, until you are twenty-seven?" His lips twitched. "Unpaid, unheralded for such a span of time?"

"If I will be a mansioner at the end of it, gladly."

"Then you may audition for me."

Perhaps the kitten had been lucky after all. Apprentice mansioners didn't usually audition, since they wouldn't be acting for years. I reasoned that Master Sulow must have a particular role in mind.

"Come in." He backed away to let me in. "I have another guest, Young Elodie. Master Thiel here wants to be a mansioner as well, along with his cat."

Did Master Thiel love mansioning, too? Were we kindred souls? I mounted the two steps and stood just inside the door.

Master Sulow sounded exasperated. "His cat! Without apprenticing, either one of them. And Meenore wants to sell ITs skewers at my entertainments."

Two tallow candles cast a dim and smoky light. Master Thiel sat on a bench, his long legs extended, his features vivid in the candlelight and shadows. What a mansioner hero he would make! He rose and bowed when I entered, spilling Pardine from his lap.

I curtsied—not a quick bob down and up, as Mother had taught me, but the elaborate reverence I'd learned from Albin.

"We meet again," Master Thiel said.

"Indeed," I said with all the stateliness I could muster.

A bowl full of apples rested on a low table. I forgot Master Thiel and mansioning. In my state I might have traded my future for those apples.

Behind me, Masteress Meenore said, "Sulow, have you been engaged to mansion at the count's feast?"

He answered, "I have, though I'd be happier if His Lordship watched in the form of a pig. A pig doesn't pretend to be more than a beast."

"I know a few humans," IT said, "who combine pig, snake, and vulture without the excuse of shape-shifting."

Master Thiel said, "Bring a cat for safety, Sulow."

"I will. And a mansioner learns to protect himself in a thousand battle scenes, isn't that so, young mistress?"

I started out of my apple reverie. "Yes, master." Surely he would offer us apples. Hospitality demanded that he must.

IT said, "Give her an apple, Sulow. I doubt she's eaten all day." IT hadn't given me a skewer, but IT had been selling them, so hospitality didn't apply.

Hospitality seemed not to apply here, either. "If she becomes my apprentice, she may have more than an apple, but nothing until then." He took my elbow and guided me past the beautiful apples, until I was backed against the wall opposite the door. "Stand here." He seated himself on a stool across from Master Thiel. "Excellent."

Masteress Meenore continued to watch from the doorway. The floor and the space around me were bare of props and scenery.

Master Sulow said, "What is your favorite part to perform?"

"Do you know *Pyramus and Thisbe*, Elodie?" Masteress Meenore asked. "I relish a good Thisbe."

I nodded. I adored that play. It always made me weep, and I had the words by heart, although it wasn't Albin's

61

favorite of my pieces. He said I was too young for it. "After your heart has been broken," he always said, "you can play Thisbe."

"Yes," Master Sulow said, smiling for the first time. "If you know the role of Thisbe, that is my choice, too."

Master Thiel said, "Nothing represents true love more forcefully." He held up an apple. "Do you mind, Sulow?"

Master Sulow laughed. "You'll have it anyway."

Why could Master Thiel have an apple and not I? I wanted to wrest it from his hand and gobble it up.

Controlling myself, I said, "May I do Thisbe's last scene?" This was the most powerful moment, when she grieves over Pyramus's body.

"By all means. I will establish the mood." He threw back his head and roared, a lion's roar, convincingly enough to make my heart race.

Oh, excellent! I clapped, which made a wet sound.

Then I kept my hands together and lowered my head, to concentrate and become my role, but the apples filled my mind. Albin said inspiration could come from any source. I wanted an apple as much as Thisbe ever wanted Pyramus.

Master Sulow coughed.

An apple would be my Pyramus. I whispered, "'O Pyramus? Is that you?'" I heard the genuine longing in my tones. I imagined an apple withering to an inedible core and wailed, "'O, O my love.'" I dropped my voice to a murmur. "'My heart, my darling.'" Tears ran down my cheeks, real tears. "'O Pyramus . . .'" O Apple. "'. . . do you yet breathe?'" Do you yet have pulp and juice? I crouched. "'What do I see? O!'" O! My apple core! "'My bloodied shawl! My love, O my love, my love, O my love, have you . . . died . . .'" Have you shriveled? "'. . . for love of me?'"

I dared say no more. I could hardly speak for sadness. I stood and curtsied.

Master Sulow shook his head, as if shaking off a vision. Master Thiel applauded. Masteress Meenore said, "Mmm. Hmm. Mmm." Had I managed to surprise IT?

Master Sulow picked up an apple, which he pressed into my hand. I bit into it. No fruit had ever tasted so sweet. Thisbe's tears still flowed as I chewed. He'd said he'd give me an apple if I was to be his apprentice. I would be a mansioner. I had performed better than ever before. Master Thiel had clapped. They'd all liked it. I swallowed. "Thank you, master. I'll toil and—"

"You earned your apple, but three paying apprentices began their service yesterday."

I paused, the apple at my mouth. Had I heard right? He'd promised.

"You should take her," IT said. "You won't easily find her like."

"Meenore, do I tell you how to deduce or induce or whatever? The three I have are trainable. They'll do." He took my elbow and walked me to the door. "I have no need of a fourth."

CHAPTER EIGHT

he door squeaked shut behind us.

"He never wanted an apprentice," I said, my elation seeping away. "He knew all along. Did you know?" I finished the apple except for the stem and seeds. I was still hungry.

"How could I?"

IT was the masteress of knowing everything.

"I do know Sulow likes his silver."

Liked money more than an apprentice who could turn herself into Thisbe. Some of my happiness came back. "Masteress Meenore, I was a fine Thisbe, wasn't I?"

"More than fine. I did not expect it."

Another realization struck. "He didn't expect it, either.

He wanted to laugh at me." Oh. I turned on IT. "And so did you!"

IT exhaled blue smoke.

I stamped away and started back toward Two Castles. I had no idea what I would do when I got there or how I would keep myself alive. Fear as well as hunger stabbed my belly. I could *be* a tragedy, not merely portray one.

The rain had lightened, but twilight was falling, and the air had turned winter cold.

Masteress Meenore landed at my side, radiating heat. I supposed IT had a home with food and a bed, if dragons slept in beds. Why didn't IT go there?

"Masteress Meenore, where may I find the nearest other company of mansioners?"

"In Pree. A month's march, and the road is unsafe."

Perhaps a caravan was going there, and I could travel along as someone's servant.

"The master in Pree isn't as welcoming as Sulow." *Enh enh enh.* "I don't see why you want to be a mansioner, Lodie—"

"*Elo*—"

"*Lodie.* Do not correct your elders. I prefer *Lodie.*"

"Elodie is prettier."

"That may be. Why would you prefer to be a mansioner when you might be a dragon's assistant?"

"I've always hoped . . ." ITs words penetrated. "Your

assistant? Or a different dragon's?" What would a dragon's assistant do?

"I will not pay you much. I am stingy."

The evening bells began to chime. *Pay pay pay pay.*

I liked the sound, but I grew frightened. Would I go to ITs lair? Would chunks of me be on ITs skewers tomorrow?

IT sniffed. "I will withdraw my offer, if you think *that* of me."

Could IT read my mind? "I didn't say anything!"

"Precisely."

I had hesitated, so IT knew. IT waddled several yards away. I missed ITs warmth.

"What will my duties be?"

IT reared onto ITs back legs and spread ITs wings without flying. "Back away."

I did, and quickly.

IT spewed a jet of flame, burnishing the yellow meadow and rusting the charcoal sky. "You will proclaim my powers of deduction, induction, and common sense." IT came down heavily on ITs front legs. "And you will thread my skewers, carry my baskets, assist me with my many responsibilities."

Proclaiming sounded well. A mansioner might proclaim.

"We will try each other out to see if we suit."

I nodded.

"If I find you wanting, I will not keep you."

If I found IT wanting, I wouldn't stay.

But where would I go?

"Twenty tins for the month. I will feed you, and you may live with me. That is my offer."

I hardly heard the sum. As soon as IT finished speaking, I demonstrated my proclaiming ability loud enough for the moon to hear. "I will serve you, Masteress Meenore, with dedication, with enthusiasm, and with whatever art nature has bestowed on me."

IT smiled, showing every pointy yellow tooth in ITs mouth.

"Is there food at your house?"

"At my lair. Bread and cheese, which you may toast. Sundry victuals."

The idea of food more substantial than an apple weakened my knees. I stumbled, then caught myself. At home my family and I would have shared four meals since I'd last eaten more than the apple.

"Masteress, would you pay to post a letter from me to my parents, to let them know I'm safe?"

"One letter. The scribes are all knaves: twenty tins to write a letter, twenty-five for posting, five for a small sheet of parchment, ten for a large." IT snorted. "Ink is free."

"Masteress Meenore, I can write my own letter."

IT exhaled blue smoke. "You will still need parchment and the posting fee." After a pause IT added, "I failed to deduce that you can read and write."

Not many could. "My mother taught me." To take my mind off home, I thought about my salary.

A hundred tins to a copper, fifty coppers to an iron bar, four iron bars to a silver. Many lifetimes before I earned my apprenticeship.

"Lodie, walking is not my preferred mode of travel. Return to the town gate, then follow the high street, Owe Street, west to the end. There is my lair. I will be waiting with your supper."

"How will I recognize your"—I gulped—"lair?"

"You will. Be alert as you go. When you reach me, tell me what your senses perceived. Mysteries abound in Two Castles. As my assistant, you must learn to notice them." IT stood on ITs back legs and lifted in two great wing strokes, ITs wing colors muted by the dusk, ITs body in flight powerful and sleek. In a moment IT rose higher than the tallest castle tower, caught a wind, and glided away.

The rain had all but stopped. I pulled my cloak out of my satchel and wrapped it around me.

Mysteries abound. I reviewed the mysteries I had already encountered: the thieving cat; barefoot Master Thiel and his jingling coins; the polite ogre hated by all; no one at the dock to meet Goodwife Celeste and her goodman, who had come to see their children; even Master Dess, who seemed perfect enough to be a whited sepulcher; the dragon willing to hire an unknown girl. An abundance.

Soon I reached the menagerie fence. I ran my fingertips from one upright log to the next, rough to the touch. I smelled wet earth, damp fur, and the rust of raw meat—some animals' feed, I hoped. My eyes sharpened as the dark deepened.

Again I heard that rising and falling call, which jangled even more eerily in my ears now that it was night. I would have been terrified if not for the protection of the fence. Any animal that escaped its cage would still be contained.

Then my hand encountered air. The gate hung open.

I fled. Although I heard nothing behind me, I didn't slow for a full five minutes. I was lucky not to slip in the mud. Finally I stopped to quiet my breathing. The open menagerie gate—one more mystery.

In this setting I could truly be Thisbe, out at night to meet my Pyramus, who would look very much like Master Thiel. I could indeed see a bloodied lioness and bolt, leaving behind my veil, if I had a veil.

Torchlight and candlelight twinkled in the town to my right and the castle to my left. Torches flanked the nearby castle gatehouse. The drawbridge was up for the night.

I took the final fork. Below the town's gate, a figure approached, striding toward me on Daycart Way.

In the daylight, thieves. At night, murderers?

A few houses remained, and he might yet enter one of them, but I couldn't wait. I darted to the town wall and stood with my back against it, hoping to disappear into its shadow.

The figure, a man, passed through the gate.

Mrrow? from near my feet.

The man halted.

I cursed Two Castles for its cats. My muscles tensed with fear.

"Who goes there?" His voice was sharp, challenging.

The cat rubbed my legs.

The man waited. I waited. The cat leaned into my calf.

Finally the man continued, and in a minute I saw him by castle torchlight. It was Master Dess! Master Dess, without his cows and donkey, but still with his kitten basket.

I almost called to him. Now that I was ITs assistant, I could return his three tins. But his voice had been so harsh, I didn't dare.

He knocked twice on the gatehouse door, then pounded—*bang! bang! bang!*—then knocked twice again. A signal?

The drawbridge dropped to let him cross. I remained where I was until he must have reached the castle. The cat made tiny noises, washing itself.

I left it behind. As I followed Owe Street west, I caught a whiff of spoiled eggs. The odor grew with every step.

The street ended at a structure such as I'd never seen before, as big as four houses and twice as tall, with a roof that reminded me of interlaced fingers, pointing upward. The fingers, made of tree trunks, twisted and curved, lashed together by iron bands. Smoke filtered in wisps between the fingers and rose in a thicker plume from a chimney on the other side of the edifice. The walls were made of wattle and daub, as an ordinary cottage would be.

The shape of the building was a rough circle, ringed at regular intervals by rainwater vats as high as my shoulders. The wooden door, big enough to admit a dragon, stood open.

ITs lair. I waited in the shadow outside for a long minute before crossing the threshold.

CHAPTER NINE

asteress Meenore faced me from halfway across the single enormous room, where stench seemed to have replaced air. I swallowed repeatedly and tried not to gag.

"Do you like my perfume?" The smoke from ITs nostrils changed from white to blue.

Blue smoke meant shame!

I begged my eyes not to water, but they watered anyway. Should I lie?

IT would know.

Soften the truth?

IT would know.

"Do you like it, Lodie?"

I breathed deep without choking. "Like it? Enh enh enh."

Enh enh enh. Enh enh enh. Enh enh enh. "My odor is terrible. But you will get used to it, Elodie."

Ah, Elodie. I shrugged off my cloak and hung it on a hook by the entrance. The lair was warm even with the open door.

"You would like to eat." IT lumbered to the fireplace, which was set into the wall across from where I stood.

How strange, a fireplace in a dragon's lair.

Wood had been laid, but there was no fire. Above the hearth, a cauldron hung on an iron rack from which also dangled a stew pot, a soup pot, and sundry long-handled spoons. To the left of the hearth sat the basket of coins and the basket of bread-and-cheese skewers. I crossed the room to lay my satchel down by the baskets.

Masteress Meenore breathed flame on the hearth logs. I took a skewer and held it out to the fire. The scent of bread and cheese improved the air.

When the skewer was toasted, I blew on it to cool it, although I could hardly wait. A human-sized bench and a tall three-legged stool were drawn close to the fire. I sank onto the bench. The bread tasted as sweet as a scone, and the oozing cheese was sharper than any I'd ever sampled.

Masteress Meenore—my masteress!—took two skewers between ITs right-claw talons. IT lowered ITself until IT reclined facing the fire, leaned on ITs left elbow, and thrust the skewers up to ITs wrist into the heart of the fire.

I gasped, although a dragon wouldn't burn. After a minute or two, IT pulled the skewers out and devoured them entirely, bread, cheese, and wood.

"The skewers are pine. I enjoy the resin."

What else did IT like the flavor of?

In ITs uncanny way, IT answered my thought, "I prefer cypress wood, but the boatwrights take it all. I will not eat oak under any circumstance. I dine also on what humans eat and pebbles when I feel too light. On occasion I swallow knives, but they do not sit well." IT cooked and ate two more claws-full of skewers, then belched. ITs smoke shaded blue again. "Pardon me."

I nodded and tucked away three more skewers myself.

IT rose. "I shall return shortly." When IT moved, I saw that ITs belly had covered a huge trapdoor. "Do not take a single coin from the basket while I'm gone. I will know."

"I'm not a thief!"

"And do not open the trapdoor." IT clumped outside.

Without ITs presence and despite the fire, the air chilled. I drew my cloak around me again and approached the trapdoor. The wood was heat-blackened but firm when I touched it. The handle was a ring of iron.

I was not a mistress of deduction or induction, but I needed neither to guess what lay below: ITs hoard. Every dragon was reputed to have one. I might be standing on wealth enough to buy the ogre's castle.

ITs wealth, not mine. I returned to the fireplace bench, sat with my back to the fire, and surveyed the lair.

Light came from the fire and the dozen torches that were spaced around the edge of the room. With IT gone, I could smell the greasy torch rags.

The walls were hung with painted cloth so faded I couldn't make out what had once been depicted. Masteress Meenore's heat had baked the dirt floor as hard as pottery.

If the fireplace was twelve o'clock, eight to ten o'clock was occupied by a high table pushed against the wall. A long bench hid under it. Mother said you could learn a household's character from its table. I rose and went to this one. The wooden tabletop, which sagged in the middle and was worn and scratched, came up to my chin.

I saw a jug, half a wheel of yellow cheese, two loaves of bread, an orange squash, a small salt bowl, and a big double-handled bowl that held a spoon and a knife. The bowl was common green pottery, the spoon wood, the knife handle wood, too—a poor folks' bowl, poor folks' cutlery.

At eleven o'clock along the wall was a heap of large tasseled pillows. The tassels lay in my hand as smoothly as silk. The pillows might have been worth a silver or two if their linen hadn't been so worn. But though worn, they were unstained. I lifted one to my nose and smelled rosemary.

Across the lair, at three o'clock, stood a double-doored cupboard. I hadn't been forbidden to open it, so I concluded I was supposed to. The contents were a stack of folded lengths of linen, clean but threadbare; sundry bowls of the same quality as the one on the table; a row of four pottery tumblers; a small pile of cutlery; four sheaves of unused skewers tied with thread; and a little box, which proved to contain knucklebones.

Nothing more. IT might have warned me away from ITs hoard to make me think IT rich, while in truth the hoard was home to a few starving mice. Or IT might be fooling me twice.

Unbidden—unwelcome—a mansioners' tale came to mind, the tale of Bluebeard. What if the hoard contained the bones of dozens of Masteress Meenore's assistants?

I stood over the trapdoor. Open it? Run?

I knelt and grasped the iron ring. And there I stayed, uncertain. I wanted to be a dragon's assistant if I couldn't be a mansioner for now, and I needed food and a place to sleep.

And IT interested me. And no one feared IT. I stood up.

The trapdoor opened. I jumped back.

IT heaved ITself up onto the floor. "Lodie of Lahnt, if I had found you below, I would have tossed you out. If I had found you napping at the fireplace, I would have tossed you out, too. I want neither a thief nor an assistant who lacks curiosity."

I returned my cloak to the hook at the door.

"So, what have you learned about your masteress?"

Imitating ITs way of speaking, I said, "I used my powers of induction and deduction to conclude there is an outdoor entrance to the hoard."

"What else?"

"I cannot tell whether or not you are rich. All depends on what lies under the trapdoor."

"Well done, Elodie."

I was Elodie when IT was pleased with me.

"Your home is scrupulously clean." I may have brought in a louse or two, a flea or three, but none had preceded me.

"Yes. I will tolerate you for the night, but you must bathe in the morning. I will burn your clothes."

My clothes that Grandmother had worn or Mother and I had made? I rushed to my satchel and hugged it. "I'll wash everything."

"Twice. No, thrice. And scrub!"

I nodded, lowering the satchel. IT stretched ITself along the floor, ITs snout near my feet, ITs eyes fixed on me. I yawned.

"You are sleepy."

O masteress of deduction! I nodded.

"Then tomorrow you may tell me what you observed on your way to me, and tomorrow night, when you are clean, you may sleep on pillows. But now it is the floor for you. I suggest under the table. I am a restless sleeper."

Don't crush me! I barricaded my dirty self behind the long bench under the table. The clay floor was even harder than the deck of the cog. I fetched my cloak and my satchel, layered everything for cushioning, and stretched out on my side, back to the wall, my head sticking out beyond the bench, so I could still see into the room.

IT went to the cupboard, then sat on the floor with the box of knucklebones in ITs claws. Hunching over, IT spilled them out. One of the bones, the jack, was yellow, according to custom. The others were their natural ivory. IT tossed the yellow bone into the air, picked up another bone, and caught the yellow one in the same claw, in one deft move. On the next throw, IT picked up two bones.

Oh, Father! Dragons play knucklebones!

Knucklebones was a popular girls' game. I had played a thousand times. Did this make IT female?

"The dragon claw is as nimble as the human hand, Lodie."

The knucklebones tip-tapped the floor. My last awake thoughts were: Here I am, full belly, bedded down near a dragon. Father, Mother, you would wring your hands. How lucky I am!

CHAPTER TEN

woke once during the night and heard a distant lion's roar, probably from the menagerie. Or from the town, with the menagerie gate open. Not from Master Sulow, because the mansions were too far away for the roar to carry.

Perhaps the ogre turned into a lion at night and terrorized the town. I moved closer to the bench. The lion would hardly attack a dragon in ITs lair, would he?

Masteress Meenore lay on ITs back. ITs legs, loosely bent at knees and elbows, bobbled in the air, in the manner of a dog completely at ease.

In the morning I awakened to chill and silence. At home in Lahnt, Father used to build up the fire before waking me. He'd kiss my ear or my forehead or my nose, whatever part of me I'd left out of my blanket.

Hugging my cloak around me, I stood and went outside. Sunny day, cold air, November in October.

IT was breathing fire on one of the outdoor rainwater vats behind the lair. IT swallowed ITs flame. "Fetch the stool."

I did.

"Your bath is ready. Here." IT opened ITs claws to reveal a milky brick of soap.

At home we saved our soap for laundering. "But—"

"Use it. While you bathe, I will scour the lair." IT left me.

I placed the stool and climbed up. The water seethed and smelled like year-old eggs, but when I put a toe in, the toe liked it, hot, not scalding. And I was first in for once—Father, Mother, and Albin hadn't taken their baths before I had mine.

Sloshing and sizzling sounds emanated from the lair. I pitied my dying fleas. In a few minutes IT emerged with a cloth in ITs claws. "I will return shortly. You have been generous with your filth . . ."

Filth seemed too strong for truth.

". . . and now I must bathe, too." IT draped the cloth over the edge of the vat. "When you are entirely clean, wrap yourself in that. Then launder your clothes, not omitting your satchel itself, until they are also entirely clean."

"Yes, Masteress."

"I have heated that, too." IT pointed at another steaming vat. Then IT flapped ITs beautiful wings and headed south.

I wondered where IT bathed and wished I could watch.

While IT was gone, I washed my things, rubbing cloth against cloth until my arms ached. When IT returned, IT steamed everything dry in a trice.

A Lahnt proverb goes, *Love your lice. Only skeletons have none.* But here I was, louse free and still breathing.

Inside the lair, IT seated ITself by the fire and took a clawful of skewers. "Did you sleep well?"

I took a skewer, too, and sat on the fireplace bench. The skewer basket was almost empty. "I was awakened once by roaring from the menagerie lion."

IT clucked ITs tongue, and the orange in ITs scales deepened to scarlet. "This is the sort of pronouncement my assistant must not make."

What had I said?

"Suppose there were no lion in the menagerie, and someone from the town heard you assert there was, and moreover that you heard it roar." IT waved the skewers. "Your nonsense would—"

"But it did roar. It's not—"

"Do not interrupt your masteress."

I blushed. "I'm sorry. But I heard it."

ITs scales dulled. "You may say 'I heard a roar from the direction of the menagerie.' You can be certain of nothing more."

I grew afraid. "Was it the ogre?"

"You may probe the possibilities." IT put the skewers in the fire. "But you must not draw unwarranted conclusions."

"Then might it have been Count Jonty Um?"

"Indeed. He is capable."

I shuddered.

IT removed the skewers and ate one.

"*Was* it the count, Masteress? Do you know?"

"Not of a certainty. Nor a likelihood. I have never known His Lordship to shift into a lion, and I have known him since his infancy."

My heart lifted. He seemed a decent ogre; I wanted him to be a good one. "Why is he so disliked and feared?" My heart prepared to sink. "Does he turn into something else, or eat people?"

IT raised ITs eye ridges. "Many who neither shape-shift nor eat people are disliked and feared. Our king for one."

A perfect example. On Lahnt no one liked him. I waited for an answer about Count Jonty Um eating people, but none came, so my fear remained. I toasted my skewer. "Are there any lions nearby that are not in the menagerie?"

"Perhaps. The menagerie houses none. The last lion in the environs of Two Castles was killed a year before my birth. King Grenville wants to procure one for his zoo, but he refuses to pay full price."

What could I have heard? I began to eat.

IT ate a skewer uncooked and went to the table. "The day is passing. Nothing done, nothing earned. Fetch a sheaf of skewers."

IT meant the skewer sticks, which I took from the cupboard, and IT set me to cutting bread into cubes. I had to stand on the bench to be tall enough.

"Now tell me, what did you see on your way here last evening?"

As I cubed, I told IT about the open menagerie gate. "I heard calls from inside." I imitated the rise and fall of the creature's voice.

IT said the cries came from an animal called a high eena.

"Masteress, a man was leaving town, Master Dess from the cog. He brought a donkey and two cows and a basket of kittens over—"

"His appearance?"

I described him and told what had happened outside the town gate. "When he knocked"—I rapped the bench— "on the gatehouse door, the guards raised the drawbridge without seeing who he was. His knocks were"—I stopped myself—"may have been a code."

IT scratched around ITs ear hole and looked unconcerned.

"What if there's a plot against the king?"

The noon bells pealed. Testily IT blamed me for the lateness of the hour.

What if IT was part of the plot?

We pushed cheese and bread onto skewers in silence. After a few minutes, I called up my courage and asked if I might write and post my letter home.

IT put down ITs skewer and waddled to the trapdoor. "Follow me, Lodie." IT pulled the door open.

I didn't move. Did IT plan to kill me before I could write to Mother and Father?

CHAPTER ELEVEN

rom halfway in, IT swiveled ITs neck and grinned back at me before disappearing down the stairs.

I stood at the top and saw a light spark on far below. The glow brightened. IT was lighting torches.

"Come!"

The stairs were stone blocks wedged into the earth. Follow IT or leave ITs service.

IT could have murdered me last night. I stepped cautiously and continued downward into a chamber almost as high and big as the one above, empty but for three large baskets beneath a table and four stacks of books on top, a fortune in books. I had never seen so many gathered together.

IT stood on the far side of the table. I approached, curious about the books but most eager to see inside the baskets.

They brimmed with coins, mostly tins but also coppers, several iron bars, and a sprinkling of silvers. I had never seen a silver before. The coin turned out to be smaller than a copper, much smaller than a tin, no bigger than one of my teeth, such a little thing to be worth a year of an apprentice's labor.

I wondered if the baskets held coins to the bottom or were only a layer hiding something else underneath.

"In a century of industry and thrift, a dragon can amass wealth." IT pulled out the baskets and thrust a claw into one after another, churning up the contents. Coins spilled onto the floor. "No bones of bygone assistants."

I blushed.

IT sat back and rested a claw on a stack of books. ITs smoke turned gray; ITs eyes paled. In a dire and doleful voice, IT said, "I cannot read."

I didn't know how to soften ITs sorrow. I ventured, "Few people can."

IT snapped, "Is that supposed to comfort me?"

I tried again. "Your vocabulary is big."

"And varied and excellent. I astound my hearers with the erudition of my speech." IT opened the top book to the middle and passed a claw across the page. "But I cannot decipher the merest word." IT took the book.

I followed ITs tail back up to the lair, where IT set the book on the bench by the fireplace.

"Nothing read, nothing learned. We will not starve if we have a holiday. Read to me, Lodie."

IT had said I could write to my family, but I didn't want to remind IT. I lifted the book onto my lap. Lambs and calves, it was heavy, both thick and wide, covered in bumpy orange-brown leather that reminded me of ITs scales.

IT stretched out with ITs long head at my feet. ITs smoke rose in spirals. I wondered what spiraling smoke meant.

"Begin."

I opened to the first page. "Masteress Meenore, this is a book about vegetable gardening."

"Mmm. Proceed."

I thumbed through. Each chapter described planting, tending, and harvesting a different vegetable. On the first page an enormous *A* in gold lettering was followed by *corn squash* in smaller black letters. In the corner of the page, with a border of gold dots, was a drawing in green and black ink of an acorn squash.

"Is the gold real?"

"Read."

I began. ITs eyes never left my face. If my mouth hadn't been moving, I would soon have been asleep. IT didn't object when I practiced my Two Castles accent, but IT wouldn't let me mansion a cabbage into tragedy or a carrot into comedy.

"Read as the farmer's daughter you are."

If I hadn't been a mansioner as well as a farmer's daughter, my throat would have given out. As it was, I finally had to interrupt myself. "Masteress, I need to drink."

IT accompanied me out to the rainwater vats. I carried a tumbler, and IT held a bowl and the ladle. The changeable Lepai weather had brought more rain, but by now no clouds remained. The air smelled of sweet grass and fallen leaves.

IT lapped ITs water with ITs tongue, as a cat does. When we finished, IT led me back inside. I told myself how interesting endives would be.

But instead IT said we would eat our midday meal. Perhaps in honor of the book, IT roasted the orange squash to have with our skewers.

"Masteress?" I asked over spoonfuls of squash. "Will you plant a garden in the spring?"

"I have no land for a garden." Then IT gave me leave to visit the scribe when I finished eating. "Thirty tins. Do not let any cats get my coins."

I counted out the tins while IT watched me narrowly. When I had enough, I spilled them into my purse, tucked the purse under my apron, and touched the spot.

"Do not touch! You are signaling thieves."

I pulled my hand away as though my apron were on fire. What a bumpkin I'd been.

"While you are out, observe and listen. Smell the air. All your senses are in my employ, Lodie."

On Lair Lane, a shutter slammed shut. A cat cleaned itself in a doorway. I spied four cats. It occurred to me that Two Castles might have not a single mouse.

Roo Street was busier than quiet Lair Lane. At a weaver's stall a man turned over lengths of cloth. I tried out the Two Castles accent I'd just practiced for hours and he simply directed me to a scribe's stall. I skipped across Roo onto Trist Street.

Ahead, outside a jeweler's stall, Goodwife Celeste held a silver bracelet close to her eyes while the jeweler pounded his fist into his palm and disputed with her husband, Goodman Twah.

I'd thought them too poor to buy jewelry.

"Mistress! It's Elodie! From the cog!"

Her hand closed around the bracelet, and she lowered her arm. "Elodie! How nice to see you."

Was it? I'd interrupted something.

"Have you become a mansioner's apprentice?"

I told her about Masteress Meenore.

"The dragon Meenore?"

"ITself."

"Look about for something else, Elodie." She put her

hands on my shoulders, the bracelet hand still a fist. "IT is moody. Today IT may be kind, but tomorrow IT could be angry and do anything. If you stay, be prepared to flee."

To flee, but not to seek her aid.

"Come, Celeste." Her goodman twined his arm in hers. "The grandchildren are waiting. Good day." He nodded at me and at the jeweler.

"Good day!" The jeweler's voice was sharp.

Goodwife Celeste and her husband headed uphill. She still had the bracelet, so her goodman must have paid for it.

I decided to be cautious in ITs company and to continue barricading myself while I slept.

In Romply Alley the scribe's table took up little space between two cheese sellers' booths. The scribe was a tiny woman with a large nose, as if the pungent cheese had directed all her growth one way. "You'd like me to write something for you?"

I said I needed no assistance.

She peered at me through small, red-rimmed eyes. "Remarkable."

Thirty tins bought me postage and a scrap of parchment. I wrote in a cramped script,

Am well, am safe. Many weavers here. A master has taken me for free. Do not miss the geese, but miss you both and Albin. Your loving daughter, Elodie

I wished I'd had room to write *loving* a hundred times. Every sentence was a lie concealed in truth. I wanted to tell them what an adventure I was having, but I had no space and didn't dare.

The scribe waved a fan over the parchment to dry the ink. "You write a fine hand, young mistress. Don't set up in competition with me."

I paid, while watching for thieving cats. The tins changed hands without trouble, and I started back to my masteress. As I turned into Lair Lane, I stopped, then ran into the lair, leaping as I went.

"Masteress!"

IT looked up from ITs game of knucklebones.

"An abecedary of vegetables!" I brushed aside the bones and put the book on the floor under ITs snout. "Look!" I opened to the first page. "*A* for acorn squash." I turned to the end. "Z for zucchini. It's an A to Z in vegetables."

ITs smoke grayed.

Gray smoke for sadness, but I rushed on. "Mother taught me to read with an abecedary. I'll teach you. We can start—"

IT sat up. "What did you see and hear and smell in the town?"

"Don't you—" I stopped myself and told IT everything except Goodwife Celeste's warning.

When I finished, IT had me read again until the evening meal, by which time I had progressed as far as *mustard.*

After we ate, IT challenged me to knucklebones. I sat cross-legged on the floor, and IT stretched out facing me with the tip of ITs tail in the smoldering fireplace.

I couldn't win. IT tossed the jack higher and straighter than I did and so had more time to pick up bones. My sole advantage lay in the variations. IT knew none, so I showed IT the ones I excelled at: round the castle, fairy fling, rolling the gnome. But soon IT surpassed me even at these.

And then, in the middle of a game, IT said, "Lodie, three scribes have attempted to teach me to read, and all have used abecedaries. But the letters fly apart. Straight lines curl. Curved lines throb. I know a single letter." ITs right claw drew a circle in the air. "O."

"Oh."

"Yes, O. The trouble must be in the dragon eye, or in my eyes."

I wasn't convinced IT couldn't learn. Clever as IT was, IT seemed meant to read.

We played a while longer, and then I slept, unafraid, not barricaded. Goodwife Celeste was certainly misinformed about my masteress.

In the morning IT gave me instructions. "Walk through the town and proclaim my powers. You will say"—IT inhaled deeply—"'Today, in Two Castles and only in Two Castles, the Great, the Unfathomable, the Brilliant Meenore is available to solve riddles, find lost objects and lost people, and answer the unanswerable. Three tins for a riddle solved . . .'"

So now I knew what three tins would buy.

"'. . . fifteen tins for a lost object found, three coppers for a lost person found—'"

I blurted, "A lost person should cost more than three coppers." A person!

"What is a person worth, Lodie?"

"Many silvers."

"And if the lost person is the son of a servant, who may never own a single silver, the son should remain lost?"

I blushed. "No. But what if the father or mother may never own a copper?"

"Then we will negotiate. You must also say, 'The fee for answering the unanswerable will be decided between the parties. The Great, the Unfathomable, the Brilliant Meenore may be found in the square. Speak to IT with respect.' Elodie, I charge you: Make the residents of Two Castles take note. This is your most important task. Make them listen."

Or soon IT would find another assistant.

Outside, the morning was as bright and cold as yesterday. I filled myself with enthusiasm and began proclaiming at the top of Lair Lane. "Today," I cried in a burst of awe, "in Two Castles and nowhere else, the Great . . ." A man hurried by, face turned away.

I rushed to the man's other side. "IT is available to solve riddles, find lost"—I wailed *lost* piteously—"objects and—"

The man pressed his cap tight over his ears. "Hush! I know Meenore."

"Sir, but do you know all IT can do? Unriddle riddles, answer—"

"I know what IT does. Every week IT heats water for my household. I pay IT fourteen tins."

"Oh," I said weakly, then rallied. "IT can perform many other wondrous feats." I skipped sideways along with him. "Find anything. *Anything.*"

"If I lose *anything* and cannot find it," he said, stopping to retie his cap strings, "I will seek out Masteress Meenore." He started off again. "Do not pursue me, girl, or I'll call the constable."

I waited until he turned a corner before proclaiming again. I proclaimed on Lair Lane, Roo Street, Daycart Way, and Mare Street along the harbor, but wherever I went, everyone already knew Masteress Meenore. A baker told me that for ten tins, IT started his oven fires when they went out. Weekly, for two coppers, IT boiled the water in the town's wells to purify them.

The midmorning bells were ringing when a smith told me, "IT makes my fire the hottest in Two Castles." He took my forearm in his grimy hand. "IT could be a fine smith if IT didn't have to be Unfathomable. Tell IT Master Bonay says so."

At her place in Romply Alley, the scribe told me that IT had once deduced that her box of quills was hidden under a rock in her garden. "How did IT know?"

I announced loudly, "IT has ITs mysterious meth—"

"Make way! Ogre coming. Dog coming."

The scribe pulled me between her table and one of the cheese seller's stalls.

Count Jonty Um's shadow darkened the alley. His shoulder brushed an awning. He stopped three stalls from me, by a cobbler. "Sit, Sheeyen. A girl turned in here, shouting about Meenore. Where is she?"

My heart rose into my throat as the scribe pushed me forward. I lurched into the street, almost fell, caught myself, and found my face an inch from a fold in the ogre's cloak.

CHAPTER TWELVE

 wheezed, "Today, in Two Castles"—I swallowed and forced my voice out—"and only in Two Castles, the Great, the Unfathomable—"

Count Jonty Um boomed, "I wish to speak with IT."

"Masteress Meenore is in the square, um . . . Count Um."

"Count Jonty Um. We will go together." He placed a heavy hand over the crown of my capless head. A finger touched each of my ears. If he pushed down, I'd sink into the street up to my nose.

"Make way," he cried. "Ogre passing. Girl passing."

Everyone stared. The scribe mouthed words at me: *Take care*. How could I take care? The ogre could squeeze my head like a lemon.

Count Jonty Um edged along to avoid upsetting tables

and bringing down displays. He'd captured me, but he took care with the townspeople's stalls. Today's dog, a brown shepherd on a short chain, managed not to knock over anything, either. Gradually my heart slowed to a gallop. Because of the ogre's hand, I feared to turn my head, but I moved my eyes from side to side.

Everywhere, people froze to watch us. I saw pity for me on many faces, but no one challenged him. Cats stared, too, from between their owners' legs, from stall tabletops, from windowsills. I heard hisses.

In the market square Count Jonty Um cried, "Ogre and girl going to the dragon. Make way."

By the time we reached Masteress Meenore, ITs customers had fled. IT swept one wing in front of ITself, then to the side, and lowered ITs head in a definite, almost graceful bow.

Did bowing, rather than curtsying, make IT a he?

I ducked out from under the ogre's hand, and he let me go. IT raised both wings at the elbow, put one back foot behind the other, and dipped, in a definite curtsy.

A bow and a curtsy. He-she-IT.

IT said, "Your Lordship . . ."

Count Jonty Um bowed, too, a quick bend at the waist that meant *I am a count, you a mere masteress.*

"Your lordship has not come for skewers. We will consult at my lair. Lodie will lead you."

"*Elodie*, if you please, Masteress." I wanted the count to know my proper name.

IT took the basket of coins in a claw, leaped into the air, and flew, barely clearing Count Jonty Um's head. IT circled low, twice, three times. Why was IT lingering?

I deduced and proclaimed, "See, one and all, how Masteress Meenore is sought by nobility. IT will answer your questions, too. Schedule your own meeting with the nimble-witted, farseeing Masteress Meenore."

IT flew off in the direction of the lair. I picked up the basket of skewers. "This way, Count Jonty Um."

"Make way!" he cried. He put his hand on my shoulder.

I gathered my courage. "You can let go, Count Jonty Um. I won't run away."

His hand dropped. We left the square, watched by everyone. When we reached a less crowded street, he boomed, "Thank you for telling me to let go. You told me to wait in line, too. I like truthful people, Elodie."

I looked up. The line of his lips had softened, his face was no longer red, and his eyes seemed wider. An easier, more relaxed face made me feel easier, too.

"This way."

A robin landed on his shoulder, ruffled its feathers, and stayed. Cats might hate him, but not all animals. The dog seemed comfortable at his side.

He must have noticed that I was rushing to stay ahead of

him, because he stopped. "You can ride on my shoulders."

What would I hold on to up there? His great ears? What if I fell and pulled an ear off with me, or grabbed his silver pendant and swung from his neck like a bell clapper? "No, thank you."

He reddened again. I had insulted him. He set off at a slower pace, a considerate ogre. I tried to think how to apologize without making the insult worse.

He sneezed hugely. "Sulfur."

The robin flew away.

"We're near the lair." He liked frankness. "Count Jonty Um, I was afraid of falling off your shoulder and pulling your ear down with me."

He began to smile. The smile broadened, mouth half open, white upper teeth shining, bathing me in sweetness.

How changed he was! Almost as if he'd shape-shifted.

The smile faded and his expression dulled again, but I had lost my fear of him.

The lair's doorway was wide enough to admit us side by side. Masteress Meenore faced us from just inside. The count sneezed again.

ITs smoke tinted from white to blue. I deduced IT thought ITs odor had caused the sneeze, as was likely.

"Welcome, Your Lordship," IT said.

"Thank you." He let go of the dog's chain and she trotted away, snuffling the floor.

IT stiffened, meaning, I was certain, that as soon as the dog and the ogre left, the lair would be scoured again. The animal made straight for the fireplace bench, where IT had placed bowls and refreshments—apples, pears, dried dates, and figs.

The count went to the animal. "Shoo, Sheeyen."

She loped to the door and curled up on the threshold.

"May I take your cloak, Your Lordship?" I said, without considering how enormous it was.

He put it in my arms, but I wasn't overwhelmed. The wool was so fine and light that the cloak weighed no more than my own. I folded it and placed it atop the coin basket by the hearth.

IT had moved the table between the fireplace bench and the fire. On the tabletop ITs precious pillows lay in a row.

"Please, Your Lordship, seat yourself." IT gestured at the table. "It is sturdy. You will not break it."

The count sat, his back to the fire, leaning forward, balancing himself so that the table didn't take his full bulk. He sneezed again and blew his nose politely on the sleeve of his tunic, which today was evergreen silk.

Masteress Meenore's smoke darkened to slate blue. IT lowered ITself on ITs haunches between the cupboard and Count Jonty Um.

IT had positioned the stool for me on the ogre's left. I sat. Deftly, IT sliced a pear and an apple and fanned the slices into a circle in an empty bowl. In the center IT placed a fig. The result was a fruit daisy. I had never seen such elegance.

"Partake, Your Lordship." IT gave the bowl to the count and gestured at the other refreshments. "Help yourself, Elodie."

"Thank you, Masteress." And thank you for my name. With my little knife I sliced half an apple and half a pear, some slices almost all peel and others almost all fruit, the peel ones for me, the fruit ones for sharing. As the lowliest here, my portion should be the most meager. I took figs and dates as well, all for sharing. They were delicacies.

Masteress Meenore helped ITself, too. I speared a date with my knife and placed it in the count's bowl. He gave me his fig, which was a kindness.

Mother, Father, Albin! Look! Albin, I will remember this for my mansioning and forever: the smallness of me, the hugeness of them, these two creatures, each with teeth the size of ax blades, sharing fruit, the meekest of food.

Our snack would have been a silent one if not for IT, who held forth on the history of castle building. I learned about the progression from castles on low ground to castles on high, from wooden castles to stone, from few windows to few windows and many arrow slits.

I nodded and said nothing. Count Jonty Um said nothing as well and hardly even nodded. I wished he would speak. I wanted to hear an ogre's thoughts on any subject: castles or cottages or the weather. Or being an ogre. Or shape-shifting. Especially the last two.

But he seemed to live inside a cocoon of silence, the air around him thick with it.

"In sum, the lords of badly defended castles rarely lived to build better ones. Have you eaten your fill, Count Jonty Um?"

He nodded. I hadn't eaten my fill, but I moved the bowls to the floor by the hearth and returned to my seat.

IT held up a claw. "I must have the details, of course, but I know why you've come, Your Lordship. You are in danger."

CHAPTER THIRTEEN

e stood fast. "No danger."

ITs tail tapped the floor, an irritated sound.

After a full minute, during which the count stared over my masteress's head, he sat again. "No danger. Nesspa, my dog, is missing." He gestured at the dog, who still slept by the door. "Sheeyen isn't mine. She belongs to the castle."

And the castle belonged to him. But I understood. Sheeyen wasn't his pet.

"Your missing dog is but one aspect of your danger." ITs smoke tinged violet.

Count Jonty Um folded his arms. "Only Nesspa concerns you."

Masteress Meenore reared up on ITs hind legs. The tail

thumps were louder; the smoke darkened. "I am not a sorcerer, Your Lordship. I cannot deduce from nothing. If you conceal your circumstances, I will return to toasting bread and cheese."

Count Jonty Um stood to leave.

I didn't want him to leave us and perhaps lose his pet forever. "What does Nesspa look like? Is it a girl or a boy dog?"

"A boy. Big, up to my knee. His coat is gold."

"He has a beautiful black nose," I said. "I saw him."

The count crouched almost to my level. "When he sees me, he wags his tail. When he sleeps, he snores, like this." He growled in the back of his throat.

I held my breath. For a moment I thought he was going to turn into a dog, but he sat again and didn't shape-shift.

IT sank back down. "Might he have run away?"

His Lordship shook his head and sat again. "He never has. He is six years old." He paused. "Things have happened, but no danger. Only hatred of an ogre."

I nodded.

"The hatred is nothing new," IT said. "What *is* new?"

"Someone is stealing from me. Not just taking Nesspa." He paused again. I suspected he thought out each sentence before saying it. "Stealing things. Linens, a wall hanging, a harness, three knives."

"Ah," IT said.

"Someone is poaching. Maybe the same person. I don't

allow hunting in my woods. My deer and rabbits used to come to me. Now they're shy. Two mornings ago when I awakened, Nesspa was gone. He always sleeps on my bed."

"A servant?" IT asked.

"They're loyal."

I swear I felt IT think a snort at the certainty. "No one has sent you a ransom note."

"No one." He opened the drawstring on the leather purse at his waist and drew out a silver, which glinted between his thumb and forefinger.

Masteress Meenore ignored it.

"When you find Nesspa, I will give you three more silvers and one for your assistant."

For me? A silver? Two more and I could apprentice.

"My fee for finding your dog is two coppers."

"The silvers . . ."

They both turned to me.

"Never mind." But I wanted my silver.

"If I discover the people or the person endangering you," IT said, "and put an end to your risk, then I will expect payment in silver."

And a coin for me, too. Say it!

IT didn't.

"Why do you say I'm in danger, Meenore?"

"The hatred, which is nothing new, as I said, has always been tempered by fear. Now someone, or more than one,

106

is unafraid. That"—IT spread ITs claws, palms up—"is your danger."

I felt frightened, but I wasn't sure why. How could anyone hurt him?

"Tell me, Your Lordship, what is the reason for tomorrow's feast?"

He looked down at his hands. "I want people to visit me. And His Highness will make an announcement."

My masteress waited in vain for an explanation of the announcement.

His Lordship met ITs eyes. "Most of all I want them to come."

"Ah. Are you permitting your guests to bring cats?"

He reddened and nodded.

Why? Cats *were* a danger.

IT said, "To persuade fools to visit you, you agreed to foolish demands."

What did IT mean?

His Lordship mumbled—actually a quieter roar—"There will be dogs in the hall."

"Naturally. If they may bring a weapon, you must have a defense."

Oh. His guests had refused to come without their cats.

He clasped his hands so tight the knuckles whitened. "I want them to stop fearing me. And hating me. My steward suggested a feast. If they come and are safe, I hope the fear and hate will stop."

But why did they fear and hate him? I had lost my fright by being with him for only a short while.

IT stood. "I will endeavor to find your dog and save your life. Elodie will live in your castle for now, as my eyes and ears."

Lambs and calves! I went to the cupboard for my things.

IT added, "Take care, Elodie. Count, His Majesty and Her Highness are visiting you, are they not?"

"Yes."

Oh no, the king!

"Elodie, His Highness is economical. He has no fear of an ogre and likes the count's wood better than his own to keep him warm, the count's food better than his own to feed his gluttony."

"The girl Elodie is to reside in my castle?"

What was wrong with that?

"Good."

I smiled as I folded my spare kirtle into my satchel. If he liked, I could teach him the mansioner's tales.

He stood. "What will she do?"

"Your kitchen will need extra hands for the feast. Elodie, your hands will do if you can peel an apple, not merely weep over it."

Naturally I could. I drew tight the satchel strings. "But Masteress, the town knows I'm your assistant."

"Tomorrow, as I cook my skewers, I will mention that I let the count borrow you for a handsome sum."

Only serfs could be loaned out, and I was no serf. I hated for the count and the entire town to think me one.

"Your Lordship," IT said, "Elodie must have the run of the castle and your grounds. Let your steward know."

Count Jonty Um took his cloak and pulled it around him.

"Elodie, this is your charge." IT raised ITs snout and blew a long column of white smoke. "Seek the dog, yes. But above all, be alert to danger to His Lordship. Raise the alarm if you are alarmed. Do not hold back."

"What about the poaching?" I asked.

"Leave the poaching to me. And if Nesspa is not inside the castle, I will find him outside."

Count Jonty Um crossed the lair and picked up the end of the dog's chain.

"Farewell, Your Lordship. Elodie, I will come to the outer ward at dawn tomorrow for your report." IT raised ITs eyebrow ridges. "Do you know where the outer ward is?"

"The area between the castle and the walls that surround it?"

"Just so, although these walls are called curtains. Do not disgrace me."

I thought of my disappointing history as a caretaker of geese. And now I was to caretake an ogre!

Outside, clouds had begun to roll in. His Lordship

started down Lair Street, to my surprise. I had expected him to follow the ridge and avoid the bustle of the center of town. After a few steps, he slowed to my pace.

I walked on his right, Sheeyen on his left. The street was deserted here, so he didn't have to call his warning.

"I'm not a serf, Your Lordship."

He nodded.

"Your Lordship?"

He stopped.

"May I ask . . ."

"Yes."

I breathed in deeply. "Why don't they like you?"

He sat on his haunches. I still had to look up to see into his eyes.

"My father was not a kind ogre." He shook his head. "My mother was not kind to people, either. They didn't eat anyone. We don't eat humans. But they liked to frighten when they shifted shape. Fifteen years ago a child died. It was an accident, but it was my father's fault." He watched my face.

I didn't blame the son!

"The townsfolk think I am like my parents. They don't know any other ogres."

So he wanted to show them the difference, and they didn't want to see. I touched his cloak over his knee. "I understand."

We continued on, passing burghers' homes. A young woman with a broom stepped out of a doorway. As soon as she saw me, she hissed, "Save yourself. Run!" and darted back inside.

I reached up and took the count's hand. We proceeded past the next house and the next. A cat crossed the street in front of us, its head turned toward the count. Sheeyen trotted along silently.

"Nesspa would have barked."

The midafternoon bells tolled. The stalls and the throngs began.

"Make way. Ogre and girl."

"Not captive," I cried. "New servant at the castle."

He turned on Sabow Street, which led to the market square. In the square he let my hand go and made purchases—first a string sack, then food and more food: lamb pottage, fish golden with saffron (the rarest spice in the kingdom), boiled eggs, legs of roasted capons, pickled blue carrots, cheese, and bread. How my stomach rumbled.

No one hated him when he opened his purse. People nodded, chatted, thanked him.

My mouth watered. When he stopped the roving marchpane seller, my mouth became almost a fountain. He bought a dozen pieces and paid out two dozen coppers.

With a bulging sack, he started up Daycart Way and resumed his cry of "Make way." He continued blaring until we reached the wealthy homes again and the crowd had thinned to nothing.

We passed through the town's south gate and continued on. To the east, the mansioners' carts caught the light of the setting sun. As we took the north fork, I heard a shout followed by a laugh.

"They're rehearsing." And I am in my own mansioner's tale, I thought, accompanying an ogre to his castle, where the drama will occur.

When we had passed perhaps a quarter mile beyond the fork, with empty, harvested fields to our left and right, the count stopped.

"Your Lordship?"

"Watch. Do not be afraid. Everyone likes this." Eyes closed, he let Sheeyen's chain go and raised his arms in a gesture of command, like Zeus in a myth, calling forth lightning. His mouth widened in a silent scream, and his eyes bulged.

I *was* afraid! Had an arrow struck him from behind? I ran around him. No arrow, but he was clearly in pain. Sheeyen sat on her haunches and howled. I picked up her chain.

He shook from side to side and forward and back, becoming indistinct, a blur of motion—a shrinking blur. He was my height, then smaller, smaller still.

CHAPTER FOURTEEN

is Lordship's arms fell to his sides. The vibrating slowed and stopped. His cloak and tunic hung in heaps and folds over the narrow shoulders of a monkey, an animal I recognized from an illustration in Mother's only storybook. The monkey was hardly bigger than a fox, his miniature ivory face fringed by coarse orange fur.

He smiled infectiously, showing his teeth and gums. His amber eyes were merry.

I had to smile back.

He removed the count's clothes and shoes while grinning as if at the silliness of lavish attire, or attire at all. When he emerged, I saw how delicate he was—thin arms, thin legs, and a scrawny chest showing through his frill of fur. All the luxury was in his long bushy tail, which curled up at the end. He stood half erect on his two back legs, with one fisted hand on the ground.

I touched his arm to feel the fur, which was as rough as an otter dog's coat. As I stroked, a spark passed between us. The monkey threw back his head and panted, laughing, I thought.

Something had to be done with his clothing. I began to fold each item while wondering how I could fit it all into my satchel and then carry it as well as the sack of food.

I rolled his belt and tucked his purse—still heavy despite all the purchases—between his hose and his tunic. Meanwhile he bounced on his bare feet, chirping like a bird, adding a screech, a *choo*, and a sucking sound.

"I wish I spoke monkey language, Your Lordship." I folded the cloak and added the huge shoes, soles up, to the pile.

The pendant lay on the ground, apart from the rest. I hid it in the toe of a shoe.

Night would fall soon. Were we safe out here, where Two Castles's thieves might kill us for the pendant and the purse? A monkey who took five minutes to transform back into an ogre would be unable to defend us, and one dog wouldn't be enough to hold off a gang.

The monkey sat in the road and pulled apart the strings of the sack.

Sheeyen tried to stick her nose in, but I pulled her away.

"Your Lordship, we mustn't stay here. Robbers and bandits may come."

He chittered and patted the ground next to himself in a gesture that said as clearly as a word, *Sit.*

The monkey was a count. I sat.

No. I was human, and he was a monkey.

The road stretched along a low rise. In two trips, tugging Sheeyen along each way, I carried everything down the western slope to a spot low enough, I thought, that we wouldn't be noticed in the dark. The monkey followed, then sat again, pulling me down next to him. Together, we watched the sunset turn the sky gold and scarlet.

Chirping, he took a packet out of the sack and opened the burlap covering to reveal lamb pottage.

"Sit, Sheeyen," I said.

Pottage was humble food, but delicious: grain mixed with beans, a chopped onion, a little shredded meat, shaped into a ball, wrapped in a square of linen, simmered with other wrapped packages of carrots, celery, beets. At home we'd eat the pottage and vegetables atop a plate of stale bread with broth spooned over. At the end we'd break off pieces of our plates and devour them, too.

Here there was no broth, but the pottage was moist, with more meat than I was accustomed to. The monkey and I shared it, feeding each other by turn, as people do.

He ate daintily but as much as if he were still ogre size. I gave Sheeyen a little at first, too, then ignored her. After a while she lost hope and slept.

"Your Lordship, are you awake inside your present shape?"

For answer he twittered, but his eyes met mine in a way I had seen in no other animal. Perhaps he could understand and remember. I had questions, and I hoped he would answer them when he could speak again.

But before I could say anything, he pulled another packet out of the sack.

Lambs and calves! This was the saffron fish, as golden as if King Midas had touched it. The monkey held a chunk to my lips. I tasted, spat it out, and wiped my mouth on my sleeve. Ugh! Gold itself would taste better. How could people enjoy saffron so much?

The monkey's shoulders shook. He took a great handful of the awful mess and crammed it into his mouth. After he swallowed, he smiled and pointed at his teeth, now dyed yellow.

I couldn't help laughing.

Next he brought out pickled blue carrots. As we ate, the stars and the moon rose. I drew my cloak tight around me. The monkey jumped up, fetched the ogre's huge cloak, and draped it inexpertly over my shoulders, making his panting laugh and ignoring my protests that it would get dirty.

I covered my head with the cloak, which enfolded me, and inside I was as snug as if I were in the lair.

We continued eating. The sack collapsed as its contents slid into our stomachs. In the back of my mind, I was aware of the marchpane still remaining. No matter how much I ate, I would make room for it.

Between bites I spoke. "Pardon me, Your Lordship"—I cleared my throat nervously—"I have a few questions. . . ."

He went on chewing.

I asked about the dog, Nesspa, what his habits were, what he dined on, whose company he kept in addition to His Lordship's.

"My guess is"—I thought aloud, deducing or inducing or using my common sense—"that you don't often change shape, because changing hurts so much." More to myself than to the monkey, I said, "I wonder why you did with me."

He reached across the sack of food and pressed my hand. Had he become a monkey because he liked me, and the monkey would show the feeling more clearly than the ogre could? A lump grew in my throat. Love lay back in Lahnt with my family and Albin. Goodwife Celeste seemed to like me, but she'd as much as told me to stay away. Masteress Meenore appeared to like or dislike me according to my usefulness.

After a moment he let my hand go and fed me a chunk

117

of bread, which, more than the saffron, told me how it might feel to be rich. If you were rich, you could chew this bread without paying attention to how sweet and tangy it was. You wouldn't close your eyes as I was closing mine and savor each bite, because you could have more whenever you liked.

I returned to my questions. How long could he remain an animal? Forever, if he liked? Or for only a few hours? Did he have to stay shifted awhile before he could switch back? If he changed into, for example, a rabbit or an owl, did other rabbits or owls know he wasn't really one of them? Did he choose the sort of animal he would change into, or did it choose him?

Question everything. Could he get stuck inside an animal? Could magic force him into a shape and keep him in it?

"Is it strange to be yourself again after you've been a monkey?"

When the sack was almost flat, he drew out the small packet and opened it. Marchpane! I made out the shapes— strawberries, roses, tiny apples, daisies.

"May I sample one?" I heard awe in my voice.

He twittered. I took that as consent. If he'd snatched the packet away, I'd have taken that as consent as well and snatched it back.

I picked a rose and nibbled it. Oh, heaven. Father! I'm eating marchpane that no one stepped on.

I held the remainder of the rose out to the monkey, who took it and gave me an apple. Soon we finished the marchpane between us. Despite his ogre's appetite, he let me have most of it. When all was gone, he lay back and stared up at the stars.

"Can you find the constellations?" I lay back, too. "They're all from mansioners' tales, you know." I pointed as I spoke. "There's Cupid as a cherub and Thisbe's apple and Zeus's lightning rod."

The monkey chittered.

I let out a long breath. "Your Lordship, I came here to become a mansioner, and I will still be one someday."

He panted softly, perhaps chuckling at my ambition.

"I will be. Albin says I have a gift, and he mansioned everywhere, before counts and kings, although not King Grenville or you." I was off, telling a monkey about Albin and Mother and Father and Lahnt and the geese, telling him more than I'd told Masteress Meenore, despite ITs endless curiosity.

When my life's story ran out, I just watched the stars and smelled the earth around us until, not meaning to, I fell asleep.

When I woke, I smelled stone and saw darkness. Terrified, half asleep, I raised my arms. My fingers encountered only air. Ah. I had not been entombed. My fingers discovered that I lay on a pallet bed. A woolen blanket covered me from neck to toe. No, three blankets. My nose and ears were cold, but the rest of me was cozy warm. Whoever put me here—the monkey? the ogre? a servant?—had considered my comfort.

My eyes adjusted to the dark. I found my satchel a few inches from my head. Nearby, someone snored a barrel-chested snore. A woman's voice mumbled from a dream.

The room was vast, vaulted, Count Jonty Um's great hall, no doubt. I hadn't been in a castle since I was a baby, when Mother and Father presented me to the earl of Lahnt, but Albin had performed in castles. I had his descriptions to draw on. Although each castle was unique, he said, they resembled one another, like cousins in the castle family.

In the dimness, I surmised I lay among the servants' pallets, with my pallet in the middle of the group. The best places clustered close to the hearth, where a few embers still glowed. Against the opposite wall, another hearth also smoldered. High above us, slitted windows made a dotted line near the ceiling. From my low vantage point, I saw small squares of blue-black sky.

There would be lower, larger windows, too, recessed into the wall of the inner ward, the courtyard at the heart of the castle, but I couldn't see them from here.

My mind refused to return to sleep. The pallet next to mine might be occupied by His Lordship's enemy, the dog thief and poacher. Or the snorer might be the one. Or the mumbler. In some neglected castle nook, Nesspa might be whining and gnawing at the bars of a cage.

What better time than now to look for him?

I rose to my knees and found that I had been sleeping in my cloak. At the foot of the pallet, my shoes pointed away from me. I pulled them on, stood, and threaded my way between the sleepers.

As I walked, the rushes scattered across the floor swished, but no one stirred. I sniffed the air. The rushes had been strewn with bay leaves. How rich! How like a castle!

I paused to decide where to go. During the day, as I'd been told, the emptiness would be filled by trestle tables and benches and bustle. But now the furniture leaned against the wall. Ahead, in a row on a dais, stood three chairs, two human sized, one built for an ogre. Of the two, one chair gleamed silver, the other gold. The third, barely visible in the gloom, was wood.

Three doors always exited a great hall. One, at the end of the wall on my left, would lead to a tower, which would hold a donjon for supplies on the lowest floor and a residence above on the next two stories. The door on the wall to my right would open into the inner ward. The third door I couldn't see, but it should be behind the screen in the corner ahead, and this would take me into the kitchen, across which I would find another door to another tower.

Where to hide a dog? Perhaps in a tower or in the stables.

Statues win no races and find no dogs. I should decide and go.

The towers adjoining the hall would be most convenient to search, but also most dangerous in case I made a noise. I rejected them for now. Tonight I'd investigate the kitchen tower.

I tiptoed behind the screen to the door, which groaned as it opened. I stopped breathing and waited, listening for sounds of waking.

What would they do if they caught me?

Silence. I slipped through and left the door ajar, so it wouldn't groan on my return.

Now I was in a short passageway; castle walls are so thick that rooms are separated by little tunnels. I entered the enormous kitchen, only slightly smaller than the great hall.

Door on my right, but not the tower door. Dimly outlined shapes of tables, stools, benches, buckets. At last, to the left of the sink, the tower door.

I pressed my ear against it. Through the thick wood, I thought I heard a thud and a whine. I pictured Nesspa, hiding from thudding feet, whining in fright.

Of course the explanation was likely more innocent. The castle steward and his family, for example, could live above the donjon. Someone might have risen to use the garderobe and stubbed his toe.

This door opened noiselessly. A stairway rose to my right. Ahead, beyond an open doorway, a light flickered in the donjon. Grain sacks piled twice my height faced me, parted by a narrow aisle. Except for the aisle, the sacks butted one another, leaving not enough room between them for a rat, let alone a big dog.

The donjon wouldn't contain just grain, however. I started down the aisle. After perhaps ten steps, the piles ended, and I saw a candle in a holder on the floor and a monstrous shadow flowing across rows of barrels, the shadow bigger by far than the ogre.

I backed away. Don't hear me! Don't see me! Whatever sort of monster you are, be deaf and blind!

Safely out the tower door, I sped through the kitchen and across the great hall to the servants' pallets, where I turned about, looking for the biggest sleeper.

There. I knelt at his side and shook his shoulder. He rolled over. I shook harder.

He raised his head. "What?" Then he leaped up, tucking his blanket around his waist. He wasn't as tall as he'd seemed from above, but he was muscular, with a hairy chest and a graying beard. He grasped my arm, whispering, "Who are you?"

"Someone is in the donjon."

"By thunder, who are you?"

"The new kitchen maid." I repeated, "Someone is in

the kitchen tower donjon. Or something. It's big."

His grip tightened. "How do you know?"

"I know." What else could I say? "I saw."

He half dragged, half lifted me out of the hall, making much more noise than I'd have dared. No one woke. In the kitchen he took a long knife from a chopping table. "This will do. By thunder, it will do for you if no one's there."

"Hurry!" I said, terrified of whatever was in the donjon and almost as terrified of this man.

But at the doorway he paused, yanked me up to his height, my feet dangling. "The steward hired you? By thunder, I'll—"

"Not the steward." My arm hurt! "The count said more help was needed for the feast. His Lordship brought me."

He let me go. I staggered sideways as he flung the tower door open. I pointed down the grain aisle at the glimmering light. He tugged me along.

I saw the misshapen shadow again. He saw the person making the shadow.

"Your Highness." He dropped to his knees. "Pardon us."

I looked beyond the shadow and saw a tall woman with stiltlike limbs, thin shoulders wrapped in a blanket, thin hands holding the blankets, trailing sleeves, a head in a cap circled by a thin golden crown. I fell to my knees, too. The king's daughter, Princess Renn.

CHAPTER FIFTEEN

"eg pardon." I bowed my head.

"You have a knife? Against me?" Her voice rose in pitch until it cracked, then started lower and rose until it cracked again. "Enemies from Tair!"

The knife thudded to the floor. "Not from Tair, Your Highness. From right here. She"—he pulled my head up by my hair—"by thunder, she said there was an intruder in the donjon."

I saw the princess more clearly. She had a heart-shaped face, cleft chin, small mouth, and a long, sloping nose. She might have been pretty if her blue eyes had been merely large, but they were enormously large with too much white. If she missed beauty, however, her mouth was sweet and her big eyes full of feeling, both fear and outrage.

"Who are you?"

He pulled back his shoulders. "Master Jak, His Lordship's chief third assistant cook, Your Highness."

Princess Renn's lips twitched in a hint of a smile. She turned to me.

"I'm *Ehh*"—I extended the vowel even longer than a Two Castles person would—"lodie, the new kitchen maid." If they were going to oust me or imprison me, they should know my proper name.

In the silence, I listened but heard no dog whimpers, no scrabbling paws, no panting.

"*Eh*lodie," the princess said, "why did you come to the donjon?"

Feigning innocence, I said in a rush, "I'm the new kitchen maid and I woke and couldn't fall back to sleep and I've never been in a castle before and thought I might look around and I'd heard that His Lordship lost his dog and if I could find it, it would be a fine thing and I came here and I didn't see you, Your Highness, I saw your shadow." I pointed.

The shadow still hulked. Princess Renn was thin, but the blanket expanded her. Her shadow suggested a bearlike creature with a tiny head.

She laughed and held out her arms, making the shadow even bigger. "La! Look at me!"

My shoulders relaxed in relief. Master Jak laughed, too,

although his laughter sounded forced.

"I am afraid myself of myself! Jak, rise! *Eh*lodie, rise! Spread your arms."

Papa and mama and daughter monster shadows filled the donjon. Master Jak's laughter turned genuine.

When our laughter subsided, the princess said, "I commend you both on your courage. *Eh*lodie! To come back after you'd seen the monster! And Chief Third Assistant Cook Jak! To brave the monster with only a knife! Jak, you may return to your well-deserved rest."

But I might not?

Master Jak picked up his knife. As he backed out of the donjon, his eyes were on me, and their expression was not friendly.

"*Eh*lodie, stay awhile. We are both sleepless, and my maid is snoring. I should like company."

How would I be company for a princess, unless she wanted to hear about mansioners' plays or the antics of Lahnt geese?

When the door closed behind Jak, Princess Renn held her candle up to my face. "La! You are a child!"

"Fourteen, Your Highness."

"You are not a minute past twelve." She frowned. "You don't sleep in a cap?"

"No, Your Highness."

"But during the day you wear one?"

"No, Your Highness. On Lahnt, where I come from, only married women and men wear caps, except in winter, when we all wear them."

"But you live here now. Are you too poor to own a cap?" She put so much feeling into *poor* that I almost wept for myself.

I shifted from my left foot to my right. Probably everyone who'd seen me since I'd arrived thought of me as The Girl Too Poor to Own a Cap. "I will save to buy one."

"You can have mine. I have others. Here." She raised her hand to her head. I saw a gold ring on her middle finger. As her sleeve fell away, two gold bracelets gleamed in the candlelight. "Hold this." She removed her crown and held it out to me.

I took it. How strange she was. Kind, very kind, but strange.

And the crown was strange in my hands, dreamlike, unexpectedly heavy for such a thin band, only an inch or two wide, without a single jewel. The metal had the sheen of moist skin, the upper rim unexpectedly sharp, the lower smooth. For a mad moment I imagined running off with it.

She donned her crown again and put the cap on me. "You have a small head." The cap's flaps nearly met under my chin. "But you'll grow into it." She inspected me, her face close to mine.

I smelled cardamom oil, the same perfume Mother wore.

Woe invaded her voice. "Oh! It's too fine. They'll think you stole it." She walked in a circle in the small clear space among the barrels. "My maid has several caps, which would do, but I don't want to waken her." She put a hand on a barrel. "Might there be caps in a barrel?"

"They probably hold pickles or some such, Your Highness." The stores were for a siege, and no one could eat caps. I took off the cap, but I wanted it. "I can turn it, Your Highness."

"What?"

I spoke louder. "I can turn it."

"La! I heard you. Turn it?"

A princess wouldn't know what ordinary folk did. "Some people, when their caps are worn, turn them on the other side where the fabric is less used. No one will think me a thief in a turned cap."

"Then I may give you the gift! *Eh*lodie, you are clever." She kissed my forehead.

Lambs and calves!

I reversed the cap and tied it back on.

"Let me." She tied the strings twice more. "There. This is how I tie my cap. Now you will not lose it. I believe in thoroughness. See?" To my astonishment she lifted the hem of her kirtle. "Two chemises underneath. Thoroughness. Now let us search for Nesspa together. For Jonty Um's sake, we'll put our sleeplessness to use. Where shall we look, *Eh*lodie?"

"The stables?" The count had probably searched there—and here—but the dog might have been taken somewhere else first.

"Excellent. The grooms will be asleep. La! Hide an animal among animals, like hiding a ring in a mountain of rings."

Nothing like hiding a ring among rings, but I didn't say so.

She held out her hand. "We'll go there now."

How courteous she was, to clasp the hand of a kitchen maid.

We left the tower. The princess walked with a bounce as we crossed the inner ward and passed between two apple trees laden with fruit.

"He will be so happy if we find Nesspa." She stopped, tugging me to a stop, too. "If we find Nesspa, I want to bring him to His Lordship. I want him to be grateful to me alone."

"Yes, Your Highness." I could give no other answer, although I wanted Masteress Meenore to be known as the finder, through me. "Do you . . ." She seemed friendly enough to answer a question. "Do you hold His Lordship in high esteem, Your Highness?" I wanted to know if anyone did.

"Certainly I do. I esteem him very much!" We walked

again. "He is taller than I, wealthy, with excellent table manners."

So much for true esteem.

"The miller's son, Thiel, is also taller than I and possesses fine table manners, but he isn't wealthy."

My Lahnt table manners might not be good enough for Master Thiel.

"Jonty Um is handsome for an ogre, don't you think? Not so handsome as Thiel, I suppose. Do I esteem Jonty Um?" She raised her arms and twirled, kicking an apple across the courtyard. "Father has betrothed me to him, *Eh*lodie. A king always betroths a princess."

My mouth fell open. Hastily, I closed it. News of the coming marriage had not reached Lahnt. I wondered if it was widely known here and if my masteress knew. Few in Two Castles could be pleased.

We started walking again.

"I shouldn't have told you. It's still a secret. Father wants wealth, a strong arm in battle, a lion if need be, and I like a strong arm, too." She laughed. "And a gentle lion. La! He is lovely as a monkey. I do not fancy him as a bird."

I didn't know what to think. Would they be happy?

We reached a door and, to the side, a descending stairway. I stopped, not knowing which we wanted, door or stair.

"You are ignorant, *Eh*lodie." Her voice was gay. "The stables are below."

Twelve steps down took us to another wooden door. I eased open the bolt, hoping not to awaken any sleeping stable hands. As soon as the door cracked an inch, I smelled the familiar farm odors.

Oh. Hot bran. I whispered, "An animal is ill." Hot bran and something else that smelled sharp and stung my nose.

"La! Very ill?"

How could I tell from the scent of a poultice? "I don't know, Your Highness, but someone is likely to be tending the beast."

I heard voices, one of them a lilting, "Honey, honey." Master Dess!

"What should we do, *Eh*lodie?"

Leave? Sneak in?

Neither. She was a princess and could do what she liked. "Perhaps Your Highness might enter, announce your presence, say you were sleepless, wanted air, and heard voices."

She nodded eagerly. "I can do that."

"You might ask what's amiss. I'll wait a minute and come in after. If anyone notices me, I'll say I lost my kitten and—"

"Jonty Um allows no cats."

Of course not. "Er . . . my pet pig."

"Do you have a pet pig?"

"No, Your Highness."

"Aha! Subterfuge." She flung the door open.

132

I jumped away from the doorway.

She strode inside.

I peeked in and saw her march through a wide aisle between animal stalls. "What's amiss?" she cried. "I was sleepless, heard voices, and wanted air."

Not quite right, but who would question her?

I slipped in, mansioning myself as a shadow. This end of the stable was in deep gloom, but I saw fireplace glow far to my left, and tallow lamps shed smoky light on a distant stall straight ahead, where two men stood.

"Your Highness?" The speaker wasn't Dess, and his accent was neither Two Castle nor Lahnt. He pronounced his *h* as *ch*, *ch*ighness.

I peered over the gate into the first stall along the aisle, where a sow and her piglets slept, nestled together as neatly as a mended plate. No Nesspa.

Princess Renn cried, "Is one of the beasts ill? Desperately ill?"

Had we happened on another affront to His Lordship, someone injuring one of his animals? The sow grunted in her sleep.

The voice with the new accent said, "Your Highness, a stable is no place for a lady."

"A princess is not a lady." She sounded indignant. "They are entirely different. Who are you?"

"Gise. Head groom, Your Highness."

I shrank into the shadow of the stall as Master Gise advanced toward her. If I moved, he would certainly see me.

"The matter is well in hand, Your Highness. Master Dess, the animal physician, is tending the beast."

Master Dess, the animal physician?

Of course he would be. Perhaps he'd been on his way to a sick animal when I'd seen him outside the king's castle.

"I should like to observe, now I'm here."

"As you wish, Your Highness."

They started off. I waited a minute or two before moving. Then I followed, peeking into horse stalls, cow stalls, and another pig stall as I went.

But if Nesspa were here, he would bark or whimper, unless he was asleep or unconscious. Or dead.

Princess Renn and Master Gise walked toward the lamplight, past a corner stall and the intersecting aisle.

"Sickness or injury?" the princess asked.

"Flying goat spiders, Your Highness," Master Gise said.

"On a goat? I must see."

I reached the corner stall. As I turned left toward the firelight, I knocked over a broom, which landed with a soft thud. I froze, my heart booming in my ears.

"What was that?" Master Gise said.

"La! I heard something fall over."

Was she addlepated? Did she want me caught?

"I'll go and see," Master Gise said.

134

I eased open the next stall I came to. Crouching, I backed in with my eyes shut, as if I'd be unseen if I couldn't see.

"It must have been only a mouse," she said. "No need to go."

"I'll be just a minute."

"Stay, Gise. I need you to hold her head. There, honey."

Thank you, Master Dess.

"The bites are blue and green and puffed, like moldy bread." Princess Renn's voice quivered. "The pitiable, hapless goat."

I opened my eyes and turned to see what animal I had joined. No beast, but a man sprawling on his side across the hay.

He lay with his back to me, his shoulder inches from my thigh. I had been lucky not to bump into him. He didn't stir, quite a sleeper to slumber through the dropped broom, Master Dess's visit, and the princess's up-and-down voice. Could he be . . . ?

I knelt over him. His chest rose and fell. Drunk, perhaps.

As I rose, I saw him better: golden hair bronzed by the darkness, firm jaw, muscular arm. And on his finger, a ring of twine.

Master Thiel?

CHAPTER SIXTEEN

es! Master Thiel. How sweetly he slept, as deeply as a child.

Was he one of the count's grooms, or did he have no other place to lay his head? My heart went out to him if he had no home.

My heart went out to him if he had a dozen homes. Quietly, I left the stall.

"Do you treat Jonty Um when he is ill?"

"Princess, His Lordship is not a beast."

"He is tended by Sir Maydsin," Master Gise said, "as you and your father are."

"La!" I heard embarrassment in her voice. "I meant when he is a beast. Have you ever tended him when he was a monkey?"

"No, Your Highness. Hush, honey. I meant *hush* to the goat, Your Highness."

Where might Nesspa be hidden? And if I found him, what would I do?

"What are you putting on her?"

"Bran, Your Highness."

If it was just bran, what was that sharp smell?

I entered a large open area. Ahead, on the outer castle wall, firelight cast a red glow and provided faint illumination. My view of the fireplace itself was blocked by carts and trestles topped with harnesses and saddles. This would be the likely spot to hide anything.

The princess's voice twanged. "Why is she rolling her neck so?"

"There are many bites, Princess. She is very sick."

A thorough search would take hours. I began by peering into the blackness under the nearest cart, but seven snoozing dogs could be there and I wouldn't see them.

I tiptoed to the fireplace and saw the expected: three stable hands sleeping on their pallets. Mustn't wake them. I picked my way silently between two of them and found the poker. But on my return, I accidentally tapped a slumberer's shoulder with the toe of my shoe.

Luckily, he faced away from me. He rose groggily on one elbow. I stopped breathing.

For a full minute he didn't move, but then he rolled

onto his stomach, and I tiptoed away.

I used the poker to probe gently under a cart. No Nesspa, so I climbed into the cart itself, which turned out to be a bench wagon for bringing guests to the castle. I felt beneath the benches. My fingers encountered no animals, but they brushed against a morsel of fabric, which I picked up. By feel it was a pouch, holding nothing heavy, perhaps holding nothing. Still, its owner might want it. By feel again, I opened my purse and stuffed it in. In the morning I would try to find the owner.

As I climbed out of the cart, I heard a bleat and then a groan from deep in the stable.

"Alack! Is she dying?"

No one answered. Then, finally, Master Dess said, "The goat is dead."

Poor creature.

"Dead? Deh-eh-eh-d!" Princess Renn wailed.

A horse neighed. I groped under another wagon, then climbed in and explored. The cart was empty but for a thin layer of straw.

"In the morning," Master Gise said, "I will have the carcass removed and inform His Lordship."

"Dead people are called *remains*," the princess said. "Why should a beast be called a *carcass*?"

It did seem unfair. I hoped Nesspa wasn't a carcass. I looked under an overturned wheelbarrow. Nothing.

"Princess," Master Dess said, "in death the goat will be treated with respect. I swear to it."

They were silent until Master Gise said, "You should return to your apartment, Your Highness."

Her voice rose. "*Should?* I think I should stay with this goat and mourn her death. You both may go."

Lambs and calves, she was good! Presence of mind, Father would have said. Master Gise and Master Dess would leave, and she and I could search together, but I'd have to warn her about waking Master Thiel and the stable hands.

"Your Highness, Master Gise lives here, and I will sleep here as well tonight."

They would pass me on the way to their pallets! I crept toward the aisle of stalls. I had to get out, and quickly.

"Then I will stay only a minute or two and let you have your rest. Will you join me in an *Eh*lodie—oh! I meant *eulogy*—to these remains."

Did Master Dess know my name? I couldn't remember. I tiptoed by the carts as fast as I could go.

"We must leave this life"—her voice rose on *leave*, a signal for me, as if I needed one—"all of us, whether goat or grasshopper, child or chicken, person or panther, human or heron. . . ." She was entirely carried away. I hoped she would continue until I escaped.

While she named more pairings, I reached the middle

aisle we had entered through and worked my way past the stalls. As I went by, I peeped into Master Thiel's stall for a second glimpse of him. The stall was empty. I halted, squinted, looked away and back again. Still empty.

". . . and even an ox or a camel or a bumblebee may be mourned. La! Perhaps not so much a bumblebee."

Had I looked in the wrong stall? No. There was the broom I'd knocked over. Had I imagined Master Thiel?

"The goat will surely be mourned. Maker of goat's milk, giver of goat cheese, happy in life, she deserves these few words in her memory."

I neared the doors.

"Now, masters, I will let you finish the night in sleep."

I was out. I flew up the stairs and waited for her in the inner ward.

What would I do if Master Gise or Master Dess decided to escort her to the donjon?

She came out alone. "Was I not quick-witted to secretly tell you to leave? Did you find Nesspa?"

I nodded, then shook my head. "I may have missed him in the dark."

She patted the top of my cap. "You did your best." She yawned. "I shall continue the search tomorrow. Go to your bed, *Eh*lodie, and I will go to mine."

I went to my pallet but not to instant sleep. A servant nearby moaned from a dream. At home, Albin was a quiet sleeper. The cottage was small, cozy. I would be tucked into bed, a pallet there, too, nestled in our little house tight against our mountain, thrice snug and sheltered.

And thrice loved.

I rolled onto my side. What had I learned tonight?

That the princess was kind and gave away caps and was going to marry an ogre despised by her subjects. That Master Thiel and Master Dess could pop up anywhere. That Master Dess was an animal physician. That a dog was not easily found. That, so far as I could tell, I had discovered nothing to help my masteress deduce or induce and nothing to keep His Lordship from harm.

CHAPTER SEVENTEEN

wareness of the meeting with my masteress must have awakened me while my fellow servants still slumbered. My eyes felt gritty from too little sleep. I sat up and straightened the princess's cap, sliding the bows from my left ear to my chin.

The fire had died down to nothing. I placed my satchel under my mattress and tidied the blankets over the lump. The pallet would be stacked, but I didn't know where, so I left it. I owned nothing to interest a thief.

Hugging my cloak, I exited into the inner ward. At the well I splashed my face, although a little water wouldn't pass for cleanliness with IT. Then I ran through the postern passage, an arched tunnel to the postern door, which opened onto the west side of the outer ward.

Dawn hadn't yet come, but the growing light revealed a fishpond to my right and a double row of fruit trees along the outer curtain, the castle's outermost wall.

Where would IT land? Each side of the castle was a quarter mile long. Had IT come down already on the other side? IT wasn't in the sky, and I might be expected to deduce where IT would land. *Enh enh enh.*

I smelled not a whiff of spoiled eggs. I started toward the back of the castle, reasoning that IT would be unlikely to land in front, where the gatehouses were and where guards might come swarming out.

As I rounded the tower, I saw ahead three fenced-in herb and vegetable gardens. Along the inner curtain bloomed Lepai rosebushes, which can flower through a light frost.

Ah, there IT was, flying from the west. IT sailed over the outer curtain, then wheeled to and fro just as the sun rose.

"Masteress!" I cried.

The tip of ITs tail flicked, in recognition of me, I supposed, but IT continued to fly, swooping here and there. When ITs face turned toward me, I saw a wild grin.

IT landed in the middle of the ward with ITs right claw outstretched. ITs left claw held three filled skewers.

I heard a terrified *yeep!* As I watched in horror, IT raised a fat brown hare to ITs flame. A minute later, IT held out the roast.

"Would you like a haunch, Lodie?"

I shook my head and kept half the ward between IT and me.

"Then come and eat your skewers. Breakfast will be gone by the time you return indoors."

I rushed close for the skewers—uncooked—then backed away.

IT sat, placed the hare on ITs thigh, and carved the meat with ITs talons.

"Are you the ogre's poacher?" I blurted.

ITs smoke blued. "I induce and deduce flawlessly, but occasionally I forget common sense. I should have let the rabbit live." IT devoured ITs meal quickly, bones as well as meat. "I am no poacher"—ITs smoke whitened, ITs discomfort over—"not since I gave up catching and toasting young maidens." *Enh enh enh.*

I smiled, although I imagined a squirming, shrieking girl in ITs claws. My fear of IT surged back.

"Lodie . . . come closer." IT held my gaze.

I went, but slowly.

"Answer me. Even if you are a budding mansioner, I will know if you are lying. Do you believe I might roast a person?"

I swallowed. I wished Goodwife Celeste had never frightened me.

ITs smoke was bright pink, ITs scales red. "Angry as I

am right now, am I flaming at you?"

I shook my head.

"I could broil you and eat you, and your parents would not know and no one here would care. . . ."

His Lordship might care. "You told me to doubt everyone."

"Yes, but test your doubt. You slept in my lair unharmed for two nights. And during one of those nights, you were grimy and flea ridden. Awareness of your dirty state troubled my sleep."

When I'd been awakened by the roaring, IT had been soundly asleep.

"Yet I did not harm even a lobe of your ear. Alas, you are almost as filthy as before, for all that you now have a cap." IT lowered ITself onto ITs belly, keeping ITs head high. "Tell me what has happened and what you have learned."

The most important news first. "Her High—"

"Wait." IT lumbered to the outer curtain at the end of the herb gardens.

I followed, munching on bread and cheese, no longer afraid.

"The castle has ears, but the outer curtain is deaf. Now, speak."

"Princess Renn is to marry His Lordship."

"Start at the beginning, Lodie."

I did. Under ITs prompting I recalled details I would have forgotten. For a mansioner, this was fine memory training. Still, I didn't remember enough to satisfy IT. I had a sinking feeling of failure, just as I used to about the geese.

When I raved over how sweet the monkey was, IT held up a claw. "Emotion is of no consequence."

But it was! "Please, Masteress, listen. He is a kindly ogre under his gruffness."

"Inconsequential." IT asked a dozen more questions about the journey to the castle, then progressed to my meeting with the princess. IT *enh enh enh*ed endlessly over the monstrous shadow.

"If people in Two Castles know she is to marry His Lordship," I said, "they must be furious. No one in the town wants to be ruled by an ogre someday."

"I agree." IT went on to questions about what had taken place in the stable.

Finally, when I thought I might pass the rest of my life in the outer ward, IT asked, "Is there anything else?"

My mind squeezed itself until I had a headache. Oh! How could I have forgotten this? "Master Thiel was sleeping in the stables. He slept through Princess Renn's shrieking."

"Or seemed to."

I blurted, "Masteress, is he in need? Without a home?" Suffering? Could I help him?

"His father left him nothing and gave the mill and the mule to his brothers, but never fear. Thiel will make his fortune through marriage. Half the maidens in Two Castles are wild for him. If you have set your new cap for him"—*enh enh enh*—"you had best have more than three tins. Thiel's blood runs noble. His great-great-grandfather, a knight, was the first owner of Jonty Um's castle. Thiel's bride—"

"What happened?"

"Lodie, do not interrupt your masteress."

I apologized.

"Debts, extravagance. Jonty Um's grandfather bought the castle from Thiel's grandfather without regard for the opinion of the town."

Another reason for people to dislike the count.

"Thiel looks much as the old man once did. I do not fancy him for you, so it is just as well you are poor."

I didn't enjoy being teased. "The stall he'd been sleeping in was empty on my way out."

"Mmm. You peered into the same stall of a certainty?"

"I dropped a broom there."

"Think. He may have moved the broom to a different stall."

I blushed. I should have thought of that. "I picked this up in a wagon in the stable." I pulled the little pouch out of my purse and opened it. The contents were only a few half-dried leaves. When I brought them to my nose, I smelled peppermint.

Goodwife Celeste?

"What is it?"

"Peppermint." Had she been in the stables and then gone? I turned the pouch over in my hand, looking for some distinctive mark, but it was plain brown wool of ordinary quality. I thought back to the cog and was certain I hadn't seen a pouch. "Do the goodwives of Two Castles carry peppermint?"

IT held the pouch up against the sun. "A healer might. A traveler might. The animal physician may have dropped it. A goodwife of the town would keep her herbs at home."

"On the cog the goodwife Celeste gave me peppermint leaves. Do you remember I told you that I met her and her goodman when I was proclaiming?"

"Naturally I remember."

I took a deep breath. "I didn't mention that she warned me against you. She said you're moody and might do anything if . . ."

IT stretched ITs neck and aimed a puff of fire skyward. The flame guttered out before reaching the ground. "Because dragons have fire, we're believed to be hot-tempered."

IT did have a temper.

"Everyone has a temper, Lodie."

"Masteress, she wears a bracelet of twine. Master Thiel has a twine ring. Is there a league of wearers of twine jewelry?"

"Mmm."

Mmm again. I returned the pouch to my purse. "Masteress, I like her, and she may not have been in the stables."

"She warned you away from me!" IT stood on ITs back legs. "I will return at the nine-o'clock bells tonight. As soon as His Lordship's guests arrive, remain with him." IT flapped ITs wings. "Do not let him out of your sight. Trust no one. Keep him safe."

How could a girl keep an ogre safe?

IT circled above me. "You can shout. A person half your size can shout. Act!"

CHAPTER EIGHTEEN

n the kitchen, Master Jak, chief third assistant cook, whom I'd awakened the night before, swore at me for my late arrival, then grinned evilly. "Onions, *Eh*lodie. By thunder, onions." He led me to the long kitchen worktable.

I scanned the room for Master Thiel, but he wasn't there.

"Sit."

I climbed onto a stool next to a sack of onions that rose to my elbow. Master Jak supplied me with a chopping knife, a peelings pail, and a big bowl for the chopped onions. He said a scullery maid would take away the bowl when it was filled and bring it back empty.

"His Lordship likes onions in his soup and onions in his stew," Master Jak said, "and he is devoted to his onion pie.

Don't stop until they're all chopped. By thunder, no weeping into them, *Eh*lodie."

I began. Soon tears were falling into my lap, and yes, into the onions. Weeping made me think of mansioning. A true mansioner won't use an onion to make her cry. I wondered if a true mansioner could conjure happiness and not cry in spite of a mountain of onions. I couldn't.

Hoping the owner wouldn't mind, I took the peppermint out of its pouch and put a leaf on my tongue. The mint helped against the onions, but not much.

The onions and I were stationed at the menial end of the table, far from the actual cooking. At the important end, yards and yards away, a baker kneaded dough, her arms floury up to the elbows. Next to her, another baker rolled out pastry. A scullery maid complained that her mortar and pestle were missing, and how could she pound the garlic and thyme without them? Master Jak told her to find a bowl and a spoon and cease griping.

At his own table, the butcher cut apart a lamb. Blood ran down grooves in the table to a pail on the floor. A small spotted dog—not Nesspa—sat at the butcher's feet, staring ardently upward.

Master Jak and three others stood at the largest of three fireplaces, tending whatever was cooking. I wondered if Master Jak's companions were the chief second assistant cook and the chief first assistant cook and the exalted cook.

I considered whether Nesspa could be stowed here somewhere. The lower half of the enormous cupboard between the two lesser fireplaces was big enough to hold a sheep. As if a fairy was granting wishes, a kitchen boy opened the double doors to get a frying pan, and I glimpsed shelves crammed with pots and pans. I saw no other likely place to hide a dog.

Sharing my end of the table, a boy—my age more or less, cap strings untied, narrow face, small brown eyes— peeled cucumbers.

He winked at me. "I'm in your debt, young mistress, for taking the onions."

I was not partial to winkers, but I winked back. "I'm new, young master. I never saw the inside of a castle before today."

Another wink from him. "A castle's big so a count or a king can bring his friends in and keep his enemies' armies out."

"How clever." I nodded encouragingly. Tell me something that will lead me to Nesspa or that I can tell Masteress Meenore.

"Thick walls, soldiers within, enough food to last a month. If we die, the rats can eat us for another month."

Ugh!

He winked yet again. "If grand folk didn't have enemies, they could live in houses."

If poor folk had money, they could live in castles. "I

never saw an ogre or a dragon before I came to town."

"How do you like them?" He picked up another cucumber.

I'd minced three onions to his single cucumber. "They're both big. I saw the ogre turn himself into a monkey. What a sight that was!"

His smile reached his ears. "He's a fine monkey."

"Do you think him fine as an ogre, too?"

"His *Lordship*"—he stressed the title—"pays better wages than any other master, and never a beating or a harsh word." He winked. "Hardly a word at all. What does that matter?"

"The people of Two Castles seem not to care for him."

"That den of thieves! None of us comes from there. They won't work for him, and we wouldn't work for anyone else."

If all the servants came from elsewhere, then Master Thiel couldn't be a groom or any sort of servant. "They say His Lordship's dog was taken right here in the castle. Who would do such a thing?"

He thrust his head at me, then drew back because of the onions, no doubt. "We wouldn't!"

He had no more winks or words for me. I nicked my finger and sucked the drop of blood that beaded up. Master Jak would see red if the onions were pink.

The castle bells rang midmorning.

A hand gripped my shoulder. "By thunder, His Lordship

wants you to be cupbearer at the feast and pour for him, the king, and the princess." Master Jak turned me on my stool. "Have you poured before?"

The king! "At home, from pitcher to cup."

"At home." He sighed and let my shoulder go. "Pitcher. Cup. By thunder."

The boy laughed. Master Jak glared at him, and he lowered his head and peeled.

"I have a steady arm." But I didn't know how steady it would be, pouring for Greedy Grenny.

"Cellarer Bwat will show you. *Eh*lodie, those you serve should have what they want before they know they want it. Watch their hands, their shoulders, their faces. Even though you stand behind them, contrive to see."

How? I would lean over and spill wine on everyone.

"His Lordship requested you. The princess will be forbearing, but if you spill a drop, even a speck of a drop, on the king . . . By thunder, don't."

What if I did? A flogging? Prison?

A woman's voice called, "Master Jak, do you have the suet crock?"

He called back. "There's another in the cupboard." He put his hand under my chin and pulled my face toward his. I saw his pores, the veins in his eyes, a drop of sweat sliding down his nose. "If you spoil His Lordship's day—if you cause him a moment of grief—you will feel the wrath of a chief third assistant cook. Cellarer Bwat will come for you in a minute." He strode away.

I lifted the half-full bowl of onions onto my lap. With the side of my knife, I scraped chopped onions from the chopping board into the bowl.

Master Jak stood over me again. "I near forgot. After the second remove, before the mansioners perform, His Lordship would like you to recite for his guests."

"Recite?" I jumped up. "Something? Truly? Oh, Master Jak!" I wiped my tears with my fist. "What should I recite?"

"Whatever you . . ." He looked down.

I did, too. Unaware, I'd let my bowl slide to the floor, spilling the onions.

I was sorry, but I didn't care. I was going to mansion!

If I wasn't first sent to jail.

Cellarer Bwat's most prominent feature, his bushy, white eyebrows, stood out from his face. If my pouring went amiss, his watery blue eyes might spring open wide and pop his eyebrows off.

His lips were pinched, his nose a mere button. His head tilted permanently in a listening attitude. He led me out of the kitchen, walking bent from the waist, as if he spoke only to seated people. As I followed, I thought about what to recite.

I could tell the touching tale of Io, who was doomed

to roam the world as a heifer. No, not a good choice, to portray a shape-shifted cow in the presence of a shape-shifting ogre.

"Don't dawdle, girl."

"My name is Elodie, Cellarer Bwat."

The vast emptiness of the great hall had been filled. Boards mounted on trestles and placed end to end formed a table that stretched two-thirds the length of the chamber. A shorter trestle table had been erected on the dais, with the three chairs drawn up to it. Benches flanked the chairs. Neither table had yet been covered with cloth, and the bare, pocked wood looked shabby.

The walls were hung with linen panels, freshly dyed, colors bright. A scene of feasting spread across the outer wall. The diners could pretend the fabric an improving reflection, their persons made beautiful or handsome as they raised tumblers, fed one another, laughed, or sang.

On the opposite wall, the hangings depicted an animal parade led by a lion, ending with a mouse. In the middle I spied a large golden dog, a monkey, a beaver, a boar, and many more. Some of them I suspected of being fantastical: a creature with an endless neck, a striped horse, an awkward beast with a lump on its back as big as a wheelbarrow. I wondered if one was the high eena Masteress Meenore said I'd heard when I'd passed the menagerie.

Among all the animals there was not a single cat.

Servants were placing trestles for side tables. Cellarer Bwat took me to the end of the long table just below the dais, where a wine bottle, a pitcher of water, a goblet, and two tumblers had been placed. On the floor stood a beer barrel with a spigot screwed into its side.

In an urgent, loud whisper, Cellarer Bwat said, "You will uncork the wine with a sharp twist of the wrist." He demonstrated in the air, then gave me the bottle.

What tale should I perform?

I held the bottle in my left hand, the cork in my right, then twisted. Half the cork remained in the bottle.

Cellarer Bwat sighed and called in an even louder whisper for another bottle. "Pull while you twist."

Should I recite the speech of a young siren, newly arrived on her rock, before she has lured her first mariner to his death? It was moving and right for my years.

Cellarer Bwat said, "You will pass the open bottle below the noses, first of His Highness, then of His Lordship, an inch below their noses, no closer, no farther, so they may smell the wine. Do not pass the bottle under the princess's nose."

"Why not, Cellarer Bwat?"

"Her upper lip will grow. Wine has that effect on ladies."

The inner ward door opened. Cellarer Bwat fell to his knees with a crack that must have hurt. He tugged me into a curtsy.

"Stay down," he hissed.

I raised my head to see who'd entered. Cellarer Bwat pushed it down. I had only a moment to take in a tall, paunchy man with shoulders pulled back, wearing a bright red cloak.

The voice was familiar, in a lower register than the one I knew, but just as prone to soaring and plummeting. The speaker could only be the king. "I had hardly awakened when the loveliest breakfast arrived at my door. Scalded milk with honey, neither too hot nor too cold." His voice rose half an octave. "Perfect! Accompanied by two scones, and they were warm, too!"

A retelling of every morsel of his breakfast followed, while Cellarer Bwat and I knelt. From the corner of my eye, I saw the other servants kneeling, too. My neck cramped.

"Now I'm hoping it will be possible to secure a slice of ginger cake on this pretty dish." Porcelain rattled. He'd opened His Lordship's plate cabinet.

"Certainly, Your Highness." A servant must have taken the plate.

Feet and ankles in leather-soled hose entered the area of floor I could see. "What are you two doing?"

"Bowing to you, Your Highness," Cellarer Bwat whispered.

"Curtsying to you, Your Highness," I whispered.

"Before I came in, of course. You may stand."

We did. My eyes were drawn to the king's cap, which was set with rubies and emeralds. He wore no crown, but the rubies formed a band, like a crown, with the emeralds dotting the top of his skull.

"I am training her to be a cupbearer. She will serve you and His Lordship and your daughter this evening."

The king's face reminded me of a pigeon's: no chin, eyes as round as coins, and a down-turned mouth. He and his daughter both had long sloping noses and nothing else alike, lucky for her.

"I see. Excellent. A beginner." Royal sarcasm. He mounted the dais and sat in the golden chair.

I noticed that his tunic, wine red and embroidered with gold thread at the throat, had an oily stain on the belly and caked food on the sleeve.

"You may teach her now. She will pour, and I will drink."

Oh no! My fingers turned to ice.

Cellarer Bwat's face reddened. "But Your Highness, she isn't ready."

"No matter. As I am the king, it will be extraordinarily good practice for her. First I should like a tumbler of water. Water goes best with ginger cake, although our southern Lepai water tastes sweetest. Beer is preferable with plain. . . ."

A servant entered with his cake. The servants who had

remained kneeling rose gradually, as if prepared to lower themselves again instantly.

Cellarer Bwat and I carried the wine bottle and other preparations to the dais table. Then we circled around to stand beside the king. Two more servants struggled up with the beer barrel. Cellarer Bwat held my elbow and guided my hand as I poured water from pitcher into tumbler. Almost inaudibly, he whispered, "Pour slowly, gent—"

"I thought *I* was speaking. I thought I was king, and people were to listen when I spoke."

"Beg pardon, Your Majesty."

How could Cellarer Bwat tell me what to do without speaking?

"No harm done. White wine is best with aged rabbit, an infrequent treat. . . ."

With the king listing beverages and foods, and with Cellarer Bwat's hand under my forearm, I held the tumbler out to His Highness.

He took it carelessly and splashed the front of his cloak. I heard a sharp intake of breath from Cellarer Bwat.

"How clumsy," the king said.

A servant rushed to him with a cloth, but he waved her away.

"It will dry." He raised the tumbler, drank, then spit into my face.

CHAPTER NINETEEN

y mouth fell open, and water and spittle dripped into it. How dare he? "Your Highness—" My voice was indignant.

Cellarer Bwat's foot came down hard on mine.

The foot reminded me that I had rarely mansioned a humble role. I made my voice silken. "Beg pardon, Your Majesty. I regret your—my—clumsiness."

"I forgive you. There is a pink wine they make in . . ."

The king went on speaking and eating between sentences. I wiped my face on my sleeve. After he finished his cake, he called for a bowl of fruit.

Since Cellarer Bwat couldn't use words to instruct me, he held my hands and arms in a viselike grip that barred mistakes. With a mansioner's concentration, I noted every move: how high we filled a tumbler with beer, how high with water, how much wine went into a goblet after the wine had been pronounced drinkable.

His Highness didn't spit on me again, but he thrust out a leg and tripped one of the servants who was going off to fetch a fresh keg of beer. The servant apologized and was forgiven instantly.

I pondered whether the king liked the servant and me better for our humiliation, or liked us less, because he knew he had been at fault, really, each time.

The castle bells chimed noon. My mind drifted back to pieces I might perform. Perhaps a funny recitation would be best. I could tell an animal fable.

After the fruit had been devoured, the king raised the bowl, so a shaft of sunlight hit it. "Such excellent porcelain. See, girl, how the light glints through it?"

He was addressing me, and I didn't dare tell him to call me Elodie. "I see, Your Highness."

"I do not own such a fine piece. I wonder if his is all so good."

Then he sent for a bowl of chicken gizzards. If Greedy Grenny kept eating until the guests arrived, I wouldn't have a moment to rehearse. He licked his fingers after eating his gizzards. His fingers and lips shone with grease.

Suppose I recited the story of Princess Rosette, whose dog stole meat from the castle cook to prevent a wedding.

The tale had three aspects of His Lordship's danger: thievery, a dog, and a betrothal.

Greedy Grenny asked if the ogre kept any apple wine. A servant was dispatched. Meanwhile, the king began cracking walnuts, his latest craving. He had downed six tumblers of water, two of beer, and five half-filled goblets of wine. His insides must have been afloat, but he had given me a great deal of practice. Cellarer Bwat's guiding hand on my arm had gradually lightened. I had learned to pour.

The apple wine arrived. With a flourish and without assistance, I uncorked the bottle and passed it under the king's nose at precisely the correct distance. The king pronounced the wine excellent. "But it is not quite the flavor to accompany walnuts." He frowned. "I must have dried cherries."

I despaired of leaving the hall before the feast began. Humble, I told myself as an idea formed, feel humble. I curtsied so deeply that my trembling legs almost gave way. "Pardon me—"

Cellarer Bwat whispered a cry of dismay.

"How dare you address me? Insupportable!"

Prison for me. But I thought I knew him by now. I used my quaking legs and pitched over to the side and onto the floor, away from the table and his legs. "Oof!"

He laughed and went on laughing, while I tried to get up and made myself fall again.

"You may rise."

I scrambled up, awkward on purpose.

"You have leave to speak."

I told him I was to perform tonight and begged for time to practice. "I would hate to disgrace Lepai."

He gave me leave to leave. Cellarer Bwat's face was purple, I supposed because he would have to pour for the king now. I pitied him, but not enough to stay.

In the postern outer ward, a woman picked pears. I didn't want an audience, so I sped toward the south side of the castle, hoping it would be deserted. As I rounded the corner, three grooms on horseback trotted my way, exercising their mounts. Next to me, wooden stairs climbed to the battlements. I could practice on high, where the wind would carry my voice away.

Sixty-nine steps brought me to the wall walk. I called, "Halloo! Is anyone here?"

No answer but the breeze in my ears. The sun was long past noon. Soon the arriving guests would end my chance to prepare.

For those who've never visited a castle, the inner curtain wall walk is wide enough for two tall men to lie across it head to toe. During a battle, soldiers are stationed here to shoot arrows at an approaching army and to drop boiling water and rocks on an army that's arrived. The soldiers are protected from the enemy by the crenellated battlement, a wall that looks gap-toothed, like a jack-o'-lantern's smile. The tooth is called the *merlon*, the gum the *embrasure*.

But with no battle and no soldiers, I had room to rehearse.

Master Jak hadn't said how long my performance was to be. The tale of Princess Rosette could take half an hour. I couldn't ready myself for half an hour's performance in half an hour!

I strode down the western wall walk, skirting a chimney opening that belched gray smoke. Confine myself to five minutes. Start in the middle of the tale, since everyone knows the whole.

"The little dog"—I cleared my throat—"the little dog, pitying his . . ." No, I should begin at a more thrilling moment. I paced.

Yes! I had it. I climbed to the walk atop the northwest tower. From here I could see the harbor and imagine my voice crossing the strait to Albin and Mother and Father.

"At midnight"—deeper for a narrator's fullness—"while the princess dreamed of her peacocks, the nurse whispered in the ear of the riverboat master."

I paced, considering how to portray the moment when the princess would be thrown overboard.

Below, someone shouted. Hooves clattered on wood. I heard rumbling. The guest wagons must be approaching. I looked down and saw a horse-drawn cart rolling up the ramp to the drawbridge.

I had to protect His Lordship. But oh, I was going to make a fool of myself when I performed.

Six more carts wound up the road, followed by two oxen towing the purple mansion. I supposed the actors were within, the mansion needed only as a conveyance because the troupe would perform inside the castle. My heart rose at the gay sight of the pennants, rippling in the wind.

I started down the steps to the lower northern wall walk. What was that tawny heap on the walk below, snug against the inner gatehouse tower? A guard's woolly cloak?

Whatever it was, it was none of my concern with the count to watch over.

The cloak moved.

I raced down the steps. The cloak thumped its tail.

CHAPTER TWENTY

he dog's back legs were hobbled. The chain around his neck had been tied to a rope, which had then been looped over the finial, a spike atop the merlon. A bowl of water lay near his head. I crouched by him and held out my hand, which he licked. He struggled to stand but toppled, though his tail continued to wag, slapping the ground so enthusiastically it lifted his entire rear.

"Nesspa?" With my purse knife I cut the cloth that hobbled him and lifted the rope off the merlon.

His golden coat was knotted here and there. I had to brush away his eyebrow hair to see an eye, which turned reproachfully up at me. *Can't you tell I'm drinking?*

When he finished, he stood, legs trembling until he

found his balance. His back was almost as high as my waist.

"Come!" The dog trotted ahead of me without tugging. What a smart beast!

I shouted, "Your Lordship," although no one could hear me up here. We started down. Halfway, he must have sniffed his master, because he began to pull. I held on, barely succeeding in staying on my feet.

The gatehouse tower stairs took us down to the passage that led to the outer ward. This was the castle's main entrance, wide enough to admit four horsemen abreast. As I ran, I saw rose petals beneath my feet.

Ahead, their backs to me, a knot of people and the count blocked the passage.

Nesspa was pulling hard enough to yank my arm from my body. "Your Lordship!" I cried, and let the rope go.

The dog cleared a path through the crowd. I followed more slowly.

"Oh! La!"

"Nesspa!" The count let go the chain of his substitute dog—Sheeyen again—and crouched.

Nesspa leaped up, again and again, to lick the ogre's face.

"Nesspie, where were you? Are you hurt?" The count's big hands felt the dog all over.

Sheeyen sniffed Nesspa's rear quarter.

"Who found you?" He looked up, saw me, and beamed his rare, sweet smile.

A man took Sheeyen's chain and tugged her away.

Might the return of Nesspa, His Lordship's protector, thwart the plans of someone here or someone arriving?

Princess Renn leaned over to pat Nesspa's head and placed her free hand on the count's sleeve. For the feast she wore an orange cloak trimmed with royal ermine and an orange cap. "*Eh*lodie, where did you find him?"

Was she angry at me? She had wanted to find Nesspa and have His Lordship's gratitude.

To let her know I hadn't tried to outdo her, I said, "I wasn't searching. I was on the wall walk, practicing for the entertainment. He was tied there."

She didn't appear angry. "You are lucky. Jonty Um, isn't she lucky?"

"I'm lucky." He frowned, while continuing to pat Nesspa. "We searched the wall walk."

I wondered if he himself had searched or his servants had. I looked away from the reunion. My masteress would want me to see everything. Behind the princess, a woman hovered, a woman in middle age, tall but not so tall as Her Highness, the woman's cloak simple but falling in the loose folds of fine wool. The princess's maid, I decided.

A princess's maid could go unchallenged wherever she liked. She might have stolen Nesspa.

Count Jonty Um stood. "Misyur . . ." He beamed down

169

at the man holding Sheeyen. "He's unhurt."

"I'm glad, Your Lordship."

Was this a friend of the count's? I scrutinized the gentleman: wide forehead, uplifted eyebrows, soft chin, swarthy skin. Warm smile, but that might mean nothing. Prosperous in a blue silk cap.

"Sir Misyur," Princess Renn said, "might we add something to the feast to celebrate?"

Ah. Sir. This was His Lordship's steward. A count's steward would be noble, a knight or better.

His friendly smile widened. "What do you think, Your Highness?"

"A frumenty with flerr sauce. Jonty Um and I love it so. My father as well."

A frumenty was an ordinary custard, but flerr berries grew only on high mountain bushes that rarely flowered. Their taste was said to be sweeter than honey, more mellow than hazelnut, and more perfumed than muskmelon.

Sir Misyur's smile faltered. "The kitchen will do its best." He led Sheeyen across the inner ward in the direction of the stable.

I heard hoofbeats from the outer ward.

"La! Jonty Um, your guests have arrived."

"Nesspa, come."

I followed His Lordship and the princess through the passage. We broke back into sunlight as the first wagon driver reined in his horses. Grooms took the bridles, and servants helped the guests step down.

A few people held squirming cats. I counted ten guests and three cats. I observed His Lordship for a frown at the cats, but his face had lapsed into blankness.

A second cart drew in. First to jump down was Goodwife Celeste's husband, Goodman Twah. With his assistance, she descended.

I positioned myself behind a groom. I'd thought them too poor and not distinguished enough to be invited, but if they were indeed poor, today their cloaks were not—marten fur fringing the collars of both, and Goodwife Celeste's was embroidered with green thread in a pattern of leaping cats. What did she mean by wearing a cat design?

She raised an arm to adjust her cap. Her fashionably long kirtle sleeve fell away, revealing a silver armband, and with it, her bracelet of twine.

A third cart rumbled across the drawbridge.

"La! Here's Thiel!" The princess left Count Jonty Um's side.

How could he be arriving, when he'd spent the night here? And how could he be a guest? Yet there he was, holding his cat Pardine as one might cradle a baby. The cat was decked out in a twine collar.

As usual, I blushed at the sight of him.

Gallantly, he let everyone descend ahead of him, seven

men and women, three young children, and four cats. Two of the men stood as tall as he. Both were fleshier and older, but their eyes were gray, too, and their jaws strong despite plump jowls. Cousins? Brothers? Neither appeared wealthy, but their cloaks were respectable. By contrast, Master Thiel wore his usual threadbare tunic and no cloak. When he jumped from the cart, I saw he wore shoes today, poverty shoes, with a drawstring at the top, like mine.

Blushing, too, Princess Renn pranced to him. "Thiel! Such news we have! Jonty Um's dog has been found. Joy!"

"Great tidings indeed," he said, smiling and moving Pardine to his shoulder.

"Come! You must congratulate him. He will want to hear from *you*." She took the sleeve of his tunic and, like an excited child, tugged him toward His Lordship.

Why would a count care what a miller's son, a mere cat teacher, said? Why had Master Thiel been invited to the feast? Because of his noble blood?

Why had any particular one of them been invited? Had Count Jonty Um invited many more, and these were the only people who had accepted? Had they come as a confederacy against him?

"Your Lordship, I hope your companion has been restored to you in good health."

"Welcome, Master Thiel. Yes, in good health."

"Now Jonty Um is happy," Princess Renn said, "and we all can be happy, too."

Happy, I thought, except for the poaching, the thievery, and the hatred of the people of Two Castles. Happy, except for every cat wanting him to turn into a mouse. Strange happiness.

CHAPTER TWENTY-ONE

hovered on the fringe of the crowd as five more carts arrived, each one met by the count with a single nod and a stiff smile. He would never win them over with those. The monkey would have done better.

The mansioners rolled in after the last load of guests descended. His Lordship didn't remain to greet Master Sulow, so I couldn't see what interested me most, the mansioners and the lucky apprentices.

In the great hall, King Grenville sat again at the dais. I knew he had left and returned, because his tunic was now blue. From here I couldn't see if this tunic was also soiled.

Once inside, we all bowed or curtsied.

"Rise. Rise. No need for ceremony with me."

I rose and looked around. White linen tablecloths, candelabra on every table, each candle already lit—during daylight! Oil lamps glowed along the walls and marched atop a line of stanchions between the serving tables and the long guest table. Roaring fires blazed in all three fireplaces. Only the sun itself could have cast more light.

A dog and a guard were stationed at each fireplace. The guests spread out, forming loose groups in the open area between the end of the long table and the door. I stood alone, wishing I could eavesdrop, but people were speaking too softly.

Nesspa barked as loud as a box of breaking pottery.

Master Thiel shouted, "Pardine!"

The cat dashed my way, then swerved to avoid me, but I grabbed him by the nape of his neck, and he hung from my hand, peaceable as a fur sack—peaceable, but with a leather purse in his mouth.

King Grenville cried, "What's afoot?"

Princess Renn answered, "Just a cat, Father."

I pried the purse from his teeth. Had Master Thiel taught him this trick? Was Pardine the only cat that knew it? Did Master Thiel indeed have my copper?

A red-faced Master Thiel hurried to me. He took Pardine, whispered in the cat's ear, and set him down. The cat walked away from us in a snaking line across the hall. Master Thiel stayed at my side.

"That's mine." A man stood over me and held out his hand.

I gave him the purse.

The man was one of the two who resembled Master Thiel. He held the purse in a tight fist, and his voice was tight, too. "Father knew what he was about, Thiel."

"Our honored father had the right to judge me, Frair, but . . ."

So this truly was one of Master Thiel's brothers who'd inherited the mill and the mule.

". . . Pardine is just a cat and—"

"*Your* cat." Master Frair's voice was harsh, a judge pronouncing judgment.

"My cat." Master Thiel's voice was velvet over a knife.

I felt afraid until Master Frair strode off to his goodwife.

And Master Thiel smiled down at me.

I smiled down at my shoes.

"Thank you for the rescue. Pardine has been carrying off this and that from my brothers since he was a kitten."

From his brothers and no one else?

"Why, you're the girl at Sulow's mansion, the girl who portrayed Thisbe. Have you found a situation here?"

I nodded, a half-truth. "My name is Elodie," I said, since he seemed to have forgotten.

"Too bad, Mistress Elodie. You should be a mansioner. Sulow never has anyone good in the child roles."

176

Lambs and calves! If only I were five years older. "Did Master Sulow decide to take you and Pardine?"

"He refused, and so I have no master."

"Thiel!" Princess Renn cried. "Come see the monkey on the wall. It is Jonty Um as a monkey. What a pretty monkey he makes."

I had forgotten to keep my eyes on His Lordship! The count stood safely with Princess Renn, Sir Misyur, and Nesspa, who'd curled up at his master's feet.

"Pardon me, Mistress Elodie," Master Thiel said, bowing and leaving me.

When would he and I ever again converse?

As I watched the count and his companions, the princess ran her hand around the outline of the monkey and chattered and gestured energetically. Sir Misyur nodded along with her words. His Lordship stood erect, treelike, his expression unreadable. If he loved Princess Renn, I couldn't tell.

If he was enjoying having visitors, I couldn't tell that, either.

Master Thiel rocked back on his heels, hands behind his back, speaking, admiring the monkey, I supposed. Pardine padded to him and rubbed against his leg. He picked the cat up. Pardine and the ogre seemed not to notice each other, but Nesspa stood and shook himself.

I looked around at the other guests. What were the

telltale signs of a poacher, a dog thief, a thief of castle sundries? I couldn't guess.

Serving maids entered with trays of tiny meat turnovers. I wondered if I should begin my cupbearing, but no one told me to, so I remained where I thought I should be, closer to His Lordship than to my post on the dais.

Goodman Twah and Goodwife Celeste moved between me and His Lordship. I went to her side. Why? Because I liked her, because I felt safe in her presence, because I could see the count from here, because I distrusted her. I distrusted them all, but she was the only one I could approach.

She must have sensed me, for she put her arm around my shoulder without looking down. Her hand tapped out a light rhythm. Mother used to mark nursery rhymes for me just this way, with a soft hand on my head or my belly.

Sir Misyur spoke into His Lordship's ear.

"Thank you all for coming," Count Jonty Um boomed. He made an awkward try at a joke. "I cannot gather myself, so there could have been no gathering without you."

"La! You are witty."

A few people laughed politely.

"Where is the humor?" King Grenville said from the dais. "Renn and I were already here. He could have gathered us."

Goodwife Celeste's hand stilled on my shoulder.

Sir Misyur cleared his throat, and a dozen men and

women ran into the hall from the inner ward and began to juggle oranges. I had seen juggling with wooden balls, never with oranges. Would they be eaten later or discarded?

"Elodie, how nice to see you," Goodwife Celeste said. "Have you become ennobled since yesterday? Are you Duchess Elodie now?"

I shook my head, embarrassed. "I am to be cupbearer to Count Jonty Um, Princess Renn, and the king."

"Cupbearer? Almost as much an advance as ennoblement. Congratulations! And you have changed masters from a dragon to . . ." I watched her swallow *an ogre* and replace it with "His Lordship."

"You are resplendent, mistress. Have *you* been ennobled?"

She looked down at her cloak. "Borrowed finery. My daughter married well." She indicated a youngish woman a little distance away, a woman of Goodwife Celeste's height and girth.

The daughter's cloak was faded and without fur. She must have lent the best to her mother. The daughter might have married well, but not well enough for two splendid cloaks.

The midafternoon castle bell tolled. The jugglers bowed or curtsied and ran out, leaving behind a faint smell of oranges. A servant, the ewerer, stood with a pitcher in front of the carved wooden screen that shielded the door to the kitchen. Another servant held a basin.

Princess Renn took His Lordship's hand, having to reach up, as a child must to hold the hand of its father. He smiled at her, a smile that seemed dutiful. They made their way to the ewerer, he shortening his stride, she lengthening hers. When they reached him, she held out her hands and scrubbed them as the ewerer poured. The water flowed over her hands and into the waiting basin.

His Lordship washed next and playfully sprinkled water on Nesspa's snout. Princess Renn sprinkled water on the count. His face reddened.

"La! You are so serious!"

The guests formed a line to wash their hands. I tagged along uncertainly and stood at the end. A cupbearer should have clean hands, no?

His Lordship proceeded to the dais with the princess and Nesspa. Each guest washed in turn, many setting down a cat to do so. When the basin filled, a servant emerged from behind the screen to replace it. Likewise, when the ewer spilled its last drops, a servant arrived with a full one.

Would the king be the only diner with dirty hands? Was he permitted, because he was king?

No. Another ewerer and another basin carrier went to him.

"Ah," he said, sounding pleased. "I regret putting you to extra trouble."

After washing, the guests took their seats. Each seemed

to know his or her place. Master Thiel, holding Pardine, sat a few guests away from his brothers and their wives, all of them near the lowly end of the table, far below the salt. He began instantly to converse with the young woman on his right.

Goodwife Celeste, her goodman, and their daughter and son-in-law were situated in the middle of the table, even with the salt.

Fourteen people filled the high table benches: Sir Misyur, the princess's maid, and the most richly dressed and bejeweled of the guests. I identified the lord mayor of Two Castles by the brass chain of office slung across his chest. The mayor and one of the women each held a cat.

Was I supposed to begin cupbearing now or wait for some signal? The ewerer and basin holder left, and I felt alone and exposed. Several yards away, Cellarer Bwat hovered over a table laden with bottles and jugs. I wished he would say what to do, but he just stared pointedly at me, his face purple again.

He must mean I should go. I ran to stand between the king and Princess Renn.

Servants rushed in bearing steaming platters. Some deposited the platters on the tables and hurried back to the kitchen. Others positioned themselves behind the guests' benches at the lower table. Three stood to my right and three to my left behind the benches on the dais, my fellow cupbearers, I supposed.

None of them did anything except join Cellarer Bwat in staring at me. I looked down to see if I'd torn my apron.

Princess Renn said, "La! *Eh*lodie, now you must pour the wine."

"Jonty Um," King Grenville said, "you chose an idiot to pour for us. Though I taught her myself this morning, she learned nothing."

"She will do, Your Majesty," the count said.

"She is not from Two Castles," Princess Renn said by way of excusing me.

My face burning, I reached between her and His Lordship for the wine bottle, which I uncorked in the fashion I'd learned. I passed the bottle under the king's long nose and the ogre's big freckled one, and poured.

CHAPTER TWENTY-TWO

nce begun, I poured well enough. Better than well enough, since the king paid no attention to me. While pouring, I observed for my masteress—and fretted for myself about my coming mansioning.

The guests and their children numbered sixty-eight, and I saw twine jewelry on twenty-four of the adults. I counted eighteen cats, but more may have been out of sight under the table.

The princess alone seemed in a festive mood. The hall was chilly, too vast to be warmed even by the three roaring fires, yet she threw off her cloak, revealing a scarlet kirtle. She talked ceaselessly, emphasizing ideas with grand gestures. Little food passed between her lips, but she shared tidbits from her bowl with everyone on the dais, sending her jeweled knife from hand to hand to the ends of the table.

Her father proffered treats to his neighbors, but he scowled when his morsels were accepted, and everyone soon learned to decline his offerings.

The count's manners seemed perfect to this farm bumpkin. He shared generously and accepted tidbits with good grace. I observed that he and Sir Misyur curled their fingers around their spoons in exactly the same fashion. The steward had taught his master well.

Except for Her Highness, such a quiet feast this was! Even the children behaved with decorum.

Courses surged out of the kitchen. I had eaten nothing since dawn and was hungry when the meal began, but the glut of food exhausted my stomach through my eyes.

Or worry replaced appetite: worry for His Lordship, worry over my approaching performance.

According to Albin, at a banquet every round of three courses, called a *remove*, was followed by an entertainment. According to Master Jak, my turn would come at the end of the second remove. After the first a minstrel sang, accompanying herself on the lute. I guessed her to be one of Master Sulow's mansioners. She warbled in a voice as soft as chamois, and even the princess quieted to hear.

The song began with a knight setting forth,

To fight the giant whose shadow
Blotted out the shining sun.

Giant, she sang, but I suspected she meant *ogre*. From my vantage point behind and to the side, I saw His Lordship's cheeks become mottled red and white. Princess Renn's hand patted his shoulder, but I doubted he was aware of her.

The knight killed seven giants in as many verses. This was the refrain:

Be the giant tall as the sky
With teeth sharp as spikes,
Eyes piercing as pikes,
And fists like hammers.
May he roar and thunder,
Yet he will die.

When she finished, the applause, muted at first, gained strength. The guests at the lower table rose to show their appreciation—and their dislike, perhaps hatred, of their host. I was astonished at their boldness.

Goodman Twah and Goodwife Celeste both clapped enthusiastically, although they lived elsewhere. What reason did they have to despise His Lordship?

He clapped without enthusiasm, ignoring the insult.

The minstrel curtsied and ran into the inner ward.

Princess Renn raised a bit of bread to Count Jonty Um's lips. "I like songs better when no one is slain."

He chewed, his face still blotchy red.

Master Sulow had certainly chosen the ballad. Why?

Three menservants emerged from behind the kitchen screen carrying the feast masterpiece: a roasted peacock. I had heard of this delicacy but never seen it, and wished I weren't seeing it now. It would have looked like any other cooked bird—if it hadn't still had its beak, and if its beautiful plumage hadn't been stabbed, feather by feather, into its crispy back.

"Jonty Um," Greedy Grenny said, "twenty-five dishes thus far, four with saffron."

"I hope Your Majesty enjoyed them," His Lordship said.

"Yes, certainly. The point is, I served only three saffron dishes when the king of Belj visited."

"Fie, Father!" The princess laughed. "Mayn't Jonty Um be more generous than you are?"

Greedy Grenny laughed, too. "He may. I prefer saffron in my belly to saffron in the belly of the king of Belj." He wiped his hands and his face on the tablecloth and stood.

The guests quieted. Servants paused in their serving.

"Loyal subjects, tonight is more than a feast of friends. Tonight will be remembered forever in the history of Lepai. My daughter—"

"La!" The princess tossed her head. Below her cap, her yellow hair flew about.

"Princess Renn has confessed to me her affection for my subject Jonty Um, the wealthiest man, er, the wealthiest *being* in Lepai, after the crown."

If silence could hush, this silence did, as though the world's winds had stilled and all creatures ceased moving.

"Even a king cannot ignore the feelings of his only child."

But she'd told me he arranged the betrothal. What a liar he was!

"I have approved their union. Dear subjects, think how safe Lepai will be with His Lordship defending us. Think how strong we will be with His Lordship leading our attacks. My daughter and His Lordship will wed, and, in due time"—he chuckled—"but not very soon, I hope, Count Jonty Um will succeed to the throne."

Princess Renn threw her arms around the king's neck and kissed his cheek. He looked pleased with himself. Why not? A happy daughter and greater riches.

I discovered I was happy, too. This ogre would be a better ruler than either the king or his daughter. King Grenville had no kindness and the princess was too flighty. Count Jonty Um's character combined steadiness and compassion.

She spun in her chair to her betrothed. Rising halfway, she kissed him on his cheek. "La! It is lucky you are tall."

His arm went around her. It was an awkward gesture, but his smile was certainly glad.

Mmm . . . I thought, wishing I could tell if he loved her. I liked the princess and didn't want her in a marriage without affection. Whatever he felt, however, he would be good to her. Perhaps that was enough.

Sir Misyur cried, "Hurrah!"

The cheer was taken up with gusto by the servants, listlessly by the guests. When the voices died away, Sir Misyur said, "My lord, tell them the sort of king you'll be!"

Count Jonty Um stood.

He should have remained seated, I thought. His shadow crossed the dais and darkened a few feet of the lower guest table.

"My friends . . ." He sounded husky. "My friends . . ."

I looked around the hall. Master Thiel and his brothers raised their knives and ate again. The brothers' wives did the same. Goodwife Celeste turned the twine around her wrist and whispered into her goodman's ear.

"Your Highness . . ." His Lordship paused, consulting the ceiling not far above him, as if words might be written there. He swayed, but steadied himself with his hands flat on the table. "Thank you. My friends . . ."

Princess Renn said, "Jonty Um, tell them not to worry." She faced the guests below her. "He'll be a good king. La!

When he's been king a week, you'll forget he's an ogre."

His flushed face deepened to scarlet. People stopped chewing. Knives and spoons halted in the air.

Let them think about something besides the princess's foolish words. I threw my wine bottle to the floor, hard, so it would certainly break. Purple sloshed on my kirtle.

The crash broke the spell. After a moment of surprise, conversation resumed. His Lordship sat without delivering a speech.

Cellarer Bwat rushed to me with a length of linen and began to mop up the wine and broken glass. I bent to help.

The king twisted in his golden chair. "Did the girl splash me?"

Cellarer Bwat examined King Grenville's cloak hem, where I saw stains as big as my hand. "Not a drop, Your Highness."

Greedy Grenny returned to his gluttony. "Of course I wouldn't have minded being splashed. I never object to anything."

Cellarer Bwat whispered, "Excellent, Elodie. Well done."

I thought this was sarcasm until he patted my hand.

A servant carved the peacock while the second wave of courses issued from the kitchen. Soon I would be called upon to perform. The tale of Princess Rosette seemed too complicated now. But what to do instead? Possibilities ran through my mind, none of them right: too long, too sad, tedious.

As I poured water for the princess, Master Thiel's brother Frair choked. His wife slapped him roundly on the back. He spit out a morsel of food.

And I knew what to mansion: a scene from *Toads and Diamonds*. The tale had no dogs or thieves and not much of a betrothal, so it was little like the present circumstance, but I knew it well enough to perform unrehearsed.

I was still frightened. How mad to debut before a king! And Master Sulow would probably be watching, too. My hands were so slick with sweat, I feared I would drop a pitcher or wine bottle. Yet my feet were numb with cold.

Two boys and a girl of my approximate age began to set up scenery against the wall beyond the end of the long table. They put out a tidy lady's chair, an enormous chair, four pillows.

I deduced the three were Master Sulow's new apprentices. They seemed unremarkable—no flourishes as they set the pillows on the chairs and brought in three large wooden pots planted with rosebushes. Not so much as a glance at the audience. If they were portraying Little Masters Humdrum and Little Mistress Humdrum, they could hardly have done better.

But maybe Master Sulow had instructed them to mansion these vacant characters. The true selves of the apprentices might be much different; they could be mansioning prodigies.

Perhaps they would gladly change places with me if they knew—charged with protecting an ogre, deducing and inducing for a dragon, soon to mansion for an entire court.

The roses they'd brought out could mean only *Beauty and the Beast*. The minstrel had sung about a giant; the mansioners were going to enact the story of a monstrous beast.

What would happen if Count Jonty Um's forbearance snapped?

Nesspa lifted a paw onto his master's knee. I knew what the gesture meant, and so did His Lordship, who stood. If he left, I would have to accompany him.

"Jonty Um, don't go. Can't you send someone? *Ehlodie?*" The princess turned my way. "You don't mind?"

His Lordship looked at me uncertainly.

I couldn't go. My masteress said I mustn't let him out of my sight. Yet how could I refuse?

"La! I forgot! *Ehlodie* is going to entertain us, but you mustn't leave either, Jonty Um. Your guests will be offended, and you want to see *Ehlodie*."

Sir Misyur beckoned a manservant, who hurried to the dais. Thank you, Princess!

Count Jonty Um mussed the fur on Nesspa's head and told the servant, "Don't let his chain go." He bent over and put his face close to Nesspa's. "Come back to me."

Tail wagging, Nesspa accompanied the servant out of the hall. Other servants took away empty dishes and platters.

Sir Misyur nodded to me.

I am a mansioner, I thought. *Toads and Diamonds.* Two sisters, one cruel and ugly, one kind and pretty. I am one. I am the other.

I left the dais and stood in front of Master Sulow's scenery. Be with me, Albin, I prayed. Let His Lordship not regret his kindness.

On shaky legs I curtsied first to the king and then to everyone else. Forgetting to keep the count in sight, I turned my back. Ah. A rose would help me begin. I placed myself so everyone could see me snap one off and pop it in my mouth. Pui! It tasted bitter. I faced forward.

Princess Renn understood instantly and ruined the surprise for everyone else. "Look, Jonty Um! The flower will fall out when she speaks."

But His Lordship's eyes were on the door Nesspa had left by.

Portraying the kind, pretty sister, I fluttered my eyelashes. In a honeyed voice I said, "Dear . . ." I made an O with my mouth, revealing the rose on my tongue.

Light laughter rippled through the hall. I removed the rose, dug a shallow hole in the floor, and planted it, as if the flower, though lacking roots and most of its stem, might grow again.

The laughter deepened. As I stood, I checked His Lordship, who still gazed at the door. Master Thiel laughed. Goodwife Celeste nodded and laughed.

I leaped sideways, turned my cap backward, and screwed my face into a grimace, transforming myself into the selfish sister. My mouth opened as wide as it could. I imagined a Lahnt moonsnake slithering out. Although I tried to say *sister*, my mouth couldn't close for the *s* or *t*. "Ih—" I placed my hands to catch the snake.

The king shouted, "Ha! She's funny."

The laughter rose again. Then it trailed off, and the room fell silent.

A cat hissed. A dog barked. My eyes followed the bark to one of the fireplace dogs, who barked again, without rising from where it sat. I turned to the dais. Nesspa had not returned, and led by Pardine, every cat in the hall was stalking the ogre.

CHAPTER TWENTY-THREE

"hoo, cats!" Princess Renn cried.

Master Thiel shouted, "Pardine! Come to me!"

Yelling and waving my arms, I ran at the cats, but they ignored me. I scooped up two. One squirmed free. The one I still held spit and tried to scratch.

His Lordship hugged himself, as if he were cold, or for protection. His face looked mottled again. His nostrils flared, and his eyes widened pleadingly.

The guests and servants were motionless, too shocked or fascinated to move.

The count's arms went up. I'd seen this before. His mouth opened wide, and he began to tremble.

Princess Renn shrieked. Pardine leaped onto the table

and crouched, poised to pounce.

I rushed to the dais, tripping over a table leg and hurtling on. When I reached the ogre, I threw the cat I held to Sir Misyur. My arms grasped the ogre's quaking body but couldn't hang on. He was too big and shaking too hard.

"Stop, cats!" I shouted. "Stop, Your Lordship! Stop! Stop!"

The count's features coarsened. His hair grew and thickened. He bent over at the waist as his torso lengthened.

I backed away. Everyone did. I heard screams.

His shoulders broadened, first straining his tunic, then bursting it. I smelled musk. His gold chain snapped with a *ping*. The pendant thudded onto the floor.

The cats froze. Pardine yowled from his place on the table.

His Lordship's front legs—no longer arms!—overturned the tabletop. Bowls and glasses slid off and smashed when the wood came down on them. Guests on the dais jumped off. I jumped, too. The princess held her father's hand and pulled him away.

He shouted, "There's peacock left. Ogre, eat peacock!"

We all scattered to the walls, leaving a throng of cats motionless on the floor or on the tables below the dais. The dogs at the fireplaces kept their places, appearing unworried.

The lion snarled.

Nothing remained of His Lordship but the flush—the lion's cheek fur blushed a faint pink.

No one stirred, every one of us likely thinking the same question: If I run, will he chase?

I watched his eyes—polished black stones with nothing of the count in their gaze. He padded gracefully to the dais's edge and roared.

The sound echoed off the walls, grew, echoed, reverberated, until I thought the castle would tumble down. My eyes dropped from the lion's eyes to his fangs and back up to the eyes. The fangs were not to be looked at!

He blinked, and when he opened his eyes again, I saw awareness in them. He choked off the roar, shook his head as if to clear it, and vibrated again.

But he didn't return to himself. He shrank.

I ran to him again and grabbed the loose skin on his back, but it melted away in my hands.

Pardine took both of us into his gaze. I felt the cat's longing: *Become a mouse. Become a mouse.*

"Don't become a mouse!" I yelled as he continued to diminish. "Not a mouse! Bigger!"

Moments passed. He shrank more. And more.

On the floor, a brown mouse trembled next to the pendant. His whiskers twitched once. Then he streaked toward the kitchen, pursued by cats. People followed, Princess Renn and I in the lead.

I ran faster than she did, but the cats outstripped me. Crashes came from the kitchen. I entered in time to see Master Jak snatch a cat while the tail of the last chasing cat exited to the inner ward.

Count Jonty Um, let me reach you! I bounded across the kitchen. Don't be eaten!

"Wait for me!" Princess Renn cried.

I burst outside. In the inner ward, all was serene under the night sky.

"La! Alack! Oh, la!" the princess wailed. "He's gone!" She sank to the ground.

I crouched, facing her in the dim light, and blinked back tears.

"They'll eat him, my tall Jonty Um."

"No. We'll find him." But I imagined a cat's bloody teeth, His Lordship's anguish, the mouse's little kicking legs. I shuddered and repeated, "We'll find him."

"Alack! Alack!" She wrapped her arms around her knees and rocked.

Master Thiel dashed out of the kitchen. He rushed to us and pulled me up. "It may not be too late."

The princess stood, too. "Go to the barracks, *Eh*lodie. I'll try the gatehouse."

Why the barracks? But I ran there anyway.

In the dark I saw the shapes of trestle beds mounded with their occupants' belongings. No movement. I left quickly and descended the stairs to the stables, a better destination. If the mouse led the cats here, they might startle a dozen ordinary mice and satisfy themselves.

A groom approached me. "What is it, young mistress?"

"Did His Lordship as a mouse . . . Did a multitude of cats . . ." They couldn't have. The scene was too peaceful. A stableboy with a mucking shovel entered a nearby stall. Another carrying a pail moved away from me down the line of stalls.

"No one's come in." The groom's voice tightened. "He became a mouse?"

Master Dess stepped out of a horse stall.

"Master Dess!" He could do anything with animals. I blurted out what had happened.

He hunched down. "Honey, honey," he sang close to the floor. "Come to Dess, honey." Still bent over, he hurried toward the doors to the outer ward.

I returned to the inner ward, now crowded with guests and servants. Sir Misyur, holding Nesspa, was dividing the servants into groups to search the castle. Master Thiel joined the group on its way to the cellar under the kitchen. Other guests called their cats, but he didn't call Pardine.

Two cats came, both ambling out of the kitchen with a well-fed air. My stomach churned.

The princess descended the steps from the battlements. Maybe she thought His Lordship would go where Nesspa had been found, but I doubted a mouse could manage the stairs on its short legs.

Silly as she often was, she seemed a tragic figure now, taking each step slowly, dejectedly, one hand on the curtain stones to balance herself.

Sir Misyur patted Nesspa's head and let go of his chain. "Perhaps the dog will lead us to his master."

But Nesspa just curled up at the steward's feet.

Some thought dogs clairvoyant. If his master were no more, mightn't he be howling?

An early star flickered in the eastern sky. Soon I would have to meet my masteress and confess my failure. Sir Misyur told me and two servants with oil lamps to search the barracks, so I returned there. We peered under every bed and poked every pile of belongings while my ears strained for a cry of discovery outside.

We left the barracks as the castle bells rang nine. A black shape winged ITs way toward the castle.

CHAPTER TWENTY-FOUR

h, how I wished I didn't have to meet my masteress. I started through the postern passage to the outer ward but had to stop in the middle, overwhelmed by a flood of tears. His Lordship had shown himself to be good, only good. If alive, he was suffering. If dead . . . I didn't want to think about it. And if he was gone forever, so was the monkey. That merriment, gone.

I should never have let Count Jonty Um and his dog be separated. Nesspa would have stopped the cats. I continued through the tunnel, sniffling as I went. Outside, I hurried to the back of the castle where Masteress Meenore and I had met before, but IT wasn't there.

I heard shouts. A plume of purple smoke rose above the battlements. I ran.

There was my masteress, ITs legs set squarely, ITs wings spread on the ground, blocking the passage that led between the outer gatehouses to the drawbridge. I wound my way among guests waiting to climb into carts.

Flames played around ITs lips. "Someone will answer for His Lordship's misfortune."

How did IT know?

"You will all oblige me by remaining to answer my questions."

Sounding not at all frightened, a man said, "Ask us in Two Castles tomorrow, Meenore. I want my bed."

IT didn't budge.

"I will not buy a skewer ever again if you don't let me go." The voice belonged to one of the men on line on my first day.

IT swallowed ITs flame.

A chorus of protests ensued. My masteress would lose the custom of all of Two Castles if IT didn't let people leave.

ITs smoke blued. IT gave in and rose into the air.

I raced back to where I'd expected IT to land.

Behind me, IT trumpeted, "Tomorrow I will come to each of you. You will not escape me."

Circle overhead, I thought. Give me a few minutes. I didn't want IT to know I'd witnessed ITs humiliation.

I wondered why anyone would tell IT the truth now or tomorrow. The guests were probably hoping for an end to

His Lordship, even if they'd played no part in bringing his end about.

But any of them might have done it. A simple gesture would have been enough. Goodwife Celeste had shown me on the cog how to start a cat stalking. She herself might have given the signal.

I reached the back of the castle and stood panting.

My masteress landed in a cloud of blue smoke. "We are both disgraced, Lodie. I saw you at the drawbridge."

"Masteress, how did you know His Lordship is gone?"

"You just said so." *Enh enh enh.* "Tell me all."

Standing close to ITs warmth, I related everything I could remember. IT questioned me again and again about who said what and where and when and with what expression, what tone of voice, what gestures. Such a misery it was to recite the tale over and over and never be able to change the ending.

As I spoke, weariness struck. I sat on the grass, certain that if I kept standing, my knees would buckle.

"Stand, Lodie. I need you alert."

I struggled up.

"Hold my wing."

I reached out gingerly, afraid of being burned, but the wing was no hotter than cozy, and it was bracing. My tiredness fell away.

"How many guests brought cats?"

"At least eighteen."

"At least?"

"Definitely eighteen." Or more.

"What were their names?"

"The cats?"

"Don't be foolish. The guests' names, the ones with the cats."

IT was being horrible. "Master Thiel brought Pardine. The mayor's wife had a cat. Goodwife Celeste's son-in-law had one. The man whose water you heat." I squeezed my eyes shut in hopes of extracting more from my memory. "I don't know who else."

"I see," IT said coldly.

This wasn't fair! IT should have hired an assistant who knew Two Castles—and left me to starve. "I'm sorry."

"No doubt."

Goodwife Celeste was right about the moodiness.

"Masteress . . . why did Master Thiel arrive with the other guests when he'd been here last night?"

"The correct question is, Why was he here last night?"

I could say nothing to please IT. "Yes, why?"

"We will ask him, now that we know the proper question. Tell me again: You saw no one signal the cats?"

I shook my head. "My eyes were on His Lordship, except when I looked down, where the snake was coming out of my mouth."

The skin above ITs snout crinkled, which I deduced or induced meant confusion.

"The imaginary moonsnake."

"Ah. Go to bed, Lodie. Perhaps you will dream something useful." IT lifted into the sky.

When would I see IT again?

I started toward the gatehouse, although, with His Lordship gone, I no longer had a right to sleep in the castle.

No one stopped me. The guards didn't even look my way. In the great hall, the tables had been taken down. Only one lamp was still lit. By its glow I saw that several servants were already asleep. Others sat up, their pallets pulled close together in clusters.

I wanted to hear the conversation.

My pallet, bulging with my satchel, was an island yards from the others. I carried it to the nearest cluster.

But as soon as I set it down, a woman servant turned around. "Sleep elsewhere."

I chose better this time, placing myself behind Master Jak's broad back, where no one seemed to notice me. Now, if only I had the cupped ears of a donkey for better hearing.

". . . beeswax candles . . . niece . . . Beeswax! Worth . . ."
I heard a sniffle, something mumbled.

". . . kind . . ."

". . . Two Castles . . ."

I leaned over the edge of the pallet, set my forearms

down, and pulled myself nearer to the voices. The pallet's wooden frame slid silently on the dirt floor.

Ah. Now I could hear.

"What was the longest he ever stayed a monkey?"

"Two weeks, by thunder." The speaker was Master Jak. "When he grew big again, he half ate the castle out of food. Never lost his ogre appetite."

"Might he . . ."

"Perhaps."

"In a hidey-hole."

"Growing hungry."

"Frightened, by thunder."

Silence fell. These people loved him. I wondered if I'd hear like talk from each cluster and from the sleeping servants if they were awake.

Someone snuffed out the lamp. People became shapes. The murmuring continued. I wished they would talk about the moment before the transformation. Master Jak had been in the kitchen, but some of the others might have served the guests. One might have seen or heard something: a nod, a word, a guest's hand flash in a cat signal.

The whispering began again.

"Misyur will read the will."

"Tomorrow?"

"Not tomorrow, by thunder. We'll keep searching tomorrow. But soon."

"What will become of us?"

Whispering voices sounded much alike. I had recognized Master Jak's only because of his *by thunder* and the masculine rumble under his whisper.

My heart skipped. Could I ask a question and have each think another had spoken?

The conversation moved along. "Will the king let His Lordship's will stand? His Highness wants this castle."

"Two castles in Two Castles, and both his."

"We'll lose our places, very likely."

"I wouldn't serve Greedy Grenny if he got down on his royal knees and begged me."

"He went back to eating after His Lordship turned into a mouse. I won't serve him either."

The murmurs turned to where servants might be needed. Slowly, slowly, I crawled off my pallet, holding my breath, hoping the whispers would cover my tiny sounds.

I wanted my voice to come from within the circle, and at last I knelt between two people. The servants discussed the merits of serving nobility or burghers. I rehearsed what to say and how to say it, while waiting for a pause. If they had gone over my question already, they'd catch me.

My knees grew numb. They spoke of monthly half holidays and wages.

Finally, silence fell.

My heart raced. I counted three beats, then whispered, "Did . . ." Mansion the accent! Draw out the vowels. Pound the consonants. "Did anyone see a signal along the table? A . . . a signal to the cats?"

I drew back.

Pause . . . Pause . . .

They were going to find me!

Pause . . .

"Or a signal from the dais, by thunder. Any of them up there could have done it."

"It happened so quick."

I inched back to my pallet.

"They were lifting tumblers, their knives . . ."

"Feeding each other."

"The princess gave away more than she ate. Not like her father."

"Everyone was laughing at the snake coming out of the girl's mouth. I laughed, too."

"Egad, Master Thiel could have done it. Hates His Lordship."

A female whisper said, "They all hate His Lordship."

"Not so much as Thiel."

"Nesspa would have protected his master."

"Thiel didn't have to signal. Likely he gave the cat instructions. That Pardine is as smart as—"

"We mustn't name folks. We don't know."

"If it was a signal, who could see a wrist flick in all those people?"

"By thunder, I would have seen."

"By thunder, you mightn't have. Somebody could have signaled under the table."

"If one cat saw the signal, all would join the chase."

"Perhaps no one signaled. A cat might just go."

"The dogs at the hearths should have protected him."

"They had bones to chew. He didn't make a pet of any of them."

The voices quieted again, and soon the broad back in front of me stretched out flat. The others settled, too.

I reviewed every remark, my thoughts snagging on Master Thiel. Could he show such courtesy and good humor and still try to murder a person—an ogre?

I hadn't thought the word *murder* before, but if His Lordship had been eaten, then murder it was, and no cat the true killer.

CHAPTER TWENTY-FIVE

woke suspecting Master Dess, who knew all animals, not merely cats. He could understand the animals that lived inside His Lordship better than the count did himself. Master Dess might share Two Castles's hatred of an ogre, or he might have been paid, and he might have known exactly what the ogre would do in the face of stalking cats.

But he hadn't been in the hall.

He might have been in league with someone who was.

Master Dess, who seemed so kind, might be a whited sepulcher, the worst villain of all, according to Mother.

Or Goodwife Celeste might be the villain. She certainly had secrets, and she'd worn a cloak embroidered with cats.

Oh, not the goodwife. She wouldn't kill. My masteress

told me to doubt everyone, but he also said to use common sense. Common sense ruled out Goodwife Celeste.

But it didn't rule out Master Thiel or Master Dess.

When I entered the kitchen, no one sent me away. The search for the mouse continued, although I wasn't able to take part because King Grenville had requested that I wait on him. I almost wept.

Master Jak let me eat a thick slice of bread and then told me that the king was in his chambers in the northwest tower. "Take this to him." He held out a tray loaded with more food than I would eat in three days. "Egad, I'm pleased His Lordship thought we needed you."

A minute later I rapped on the tower door. A guard admitted me to the first story, which held the castle armory. I knocked again on the second level, and His Majesty bellowed for me to enter.

I never thought I would see a king's hairy legs. He stood at his window embrasure in a silk undershirt that hung to just below his knees.

No guards, only His Highness and I. My heart thumped.

Holding the tray in an iron grip, I curtsied. The dishes rattled, but nothing spilled.

The room was a parlor, not a bedchamber, which must be upstairs. The biggest area was occupied by two benches that faced each other, both piled with pillows, with a low, rectangular table between. A chest butted against one wall and a small cabinet against another. A round cloth-covered table and two chairs kept company by the fire-place, where a fire blazed. I placed the tray on the round table and hoped that was right.

His Majesty stumped to the chair nearest the fire and sat. "Girl, make the snake come out of your mouth again."

I didn't understand. "Your Majesty?"

"When you crossed your eyes and pretended a snake was coming out." He bit into a slice of bread and spoke with his mouth full, white bread and yellow teeth. "That was comical. Do it again."

I stared. He began to frown. I crossed my eyes and held out my arms for the imaginary snake.

He laughed. "A pity you were interrupted. What comes next?"

For once I didn't want to mansion, but I enacted the rest of the tale. When the prince rode in to see the pretty sister, I straddled the spare chair and made it clatter back and forth on its wooden legs. I snapped at the chair's imaginary withers with an imaginary whip.

The king even stopped eating to laugh. When I finished, he said, "To think of you here, performing for me alone! How lucky I am. Again, girl. No, wait. Take my tray and find my daughter. She must see it, too. Bring her a breakfast as well, and I should feel so very fortunate for a leek pie in brown sauce."

The kitchen was half empty. At the long table Master Jak cut butter into flour.

He nodded when I told him what the king wanted. "My pies are half ready. Come back in twenty minutes, and you shall have it. The princess is in the great hall. By thunder, Her Highness has a new idea every moment, and Sir Misyur must listen."

But instead of entering the hall, I cut through the inner ward to the count's apartment, where the door stood open. Inside, a guard sat on a stool along the inner wall with a tureen lid in his lap. Between his feet lay a wedge of cheese.

His chin came up when I entered, and he blinked sleepily at me. Then his hand flew to the hilt of his sword. "What is it, girl?"

I went to him. "I was sent to find Her Highness."

Nesspa lay by the fireplace hearth. His tail thumped the hearthstones. I went to him and patted his head.

What if the mouse was in the walls in this room, comforted by Nesspa's presence?

What if this guard was the cat signaler?

"Not here."

I could see that. "What will you do if a mouse comes out?"

"Clap this over it." He raised the lid.

"Then what?"

"Bring it to Master Dess in the stables."

"What will Master Dess do?"

"He's magic with animals, says he'll know a mouse that isn't a mouse."

"Can he turn the mouse back into His Lordship?"

"Dunno. Maybe he'll cast a spell."

"What is he doing with the real mice?"

"What one does with mice."

Feeds them poison. That's what we did at home, and I'd hated it. But Master Dess might make a mistake! He might even make a mistake on purpose!

I hurried to the stables, guessing that I had ten more minutes at least before Master Jak would be ready.

Master Dess stood crooning in a horse stall just beyond the big aisle. I approached, and he beckoned me in with him. Master Gise, the head groom, entered behind me with a bucket.

"Another mouse." He handed the bucket to Master Dess. "Who is she?" Meaning me.

"A lass from Lahnt. His Lordship took her in."

As the bucket passed between them, I saw a frantic mouse scrambling at the bottom, trying to climb out.

Master Dess reached for it.

He would have his pick of common poisons. Farm folk knew them all: frogbane, tasty false cinnamon, ground boar tusk, apple-pit powder, and the many poisonous mushrooms.

Albin had schooled me in the more exotic poisons that appeared in mansioners' tales, such as murder milk. I knew the poisons that killed quick and the ones that killed slow, those that caused fever or stomach pain or sleep. It had amused Albin to school a child in such gruesome arts.

The mouse stilled in Master Dess's hand.

Let it be His Lordship, I prayed.

Master Dess looked into the mouse's eyes, then shook his head.

Now he would kill it. I snatched it from him and began to run out of the stable with the squirming creature. I'd saved this one, but how many had already died? Had Count Jonty Um been among them?

I was halfway to the door. What would I do with the mouse?

It answered by wriggling out of my hand. I lunged, but it raced into a stall. I gazed after it and fought back tears.

"Honey . . . Girl . . ." Master Dess came to me. "I wasn't going to kill the poor mouse."

"You weren't?" I felt shaky with relief.

Master Gise walked toward us. "His Lordship doesn't let us kill mice."

I should have guessed.

Master Dess touched my shoulder. "Someone will find

the mouse again, or not. It wasn't the count."

"Have you examined the other animals, Master Dess, not just the mice?"

He nodded. "All the beasts."

"I'll see if more mice have been found." Master Gise started out of the stables.

I guessed I still had a few minutes. "Er . . ."

"Yes, honey?"

"The night we arrived in Two Castles . . . you heard someone outside the king's castle, do you remember?"

"That was you, girl? Why didn't you speak out?"

"Um . . . you sounded angry. I—"

"I was angry, honey! After your coin was stolen, a thief took one of my cows, a good cow I had for five years."

"Have you gotten her back?"

"Not yet." His voice was as grim as it had been then.

"I'm sorry." A mystery solved. But the stolen cow was unsolved for Master Dess.

I left the stables.

In the kitchen Master Jak was spooning sauce over the leek pie. He made room for it on a tray that was as heaped with food as the king's breakfast tray had been. "You are prompt to the minute, *Eh*lodie. Hurry. No doubt his royal gluttony is impatient."

As I passed behind the screen to the great hall, my nose caught a faint but biting odor.

Master Thiel sat cross-legged on the floor before one of the fireplaces. The source of the stink, a glue pot, rested on the hearth, and he held together two pieces of a broken bowl.

Master Thiel. Always where least expected.

A glue jar and his satchel lay at his elbow, the satchel bulging with the tools of a plate mender's trade. He was a plate mender?

I surveyed the great hall. The sleeping pallets had been stacked, and the dinner tables were not yet set up. A manservant crisscrossed the hall, strewing rushes from a burlap sack. Seated on a low stool on the dais, Sir Misyur hunched over a writing board on his lap. He dipped his quill pen in ink and scribbled something on a sheet of parchment.

Looming above him, the princess balled the cloth of her skirt with both hands. "Have they checked the wall walk again, Misyur?" Her voice careened up and down the scale. "Have they combed the cellars?"

I should have gone straight to her, but instead I went to Master Thiel. When I reached his side, I crouched and whispered, "Where is your cat, Pardine?"

He smiled, and I almost lost my balance. "Pardine is rented today to a burgher's wife whose own cat recently died." His expression became serious. "Did you think I'd bring Pardine here after yesterday's calamity?"

I blushed. "No, of course not."

"I came to help, but Sir Misyur said all is well in hand, so I decided to mend a dish or two. Even lords need their plates mended from time to time."

I nodded and backed away to the middle of the room, not tripping over my feet purely by accident.

"Misyur," the princess said, "why are you writing when—"

Sir Misyur craned his head up toward her, a tic pulsing at the corner of his eye. "I am recording where the search has been made, what has been found, where—"

"If not the wall walk or the cellars, he would hide in a donjon, where food is plentiful."

"Your Highness," Sir Misyur said, "two maids are circling the wall walk this very moment. Four menservants—"

I coughed. Both of them turned.

"His Majesty requests you." I curtsied.

She let her skirt go and waved her hand. "Requests which of us? No need to bow, *Eh*lodie."

I straightened. "You, Your Highness. He instructed me to bring a breakfast for you." I held out the tray.

"But I'm not hungry, and I'm helping! We're finding Jonty Um." Her huge eyes filled, reminding me of blue-yolked poached eggs.

How wicked I was to have such a thought!

"I'm coming." Her hair bounced below her cap as she leaped off the dais. "My father would not like to know I jumped."

I smiled. "I won't tell."

The king's first words were addressed to me. "Half an hour is not long for a king to wait for his command to be obeyed. How lucky I am to be a king."

Instantly Princess Renn said, "La! I came as soon as I was told."

I flushed. She turned to face me. Under pretense of taking the tray, she mouthed, *I'm sorry.*

Perhaps he did worse to her than he did to servants.

She placed the tray on the table. "I'm sure the cook was slow, Father, not *Eh*lodie."

"The girl has a name? A name in three syllables?"

This made me as angry as anything else he'd done.

"Yes, Father. *Eh*lodie."

"How grand of her. Come here, girl."

I moved a little closer.

He frowned. "Has she come near, Renn? Do you believe she has approached me?"

"No, Father." She murmured. "Perhaps she is afraid."

"Of me? Come, girl. I won't spit at you again."

Not comforting, but I advanced and stopped a few inches from him.

"Most mansioners paint their faces, if I am not mistaken. Extend your face, girl."

I put my face forward and dug my nails into my palms.

"You don't mind my finger in your jam, do you, dear?"

"No, Father."

He dipped his forefinger in. I closed my eyes. He might accidentally or purposely poke one of them out.

"One sister is pretty. . . ." His finger rubbed jam into my left cheek and stroked it across the left half of my lips. "And the other is not." After a moment he smeared something warm on my right cheek and across the right half of my lips.

I licked my upper lip on the right. The brown sauce.

"Mustn't." He applied the sauce again. "Ah. Stand away so my daughter may see."

I opened my eyes.

"Is she not improved?" He didn't pause for an answer. "You would have benefitted from my assistance yesterday, girl. Now perform the piece again."

Shamed tears flooded my eyes. Do not cry, I thought, or he will be glad. I blinked them away and reenacted the scene. I did it well, too, to spite the king and please his daughter.

She didn't laugh until I had the prince search the floor for jewels, my nose just above the wooden planks. But then she did and kept laughing until I finished.

"I am delighted to hear your laughter." His Highness speared a chunk of his leek pie and put it in his mouth. "All but the pie is for you. You are too thin, my love."

She took a hard-boiled egg and picked at it with her fingers.

I backed away. If they ignored me for a few minutes, I would slip out.

"I want you at your prettiest. With the ogre vanished, you still need a husband."

I froze.

"I have chosen a better one."

She swallowed and blinked. "So soon?"

"The night of grieving is over. Now is the day of joy, my dear."

"La! Only it is so soon."

He frowned.

"Is he tall and rich, Father?"

"He is rich. He will be tall. His father, the earl of Profond, is tall."

She swallowed again. "How old is the son?"

"He was born six months ago. Love is deep when it starts early."

"Cruel!" The word exploded out of me. My hand flew to my mouth to snatch it back, but it seemed to fill the entire tower.

CHAPTER TWENTY-SIX

"—cruel?" the king said mildly.

I looked down at my shoes peeking out from my hem. How worn they were, water stained and grimy. What would His Highness do to me?

"Am I cruel, daughter?"

"You are never cruel. Does the son have ringlets in his hair?" Her voice lightened. "Ringlets are charming."

"I am told he has golden ringlets."

"Will he be handsome, do you think?"

I looked up.

She threw her arms around the king's neck. "You are goodness itself." She raised her head. "*Eh*lodie, my husband will be tall and rich, and he will never turn into a mouse. How happy I am."

King Grenville patted her back. "I'm glad, child."

"And how sad I was a moment ago."

"Eat, my love. The sausages are very fine."

She returned to her seat. "If they are fine, we must share them." She cut off a chunk and fed it to him.

While chewing, he continued. "The count would have been a great help against Tair, but the earl is eager to put money into the undertaking." He seemed to remember my presence. "Girl, you may leave. You will do well to stay out of my sight unless a real snake is exiting from your mouth. That I would like to see."

His laughter followed me out the door.

In the inner ward, I went straight to the well. The jam came off easily, but the sauce had hardened. On my chin I needed to chip away a congealed bit with my fingernail. When I thought I had rinsed the food away, I scrubbed again. I felt dirty under the skin.

From the well I returned to the great hall to ask Sir Misyur how I might help in the search—not to see if Master Thiel was still there, which he wasn't.

Several servants carried trestles to the middle of the hall, in readiness for a meal, I supposed.

"Elodie," Sir Misyur said, looking up. "Nesspa must want a walk. Will you be so kind as to take him to the outer ward."

I got him from the count's apartment, and he pulled me into the postern passage, which was long enough to be dark even in midday.

"Young Mistress Elodie?"

My heart lurched with fright until I recognized the voice. Then it simply lurched. In the gloom, I saw Nesspa leap up to lick Master Thiel's face.

"May I walk with you?"

I nodded, although he couldn't have seen my head bob.

Outside, Nesspa ran here and there, sniffing as I let out his chain.

Master Thiel slung his sack over his shoulder. The coins in his purse jingled. "There is a question I would like to ask you."

The start of a Lahnt love song ran through my mind: *A secret meeting and a secret, a sweet greeting . . .*

"You may ask." How grown-up I sounded!

"In Master Sulow's mansion, what were your thoughts when you pretended to be Thisbe?"

This was his question?

I sighed. "I was very hungry. Remember the bowl of apples? I pretended an apple was Pyramus. I adored that apple."

Nesspa sniffed a patch of grass, then barked and scuffed up clods of dirt with his back legs, after which he tugged me away, following a new scent.

223

"And last night, when you mansioned the princesses?"

"I simply thought about the fairy tale. When I was the princesses, I imagined myself in their stead." The words repeated in my mind: *I imagined myself in their stead*. The words were important, but I didn't see how. *I imagined myself in their stead*. "Why do you ask?"

"I hope to be . . ."

I looked up.

He was blushing. ". . . something more than a plate mender or cat teacher. Despite Sulow's first no, becoming a mansioner may be within my grasp, and it would be"— he paused—"an exciting life."

No one could be a true mansioner who wanted the life, not the mansioning.

Nesspa raised his head. He sniffed the air, then howled deep in his throat and ran, pulling me helplessly along.

Master Thiel grabbed the chain just above my hand. Between the two of us, we controlled the dog, who continued to strain toward the south ward, keening eerily. We followed, Master Thiel so close to me that my shoulder jogged his side. He smelled of hay—another night in the stable, perhaps.

Was Nesspa taking us to the ogre, safe out here by some miracle?

When we neared the southwest tower, I heard groans above Nesspa's whines. Master Thiel and I stopped restraining the dog and raced behind him.

We rounded the tower. Not many yards away, an ox lay on the ground, bleeding into the grass.

"Get Master Dess from the stable," I yelled. Master Thiel could run faster than I could.

His face was pale, as mine must have been. "Can—"

"Go!" I cried.

He left me at a run.

The blood was seeping from gashes that striped the beast's neck and shoulder. He struggled to his knees, then collapsed on his side, panting heavily. Nesspa wagged his tail and licked the wound.

"Poor thing." I stroked the ox's face. Lepai oxen are mild-tempered. "What happened to you?"

Masteress Meenore could have done this.

A lion could have done it. My hand stopped in the air above the beast's cheek. Had the count turned back into a lion?

Or might this ox be His Lordship?

Master Dess arrived soon, carrying a sack, but Master Thiel didn't come with him.

"Honey, honey. Dess is here." He pressed linen from his sack into the cuts, layer upon layer of cloth until the blood stopped showing through.

"Master Dess . . . is the ox—"

"Just an ox. Girl, put your hands here. I need to move

him." He had me take his place pushing down on the bandages.

"Like this?" I wished my hands were bigger.

"Yes, and don't stop pressing."

No one could move an ox if the ox didn't help, but Master Dess got his hands under the beast and murmured in his ear. The ox groaned and rolled backward a few inches.

"Now your mouth, honey, honey." He eased it open. "Keep holding, girl, girl." He placed a large leaf on the beast's tongue. Then he gently closed the mouth and released me from my task. "If you and Master Thiel hadn't found him, the beast would soon have been beyond my help."

"He'll live?"

"Likely he will." The ox squirmed. "There, honey. I'm here. I'll stay with him now."

I had been dismissed, but I hovered. "Did a lion attack him? Did—"

"I don't know." His voice was harsh again.

I brought Nesspa back to His Lordship's apartment. Afterward I paused in the inner ward, uncertain what to do next.

Voices came from the kitchen. I heard "lion" and stood in the doorway. News of the ox couldn't have reached anyone yet except by way of Master Thiel's tongue.

Master Jak set me to peeling and slicing turnips. The kitchen servants were jubilant, despite the ox. All were certain that His Lordship had been the lion. He lived and would return soon in his usual form. I wished I shared their certainty, but I kept thinking of my masteress killing the hare in almost the same spot as the ox had fallen.

A maid said, "What if he remains a lion? What if he cannot change back?"

"He stopped being a mouse, didn't he?" Master Jak said. "And he never harmed a hair on a human being before, though he was big enough as his ordinary self."

"But," the butcher said darkly, "they'll think the worst in Two Castles. When he's an ogre again, someone will try to kill him." He whacked his chopper down on the neck of a struggling chicken. "By cat or arrow or ax, eventually someone will succeed."

CHAPTER TWENTY-SEVEN

hen my turnips were all peeled and sliced, I slipped into the great hall, which was deserted now. I claimed my satchel and left, exiting the castle by the postern entrance.

I started down the track that would take me to the road to town. But after a few steps, I stopped. I couldn't go to IT if I believed IT could have mauled the ox.

Did I?

I stared up at the sky, which was milky with haze across the sun. Not far from here, IT had dropped out of the air to shelter me from the rain.

IT wouldn't hurt an ox. I didn't deduce or induce or even use common sense to decide. Lambs and calves, I trusted IT.

At the menagerie the gate was open again or still open,

but this time two guards flanked it, facing inward.

Although I had planned to go directly to my masteress, I went in under the noses of the guards, who seemed not to notice me. Beyond the ornamental shrubbery, a peacock strutted, its feathers fanned open. I recalled the roasted peacock at the feast.

"One tin for entry!"

To my right a plump man sat on a high stool with a basket in his lap—the menagerie keeper, no doubt. I dug in my purse.

"Everyone must pay. Except the king and the princess and anyone they say doesn't have to pay. Did one of them say that to you?"

I was tempted to lie, but I shook my head.

"An honest girl needn't pay. Honesty is worth a tin. Parade of people today."

Who?

"The princess didn't pay," he said. "And she told me to let that pleasant young man, the miller's son, in for free. They arrived early." He slid down from his stool and turned out to be no taller than I. "Come." He headed toward an avenue of cages and pens. "You want to see the monkeys. Everyone did. No one lingered. They've all gone. I'll go with you myself. Perhaps the creatures are shedding golden hairs."

"Who else visited?"

"His Lordship's steward and the animal physician. Master Dess visited all the animals, stayed awhile at each cage. And half the town came—the tailor, Master Corm, the baker, Master Gatow, and . . ."

Naturally they'd come. As the menagerie keeper listed the townspeople who'd stopped by, I clenched my jaw with impatience. He walked so slowly, and I, too, wanted only to see the monkeys. If His Lordship were anything else, I wouldn't be able to tell, but I might recognize him as a monkey.

Still, I looked around. I had never visited a menagerie before. Some animals were shackled as well as caged, and both the cages and the pens needed cleaning.

I asked the menagerie keeper to point out the high eena, which turned out to be a striped beast, the size of a wolf, who stood motionless in a corner of its cage.

Before reaching the monkeys, we passed an assortment of other beasts: a huge creature with a murderous-looking horn, a yellow-and-blue snake, a dozen ratlike animals with long snouts, and more.

The monkeys' cage was at the end, holding three adult monkeys and a lively monkey child, who climbed the bars of the cage. Two adults sat together, one of them picking through the fur of the other. Across the cage, the third adult lay on its side and seemed to be asleep.

"You've always had three?"

"The third came last year, and the little one was born here."

The monkeys ignored us. Not one smiled at me. I felt a pang in my chest.

"Master, is there more than this?" I gestured at the line of cages and pens.

"No more animals, except the fleas."

We started back to the gate. When we reached it, I bade him farewell and thanked him for his kindness.

"No trouble. Had to get down from my stool anyway. End of day. Feeding time."

"Master? Do you lock the gate at night?"

"Not I. No key. His Majesty's guards do it after I've gone."

The guards might forget sometimes, I supposed. I curtsied and left him. When I reached the lair, I found it empty, so I hurried to the market square, where the marchpane vendor said IT hadn't sold skewers today.

"IT came earlier," she said, "and bothered people with questions about the ogre's feast."

I decided to wait in the lair, but on Sabow Street I saw a column of black smoke ahead and remembered that IT sometimes made the fire hotter for Master Bonay, the blacksmith. I followed the smoke.

ITs shoulders and trunk filled the doorway of the smithy. ITs head was inside.

The shop abutted the town wall, set apart from the line

of houses across the way. And no wonder it was alone: The entire building glowed fiery gold.

Master Bonay stood nearby, holding his poker in his right hand. He turned as I approached, although I don't know how he heard me over the rush of fire. "Ah, the dragon's apprentice."

"Assistant, master."

Ash drifted down on us.

He grinned. One of his front teeth was gone, but the others shone white against his sooty face. "A great day. Meenore the Unfathomable, the Stingy, lights my furnace for free."

Smoke eddied from the side of the shed as well as from the chimney. Curious, I went there and discovered a window. I waved to clear the smoke, peered in, and gasped.

A thick jet of white fire shot from ITs mouth into the forge, the flame roaring as it spewed forth.

How could IT create such an inferno?

Nearby, a man worked a bellows. I marveled that he didn't melt.

Master Bonay spoke into my ear. "I used to pump the bellows." He chuckled. "Better to be a master than an apprentice."

Undoubtedly. I crossed the street to where the heat was less fierce. Master Bonay joined me there, and we waited several minutes while, gradually, the noise dwindled. The shed's incandescence dimmed. A few minutes more and my masteress backed away from the doorway.

"Bonay?"

"Behind you."

IT turned. ITs eyes were paler than I'd ever seen them.

"Bonay?" A set of almost transparent eyelids lifted. IT had two pairs of eyelids. "There you are. Lodie, you are in time to hear Bonay answer my inquiries."

How did IT know I hadn't come on some urgent matter?

"Fire away, Meenore." Bonay laughed at his own joke.

Enh enh enh.

The smith hadn't been a guest at the castle. Why was IT questioning him?

"Do you believe the ogre is now a lion, Bonay, a lion who mauled his own ox?"

"I believe it. I heard a lion's roar a few nights ago—"

As I had.

"His guests saw him turn into a lion. Only a fool would *dis*believe." He shrugged. "Makes no difference to me if His Lordship the lion is still prowling." He raised his poker. "I have this and my cat."

"Tell me, Bonay, if you have your cat and your poker, why wear an aegis?"

What was an eejis?

Bonay looked down at the bracelet of twine on his left wrist.

"Lodie," IT said, "you've wondered about the twine. We have a saying in Two Castles: *Innocence bares its wrist and trusts its luck. Guilt wraps its wrist and trusts no one.*"

I understood. The twine bracelets were a protection from harm—for people who had done harm.

Goodwife Celeste wore twine, and so did Master Thiel!

"Guilt isn't the only reason to wear a bracelet, Meenore. I need protection from fire, a roof beam collapsing."

"I fly over town at night when the mood strikes me. Most houses are asleep, but your shed is awake. Who is giving you silver and gold, Bonay?"

The apprentice emerged from the shed. "The fire is hot enough, Master."

"You may use the tongs, Gar. You're ready. I'll come in to see what you've done."

The apprentice disappeared back into the shed.

"This is none of your affair, Meenore."

"We have a bargain."

He relented. "Burghers in debt bring me silver sometimes. Occasionally gold."

Violet smoke rose from ITs nostrils. "Burghers in debt take their precious metals to a jewelry smith. Who really brings you silver and gold? Do not lie to me."

"I didn't agree to be insulted. I answered your question. My obligation is discharged." He shifted the poker from his left hand to his right. "You are all smoke and no fire, Meenore."

IT grinned. "Two Castles boasts three blacksmiths, but the king sends all his sword work to you. Why is that, Lodie?"

Bonay's face was still sooty, so I felt rather than saw him pale. I cast about for an answer.

"I pay for your services!"

"And the others would as well. Lodie, Bonay has the king's custom because Bonay's fire is hottest."

And the fire was hottest because Masteress Meenore heated it.

"I will ask once more: Who brings you silver and gold?"

"Do not say I told you."

"I make no promises."

Bonay dug his poker into the dirt and rocked it back and forth. "Thiel brings me silver."

I swallowed a gasp.

"And when they come to Two Castles, a Goodman Twah and his Goodwife Celeste bring both gold and silver. They come infrequently, but they bring a great deal. I don't have to pay them as much as I pay Thiel, who bargains hard."

"Anyone else?"

Anyone else I admired? The princess? Sir Misyur? Master Dess?

"Just those three—Thiel and the old couple."

My masteress wouldn't let me into the lair or listen to any of what I had to tell until I had washed myself and laundered my clothes. The sky had darkened to night by then, and I was damp and cold, but the lair warmed me.

An area between the cupboard and the door had been curtained off. Curious, I approached the curtain.

"Leave it be, Lodie."

I backed away.

The cheese and bread were in bowls on the fireplace bench.

"I have new cheese. Tell me how you like it." IT threaded skewers and toasted them in the fireplace, one for IT, two for me. "And we still have a few figs and dates from His Lordship's visit. They are in a bowl in the cupboard. Fetch it."

I wondered if IT had saved the delicacies for me.

When the skewers were toasted, I sampled the new cheese, which was sharper than any I'd ever tasted. "Mmm. Delicious."

"Make more skewers if you like." IT settled on ITs belly, ITs head and neck along the floor between me on the bench and the hearth, ITs eyes on me. "And tell me everything."

I did so, ending with my visit to the menagerie.

IT raised ITs head. "When you found the ox, you saw nothing of a lion?"

"Nothing."

"The grass around the ox had not been disturbed? You saw no tracks?"

"The grass was bloody, but not torn up."

"Why is this detail important, Lodie?"

I imagined a lion, stalking a grazing ox. The ox smells something amiss, lifts his head, turns. Sees the lion. The ox gallops. The lion is faster and springs. The ox swings his horns, misses the lion. The lion's teeth rake the ox's shoulder. The lion's claws scratch.

I closed my eyes tight and screwed my face into a grimace, feeling the pain of the ox.

The ox whirls, trying to get free, sending up great clods of dirt and grass.

"Oh!" I opened my eyes.

"Yes, Elodie?"

"There was no lion."

CHAPTER TWENTY-EIGHT

as there a dragon? Did I do it?"

I didn't have to think. "There would have been a struggle as well. You didn't do it. But I knew that already."

The ridges above ITs eyes rose. "Ah. You have already exonerated me." IT sat up and picked ITs teeth with a skewer. "Undoubtedly the attacker planned to create signs of a struggle. If Nesspa had not barked and given warning—unintentionally, certainly—you might have caught him or her at it. Someone wants the folk of Two Castles to believe in the lion, and most do believe, save us deep thinkers."

"Then who or what attacked the ox?"

"Yes, who? Who indeed?"

I considered. "A person with a rake. Someone the ox

trusted. Someone he wouldn't run from."

"But who? You stayed in the castle. You may know better than I."

"The stable master Gise . . . The grooms and stable hands. Master Dess, the animal physician . . . no animal fears him. And the beasts may be used to Master Thiel if he often sleeps in the stable."

"You are ready to accuse handsome Thiel?"

To cover my discomfort, I helped myself to a handful of cheese squares. I no longer knew what Master Thiel might do.

IT said, "He was with you. He couldn't have interrupted himself. May he be exonerated too?"

I hoped he might be, but I wasn't sure. "Perhaps he was frightened off before I came."

"Then someone else would have discovered the ox."

"Anything might have startled him." I frowned, searching for ideas. "The grooms exercise His Lordship's steeds in the outer ward. At the sound of hooves Master Thiel—or anyone else—would have run without looking back, but the grooms might not have rounded the tower. Then he might have gone with me to discover the ox, which he knew was there."

"That is cold-hearted enough for Thiel. Anyone else?"

I hesitated, hating to say the words. "His Lordship as himself, not as a lion. But why would he maul his own ox?"

"I doubt he did. Common sense deems it unlikely."

I felt tears coming. "He is likely dead, isn't he, Masteress?"

"Common sense says yes, but induction and deduction have not yet proved the result."

I swallowed the tears. "He may be alive?"

"Or dead. We may never know."

I felt like a bird that kept rising and then being thrown to earth.

"I will hate not to know. Not knowing will gnaw at my liver. Dragons have livers, too, Lodie."

"Masteress, whoever mauled the ox wanted to endanger His Lordship, right?"

"I can think of no other reason."

"Does that person know for certain that His Lordship lives?"

"It would seem so, but that conclusion is not proven either."

I sighed, then yawned in spite of myself.

"Lodie . . . when Thiel was mending His Lordship's plates, did you notice his satchel?"

I missed nothing when it came to Master Thiel. "It was at his elbow."

"Did it lie flat?"

"No. I saw the angles of his tools through the cloth."

"Think, Lodie."

I was too tired to think.

IT waited.

The plate mender rarely came to our cottage on Lahnt. Poor people learned not to be fumble-fingered.

What were a mender's tools? A glue pot. Thiel's had been on the hearth. A glue jar. Next to the sack. Two or three clamps, which would occupy little space. I could think of nothing more.

No!

Yes. "Some of His Lordship's goblets and bowls and such were in the sack." I marveled. "With Sir Misyur in the hall, too."

"Thiel is a master thief, light-fingered enough to steal a man's beard."

I smiled at the idea.

Enh enh enh.

"And Pardine is a master thief among cats," I said. "He must have taken my copper."

"Very likely."

"Do you think Master Thiel is the thief His Lordship told us of, who made off with the linens, the wall hanging . . ." I'd forgotten what else.

"Also very likely."

He had probably taken Master Dess's cow, too. But we still didn't know who the poacher was. Or, most of all, who had signaled the cats.

"How can Master Thiel make people like him and then rob them?"

"Speculation exhausts the mind, Lodie."

"Do you think His Lordship discovered Master Thiel's thievery?"

"Possibly."

"And so Master Thiel set the cats on His Lordship and mauled the ox?"

"Perhaps, Elodie."

"Elodie? But I'm speculating!"

"You are deducing."

Deducing when IT called it so, speculating when IT called it so. How happy I was to be back in ITs company!

"Be wary of Thiel."

I imagined him, not only his form but also his friendliness, his way of setting everyone at ease. "Is he the one you think the most likely?"

"There is an entire town and a castle to choose among."

I couldn't help yawning again.

"You would like to sleep?"

ITs voice had a lilt I hadn't heard before. IT plodded to the new curtain and drew it back.

"Lambs and calves!" Three big pillows mounded under a linen sheet (no blanket needed in the lair). A small pillow lay at one end of the bed—a pillow for my head, such as rich folk had. I ran my palm across the linen, which was smooth as butter. The pillows were soft as white bread.

"I layered straw under the pillows."

I sat. "I'll float!" I had never slept in such a fine bed.

"The straw is fresh. The pillows are stuffed with down, and the linen is scrupulously clean, as are the pillow covers. Good night, Lodie." IT pulled the curtain closed.

"Good night, Masteress Meenore." I shed my kirtle and slid under the sheet in my chemise. My last memory before sleep is of pushing the little pillow aside.

I woke up remembering what I'd failed to report last night.

IT had cooked pottage for breakfast, and IT watched me closely as I put the first spoonful into my mouth. "Do you like it?"

I nodded and managed not to spit out the mouthful, but there were limits to my mansioning.

IT took my bowl away. "I will prepare skewers. What did I do wrong?"

"The beans have to be cooked first."

"Ah. I enjoy them raw."

Certainly, if you can cook them in your stomach.

"You may cube the cheese."

I began to cut. "The princess is betrothed again." I explained.

"Mmm."

I hated *Mmm*! "What do you conclude, Masteress?"

ITs voice tightened, became *mistressish*, as Father would say. "It is not for an assistant to question her masteress."

Mmm, I supposed, was sacred, so I asked something else. "Did you discover anything yesterday before I came?"

"I passed the morning," IT said, not minding this question, "circling the castle, flying low, scanning for a fleeing mouse or any creature behaving in an untoward manner. But if His Lordship in any shape had been north of the castle while I was south or vice versa, I would have missed him. I cannot deduce that he was not there."

"In the fields a hawk or an eagle might have caught him."

"In the afternoon I visited Thiel's brothers. After I threatened to boil away the water in their millstream, they were happy to answer my questions." *Enh enh enh.*

I smiled. "What did they tell you?"

"That Thiel does not live with them, that they know not where he lives, that they saw no one signal the cats, and that they gave no signal themselves. They were abundantly supplied with *no*s, both of them. I peered in a window of the mill house. Every comfort in full measure. Whatever one thinks of Thiel, the old miller was unkind to him."

"If his father had left him anything, he might not have become a thief."

"He stole before his father died, Lodie."

Oh.

The nine-o'clock bells rang.

"Then, in the square, I interrogated this one and that. The townsfolk expect a lion to run up and down the way, dining on people as he goes. They are worth nothing, the lot of them. If His Lordship becomes His Lordship again, he will not last long. He would do better to come back as a lion and really eat them."

CHAPTER TWENTY-NINE

hen we had finished our breakfast, IT announced that we would visit Master Sulow and his troupe. "You say mansioners are observant. We shall find out."

Master Sulow had seen my performance at the banquet. Had he liked it? Had he hated it?

As I walked to the mansions, missing ITs warmth, IT flew to and fro, ITs shadow scribbling across the landscape. Both of us looked for any animal not acting as it should. Most likely we were too late, but we looked.

Finally the meadow ended. I was close enough to see the cats lolling under the mansions.

My masteress landed and lumbered along at my side. "The villain, whoever he or she is, must object to my questions. You may be in danger. I am near invulnerable, but he or she may attack me through you."

I shivered, then felt surprise. IT would be injured if I were hurt?

"My wing is an impervious shield. Seek its shelter if need be. Do not stray far from my side until the danger is over."

I swallowed over a lump in my throat. IT wasn't using common sense. No one would think of harming me to stop IT.

As before, we reached the mansions from the rear. I heard voices calling to one another, the beat of a hammer, the thud of a mallet. Someone laughed. Then came a cry like none I'd ever heard—a bleat, a bray, a deep wail—all three at once.

"That, no doubt, is Master Sulow, portraying himself as a donkey." *Enh enh enh.*

We rounded the side of the purple wagon.

Master Sulow, wearing a bull's mask, strode back and forth before the black mansion. He sounded like nothing human even as he began to blare words: "Whoever imprisons me will die. I am the whelp of a woman, son of a god."

I had it. This was *Theseus and the Minotaur.* Just as at the count's feast, the next entertainment would be about a beast, this time the bullheaded minotaur, portrayed by Master Sulow.

The front walls had been removed from three mansions.

Within the green (for love), trees had been painted on the side walls, and cutouts of trees stood before the back curtain. In the purple (for pomp), a cutout of a castle blocked most of the curtain, and the stage was bare. In the black (for tragedy), the prow of a ship with a single black sail projected from the left-hand wall. Wooden ocean waves, painted blue-green, scalloped the floor.

In front of the mansions a low wooden fence, unfinished, zigged and zagged and was the source of the hammering and pounding. The apprentices I'd seen at the castle were busy building it, one of the boys steadying the fence while the girl hammered and the other boy held a pail, probably containing nails.

Beyond the fence, four rows of benches had been set facing each open mansion. These seats would accommodate those willing to pay extra for comfort. The rest—called the *tin audience*, because they paid only a tin or two—would stand.

A group of journeyman mansioners and older apprentices stood by the closed yellow mansion, closed because there was no comedy in *Theseus and the Minotaur*. I recognized the minstrel from the ogre's feast. The journeymen spoke lines to one another, softly enough that they didn't compete with their master, who was trying his lines one way after another. Now he alternated an animal and a human voice. The first made me fear the beast; the second made me pity him.

Experimenting further, he began softly and rose to a

rage, animal the whole while. Next he gave an all-human reading drenched in bitterness.

He surpassed Albin and all the mansioners I'd admired in Lahnt. Not merely surpassed. The gulf that separated genius from talent stretched between. If he'd accepted me as an apprentice, how much I could have learned!

And if I'd stayed with Master Sulow, I wouldn't have grown to love His Lordship. I'd be free of the grief that traveled everywhere with me.

But I wouldn't have discovered inducing, deducing, and using my common sense.

Master Sulow removed his mask. "Meenore! Young Elodie or Lodie or any other name you prefer!" Holding the mask, he bowed elegantly. "How long have you been watching my wretched attempts?"

Had he truly been unaware of us?

I curtsied. IT inclined ITs head.

"Come! I will not refuse you food today." He led us to the yellow mansion and opened the door. "Please come in, Lodie."

"Elodie."

"Serve us out here, if you please, Sulow. Your mansion is impossible for me, as you know."

I was being protected. I felt embarrassed, as if Master Sulow would guess that Masteress Meenore didn't trust him.

He entered the mansion and returned in a few minutes

with a tray that held a bowl of apples (again), a smaller bowl of dried apricots and walnuts, a sliced honey cake, and a bowl for each of us. He set the tray on the bench in the first row before the purple mansion. Gallantly he motioned me to sit.

I did, and he took his place on the other side of the tray. IT settled ITself before us, positioned to see Master Sulow and his mansioners and to raise a wing between me and an attacker.

The three of us followed the custom of serving one another.

"Tomorrow afternoon we perform the whole of the minotaur tale, not merely Theseus's scenes. It is rarely performed in its entirety, Elodie."

Ordinarily I would have wanted to see the play more than anything, but now I wanted most to find His Lordship—or His Lordship's killer.

IT put an apple in Master Sulow's bowl and ate one ITself, core and stem. "Why more mansioning on the subject of a monster?"

"*More* means more than one, Meenore. We were unable to perform *Beauty and the Beast*."

I burst out, "Your minstrel sang about a giant slayer and a giant. A giant is a monster."

"Young Elodie, my audience is in a mood for monsters. Meenore, would you grill white cheese if your customers preferred yellow?"

"I can turn white to yellow with my flame, and a mansioner as skilled as you can turn anything to anything."

I smiled with pride. How clever my masteress was.

"No one has eaten any walnuts." Master Sulow put two in my bowl and three in ITs.

I passed one back to him.

He cocked his head toward his three apprentices. "One will be a tolerable mansioner if I heckle and hound him ceaselessly. The girl shows promise as a carpenter, which I can always use, but the third might as well be a piece of cheese for all the good he will do me. If you hadn't come, Meenore, I would have sought you out."

My stomach fluttered.

"Why?" IT asked.

"To apologize. I own up when I'm wrong, unlike some conceited dragons."

"I am never wrong." *Enh enh enh.*

"To apologize to Elodie." He turned to me.

My heart fluttered.

"I regret that your improvisation for His Lordship's guests was cut short."

"Th-thank you."

"I should have taken you when I saw your Thisbe. I'll be honored if you apprentice with me."

CHAPTER THIRTY

ambs and calves!

IT said something and Master Sulow answered, but I didn't hear. Instead, my mind numb with astonishment, I turned to watch the other mansioners, who were laughing among themselves. I counted a dozen of them—young, old, fair, uncomely—because there were roles for all sorts.

My masteress snapped, "I pay her!"

I came to attention.

"Alas, the guild does not allow me to pay an apprentice."

"Then make her a journeyman."

A journeyman? I gripped the bench with the hand that didn't hold my bowl.

Silence fell between them.

But IT had said I was in danger and had to remain with IT. Had IT changed ITs mind?

"I will pay her. And you, Meenore, may sell your skewers here."

This was my soft bed sending me a pillowy dream. I was still in the lair. I could say anything. Real mistakes were impossible in a dream. "Pay me how much?"

"The beginning rate for a mansioner is two coppers a month. The guild will not let me pay less."

From my masteress I would accumulate a single copper in six months.

Quickly he added, "The guild will not let me pay more, either."

Talk of the guild didn't sound dreamlike. "Why are you willing to pay me?" I wanted to hear him say I was that good.

He said so. "The mayor laughed, and I've been trying to extort a smile from him for fifteen years. The women left off looking at Thiel and watched you."

"Lodie has not the temperament of a mansioner."

I thought IT wanted me to be a journeyman.

"Meenore, let me decide that."

Let *me*!

"She is helping me discover what befell His Lordship. I will not release her until we are done."

"And then, Masteress?" I asked.

"Then you may decide." IT knew I wouldn't leave until the count was found or until we were convinced he would never be found.

But then I would leave. I would rather be a mansioner than even a dragon's assistant.

How my spirits rose! I still pitied His Lordship, but I couldn't feel sad. La! as the princess would have said. La! La!

"You may hasten our inquiries, Sulow, by answering a few questions. We visited today for that purpose, not for you to wheedle my assistant away from me."

Master Sulow transferred the tray from between himself and me to his other side, signifying that sociability had ended. "Ask what you like. I'll answer as I choose."

If Master Sulow had had any part in setting the cats on the count, I wouldn't mansion for him.

"When you were in the kitchen waiting to perform, what did you notice?"

"No one wanted to serve His Majesty. One maid destined for him dropped her tray and wept."

"How long did you spend in the hall itself?"

"I was present to hear my minstrel and then again to watch my apprentices set up, and of course I saw Elodie." He stood and sketched a brief bow for me.

I curtsied.

"Thus I was there when the cats stalked His Lordship. I

could have started them stalking myself, but why would I? Elodie could have as well."

I? I?

But I couldn't have. Everyone was watching me. Master Sulow knew that.

"I don't fancy an ogre owning a castle," Master Sulow said, "but he paid me handsomely. Meenore, nothing passed in the hall to show where His Lordship is now."

"Would *you* have liked the count to become king?"

"An ogre in place of a tyrant? The ogre is far more generous."

"Master Sulow," I said, "did Master Thiel catch your eye?"

"Thiel? Yes. While His Lordship was shape-shifting, Thiel slid a silver spoon up his sleeve."

Thieving even then.

"And two wine tumblers as well. But I didn't see him signal the cats."

"Four nights ago," I said, "were you practicing a lion role? Did you roar in the middle of the night?"

"Several nights ago, yes. I don't remember how many."

"Were you practicing in your mansion, master?"

"No. When I'm sleepless, I march above the town and rehearse at full voice."

"More than one person heard a lion that night," IT said. "Have you told anyone of your late rehearsing?"

"No one."

The townsfolk who heard wouldn't have known it was Master Sulow. They would have thought it was His Lordship as a lion. Had Master Sulow set the ogre trap?

He told us nothing else I thought of interest. When IT had exhausted ITs questions, he gave us leave to speak with his apprentices and the minstrel.

The apprentices said they'd been too intent on their preparations to attend to anything else. They claimed not to have been aware of the stalking until the ogre began to vibrate, which they felt before they saw.

The minstrel had been on her way back to the mansions when the trouble began, but she told us about her observations while she sang. "One in the hall hardly watched me. An elderly goodwife kept her eyes on you, young mistress. Whenever you poured for His Highness, she fidgeted and whispered to her goodman, which was rude while I was singing."

"Where did this goodwife sit?" I asked.

The minstrel gave the answer I already knew: She sat in Goodwife Celeste's seat.

CHAPTER THIRTY-ONE

he noon bells were ringing when we left the mansions. I walked upwind of IT. "Masteress, why do you think my temperament is wrong for a mansioner?"

"Sulow spoke to the heart of it. He gives his audience what they want. You will give them what you want."

Was that true of me? For now I hoped only to perform.

"Next we will speak with Master Thiel." IT set off through a field, heading south.

"At His Lordship's castle?" The castle lay to the south. I was eager to go there and learn any news that might be. Perhaps the count had returned.

"Master Thiel will not soon revisit the castle in daylight. By now someone has counted the silver and the plate. Lodie, I have not half the day to walk with you to His Lordship's woods. You must ride."

"But we have no donkey."

"Common sense! Ride on *me*."

"You?"

IT lowered ITself to ITs belly, then rolled onto ITs side. "Keep your cloak under you. My skin grows hotter as I fly. Now climb on."

I balanced myself, one hip against it, one foot on the ground. IT stood and slid me into place with ITs shoulder. I crossed my legs so all of me was on my cloak. If ITs skin was going to be too hot to touch, there would be nothing to hang on to.

I'm not frightened, I told myself, and clasped my hands so tight the skin whitened. IT ran and flapped ITs wings, bouncing me hard while I could still cling to IT, but the moment we were aloft, ITs flight evened.

Mother! Father! Albin! I'm a bird!

The day was calm, but flying made a wind. What power, to create a wind! The air ballooned the princess's cap, lifting it half off my head.

ITs wings pumped. My view flickered. Wings raised, and I saw the landscape, blurred and tinted, through ITs wing segments. Wings down, and my sight cleared. Below lay the count's castle. I leaned over and almost fell.

How reduced the castle seemed from above! I saw it as

if drawn on parchment: six squares for towers on the outer curtain, four circles for the inner towers; big horseshoes for the inner gatehouses, smaller horseshoes for the outer ones; straight lines for the curtain walls, except the front wall, which bulged outward, edged by the meandering moat.

Two people—sparrow size—walked along the inner curtain wall walk, four along the larger outer. Several stood here and there in the inner ward, several in the outer. The search was still in progress. His Lordship hadn't returned, but they hadn't given up hope.

South of the castle the hills rippled higher and higher toward the distant mountains. Below us lay pastures and cleared fields and fields that had not yet been harvested. Beyond was forest, evergreen and autumn orange. I wondered if all I saw belonged to His Lordship.

Approaching the forest, IT flew lower, and ITs wing strokes shortened. My ride became bumpy again. I would have fallen if IT hadn't tilted to save me.

IT landed and ran. I jounced up and down but, luckily, not sideways. Wings still beating, IT careered directly at the woods.

I had seen IT land more neatly than this. IT was toying with me!

So I refused to be frightened. I leaned back and thought about how I'd roll off if we crashed into the trees that were rushing at us. At the last moment IT turned aside, slowed, and stopped. IT lowered ITself and folded ITs wings.

Enh enh enh.

I slid off, stood, lost my footing, and toppled, becoming filthy yet again.

IT furrowed ITs eye ridges. I dusted myself off.

IT whispered, "Kindly mansion Princess Renn's voice, but softly."

Her voice wasn't soft. Still, I tried. "La! Perhaps I can. No, I can do better." I thought about what she might say. "La, Masteress!" I raised and lowered my pitch without increasing my noise. "How brave you are to fly!"

"Please call to Thiel. Not softly."

"What should I say?" I whispered, too.

"Desire him to come to you—to her."

Why? I invented a reason. "Thiel?" I cried, loud enough to be heard a mile away. "Thiel? La! I cannot catch my breath. I have such news! La, Thiel, come!"

"You have set the trap. Now we must wait."

A flock of geese passed overhead. I watched the ground, looking for a mouse. Dead leaves rustled in the woods. I raised my head and saw a shadow among the trees, and then Master Thiel emerged.

"Good day, Masteress Meenore, Mistress Elodie." He sounded as if he'd expected us. "Young mistress, you had only to call me in your own voice and I would have come. You are a treat, however, at imitating Her Highness."

I blushed. It made no difference that I knew him to be a thief. In his presence I had to blush.

"Lodie," IT said, "not far into the woods you will find a sack, guarded by his cat. Please fetch it. If the cat snarls, kick him."

"Pray leave the sack, Mistress Lodie, and don't kick Pardine."

I started into the forest.

"The sack holds a brace of partridges," Master Thiel said. "Are you here to rob the poacher?"

"Return Lodie's copper, answer my questions, and you may keep the partridges."

I turned. "And return Master Dess's cow."

He snapped his fingers, and Pardine pranced by me with a sack in his mouth. I left the woods, too. Master Thiel took the sack, hung it from his belt, and lifted Pardine into his arms. I noticed again his twine ring. If anyone needed an eejis, Master Thiel was the one.

"Young Mistress Elodie, the cow is gone."

Oh. For Master Dess's sake, I hoped she'd been taken to a farm and not eaten.

"Ask what you like, Meenore. I am an honest man."

IT snorted. "Bonay has told me what goods you bring him."

"I appeal to you, Mistress Elodie. My father left me to starve. I think it my duty not to."

I blushed.

"Here is my first question: Why would you *not* set the cats on His Lordship?"

"Rather ask why I would. Why would I hurt someone, even an ogre? I wouldn't. I didn't." He paused. "What would I gain?"

That was the real question with him.

"What would he gain, Lodie?"

I touched the purse at my waist, which still lacked the stolen copper. "Revenge on His Lordship for owning your grandfather's castle. Because you, too, hate ogres and—"

"I hate no one."

I rushed on before his innocent look stopped me. "And you don't want an ogre to be king."

"What else, Lodie?"

Induce. Deduce. *Think.* "His Lordship discovered your poaching and was furious."

"I am never discovered"—he bowed to my masteress—"except by a masteress of discernment."

Enh enh enh.

"I didn't harm His Lordship."

Pink smoke curled up from ITs mouth. "You harmed him. In these woods the beasts were his companions. Now, tell me where you think he would hide and how he would act."

"As a mouse?"

"And after, if a cat didn't eat him."

"As a different animal? My dear Meenore, you should ask Mistress Elodie. Sulow says I have no talent for mansioning."

"I am asking you."

"I can't tell you that, but I can tell you something. I didn't think of it until this morning. Walking here with Pardine, I reviewed the lamentable events of that afternoon, and I remembered seeing Sir Misyur flick his wrist."

No! Sir Misyur loved the ogre. I looked at Masteress Meenore, but ITs expression showed nothing.

"I almost missed it and didn't pay attention then. I was laughing too hard. Mistress Elodie, you and he might have been conspiring to keep us from seeing."

What?

IT said nothing.

"I apologize. You would not conspire. Sir Misyur gestured to the servers to delay the next remove. He could see no one wanted an interruption while you performed. His signal to the cats was in addition to the gesture to the servers. It was slight, but a cat teacher couldn't miss it."

"Plausible," IT said.

Impossible, I thought.

"I have more proof. The lord mayor read the count's will last night. He left everything to Sir Misyur. The news is all over town."

I could hardly take it in. Before I could form a thought,

ITs tail whipped around Master Thiel's waist and ITs smoke turned purple.

"Let me go, Meenore. Ouch! What have I done?"

"You have told His Majesty about Sir Misyur's wrist flick, or you have told someone who will tell His Majesty."

"I thought of it only this morning and I've been here. Let me go."

"You concocted the wrist flick when you heard about the will, and you will make sure His Majesty is informed as soon as you may. Lodie, why will he do so?"

I felt as confused as a mansioner who's entered the wrong tale.

"Your scales are hot!"

"How unfortunate for you. Lodie?"

"Because Master Thiel doesn't want Sir Misyur to inherit."

"And what else?"

I spoke slowly, reasoning it out. "Because . . . neither . . . will . . . His . . . Majesty . . ." I had it! "His Majesty will seize the castle. People will believe Sir Misyur guilty because he had riches to gain." I felt breathless. "Master Thiel will receive a reward for his lie."

"I have not told His Majesty. Whatever you think of me, I cannot. Let me go and I'll say why."

IT freed Master Thiel with a snap so sharp that he spun twice on his heels.

"Do not try to run or I will snatch you up again, and I will not be gentle next time."

Master Thiel regained his balance. "Word is all over town. His Highness is deathly ill, poisoned during the feast. He sickened in the middle of last night."

CHAPTER THIRTY-TWO

aster Thiel smiled. "The news is distressing to His Majesty's subjects."

How unfeeling he was. I shivered. Greedy Grenny was horrible, but I didn't wish him poisoned.

My masteress gripped Master Thiel's arm with a claw. "Who is blamed?"

"Master Jak and the taster are imprisoned."

IT let Master Thiel go. "Lodie, we must leave."

"Then I may check my traps, unhindered?"

"Yes. No." The tip of ITs tail circled his ankle. "Give Lodie her copper."

He produced a copper from his purse. "Pardine couldn't tell how pretty you are, or he'd have left you alone." He bowed.

I didn't blush. I was finished. "Is anyone else ill?" I asked. "Any of the others on the dais?"

"I've been told that Her Highness was a little ill, nothing serious. Her father did not share much of his meal with anyone."

"Gluttony and selfishness to good purpose for once." IT lowered ITself. "Lodie, take your seat."

IT landed in a pasture distant enough from both the forest and His Lordship's castle to be hidden from both. I jumped down.

"I must deduce and induce and use my common sense." IT extended ITself on the ground and closed ITs eyes. Only ITs tail switched slowly back and forth. Wisps of smoke rose from ITs nostrils.

I sat on the browning grass. On the farm at this hour, Father and Albin were likely leaving the apple orchard for their midday meal. Our dog, Hoont, would be dancing between the two men, an apple in her mouth, begging to be chased. At home Mother would be stirring the pottage pot. If I were there, I'd be setting out bowls and spoons.

IT raised ITs head and opened ITs eyes. "Lodie, did you see Sir Misyur pass any delicacies to the king?"

"Do you think he and not Master Jak or the taster poisoned him?"

"Answer my question."

"Several times. Sir Misyur was at the end of the dais

table, and His Highness was in the middle. People picked at the food as the bowl went along. They would be poisoned, too."

"They may have been. Thiel may know only of the king, or he may have chosen to tell us only of the king."

"Sir Misyur rose and went to the kitchen more than once to make sure all was well."

IT shook ITs head. "I'm rarely wrong about a character. I've long believed Sir Misyur a good man."

"He could be a whited sepulcher."

"Indeed. I will now think aloud. If you hear a flaw in my reasoning, stop me."

"Yes, Masteress." I felt both nervous and honored.

"Sir Misyur has served His Lordship for seven years. If he knew he was to inherit, why wait to harm him?"

"Maybe—"

"Do not interrupt. Perhaps Sir Misyur has learned only recently that he was to inherit."

"Maybe—"

"Lodie! Sir Misyur, fearing he would no longer inherit when His Lordship married Her Highness, set the cats on the count. He also surmised that His Majesty would not countenance the inheritance. Wanting to keep his wealth, Sir Misyur resorted to poison. In this conjecture, Master Jak and the taster are innocent."

I nodded. These were horrible speculations.

"Don't nod. Sir Misyur wouldn't behave so reprehensibly."

I agreed but didn't nod.

"Let us suppose someone else expects to inherit and signals the cats, then discovers he or she isn't to inherit. . . ." IT shook ITs head. "Two culprits are possible, but not as elegant. A solution should be elegant, Lodie."

I didn't understand, but I had an idea of my own. "Masteress?"

"Yes?"

"What if Master Thiel wormed his way into King Grenville's good graces with gifts of stolen silver or plate or spices or even"—I pointed back the way we'd come—"a brace of partridges. What if he promised to destroy His Lordship . . . ? The king could seize the castle after the count was gone, no matter who was to inherit. Master Thiel would demand riches, perhaps a title, in exchange."

"Possible."

"What if His Majesty refused to fulfill his side of the bargain? Master Thiel might be angry enough to poison him. King Grenville may have been poisoned not at the feast but soon after."

IT said, "Master Thiel may indeed have poisoned the king. He has the malice for it. Master Thiel is my favorite."

"What about the mauled ox?"

IT said, "Master Thiel may have injured the ox earlier and wanted to be with you for the discovery."

"But you said we interrupted the mauling."

"We lack sufficient information." IT rolled onto ITs side for me to climb on. "We will dine at home and then visit your esteemed goodwife, her goodman, and their children. Are you ready?"

I said I was.

In the lair we set to making skewers. Three were complete when a guard wearing a red cloak appeared in ITs open doorway. Her green scalloped cap signified she served the king.

"Elodie of Lahnt?"

I felt IT tense.

"Yes?"

"You are wanted at Count Jonty Um's castle."

Good news! I hurried to the hook for my cloak. "Masteress, His Lordship is back!" He'd sent for me.

IT said, "Why is she wanted?"

I turned from the hook to the guard.

"For poisoning His Majesty."

My knees weakened and I leaned against the wall. Of course they suspected me. I'd poured for him.

She continued, "And for signaling the cats against His Lordship."

CHAPTER THIRTY-THREE

ou can't be serious!" IT said. "She's a child."

They couldn't suspect me of signaling the cats! "I was performing when the cats began to stalk. An imaginary snake was coming out of my mouth. I was reaching for it with both hands. Everyone saw."

The guard said, "She must come."

"I am a fool," IT said. "Who is her accuser?"

The guard hesitated. "Cellarer Bwat. Her Highness sent for you." Her voice softened. "His Majesty's illness has brought her very low."

"He still lives?"

Silence. Why tell a poisoner whether or not she had succeeded?

I still leaned against the wall. "My masteress has

commanded me to go nowhere without IT. I cannot disobey."

"True. I will accompany Elodie."

"She may not bring anyone with her. Apologies, Meenore. You shouldn't have befriended a spy of Tair."

That's what they thought? "I'm not! I've never—"

"Meenore, you might have deduced what she is." She advanced. "Come."

Three more guards filled the entry.

I pushed myself away from the wall and wrapped my cloak around me. "I've never been to Tair. I grew up on a farm in Lahnt."

She took my arm. "And learned to mansion on a farm?"

She walked me out or else my knees would have given way. I looked behind me. IT held the heel of a loaf of bread in one claw, ITs knife in the other. Green smoke rose from ITs nostrils. Green smoke for bewilderment? ITs mouth hung open, and ITs eye ridges were furrowed.

Could IT believe me a spy? Did IT suspect me of poisoning the king, signaling the cats, mauling an ox?

The guards set a quick pace. The one who'd addressed us, the only female, held my right elbow. Another guard had my left. I staggered along between them.

Mother! Father! Fear pounded in my ears. "If I am deemed guilty, the real poisoner won't be caught."

They didn't slow.

"More people will die." I had no idea if this was true.

What would happen when we arrived at the castle? Would a trial take place immediately?

Who would judge me, with His Highness sick, perhaps dying? The mayor? The princess? Sir Misyur, who might have done everything?

Bells chimed—the three-o'clock bells, not the long tolling that would mark His Majesty's death. I was glad at least that the lair lay at the southern edge of Two Castles and there were no witnesses to my disgrace. But the secret wouldn't be kept. Soon my accusal would be known in town. Eventually word would reach my family, who thought me safely apprenticed to a weaver.

The menagerie lay ahead. If only I could shape-shift.

I stumbled. The pressure on my right arm grew, although I hadn't been trying to break free. The guard on my left complained that they were missing their meal. I had missed mine, too, and was hungry through my fright.

A guard behind me said, "Master Jak will have put something aside for us."

Master Jak? I thought he and the taster were imprisoned. No, of course not. I was the one who would be imprisoned. Master Thiel had lied. Why would he lie about this?

To persuade Masteress Meenore to let him go.

The count's castle rose ahead. I made myself heavy and stopped walking.

The red-cape guard snapped, "None of that!"

"I'll take her." The guard on my left slung me over his shoulder as if I were a sack of wheat.

My head jounced with every step. "I'll walk!" I cried, but he didn't put me down.

Someday I will mansion this, I thought.

Sir Misyur and Her Highness were waiting at the door to the northeast tower when I arrived, along with guards who stood so still they might have been nailed in place. My guard set me on the ground and pushed down on my cap to force a curtsy. I would have curtsied!

Sir Misyur only looked at me dolefully, but Her Highness cried, "*Eh*lodie! How could you have hurt him?"

"I didn't! I wouldn't—"

She slapped me across my face. My head swiveled with the force of the blow.

"La! Didn't I give you my own cap?"

I put my hand up to my cheek. "Please, Your—"

"You will have an opportunity to speak," Sir Misyur said. "Until then, you'll be confined to the tower."

"You'll be comfortable in spite of your crime. I give you a princess's word. You won't suffer."

"Does your father still breathe?" I shouldn't have asked,

274

since they believed I wanted him dead.

No one answered. I was led inside.

As I went in, I heard Sir Misyur say, "A mansioner can easily mansion innocence."

The door thudded shut. I didn't hear a lock turn. What need to lock a guarded door?

Facing me was the door to the donjon, closed now. On my right rose a narrow circular stairway in its own little tower attached to the big one. The stairs were dimly lit by occasional slitted windows.

My left-hand guard pulled on my elbow. He and I advanced together with Mistress Guard in the rear. The other guards remained at the bottom. After climbing once around, we reached a short landing and another shut door. The stairs continued, and so did we to the third and top story. A landing here, too, door on my left. Facing me, a ladder led upward to a trapdoor, which must have opened onto the wall walk.

Mistress Guard lifted the latch and pushed the door open. "In you go." She shoved me inside.

The chamber was large and comfortable. In other circumstances it must have been guest quarters. A fire burned brightly and an oil lamp had been lit, no doubt the princess's doing to keep me from suffering, as if light and heat could lessen my misery. A low door across the room would certainly lead to the privy.

The guards exited. The door groaned as a crossbar was pushed home. On my side, the key to the ordinary lock was in the keyhole, useless because of the crossbar.

Furnishings were a small table, a low-backed chair, a case of shelves that held no more than a sewing box and a clay bowl, a barred window too high in the wall for me to see out of, and a bed, a rich man's bed, suspended from the ceiling by ropes and surrounded by drapes to keep out the cold. For extra warmth, a second blanket lay folded at the foot. I threw myself facedown across the coverlet and wept.

I don't know how long I cried. For a while I seemed made of brine. I wept for the ogre, the king, the ox, the princess, Nesspa. And me. Thoughts of yesterday's happiness were torment. I was unlikely ever to become a mansioner.

More than a few tears were caused by thoughts of my masteress. Why hadn't IT flown with me to the castle? IT could have ripped me away from my captors.

Because IT doubted me. IT hadn't ridiculed Master Thiel's suggestion that I had plotted with Sir Misyur, and IT had called ITself a fool when the guards came, a fool for not deducing that I was the whited sepulcher.

That hurt most of all, ITs disbelief in me.

CHAPTER THIRTY-FOUR

 heard the crossbar drawn back. I wiped my eyes and emerged from within the bed drapes. Two guards entered, their faces as blank as new spoons. One bore a tray on which rested pottage, bread, and a tumbler of cider. My empty stomach growled. The second guard blocked the door and seemed to have come solely to protect the first. From me!

The food bearer placed the tray on the table.

"Thank you."

No answer. They left.

Hungry as I was, I set the tray on the floor and pushed the table to the wall under the window. I climbed up but still couldn't see out. I placed the chair atop the table.

Taking care, I climbed onto the table again and stood on the chair.

Night had arrived, a bright, starry night ruled by a gibbous moon. *Gibbous*—rounded—a word Albin taught me.

The window bars bowed outward, so I could see down as well as out. Directly below me was the outer ward bordered by the outer curtain. The town lay too far to the west to see, but in the distance I made out the shiny black strait.

I climbed down and turned my ladder back into table and chair. The kitchen had given me no knife. How frightened they were! But I had been provided with a bowl of water, so I could clean my fingers before eating. I did so now. Afterward, I broke off a corner of bread, then dropped it back on the tray.

His Majesty had been poisoned. Whoever had done it might still be in the castle. Death by poison would prove me guiltless, but my cleared name would be no use to me.

I set the tray by the door, where it tempted me. If I had to keep looking at the food, I would eat it. I climbed up to the window again, poured out the cider, and tossed the bread and pottage. I hoped a hungry night creature wouldn't dine and die.

We'd had no frost yet, so the crickets still sang, untroubled by the plight of a human girl. A dark shape blew across the sky from north to south, turned and returned, angling my way, trailing purple smoke. My masteress!

My masteress, angry. I gripped the bars. How would I convince IT of my innocence?

IT crossed over the outer curtain and flew lower until IT was level with the tower's second story. ITs right claw held a sack.

Again it wheeled back and forth, coming closer with each pass. I feared IT would break a wing on the tower. But IT whipped around and anchored ITself to the stone. Claw over claw, clinging to cracks, IT climbed to me.

"Lodie? Have you—"

"I wouldn't poison anyone. I'm not a whited sepulcher." I was weeping again. "I love the ogre."

"Have you eaten anything here?"

I shook my head. "Nothing. And I'm not a spy."

"Nothing? No drink?"

"None."

IT smiled. I wiped my streaming eyes and dripping nose with my sleeve and smiled back. I had never seen IT look so happy.

"I couldn't warn you not to eat in the presence of the guards. You believe I suspected you?" ITs smoke tinted pink. "You think me an idiot?"

"No. But you called yourself a fool. I thought, a fool for trusting me."

"A fool for not realizing you would be accused. I never for

a moment believed you to be a spy or a whited sepulcher."

I tried not to sound reproachful. "Where have you been?"

"I found Dess and your Goodwife Celeste. They could tell me nothing about Jonty Um, but both have an understanding of poisons and their antidotes. They're in the king's chamber now, along with the physician, Sir Maydsin, who is worthless in my opinion. Dess slipped out to inform me His Highness will likely live."

Relief swept through me. "Do they think I poisoned the king?"

"Dess and Goodwife Celeste?"

I nodded.

"They didn't say."

"Will the guards release me since His Highness is better?" I shook my head. "No. They won't." His Highness had still been poisoned.

"He'll preside over your trial."

And wouldn't be merciful.

"Whatever sort of monarch he is," IT said, "he will be fair. He wants to discover the true poisoner as much as anyone."

How would he do that? "Masteress, would you bring me a few skewers and a jug of water?"

"I have." IT let go of the tower with ITs right claw and held out the sack, which barely fit between the bars. Something inside jingled.

IT grasped the window bars with both claws. "Climb

down, Lodie. You are too precariously perched."

I did. In the sack, along with the food and drink I found a leather purse—containing two silvers and three coppers.

"Masteress!" I cried.

"Speak softly."

I lowered my voice. "Masteress!"

"It is unwise to be in prison without a full purse. You may succeed in bribing a guard, but do not attempt to bribe more than one at once. Each will not trust the other."

"Thank you!"

"If you don't use the coins, I expect them back."

I was affronted. "I'm not Master Thiel." I pushed my old purse into the new one and hung the new one on my belt.

"Lodie, I can visit you only at night, but I will watch your window at intervals during the day. If you need me, tie your cap to a bar. I'll come somehow."

I nodded while pulling a piece of cheese off its skewer.

"You may hear a lion roar again tonight if the wind is in the right direction. Sulow has agreed to roar."

"Why?"

"Perhaps we can draw out our villain."

"Masteress, why did Cellarer Bwat accuse me?"

"Common sense tells me that he knew someone would be named. He didn't want the someone to be himself or any of his friends among the servants, so he offered you, a stranger."

I wondered whether Sir Misyur or Her Highness had asked him or if he'd come forward unasked.

"Farewell, Elodie. May your sleep be sweet."

"Thank you, Masteress." I wished IT could stay. "Good night."

"Do not climb up to the window unless you must." IT let go of the bars and was gone.

I threw a log on the fire and toasted three skewers. With each bite I took in ITs friendship.

When I finished, I returned the remaining skewers and the half-empty jug to the sack, which I hid between the head of the bed and the wall.

I lay down. Firelight made the ceiling glow orange-gray. For how many nights would I look up at it? For how many years?

Two guards brought my breakfast, one of them a chatty, fatherly sort who informed me that the king had eaten his breakfast and his face was no longer so waxen. Goodwife Celeste, Master Dess, and the physician attended him in turn, although they would depart soon if his improvement continued.

"Her Highness rarely leaves his side, and Sir Misyur comes often as well. Aren't you going to eat?"

"Later. I never wake up hungry."

"Children need nourishment."

I wondered if he might be the poisoner, or if someone had instructed him to see me eat. "It tastes bad unless I'm hungry."

The other guard said, "Let her starve if she likes."

The kindly guard gave up, and they left. As soon as they'd gone, I climbed up to the window. A steady rain poured down. I tossed my breakfast—pottage again—out the window and consumed a skewer. I would need to husband food and water until IT came tonight.

King Grenville's skin had been waxen. Martyr's mint caused waxy skin, and so did false cinnamon. Both were grown in Lepai. False cinnamon tasted enough like the true to go unnoticed. Martyr's mint, despite its name, had no flavor at all.

But false cinnamon acted quickly, and His Highness had been poisoned at the feast. He certainly had been well the next day—well and spiteful enough to paint my face with gravy.

In addition to waxy skin, martyr's mint caused slow and light breathing, stomach bloating, listlessness, no pain. And death.

Enough thinking about poison and death. To distract myself, I passed the morning reciting tales and mansioning every role. When the knock came for the midday meal,

I was bellowing, "Fee fie fo fum, I smell the blood of a Lepai man." Not the most sensible line for one suspected of being a spy for Tair.

The door opened, and there was the princess herself, holding my tray. No guards, but I knew they were outside at the ready.

I curtsied while hoping the thick door had contained my words. "Your Highness . . . beg pardon, I was mansioning. Do you know—"

"*Eh*lodie." The lowest note came last, sorrowfully.

I took the tray and set it on the table.

"I shouldn't have struck you." She smiled. "You've heard?"

I nodded. "His Majesty is better. Your Highness, I didn't—"

"Let's not speak of it. I'm still glad I gave you my cap. La! I do not miss it. And until . . ." She shook her head. "I've always been happy to see your head in it."

"Thank you." I wasn't sure what to say. "I've never had such a fine cap." I remembered my manners. "Please sit." I pulled my chair away from the table for her.

"That's your chair." She sat on the bed. "I'll keep you company while you eat your meal. Lamb stew. Won't you try it? I had mine, lamb stew also, quite tasty."

What excuse could I give her for not eating? I wondered if I could trust her with the truth.

Wait! Why did she want me to know her meal had been the same as mine?

"Your Highness, I finished my good breakfast just half an hour ago."

"La! Breakfast? Hardly enough to feed a squirrel. Come, you must have more now."

Could she be the poisoner?

She couldn't be. She would expect me to share with her.

Oh. My tray had but one spoon.

Still, she couldn't be.

Whatever she was, I had to prevent her from forcing food on me. Mansion! My eyes filled with tears. "You have always been kind to me. I promise to eat as soon as hunger returns."

"I won't leave until I see you swallow a morsel or two, for my own consolation. No one will say we starved a prisoner. La! I'll entertain you while you eat. My father . . ."

She *was* the poisoner. I gripped the table, which seemed to spin. Princess Renn was the whited sepulcher.

CHAPTER THIRTY-FIVE

rincess Renn had come to see me eat, because she knew I hadn't touched my meal last night or this morning. If I had, I would be sick or dead by now. I rinsed my fingers in the water bowl, slowly, slowly. Her mouth moved. I restrained myself from screaming and heard not a word.

What poison would she give me? Something quick, that wouldn't hurt, because she didn't want to cause suffering.

How much would kill me?

I had an idea what it might be, and I couldn't eat a bite. When she paused, I said, "Your Highness, alas, my hunger is banished for now." I shivered. "Do you feel a chill?" I held my hands out to the fire, which was blazing, and leaned in as well to redden my cheeks.

She took my shoulders and turned me. "Are you ill, dear?"

I shook my head. "Only cold, and my throat is sore."

"Food will warm you."

I bit on my cheek, hard. "You are too good, but I cannot choke down any." I coughed and wiped my mouth on my sleeve, taking care that she saw the blood.

Her face relaxed. "La, it *is* chilly."

Oh, my cheek hurt.

She held my hands, which were still hot.

I saw her gold bracelets again, but none of twine. Perhaps she thought she didn't need an eejis.

"*Eh*lodie, my father will be just, and I'll see to it that you don't suffer here. I'll leave you now." She twitched the bed-curtains aside. "I see you have enough blankets to make you warm."

She'd made sure of that. I had guessed right about the poison.

She left.

I sniffed my bowl. The scent was faint but detectable: eastern wasp powder. Rare and expensive, but she was a princess. The poison acted in an hour or two, caused chills, fever, tremors, a tight throat, death. A single swallow would be enough to kill me. But I would feel no sharp pain, no agony. No suffering.

If she was her father's poisoner, too, she would have

used something slower on him, because his symptoms had appeared much later.

I climbed to the window, tied my cap to a bar, and descended for my stew and tumbler. As I was about to tip them out, I realized the danger. Even in the rain, she might come out to look for spilled stew.

I threw the meal into the fireplace and began to pace. My masteress said that one culprit was elegant, but there had to be two in this case. Master Thiel had certainly been the poacher and the thief of castle valuables. I would assume Her Highness responsible for everything else: stealing Nesspa, signaling the cats, poisoning her father.

Why do any of it?

Put myself in their steads. That's what I'd told Master Thiel about mansioning, and I'd thought the words significant. Now I knew the meaning: put myself in Princess Renn's stead. She might poison her father because he was about to betroth her to an infant, and she wouldn't be allowed to say no.

But the new betrothal had come after the feast, and he was poisoned at the feast.

I felt bewildered.

Let the king go for now. Why set the cats on the count?

She told me that the king had betrothed her to the count. Put myself in her stead. Suppose she hadn't wanted to wed an ogre, but she had pretended to love him.

And signaled the cats.

To simplify the task, she stole Nesspa. She must have been horrified when I found him. But then, luckily for her, he needed to leave during the feast.

How had she stolen him?

With treats.

How had she kept him hidden?

The answer broke on me like a mallet on the head: by poisoning him, just enough to keep him docile. When I found him he was alert, but he didn't have to be quiet on the wall walk where no one would hear him. Likely she had dosed the other dogs in the hall, too, and that was why they did nothing to stop the cats.

I had tied my cap to the window only a few minutes ago, but I climbed up to look for IT.

The rain prevented me from seeing as far as I had yesterday, and I didn't see IT.

I climbed down.

She must have lulled the ox with poison, too, then raked its shoulder. Why?

She'd spoken about thoroughness when she tied her cap laces three times under my chin. If she did a thing, she did it more than once, or in more ways than one.

Why?

Think elegantly.

If His Lordship (as a mouse) had been seen being

devoured by a cat, she would have had to do nothing more about him. But when the mouse escaped, she had no certainty, so she mauled the ox and frightened the town into believing the ogre a hungry lion. If he returned in his ordinary form, the people of Two Castles would find a way to kill him.

I wished IT would come.

Now for the king's poisoning.

Perhaps at the beginning she didn't want to kill anyone but an ogre. Causing a monster's death wouldn't be evil, according to her. She didn't intend for Nesspa to die. He would have been freed when she was safe from His Lordship.

But when her father announced her new betrothal, she realized—while I was alone with the two of them—that he would go on making matches for her. She decided that he had to die, too. She couldn't have much daughterly affection for him, horror that he was.

That meant he wasn't really poisoned at the feast. She might even have dosed him while I watched. I shuddered.

How?

The fashion of long, flowing sleeves! Perfect for concealment. Prepared for anything as she was, she could have kept a hidden pouch of poison on her always.

With closed eyes, I recalled the scene. I saw her spear a chunk of sausage on her knife with her right hand. Her left passed over the meat to gather up her right sleeve and keep it from trailing through the food. Likely the poison was in her left sleeve. She sprinkled with her left hand.

I remembered the missing mortar and pestle on the morning of the feast. She might have taken them to grind her poison.

Where was my masteress? As soon as King Grenville recovered enough to do without constant watching over, his daughter would feed him something else. In his weakened state, he would certainly die. Everyone would think he'd merely taken a turn for the worse. Cures for poisoning were uncertain.

IT had to come soon!

I returned to my deducing. Princess Renn must have been behind Cellarer Bwat, my accuser. She had probably hinted to him that I might be to blame, hinted so subtly he thought the suspicion his own.

As I mulled it over, I saw she had reason to fear me. I'd witnessed her dismay when His Highness revealed her new future husband. She had directed me to search the stable when she knew Nesspa was elsewhere. I had discovered the mauled ox. And I was the assistant to a dragon skilled at unraveling mysteries. Thorough again, she thought imprisoning me not enough. She had to poison me, too.

I wondered if His Lordship had seen her set the cats on him. Poor count. If he loved the princess, what a blow that would have been.

Had she poisoned him as well as signaled the cats? I remembered his face had been mottled red and white when the minstrel sang, and he'd swayed when he tried to address everyone after the king announced the betrothal. Also he'd hugged himself as if he were cold just before he shifted into the lion.

Poison might have made him less able to resist the cats.

Again I climbed to the window. Below me a hooded figure rounded the tower, walking slowly, hugging the wall. Even from above I recognized Princess Renn's thin shoulders and awkward gait. She was seeking the remnants of my meal.

A moment ago I'd wanted my masteress instantly. Now IT mustn't come!

With trembling hands, I pulled in the trailing cap laces, untied the knots, and took in the cap.

Then I waited, waited, waited.

Surely she must be gone by now. I peeped out.

She was kneeling on the wet ground, her shoulders shaking. As I watched, she raised her head. I retreated, but not before seeing her red eyes, her tragic expression.

The next time I looked, she was gone. I tied the wet cap back in place. A form, grayed by the weather, flew toward me from Two Castles. Soon IT would pass over the outer curtain. I waved. IT would find a way to save the king.

IT wheeled back and forth as IT had last night, but at a greater distance from me. Why?

Abruptly IT flew straight up.

"Come back!"

IT rose higher, then twisted in the air. While frantically beating ITs wings, IT fell and disappeared behind the outer curtain.

CHAPTER THIRTY-SIX

 gripped the bars. IT must have taken an arrow in ITs belly. I heard myself sobbing as if from far away. Could IT survive the arrow or the fall? I squeezed my eyes tight, making colors swirl behind my eyelids—rather than images of ITs death.

Oh, my masteress, I thought again and again.

I untied my cap and climbed shakily down from the window. Then I sat with my head down on the tabletop, but after a minute I stood, refusing to cry anymore. I would hope IT lived, so why cry?

IT couldn't save the king now. I would have to attempt the deed myself.

But His Majesty wasn't worth saving compared with my masteress. How could I save IT?

Master Dess might be able to heal IT if I could get to him.

I hadn't tried to escape while I was relying on my Great, my Unfathomable, my Brilliant Masteress Meenore.

I circled the room, looking at everything. The fire poker. Stand on the table, yell for the guards, and smite them on the head as they entered.

No. The first guard would catch my arm before I could strike. I would only anger them.

Might I mansion myself out of here?

I continued to circle.

When would the princess come to see how sick I was?

Had she already poisoned her father again?

I circled the other way. An idea began to form. I thought it out, although I had no time for all this thinking.

I would say this. If a guard said that, I would say the other. They wouldn't be surprised to see me healthy. Her Highness could hardly have told them to expect me to be ill.

Three more circuits, and I was ready. I wrung out my soaked cap and put it back on, although the dampness was unpleasant. Then I eased the key out of the keyhole and tucked it into the heel of my shoe where I could get at it quickly.

I swallowed over a lump in my throat. Masteress Meenore would want to hear about this, if I did well.

The bottom of the bed draperies had a two-inch hem. I found a dropped stitch and pulled, widening the opening.

I knocked on the door. In a gay tone, I cried, "Hail! Open, if you please!" I leaned my ear against the door but heard nothing. If they ignored me, I was lost. His Majesty and my masteress as well. I called again.

A minute or more passed before I heard the bolt pulled free. I backed farther into the room and clasped my hands pleadingly.

The door opened. The guards had changed since Her Highness had come. Luck was with me—half with me, at least. I recognized one of the guards, a young man who had been posted at a fireplace in the great hall and had watched my performance. I remembered seeing him laugh. The other guard was older, with lines of discontent around his mouth.

"Thank you, masters. Time passes slowly in here." I bit my lip. "And I'm frightened." I truly was. My legs could hardly support me. "So I've been practicing my mansioning."

The older guard folded his arms across his chest.

I smiled up at them both. "But I need help with a man-sioner's tale that has four characters. A princess." I ran to the table for my spoon. "Here is my scepter." I flourished it. "A beautiful princess." I batted my eyelashes. The younger guard grinned. The older one settled back on his heels.

"The second character is a witch, who has the princess in her keeping." I pulled a blanket off my bed and threw it around me, making a hooded cape. Rounding my shoulders as a hump, I pulled my cap laces forward to suggest a few strands of chin hair. In a crackly voice I said, "I am the witch."

I wished I could do this quicker, but I had to persuade the guards to forget themselves.

Straightening, in my own voice, I said, "I need two princes. I can't portray them."

The younger guard grinned and said, "I've always . . ."

The older guard sent him a reproving look. My heart sank.

But the young guard came to my aid. "Dure, it's dull enough out there." He indicated the door with his head. "Where's the harm? She can't get past us."

Dure's mouth relaxed.

"Alas, they are impoverished princes, their father being a spendthrift. One prince is as kind and warmhearted as the sun, the other as handsome and brilliant as a star."

This was the first tale Albin had ever taught me, and I was using his exact words, pausing where he used to pause.

"Which would you like to be, masters?"

The young guard laughed. "You be the handsome one, Dure. I'm handsome already."

The older guard shrugged. His voice was like rough rocks rubbing together. "Onnore, you could persuade a hedgehog to fly. I will be the handsome one, young mistress."

I sat in the chair, pulled the blanket onto my lap, and tossed my head prettily. "I am sitting in a castle window, sewing." I held an imaginary needle and pushed it in and out of the blanket. "You ride by on your prancing chargers."

They didn't move.

"Walk past me, please."

They did so, awkwardly.

"With pride. Remember, you are princes."

They threw their shoulders back.

"I am so comely you both fall madly in love with me."

Dure snorted.

"Truly, I am half in love already, little mistress," Onnore said gallantly.

"You both return to stand under my window."

They actually came back.

"Each of you wishes to marry me, so you begin to argue."

Neither one said a word.

I pursed my lips and smoothed the hair on my forehead below the cap. "Why do you think *you* should have me, Prince Dure?"

I watched him think. "Because I am so handsome." He chuckled. "Onnore, you are not half as handsome as I."

"But I am as warm as the sun." He laughed. "I can melt your handsomeness."

"Yet I can outwit you and stop you from melting me."

I let them make a few more arguments. The minutes ticked by.

With each rebuttal they laughed harder.

Finally I cast my imaginary needle over my shoulder and turned the blanket into a hooded cape again. I cackled, "You princelings who love my Soulette, I will not give her to just anyone. The man who can find the magical purse filled with coins . . ." I untied my purse from my belt and shook it so they could hear jingling. I took a silver coin halfway out, then dropped it back in.

There is a saying in Lahnt: *Silver blinds men more powerfully than the sun.*

Dure's mouth dropped open. Onnore rose on his toes.

"That man and no other will have my Soulette." I closed my fist around the purse. In my ordinary voice I added, "Both princes, stand at the door, if you please."

They went willingly and stood with their backs to the door. Dure crossed his arms again, his guarding pose.

"Stand there to prevent my escape. Now close your eyes, so I may hide the magic purse."

They closed their eyes, but I suspected they would open them a slit in a moment. I hid my fist in the folds of my skirt.

Princess Renn would certainly check on me soon. Wait, Your Highness, I pray you. Do not come yet.

Noisily I pulled the chair and table to the window and climbed up but didn't leave the purse there. Next, I hurried to the bed and closed the drapes around me. I lifted the mattress and let it fall, smoothed out the bedding, and then—silently—inserted the purse into the hole I'd made in the drapery.

After slipping out between the bed-curtains, I stamped to the case of shelves, which I moved away from the wall, paused, pushed back. I opened the wooden box, then closed it with a loud click. I dragged the table and chair to the middle of the room, laid a fresh log on the fire, and announced in my witch's voice, "There, my sweetlings."

Master Onnore, who was tall enough not to need the chair, shoved the table against the wall and climbed up. He ran his hand along the windowsill, although he could see there was no purse. He looked back to make sure I hadn't left. Then he peered down, seeking the purse below in the outer ward.

Master Dure stood at the shelves, opening the box, looking in the bowl, feeling under each shelf. He, too, glanced at me after every few seconds. Finally he moved the case of shelves aside and slid his dagger between the floorboards.

Master Onnore rushed to the fireplace and used the poker to assure himself I hadn't tossed the purse in there. He would have been comical if the circumstances hadn't been so dire.

Together they advanced on the bed and drew open the

curtains. After a minute or two of carefully shifting bed-clothes and looking at me, they ripped open the mattress and forgot me in pawing through the feathers. I counted to a hundred, then inched the door open, slowly, slowly, until I had just enough room to slip out, and slid it closed behind me—

And heard the princess from below. "I've come with a refreshment for the poor girl. I will take this one to her as well."

My heart pounded, but I fitted the key into the lock and turned, hearing a quiet clink. Then, key still in my right fist, I lifted my skirt and started up the ladder to the wall walk above the tower.

"La! I can climb stairs unaided."

I saw the glow of a torch on the staircase walls below. With all my strength, I raised the trapdoor, climbed out—

And faced low boots and stout calves.

The guard pulled me up by my armpits. I passed a big belly, saw a red beard, green eyes. "Be still. I've got you."

"Her Highness is hurt!"

Princess Renn cried from below, "La! Help! Oh, la!" She had discovered the locked door.

The guard grabbed my left hand and started down. I bent over but didn't step back on the ladder. Other cries rose from below.

"Come." He let go my hand and reached for my ankles.

I jumped back.

The cries continued, the princess's most shrill of all.

Would he come up for me or go down to her?

He descended. I tossed the key over the battlements and raced away. The rain had become fog. If more guards were on the wall walk, the mist might hide me.

The king's chambers were in the northwest tower, on the other side of the gatehouse wall walk.

Let them not expect me to go there. And let me not be too late.

I didn't think His Highness's trapdoor would be guarded, and it wasn't. Why guard it without a prisoner inside? I raised it a crack. Guards would certainly be posted inside or outside the king's chamber, or both.

Luck was with me. No guards on the landing. I lifted the trapdoor just enough to admit me and then gentled it back into place and stole down the ladder. The king's bed hadn't been in the room I'd visited or on the story below, so it had to be in the top chamber, as my prison bed had been.

The tower seemed to sway. I put my hand on the door-knob to steady myself. I swallowed repeatedly before I knew I could speak.

"La, Father! Here I am. . . ." I turned the knob and opened the door. "La! I have extraordinary . . ."

I ran in. An impression of startled faces. "Your

Majesty . . ." I fell on my knees—and was lifted by two guards the instant my knees touched the floor. They began to drag me out.

"I didn't poison you, but I know who did. She'll do it again."

His Highness held up his hand. "How fortunate I am that prisoners break in to bring me truth." His voice had diminished to a whisper. "Pray tell, who?"

Goodwife Celeste sat on a stool near the king's bed. "Elodie!"

Sir Misyur turned away from tending the fire. "Elodie?"

Master Dess sat in the window recess, stroking a small dog in his lap. A third man, likely Sir Maydsin the physician, held the king's wrist, taking his pulse.

The guards loosened their grips but didn't let me go.

His Highness leaned forward. "Name the lady you wish to put in your place."

Say it! I told myself. He may kill me, but say it! "Has . . ." I had to catch my breath. "Has your daughter given you food today?"

"My daughter?" He laughed. Coughed. Laughed again. "You may release her."

The guards obeyed but remained close.

"Master Dess!" I cried. "Beyond the eastern outer curtain, Masteress Meenore lies wounded. IT may have an arrow in ITs belly."

"Your Majesty . . ." Master Dess bowed and hurried from the chamber.

"Misyur, will you be so kind as to find my daughter, and don't tell her what this is about. This girl is always droll. Renn will be amused. We'll hold the trial here."

Sir Misyur bowed and left.

"My daughter did share with me a delicious rabbit pie." He addressed himself to Goodwife Celeste. "She came after you left me for my nap. She is always welcome, but especially when she brings food."

Goodwife Celeste looked startled.

How much poison in the pie? How soon would it strike?

"Now, while we wait, the girl will mansion the tale with the snake." He waved the guards away. "Give her space."

How could I mansion now? I didn't want to!

Goodwife Celeste nodded at me. I began by turning my cap backward for the bad sister. The imaginary moonsnake oozed slowly from my mouth. How hard it was to concentrate.

When the snake had emerged, I leaped from side to side to get away from it.

The king laughed. The guards laughed. The king coughed. Goodwife Celeste frowned.

After an especially wide leap, I turned my cap to the front to be the kind sister.

"La, Father!" The princess entered with Sir Misyur

and two guards, neither of them Master Dure or Master Onnore. "*Ehlodie?*"

The king patted the bed next to him. "Sit by me. The girl is even more diverting than I thought. She claims you poisoned me."

"La!"

"It is in her left sleeve! You'll see. She tried to poison me, too." Oh no! "She was bringing me—"

"My dear, oblige me by holding out your left arm."

I was frantic. "If the guards eat my meal, they'll die!"

"Make her quiet," King Grenville said.

A guard put his hand across my mouth.

"Father! You mistrust me?"

"I trust you. You are my beloved daughter, but hold out your arm."

She held it out. He rolled up the long sleeve inch by inch. No poison.

CHAPTER THIRTY-SEVEN

t had to be there. What had she done with it?

"The other arm," the king said. "I will be thorough." He revealed her right arm to us all. No poison.

I bit the guard's hand. He squawked and let go. "Her purse!"

The guard covered my mouth again.

The king laughed. "She is so funny. Your purse, my love."

The purse contained only keys.

"That is enough. I am tired of this sport. We cannot keep girls who won't stay in their guarded towers. Tomorrow—"

Keys! I'd put the tower key in my shoe. I bit the guard again, and he let go again. "Look in her shoes! I'm—"

The guard muffled me again.

"Father!"

"Dear, you needn't remove your shoes. Tomorrow the girl will die. Poison will be her—" He coughed and put his bedsheet to his mouth. It came away stained with blood, and blood etched a line down his chin.

The guard dropped his hand from my mouth.

What would she do now?

"Father, are you ill again?" She began to untie his cap, a daughterly gesture.

He turned frightened eyes to Sir Misyur. "Look in her shoes." The inside of his mouth was bright red.

She jumped off the bed and stood.

"Your Highness," Sir Misyur said, "take off your shoes."

She stamped. "I will not."

Sir Misyur nodded to a guard, who approached her.

"You see . . ." She laughed awkwardly. "There is a darn in the heel of my hose. I would not have you see it."

"Beg pardon, Your Highness." The guard knelt at her feet. He lifted her right foot by the ankle.

A pouch was in the toe of the right shoe.

"Let me have it." Goodwife Celeste took the pouch and sniffed inside. "Eastern wasp powder." She looked at Sir Maydsin. "Deadly." She rushed out of the chamber, crying, "I have a remedy. I'll fetch it."

"La!" Her Highness pulled herself to her full height. Her voice achieved extraordinary heights as well. "I was kind enough. . . . I was kind. . . . I am kind. . . ." Her eyes swam, and her nose reddened. She buried her face in her long sleeve. "Alack!"

Sir Misyur told the guards to take the princess to the tower where I had been kept.

"If the guards there ate my food, they've been poisoned, too."

"Send them here," Sir Misyur said.

The princess was escorted out, bent over, sobbing.

"Pardon . . . may I leave to find my masteress?"

Sir Misyur nodded.

A Lepai finch flew in the window and landed between Sir Misyur and me. It fluttered its yellow feathers, then began to vibrate—and grow.

I saw Sir Misyur's smiling face and his tears. I wept and smiled, too.

What brought him back now? Where had he been? *What* had he been?

Sir Misyur removed his cloak and draped it around the ogre as he became himself again. "Welcome home, Your Lordship."

I heard distant barking. Nesspa had sensed his master's return.

"Thank you. Elodie, your masteress wants you."

"Is IT injured?"

"The animal physician is with IT."

I ran out of the room and pelted down the tower steps. The day was ending, and the rain had resumed. With my feet squelching in mud, I raced across the inner ward, between the inner gatehouses and the outer, across the drawbridge, along the moat, around the outer northeast tower. And there IT lay sprawled, ITs belly and legs on a mound of hay, ITs head and neck extending across the ryegrass.

Master Dess sat on the hay mound, dabbing ITs belly with linen.

"Elodie!" IT lifted ITs head. White smoke rose in spirals. "You escaped! I congratulate you."

"Master Dess, is my masteress badly hurt?"

IT began to rise, stopped, and asked Master Dess if IT might.

"Yes, honey, honey. Elodie, I wish all my patients would pull their arrows out with their teeth and then eat them. I stopped the bleeding. Took just a moment."

IT sat up, looking pleased with ITself. "Pine arrows and quartz arrowheads. Quite tasty."

I marched straight to IT and hugged ITs front thigh. Leaning my face into ITs belly, I inhaled sulfur. Lambs and calves, IT stank! Heavenly.

"Mmm," IT said. "Mmm, Lodie. If you must. Mmm."

Finally I stood back. "Her Highness signaled the cats

and poisoned the king and mauled the ox and tried to poison me."

"Honey!"

"The whited sepulcher," IT said. "The poison was secreted on her person?"

"In her shoe."

Of course I bathed before entering the lair. IT toasted skewers for me and then insisted I sleep, despite my protests that I wasn't tired and had much to tell and much to ask.

In the morning IT declared a holiday. After breakfast I sat on a pillow on the floor, and IT reclined on ITs side before me, ITs right arm bent at the elbow, ITs big head resting on ITs right claw—a feminine pose, I thought.

"Did you put out your cap to call me? I hoped to approach close enough to see and then fly off again if all was well."

I nodded. "I was watching when you were struck. I thought . . . I couldn't tell. . . ." If IT had been slain.

"Elodie, I told you to stay out of the window." IT touched my shoulder gently with the flat of ITs left claw. "Princess Renn must have suspected I would come to you. Hence the archers."

In a shaky voice I said, "They would have been considerate if they'd shot straight into your mouth."

Enh enh enh.

"I wonder why His Lordship arrived at the castle when he did."

"There is nothing to wonder at. I found him." ITs smoke curled in a lazy spiral. "Logic took you to the menagerie, Elodie. Logic took me there as well. My first two visits bore no fruit, but two failures did not rule out future success, and indeed His Lordship arrived there last night. I discovered him as an additional monkey and brought him here, where he became himself again. Do you know that he had been poisoned, too?"

"I thought he might have been."

"I didn't know. May I enter?" His Lordship stood in the doorway, carrying a large basket, Nesspa at his side.

My masteress heaved ITself up and invited him in.

The count let Nesspa's chain go, and he ran to me, tail wagging. I patted the top of his big head.

With the help of His Lordship, IT moved the table— His Lordship's bench—back to the hearth. I put pillows on top while he placed the basket on the fireplace bench, now our low table. Then he seated himself carefully and removed delicacies from the basket. I toasted skewers. When all was ready, I perched on my stool at one end of the table. My masteress sat at the other. Nesspa stationed himself at the count's leg.

IT and I had just eaten, but we feasted anyway and shared according to custom, with no danger of poison.

Nesspa was too polite to beg, but hospitality was extended to him, too, from my hand and His Lordship's, but not from my masteress's claw.

I had almost the appetite of an ogre, and this ogre had brought marchpane. Still, I finished before him.

When even he finally put down his knife, I said, "You didn't know you were poisoned?"

"No." His ordeal had not made him more talkative.

"But you were ill?" I asked.

He nodded.

"His Lordship has told me some of this, Lodie. Until last night he was in a mouse hole in his bedchamber wall, at first ill almost to death, then improving slowly."

"Why didn't the poison kill him?" I turned to him. "Kill you, I mean. You were so tiny!"

"I am strong, even when I'm a mouse." He made a fist and held it up.

"Did you run to the menagerie as a mouse?" And no cat caught him?

"As a flea. At the menagerie I became a monkey."

"Your Lordship . . ." I hesitated. "Pardon my questions."

"People don't ask enough questions." He shrugged. "They just guess."

Encouraged, I said, "Can you change whenever you want, to whatever you like?"

"Unless there are cats." He patted Nesspa's head. "Then

312

I can't resist becoming a mouse."

I had been curious about this ever since I first saw him as a monkey: "Are you yourself inside the animal?"

He stared at the ceiling and said nothing for a minute. "I am thinking." He was quiet again. "Are you yourself inside a dream? The monkey is a happy dream."

IT said, "Mmm," but not ITs usual *Mmm*. This one was softer, a feeling *Mmm*, not a thinking one.

"I wake up inside the beast from time to time, to decide if I want to shift back. When I was the mouse, I was awake because I was sick."

"Your Lordship," IT said, "did you realize Her Highness had signaled the cats?"

He shook his head.

I dared to ask the question I most wanted to know. "Your Lordship . . . er, did you love her?"

He blushed. "I did not."

Good!

He went to the middle of the lair, where he paced in a small circle. Nesspa followed him, whining uneasily. After a few minutes His Lordship stopped and Nesspa nuzzled his legs. "I should not have agreed to the marriage . . . but I wanted to be king so people would learn an ogre can be good." He paced again and spoke while walking. "I liked Her Highness. I thought she loved me. I was grateful." He went to Masteress Meenore. "I am to blame."

CHAPTER THIRTY-EIGHT

nh enh enh. "And I am to blame for lighting the forge of a dishonest smith, although I was unaware of his dishonesty, and Lodie is to blame for allowing herself to be the victim of a thieving cat."

I smiled, but His Lordship looked puzzled.

IT continued. "I suppose that your cook is to blame for preparing food that could be poisoned." *Enh enh enh*. "Perhaps the builder is at fault for building the castle you would eventually hold a feast in."

I don't think His Lordship had ever graced my masteress with his full, sweet smile before, but he beamed it on IT now. ITs white smoke curled into spirals, and I understood what spirals meant—dragon happiness.

"Elodie," IT said, "I have not yet told you all. His

Lordship was with me, as a flea again, when I was shot. He returned to the castle to plead your case after Dess told us where you were."

"Thank you, Your Lordship."

He inclined his head. "I knew you would not poison anyone." He stood. "I must leave. Misyur worries if I am gone too long. Meenore, I owe you payment." He untied a brocade purse from his belt. "What is your fee?"

Promptly IT said, "Ten silvers."

Astounded, I blurted, "So many?"

IT glared at me.

His Lordship counted out coins into ITs claw. "And a silver for—"

IT snapped, "You may give that to me, and I will hold it for her."

I glared at IT.

His Lordship gave my silver to IT. "Come, Nesspa." They left.

"You are my assistant, and you are a child." IT placed the silvers in a stack on the cupboard, then lumbered to the coin basket. "You may have these."

I went to IT and received four coppers, a fiftieth of a silver but more money than I had ever owned and much more than my promised salary. "Thank you." I stacked my coppers next to ITs silvers.

Together we dragged the table back to its place against

the wall. IT stretched out again, and I returned to my pillow near ITs head. "There is more to my tale, Lodie, and more to yours."

I sat cross-legged on the pillow. "What happened after you found His Lordship?"

"He spent the night on my floor. He is no cleaner than a human. In the morning he stayed here while I visited your goodwife and her goodman, who are not thieves but the real spies for Tair. Their trade with the smith provides them enough to live on. They said none of this outright, but the goodwife hinted, and I deduced."

Spies? I chewed on it and felt relief. A spy but not a murderer, a spy who'd saved the king's life with her knowledge of herbs.

"Do we have to tell His Majesty?"

"We have no proof, and I will not reveal them to Greedy Grenny. I believe I persuaded the goodwife that I am *not* moody." IT scratched ITs snout. "Now tell me what ensued after I left you."

I did. IT made me act out my mansioning to the guards, and this time I had to mansion their parts as well. IT *enh enh enh*ed heartily.

However, IT stopped laughing when I mentioned leaving my purse.

"You left the coins I gave you?"

"They may still be there." I sat down again. "There's a

saying in Lahnt. *Gold—*"

"Spare me your quaint sayings. Tomorrow we will go to the castle and reclaim your purse."

"I'd like to apologize to the guards." And learn if they'd eaten my meal and been poisoned.

"They may not wish to hear you."

"And we must find out if His Highness survived." How awful that I hadn't thought about this since leaving the castle.

"Yes, we must. But you have not finished your recitation. What did you do when you were outside your prison door? Surely there were more guards."

I continued the tale. IT continued ITs questions. When I'd finally answered them all, IT said, "By coming to see why you were not dead, Her Highness as much as told you she was the poisoner. She saved you the trouble of deducing."

Indignantly I said, "I deduced! I worked out why and how she did it."

"Mmm. Mmm." IT closed ITS eyes, then opened them. "You did. You did well, Elodie."

I felt as if an audience of a thousand had just clapped for me. IT lumbered to the cupboard, where IT removed a skewer from its bundle. "Perhaps Misyur will make me a gift of the remainder of the arrows that were to be shot at me." IT used the skewer as a toothpick and then ate it. "I imagine you will go to Sulow soon, tomorrow or even a few minutes from now, to become his new mansioner. I suppose you will not delay."

Oh! I hadn't given Master Sulow a thought. "Could I do both, proclaim and deduce and induce and mansion, too?"

"I do not want a sometime assistant. You needn't worry. I will find another."

I had more pride than that. "Who will replace me?" Nastily I added, "Is another cog coming from Lahnt?"

"Ah," IT said, sounding pleased.

Oh. Oh. I was saying I didn't want to be replaced. But I was a mansioner. I went to the lair entrance. A brisk wind blew cloud tatters across the sky. I stepped outside. Cold. I stepped inside. Warm. Outside again.

Master Sulow had no warmth. If he'd been my master when I'd been imprisoned in the tower, he'd likely have left me there.

Pacing back and forth between the rain vats on either side of the lair, I debated with myself.

My masteress said I didn't have the temperament to be a mansioner, and in truth, I'd hated mansioning the moonsnake over and over for the king. But perhaps I'd merely hated the king.

And perhaps there was more than one way to be a mansioner, not simply as a member of a troupe. Since I'd been in Two Castles, I'd mansioned for Sulow, for the court, for the king, and for two bewildered guards.

But in a troupe, mansioners became better at the roles they repeated. Albin said a mansioner finds something new in a part each time she steps into it.

I felt pulled in two. I stopped thinking, wrapped my cloak around me, and stared up at the sky. The princess's cap kept my ears warm.

Her cap! The cap of a poisoner.

I stepped back into the lair, extending my arm and holding the cap in my fingertips. At the fireplace I threw it in.

My masteress reached in and pulled it out before it was even singed. "I deduce you no longer want it." *Enh enh enh.*

"I'd rather go bareheaded."

"Then I suggest you sell it. People will fight to own a cap that once belonged to the poisoner princess. Trade it for half a dozen caps, or I will sell it for you if you like."

"Sell it, please." I wanted nothing more to do with the thing.

IT folded the cap carefully. "I will get a better price than you will. Now read to me. I believe you stopped at *mustard*."

I found the book in the cupboard. IT had marked my place with a skewer. Outside the wind blew. IT rested ITs head on ITs front claws, ITs eyes on me.

Mother, Father, I thought. A lair is my home.

EPILOGUE

I did not go to Master Sulow later in the day, and during the night, while I slept in my cozy bed, my mind made itself up. I awoke knowing that, for now at least, I would remain with Masteress Meenore and mansion when the opportunity arose.

Did I mind? Did the decision feel like a sacrifice?

A little. Very little.

Master Sulow was a mere human. His breath never spiraled or turned green. With IT I would have more adventures than I'd get peering out from under Master Sulow's thumb.

Not only more adventures, more consideration of my ideas and more friendship.

I told IT my decision over breakfast, and ITs smoke

spiraled satisfyingly. "A commonsensical choice. You still have much to learn about deducing and inducing."

In the morning we visited Count Jonty Um's castle. Sir Misyur came to the outer ward to talk to us.

The king would live. Goodwife Celeste had saved him with broth and coarse herb bread. He'd slept a quiet night and was now closeted with His Lordship. Sir Misyur believed His Highness wanted assurance of His Lordship's aid in any war against Tair. I thought the king would be disappointed. The count seemed to be a peaceable ogre.

Princess Renn had company in her tower. Master Thiel had charmed his way into visiting her. I supposed he must be stealing the gold rings from her fingers and the bracelets from her arms.

Master Onnore and Master Dure, the two guards, had not eaten my food. They'd been too occupied in searching for my purse—which they'd failed to find—and then in searching for me.

Sir Misyur dispatched a guard to the chamber, who returned with my purse, its wealth untouched. My masteress gave me back my cloth purse and kept the rest.

In the afternoon IT sold Princess Renn's cap for twelve coppers, and I bought myself a kirtle, an apron, and a pair of shoes, all used, of course, but all in the Two Castles fashion, and my own cap—pink with red roses, hardly faded, embroidered around the crown. My custom went to a mending master on Roo Street, not to the mending mistress on Daycart Way who had insulted me, although I paraded back and forth by that mistress in my new finery. She seemed not to notice.

I had three coppers left from my purchases, which I knew I should save to send home, but I wanted to buy something for IT, who called ITself stingy but had shown me only generosity.

On the wharf I found a boat wright willing to sell me a block of cypress wood for a copper, a kingly sum for a snack, but I paid.

IT was selling skewers, so I headed for the lair to hide my gift. On my way I met Goodwife Celeste again, this time at the baker's oven. When she saw me, she hugged me hard, then held me at arm's length and scrutinized my face.

"You are well?"

I smiled. "Very well."

"Safe?"

I nodded.

She shook her head. "IT should never have sent you to the castle alone. Thoughtless of IT."

Thought*more*, I would say.

She let my shoulders go. "We're leaving shortly, but we'll be back. I'll look for you."

"I'll be happy to see you." And sad to see her go.

She took her loaf from the baker, and I continued toward

the top of town. At the corner I encountered a crier for the king, trumpeting that His Lordship had been a lion only momentarily and only during the feast, and that he had never mauled an ox or any living thing. I saw another crier on the next corner. Greedy Grenny was making amends.

In the lair I hid the wood block, which was as thick as my thigh, under my mattress and brought it out while IT was toasting skewers for our evening meal. I placed the gift on the hearth next to IT.

"For me?" IT dropped three skewers into the fire. Smoke rose from ITs nostrils in a green spiral.

I used the poker to rescue the skewers. "You said you like the taste." IT liked cypress and hated oak. Oh no. Had I gotten that backward?

IT touched the wood with a talon. "For me?"

"For you to eat, if you like, Masteress."

"For me?"

I nodded. "If you don't like, perhaps we can put it in the fire or use—"

"Burn cypress, Lodie?" IT picked up the wood and hugged it. "That would be an outrage." ITs inner eyelids closed while IT nibbled a corner. "Excellent quality. I have not received a gift in . . . forty-two years, and that was a trifle." IT stroked the wood.

I smiled at ITs pleasure.

"You bought this with your cap money."

I nodded, although IT hadn't asked.

"Of course you have no other source of funds. You thought of me." Trailing smoke spirals, IT waddled to the cupboard, opened it, and laid the wood on the top shelf. "I will savor it slowly, or perhaps I will simply save it."

King Grenville never thanked me for saving his life. Maybe because I'd revealed his daughter as his poisoner, he felt no gratitude. Or maybe his gratitude was aroused only by a well-cooked dish.

His criers were believed about Count Jonty Um. The tide of popular opinion had turned. By now everyone knew of Princess Renn's attempts on the lives of her father and her betrothed, and the count was pitied and no longer feared.

But the town's goodwill might have come too late. Other than his visit to us, His Lordship stayed away for the next week. The princess and her father removed to their own castle, where she was again imprisoned.

Soon after their departure, more news broke on the town: Master Thiel was to become Prince Thiel and to marry the princess. He had persuaded the king that he would keep Her Highness from poisoning anyone ever again. The couple would be given a burgher's house to live in, and Pardine would be Prince Cat of the kingdom.

I supposed His Majesty no longer wanted his daughter under his roof, and I doubted they would dine together often. On King Grenville's death, King Thiel would rule.

Sentiment in Two Castles was divided. The victims of Master Thiel's thievery were outraged, the rest pleased.

My masteress told me ITs opinion over a mutton stew I had cooked. "When Thiel is king, he will not send Lepai to war. Until then, if King Grenville expects his son-in-law to lead anyone to battle, he will be disappointed. Thiel loves himself too much to risk even an eyebrow hair."

I thought Princess Renn wouldn't poison anyone again for a while at least. I believed she truly loved Thiel—tall, handsome, and now rich Prince Thiel, whose table manners were excellent. But if he angered her, he had better not eat his meals at home.

A monkey and a dog appeared in our entrance. Nesspa, trailing his chain, trotted to the fireplace where the stew pot hung.

The monkey loped in, chittered, stroked my hair, and smiled his toothy smile at me. I jumped off my high stool and curtsied. The monkey took my masteress's front claw and stroked it.

"Welcome, Your Lordship." From ITs pink smoke I knew IT was enduring the petting.

The monkey ran to the middle of the room and began to vibrate.

When the shift was complete, I asked, "May I give you stew, Your Lordship?" I hoped we had enough.

"Thank you." He piled pillows on the floor and sat on them with his legs under our table. I ladled stew into ITs largest bowl and held a morsel of cheese out to Nesspa. Then I poured tumblers of apple cider for us all.

While we ate and drank, my masteress spoke at length about the making of books.

Finally His Lordship put down his spoon. "I have something to say." His chest rose in a huge breath. "The townspeople have forgiven me for being an ogre. Seven smiled at me today."

"That's wonderful, Your Lordship," I said.

"Yes." He smiled, not the huge, sweet smile that transformed his face but a small smile that mixed pleasure and sadness.

We waited.

"Now I would like to travel."

"Where will you go?" I asked, feeling a lump form in my throat. I was losing Goodwife Celeste, and now I would lose His Lordship.

"To Tair. Several of us live there. Humans are not so clannish in Tair."

Nesspa curled up against the wall next to the cupboard.

"When do you depart?" IT asked.

"Soon. I want you both to come." He blushed. "If you will. An ogre can use someone to induce and deduce and someone to mansion."

I had no fondness for Two Castles, and one way to reach Tair involved crossing Lahnt. I might see my parents and Albin. How heavenly that would be.

Father and Mother would overcome their fear of a dragon and an ogre. They wouldn't be like the people here.

My masteress said nothing.

His Lordship's blush deepened. "I will pay you to come."

IT tilted ITs head. "We will consider your proposition. You will pay handsomely?"

"Yes."

"Lodie?" IT asked.

I nodded.

The next day, while I proclaimed, my masteress and His Lordship conferred in the lair about the coming journey. Two weeks later I had been ITs assistant for a month, and IT paid me my first wages, slowly and solemnly counting the twenty tins into my hand. I slid them into my purse, which jingled delightfully. How astonished Mother and Father would be at this wealth.

But I owed three tins to Master Dess, and I had been tardy in repaying him. I found him in the stables of the Two Castles Inn, tending a lame horse.

"I forgot, honey!" he said when I produced the coins—carefully, although Two Castles was a more honest place now that Master Thiel was with the princess.

"Master Dess, I'm going to Tair."

"Ah." He patted the horse's flank. "The cows in Tair are striped, honey, small for cows, but their milk is sweet as honey. I wish you a safe journey."

The following day His Lordship left his castle in Sir Misyur's trustworthy hands and took with him on the cog only enough valuables to half fill the hold. Much of the rest of the hold was stuffed with ITs hoard.

His Lordship, my masteress, and I stood on the deck along with Goodwife Celeste and Goodman Twah, who had delayed their departure to cross with us. I was glad to know the goodwife had peppermint leaves in her purse.

IT said, with satisfaction in ITs voice, "There are those who keep to their lairs and those who travel. We travel."

The cog master raised the gangplank.

I closed my eyes and imagined the mountains of Lahnt and our valley hidden among them. Home and then away again with my two friends—deducing, inducing, using my common sense, and mansioning.